ANDBOOK
OF CARE

This book belongs to

LORNA KIRBY

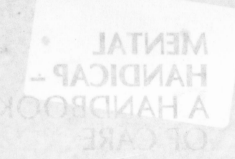

I wish to dedicate this book to the residents
and staff of the following:

St Mary's Hospital, Drumcar, Ireland

Gogarburn Hospital, Edinburgh, Scotland

St Joseph's Hospital, Rosewell, Edinburgh,
Scotland

MENTAL HANDICAP – A HANDBOOK OF CARE

EDITED BY

EAMON SHANLEY

RNMH RMN CPNCert RNT BA(Hons) MSc PhD
Senior Lecturer, Department of Molecular & Life Sciences,
Dundee College of Technology, Dundee

Churchill Livingstone 🏛

EDINBURGH LONDON MELBOURNE AND NEW YORK 1986

CHURCHILL LIVINGSTONE
Medical Division of Longman Group UK Limited

Distributed in the United States of America by Churchill
Livingstone Inc., 1560 Broadway, New York, N.Y. 10036,
and by associated companies, branches and
representatives throughout the world.

First published 1986
  Reprinted 1989

ISBN 0 443 02793 5

British Library Cataloguing in Publication Data
Mental handicap — a handbook of care.
  1. Mentally handicapped — Care and treatment
  I. Shanley, Eamon
  362.3'8   HV3004

Library of Congress Cataloging in Publication Data
Mental handicap.
  Includes index.
  1. Mentally handicapped — Rehabilitation.
2. Mentally handicapped — Services for. I. Shanley,
Eamon. [DNLM: 1. Mental Retardation — rehabilitation.
WM 308 M5488]
RC570.M376 1985   616.85'88   85-19467

Produced by Longman Singapore Publishers (Pte) Limited
Printed in Singapore

Preface

The book was written primarily for those who provide care for people with mental handicap and for those preparing to work with them, e.g. RNMH, CSS, CQSW, BA and BSc students.

It is the simple hope of this book that through its pages it may help improve the care given by nursing and social work staff to those people for whom they have such a responsibility.

The book reflects the wide diversity of work that both nursing (mental handicap) and social work staff are involved in, ranging from the provision of substantial amounts of care to people with multiple handicap to dealing with the grief reaction often experienced by parents and siblings. In addition to describing the provision of care it includes details relevant to the understanding of mental handicap as a subject, e.g. causes, conditions and issues such as legal and ethical aspects. Overall, however, the emphasis of the book is towards the description of practical means of improving the quality of life with the focus on self help. The fact that each chapter is written by an individual with particular interest and competence in that area allows the wide range of practical skills acquired through experience to be contained within this volume.

Finally we acknowledge that throughout the book terms such as patient, resident, client, mentally handicapped person, person with mental handicap are used in referring to people with mental handicap. Although it is increasingly felt that the most desirable term to be used is 'person with mental handicap', it was decided that the other terms cannot simply be omitted as they are in constant use in daily practice, and it will be a long time before terms in common usage are replaced.

Dundee 1986   E.S.

Contributors

Mary Boyle

Clinical Teacher, Mental Handicap and Paediatric Areas, South Lothian College of Nursing, Edinburgh. JBCNS Behaviour Modification

Bronwen Burford BA

Movement Therapist, Gogarburn Hospital, Edinburgh; Co-ordinator, Movement Therapy Study Group in Scotland

Philip Darbyshire RNMH RSCN DN(Lond) RNT

Nurse Tutor, Paediatric and Mental Handicap Areas, South Lothian College of Nursing, Edinburgh

Raymond Goodall RNMH

Charge Nurse, Gogarburn Hospital, Edinburgh

Isobel Hessler RGN RNMD RCNT RNT

Nurse Tutor (Mental Handicap), St Joseph's Hospital, Rosewell

Gail Ketley-King BA(Hons) CQSW DSW

Hospital Senior Social Worker, Paediatric Assessment Centre, Leicester Royal Infirmary, Leicester

Kevin Millar RNMH RGN

Nursing Officer, Gogarburn Hospital, Edinburgh

Robert Paterson RNMH RGN DipN(Lond)

Director of Nursing Services, Greaves Hall Hospital, Southport

George Petrie RNMH RGN DipN(Clin Teaching) RNT

Senior Tutor, Mental Handicap Nursing, South Lothian College of Nursing, Edinburgh

Frank Quinn RNMH RGN RMN DN RNT

Senior Tutor, Nurse Teaching Department, St Joseph's Hospital, Rosewell

Eamon Shanley RNMH RMN CPNCert RNT BA(Hons) MSc PhD

Senior Lecturer, Department of Molecular & Life Sciences, Dundee College of Technology, Dundee

Jois Stansfield MSc

Lecturer in Speech Pathology and Therapeutics, Queen Margaret College, Edinburgh

Contents

Contents

Eamon Shanley

1

Introduction to mental handicap

- *Different emotive value attached to terms describing the mentally handicapped*
- *The term 'mental handicap' has least negative implications*
- *No definitive method of classifying and counting the mentally handicapped*
- *Care staff may be guilty of reinforcing stereotype images*
- *Institutionalisation can affect both care staff and residents*

WHAT'S IN A NAME?

What exactly is meant by the term mental handicap? Although it is commonly used it is open to different interpretation. According to Osgood et al (1957) words have three dimensions: evaluative, potency and activity. Of the three the evaluative dimension is the most important. For example in describing someone like the Prime Minister the word 'strong-willed' might be used by an admirer whereas the word 'stubborn' might be used by a detractor. Both people are describing the same person yet one is making a positive evaluation by using the word 'strong-willed' while the other is being negative. The meaning of the word is more or less the same, but the evaluative component is very different.

The words people use to describe others often contain some sort of judgemental component that reflects whether they see them as good or bad as well as conveying a meaning. The terms used to describe people who are mentally handicapped are particularly prone to carry a strong evaluative component and in the past included moron, feeble-minded, imbecile and idiot. These terms have become associated with such marked negative evaluation that they are no longer used by the caring professions although still used freely by the general public. Professionally there is a distinct geographic variation in words used to describe a person with mental handicap. In England and Wales the official term used to be

1

'mental subnormality'; in Scotland until recently the term used was 'mental deficiency'; in the Irish Republic the term is 'mental handicap'; in the U.S.A. 'mental retardation' has been used although there is a move towards 'developmentally disabled'; in mainland Europe some countries use the term 'oligophrenia'. All of these terms describe the same phenomenon yet they vary in terms of their evaluative component. While one term is acceptable in one area it may be considered offensive in another. At present the term 'mental handicap' seems to convey the least degree of negative evaluation in the U.K. (in 1983 England adopted 'mental impairment' as its legal term whereas Scotland in 1984 adopted 'mental handicap') and for that reason it will be used throughout this book. It should also be borne in mind that mental handicap is a general term encompassing a wide range of disability and impairment, and the categorisation of different levels of mental handicap is subject to wide variation. In Scotland nursing staff classify people with mental handicap according to their degree of independence, i.e. how much they can do for themselves. The terms are high, medium and low dependency (G.N.C. circular 1980/8):

High dependency — applies to individuals who have a severe degree of mental deficiency to the extent that they cannot guard themselves against common physical dangers and depend on others for care and protection.

Medium dependency — applies to individuals who have a medium degree of mental deficiency such that they require some care and consistent supervision.

Low dependency — applies to individuals who have a slight degree of mental deficiency such that they require some supervision but since they can benefit from education and training they should be able to adapt to society to a considerable extent.

One may assume that individuals with higher degree of dependency are capable of benefiting from education and training in adapting to society though perhaps not to the same extent as those of low dependency.

Historical background

Until the time of the Industrial Revolution in the mid-18th century there had been little or no established provision of facilities for mentally handicapped people. In fact there was little or no provision for any special groups. Reliance was placed on the social network of family, friends and neighbours with any outside help coming from religious organisations. This social network was disrupted and put under great strain with the change from a rural-based society to an urban society. Expanding towns were barely able to cope with the developing industrial labour force, let alone the associated social problems. Separation of the able-bodied from the sick and destitute was the solution adopted, so those unable to support themselves were segregated from the productive labour force and accommodated in 'Workhouses'.

During the 19th century the policy of segregation continued and there was the development of the idea that as the less intelligent and those with other 'undesirable' characteristics, mainly the working class, had more children than the more favourably endowed (aristocracy, landowners and factory owners) there would eventually be a deterioration in the intelligence and 'fitness' of the general population. Selective breeding in animals had been pioneered during the agricultural revolution and had resulted in better quality, more valuable livestock. The theory was considered equally applicable to humans. People with low intelligence mixing with others of low intelligence were likely to marry one another and produce children of low intelligence. These children were more likely to remain and marry within this culture thus creating a population with low intelligence. Darwin's theory as presented in his book *Origin of Species* added weight to the fear of a deterioration of the intelligence of the general population by stating that it is a natural law that only the fittest of the species survive to produce offspring thus passing on genes with a greater likelihood of survival. It was felt that in the case of human beings the most unfit were procreating faster than the fittest. In 1909 Tredgold stated that it was 'imperative . . . to devise such social laws as will ensure that those unfit do not propagate their kind.' An organisation called the Eugenics Society had been formed in the mid-19th century to seek ways of preventing degeneration of the human species, and the issue of controlling genetic factors in humans has been with us since that time. In the 1930s a Government Committee on sterilisation considered the feasibility of compulsory sterilisation in Britain. During this decade the theory of genetic control was taken to its logical conclusion in Nazi Germany. Extermination of individuals with undesirable characteristics, mentally ill, mentally handicapped and the aged among others, was undertaken on a massive scale. After the Second World War Butler (1951) in the U.S.A. reported that in 21 states, sterilisation of mentally handicapped people was practised on the basis of the IQ score. Thankfully less drastic and more humane ways of preventing the transmission of undesirable characteristics from one generation to another have become possible, based mainly on genetic counselling and methods of birth control. In the future, genetic engineering may play a part. Unfortunately each one of these methods is accompanied by ethical problems which become increasingly difficult to resolve with advancing technical knowledge.

Over the past hundred years the policy of segregation found expression in various Acts of Parliament, chief of which was the 1913 Mental Deficiency Act. Many of those detained under this Act while having some degree of mental handicap were primarily misfits in that they may have committed minor crimes, have been illiterate, pregnant, unemployed or destitute. Soon hospitals filled up with many such people who varied from dull to average intelligence. With little chance of the inmates ever getting out again and a comparatively high level of intelligence among them, mental handicap hospitals became working communities. They were relatively self sufficient in that they supplied much of the labour force on farms, kitchens, maintenance and for domestic tasks including helping to look after more highly dependent residents.

This situation was dramatically altered by the Mental Health Act (1959) for England and Wales and the Mental Health (Scotland) Act (1960) which resulted in a mass exodus from mental handicap hospitals of the most capable. These Acts did away with the legal restrictions on most residents and facilitated easier discharge. As a result the character of the hospitals changed with a greater proportion of highly dependent residents and less 'assistance' from the more able residents.

Today there are even fewer low dependency residents and renewed efforts are being made to depopulate mental handicap hospitals in a drive towards habilitating them in accommodation outside hospitals (see Ch. 5).

IDENTIFYING THE MENTALLY HANDICAPPED

Until quite recently, identification of those with mental handicap had been based on a measure of intelligence — those with low intelligence were considered to be mentally handicapped. In attempting to specify precisely what constitutes mental handicap, great importance was attached to people's intelligence quotient (IQ) scores. Since the 1960s, however, more attention has been given to other measures that reflect a person's level of competence in performing skills such as eating, dressing, communication and social skills. These behaviours do not necessarily coincide with the person's score on an intelligence quotient test.

There are three main systems in use in the classification of degrees of mental handicap: the World Health Organization (WHO) system, the system based on the Mental Health Act (1959) for England and Wales and the one advocated by the American Association for Mental Deficiency. In the WHO system the IQ scores are the main criteria and the degrees of handicap are determined as follows:

Mild retardation   50–70
Moderate retardation   35–50
Severe retardation   20–35
Profound retardation less than 20

The British system, based mainly on the legal classification of the Mental Health Act (1959), later superseded by the Mental Health Act (1983), is divided into two levels, namely subnormality and severe subnormality. Severe subnormality is defined as a 'state of arrested or incomplete development of mind which includes subnormality of intelligence and is of such a nature or degree that the patient is incapable of living an independent life or guarding himself against serious exploitation or will be so incapable when of an age to do so.' Subnormality is defined as 'a state of arrested or incomplete development of mind (not amounting to severe subnormality) which includes subnormality of intelligence and is of a nature of degree which requires or is susceptible to medical treatment or other special care or training of the patient.'

The British Psychological Society interpreted the severe subnormality range as being under an IQ of 55 and the subnormal range as being between an IQ score of 55 and 70. However others (Goodman & Tizard, 1962) take the cut off point between severly mentally subnormality and subnormality to be 50.

The third system of classification, the American Association of Mental Deficiency, is the most comprehensive of the three and warrants close consideration. In attempting to define what constitutes mental handicap three characteristics have been identified (Grossman, 1973):

a. a significant low measure of intelligence
b. a marked deficiency in adaptive skills
c. existence of the state of mental handicap before adulthood is reached. (This excludes states of intellectual impairment caused by such conditions as dementia, or trauma either physical or chemical which affect adults.)

Significantly low measure of intelligence

Development of IQ tests

Binet test. Binet, a French psychologist, attempted to identify less able pupils in Paris schools. In 1903 he devised a series of tests for children of different ages, e.g. one test for 5-year-olds and another for 6-year-olds etc. If a 10-year-old was unable to do the test for 10-year-olds, but could do the one for 8-year-olds he was considered to be of below average intelligence. Similarly if another 10-year-old could complete the test for 12-year-olds, he was considered above average intelligence. The relationship between a child's score and the average score for that age was later expressed by the formula:

Intelligence Quotient (IQ)

$$= \frac{\text{Mental age (MA)}}{\text{Chronological Age (CA)}} \times \frac{100}{1}$$

In the case of the 10-year-old child being able to complete the test for 12-year-olds the child's mental age is considered to be 12 years while his chronological age is 10 years. Applying the formula to this information:

$$IQ = \frac{MA}{CA} \times 100$$

$$= \frac{12}{10} \times 100$$

$$= 120$$

Thus the child's IQ score is calculated as 120.

The test devised by Binet was later modified at Stanford University and renamed the Stanford-Binet test. From the age of 2 years to 5 years there is a test for every 6 months and a sub-test for every month. From the ages of 6 to 14 years there is a test for every year with a sub-test for every 2 months.

Examples of items on the Stanford-Binet tests are as follows:

for a 3-year-old — stringing beads, identifying pictures of everyday objects.
for a 9-year-old — what is foolish about this statement: 'a person had two heart attacks;

he died from the first but recovered from the second'?

for a 14-year-old — 'which direction would you have to face so that your right hand is towards the north?'

Occasionally the Stanford-Binet is used for adults. However the above formula is inappropriate. Up to the age of 16 years a person's ability to do IQ tests increases. After 16 years of age the IQ score declines gradually. In calculating the IQ scores of people over 16 years of age the chronological age (CA) is taken as 16 years. For example, if a person aged 60 can do the IQ test that an average 10-year-old can do, his IQ score is calculated thus:

$$IQ = \frac{MA}{CA} \times \frac{100}{1}$$

$$= \frac{10}{16} \times \frac{100}{1} \text{ (Note the chronological age is written as 16 \textit{not} as 60.)}$$

$$= 62$$

If 60 was used as the CA his IQ score would have worked out at 17 which would place him in the profoundly mentally handicapped category. Plainly a person with a mental age of 10 years cannot be considered to be profoundly mentally handicapped.

An important development which overcame this shortcoming in calculating IQ scores for adults was introduced into the Stanford-Binet test. As a result the person's test score is now compared with a table of scores which takes the person's exact chronological age into consideration. Applying the above formula is no longer necessary though knowledge of the principles involved is important.

Wechsler test. The main advantage of this intelligence test is that each test assesses the person's practical as well as verbal abilities, whereas the Stanford-Binet test depends mainly on verbal ability.

Three different tests were developed by Wechsler and his associates. They are:

Wechsler Primary and Preschool Scale of Intelligence (WPPS)	4–6 years

Wechsler Intelligence Scale for Children (WISC)	5–16 years
Wechsler Adult Intelligence Scale (WAIS)	15 years +

In the Wechsler Intelligence Scale for Children the two sections are:

Verbal	*Performance*
Information, e.g. how does yeast cause dough to rise?	Digit symbol
	Picture completion
	Block design, e.g. 9 blocks each with red, white/red & white sides. Given certain designs to copy. Timed.
Comprehension, e.g. what does this saying mean: 'one swallow doesn't make a summer'?	
Arithmetic	Picture arrangement, e.g. Place story cards in sequence. Timed.
Similarities	
Digit span	
Vocabulary	Object assembly

Apart from the advantage of the Wechsler Tests having two sections, i.e. verbal and performance, each subscale, e.g. information, can be scored separately as can each section. The person's scoring on particular subscales may be much more useful than a single score as offered by the Stanford-Binet in identifying areas of deficiencies.

IQ and age

If a person has an IQ score of 95 at the age of 8 years and a score of 90 at the age of 10 years, has there been an actual decrease in the level of intellectual functioning?

On looking at the drop in IQ score the immediate deduction may be that the person's level of intelligence has declined. On the contrary the person's level of intelligence has actually increased!

The formula IQ MA × 100 can show us why.

Applying the formula when the child was 8 years old

$$95 = \frac{MA}{8} \times 100$$

$$MA = \frac{95 \times 8}{100}$$

$$= 7.6$$

$$= 7 \text{ years 7 months (approx.)}$$

The child's mental age at the age of 8 years is 7 years 7 months. When the child was 10 years old his mental age is calculated thus:

$$MA. = \frac{90 \times 10}{100}$$

$$= 9$$

At the age of 10 years the child's mental age was 9 years.

Degrees of mental handicap according to standard deviation

Apart from viewing IQ scores in terms of mental age another way of interpreting IQ scores is in terms of standard deviation. The basic principle is the same. It involves comparing an individual's score with the scoring of others. However the standard deviation method is based on statistical interpretation of scores on a normal distribution.

The significance of the standard deviation (s.d.) is that approximately 68% of people get a score within 1 s.d. either side of the average score (mean); 96% of people score within 2 s.d. and 99.7% of people score within 3 s.d. (Fig. 1.1).

Putting numbers on these statements, in the Wechsler test 1 s.d. is equal to 15 points. Therefore 68% of people score between 85 and 115(100–15 = 85; 100 + 15 = 115).96% of people score within 2 s.d. of the mean score within 70 and 130 points (100–30 = 70; 100 + 30 = 130). 99.7% of people score between 55 and 145.

As the standard deviation in the Stanford-Binet test is 16 the distribution of scores is somewhat different, i.e. 68% of people score between 84 and 116 points; 96% of people score between 68 and 132 points; 99.7% of people score between 52 and 148 points.

People who score more than 2 s.d. below the mean (average) on either tests are classified as being mentally handicapped, i.e. below 68 on the Stanford-Binet and 70 on the Wechsler tests.

More specific classification of degrees of mental handicap is as follows:

those who score between 2 and 3 standard deviations are mildly handicapped
those who score between 3 and 4 standard deviations are moderately handicapped
those who score between 4 and 5 standard deviations are severely handicapped

Table 1.1 summarises the use of IQ as a means of classifying degrees of mental handicap.

Table 1.2 indicates an alternative system

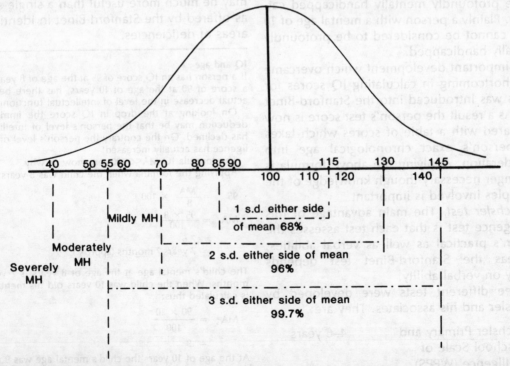

Fig. 1.1 Normal distribution curve.

Table 1.1 IQ scores as a guide to classification according to standard deviation (s.d.)

Level of mental handicap	Stanford-Binet (s.d. = 16)	Wechsler (s.d. = 15)	% of mental handicap population	Mental age at adulthood	Degree of assistance required
Mild	68–52	70–55	86.7	8–11yr	With supervision capable of living independently
Moderate	51–36	54–40	10	5–8 yr	Requires some assistance
Severe	35–20	39–25	3.3	under 3 yr	Requires considerable help
Profound	Under 20	Under 25			Requires total care

Table 1.2

Level of mental handicap	IQ scores	% of mental handicap popn	Mental age at adulthood
Mild	50–70	75	8–11 yr
Severe	<50	25	<8 yr

used in Britain of classifying degrees of mental handicap.

Marked deficiency in adaptive behaviour

While measurements of adaptive skills are technically nowhere near as precise as those that measure IQ such measures fulfil a much more useful function in that they identify the skills a person has acquired for day-to-day living. They offer a basis for planning the development of these skills. One such measure developed by the American Association for Mental Retardation is the Adaptive Behaviour Scale. It focuses on the person's ability to adapt to the natural and social demands of his environment. It can be used for children and adults from the age of 3 years to 69 years and for groups other than people who are mentally handicapped, e.g. emotionally maladjusted people. Other measures of adaptive skills include the Progress Assessment Chart, the Progress Evaluation Index and the Social Competent Index.

Adaptive behaviour scale

This scale consists of two parts which identify different domains or areas of behaviour. Part 1 is composed of the following:

1. Independent functioning
2. Physical development
3. Economic activity
4. Language development
5. Numbers and time
6. Vocational activity
7. Self destruction
8. Responsibility
9. ~~9.~~
10. Socialization.

Each domain is composed of a number of sub-domains, e.g. independent functioning is made up of the following sub-domains:

1. eating
2. toilet use
3. cleanliness
4. appearance
5. care of clothing
6. dressing and undressing
7. travel.

Each of these sub-domains are further broken down, e.g. 'toilet use' is subdivided into 'toilet training' and 'self care at toilet'. 'Self care at toilet' is in turn broken down to the items that the person is evaluated on, such as: 'lowers pants at the toilet without help' and 'washes hands without help'.

The person is scored on each of these items and scores obtained for each area of behaviour. The scores may be compared with the scores of other mentally handicapped people with similar levels of functioning in similar situations, i.e. in institutions, home etc. (reference group). The 10 domain scores may be presented as a profile in which the individual's level of performance can be compared with his reference group in terms of percentiles. For example a score of 75 in 'Independent functioning' for a 16-year-old falls at the 29th percentile which is as good as or better than 29% of handicapped people living in hospitals or residential settings.

Part 2 is concerned with maladaptive behaviour and is made up of 14 domains which are divided in a similar manner to Part 1. The domains or areas of behaviour are:

1. Violent and destructive behaviour
2. Anti-social behaviour
3. Rebellious behaviour
4. Untrustworthy behaviour
5. Withdrawal
6. Stereotyped behaviour and odd mannerisms
7. Inappropriate interpersonal manners.
8. Unacceptable vocal habits
9. Unacceptable or eccentric habits
10. Self-abusive behaviour
11. Hyperactive behaviour
12. Sexually aberrant behaviour
13. Psychological disturbances
14. Use of medication.

'Violent and destructive behaviour' is divided into 6 sub-domains that include 'threatens or does physical violence'; 'damages personal property', and 'has violent tantrums'. Examples of the type of statements contained in Part 2 can be seen in the content of the sub-domain of 'has violent temper' or 'temper tantrums'. These are:

cries and screams
stamps feet while banging objects or slamming doors, etc
stamps feet screaming and yelling
throws self on floor, screaming and yelling
others (specify).

The person using the Adaptive Behaviour Scale decides whether each statement is true for the person being assessed and if so whether the behaviour occurs occasionally or frequently. The person is scored accordingly on these items.

Like the IQ scores, a major problem associated with the Adaptive Behaviour Scale is the interpretation of the scores. Interpretation should entail detailed consideration of the individual's physical and social environment particularly the attitudes and expectations of parents or staff.

Progress Assessment Chart (PAC)

This instrument has been largely superseded by more sophisticated methods of assessment of performance skills though it still retains its attraction in the use of the easy to read PAC wheel. The person's competence in particular skills is indicated by shading in the relevant parts of the PAC wheel, which gives a clear, albeit simple, indication of the areas that the individual has problems with.

There are five versions of the PAC, ranging from Primary PAC which caters for very young children or severely handicapped adults, to PAC 2 which deals with adolescents and adult mentally handicapped people. In each version the PAC is concerned with four areas of behaviour, i.e. self-help, socialisation, communication and occupation. Each of these areas are sub-divided, e.g. self-help is composed of four parts; eating, mobility, toilet and washing and dressing. Dressing contains six statements:

co-operates passively when being dressed
holds out his arms and feet when being dressed
assists in getting dressed
pulls off socks
removes and puts on simple articles of clothing
unbuttons accessible buttons.

Progress Evaluation Index (PEI)

With this assessment tool the individual's performance may be assessed regularly and compared with the average performance of his reference group. Here the emphasis is on assessment, goal setting and evaluation on a continuous basis.

Progress Competence Index (PCI)

This measure allows a person to be compared in percentage terms with average performance levels according to age and intelligence.

ASSESSING THE NUMBER OF MENTALLY HANDICAPPED PEOPLE

Finding out the number of mentally handicapped people there are in the general population is beset with problems; firstly there is the problem of the ill-defined nature of mental handicap. Do you depend on IQ score in identifying mentally handicapped people? If so, which system of classifying degrees of handicap do you use? One way is according to standard deviation, mentioned earlier, the other is according to the World Health Organization (WHO) system of calling those who score between 50 and 70 mildly mentally handicapped and those who score below 50 severely handicapped. Instead of using IQ scores you may wish to use a measure of social competence. Again you are faced with the problem of which one to use.

Counting methods

The next decision concerns the methods of counting. There are three main approaches that have been used. The first two methods involve carrying out surveys. One involves counting those who are in contact with agencies either state or voluntary such as social work departments, hospitals for mentally handicapped people, Dr Barnado's etc. The second way is to conduct household surveys, i.e. to go into representative areas and find out directly from people the number of mentally handicapped people in each household. Of the two the latter is considered to be more accurate as many mentally handicapped people, particularly the less severely handicappped, have little or no contact with any services.

The third method depends on statistical processes. It has already been shown that in the Wechsler IQ test the vast majority of people (96%) score within 70 and 130 points (2 standard deviations either side of the mean). Accordingly, about 2% of people score over 130 points and 2% score under 70. The 2% who score under 70 are considered to be mentally handicapped. While this statistical method of calculating the numbers of mentally handicapped people is convenient the figure of 2% is useful only as a rough estimate. More detailed information is required as a basis for any planning of services.

An illustration of the difficulties encountered in the area of obtaining an accurate estimate of the numbers of mentally handicapped people can be seen in a review (Conley, 1973) which lists 9 studies, 7 of which used different IQ scoring in classifying degrees of mental handicap and the remaining 2 different combinations of IQ and social competence criteria. In the U.K. Kuchlick & Blunden (1974) in reviewing 11 surveys found that 6 had different IQ criteria and the remainder simply used the criteria of those who were known to the agencies as being mentally handicapped.

Another illustration of the problem in defining degrees of mental handicap can be seen in Mittler's (1979) results: 75% of mentally handicapped people are mildly handicapped (IQ 70–50), 25% are severely mentally handicapped (under 50) of which 5% of total mentally handicapped population have IQ scores below 20 points. Ingall (1978) using the Wechsler scale and the standard deviation system of classification showed that over 85% of people with mental handicap are mildly handicapped (IQ score 70–55), 10% are moderately mentally handicapped (IQ score 54–40), and the remainder are severely or profoundly handicapped.

Estimation of the number of the more severely mentally handicapped is somewhat easier than for the less severe. Most of those at the severe end of the spectrum are identified early and contact is made with the helping services. Thus the person's name gets on the register. At the less severe end of the mental handicap range the majority do not have contact with services and are not included in the statistics. This may help account for the disparity between the figures based on registers of mentally handicapped people used in planning services and the figure based on standard deviation of IQ scores. For example the Sheffield register (Martindale, 1976) has 0.49% of the population on its books (almost

1 in 200) while according to the Wechsler IQ test the number of mentally handicapped people in the general population is much larger with 2% (1 in 50) scoring under 70 points thus falling into the category of mental handicap. As can be seen from this brief exposition a major difficulty for planners of services and facilities for mentally handicapped people is in ascertaining the numbers for which services should be provided (see Ch. 4 for more detailed discussion).

ATTITUDES TO PEOPLE WITH MENTAL HANDICAP

When we talk about attitudes to something we usually mean that there is a particular underlying pattern or way of thinking that colours the way we relate to that thing. The human brain is incapable of dealing separately with each bit of information that we receive through our senses, so we tend to group pieces of information together into something that makes sense to us. Millar (1956) suggested that we can usually deal with about seven new pieces of information at any one time. An example of this is the immediate recalling of a series of numbers. Most people could recall seven though some may recall more or less than this number. Studies of memory (Baddeley, 1926) have shown that if people learn to group information into existing categories they can improve their recall considerably. Mnemonics is a good example of this technique.

While the process of grouping information and concepts into meaningful divisions makes for greater efficiency in dealing with our world it does have its disadvantages. The production of stereotypes is an important example. Stereotyping involves the formation of opinions on people based on a limited amount of information. Stereotypes have been formed on different nationalities, e.g. Scots, Irish, French. This allows us to deal with individuals about whom we have very little other information. In a similar way we form opinions about people who are mentally handicapped. Although stereotyping is more obvious among the general

public than among those of us who have greater contact with people who are mentally handicapped, staff's behaviour may still show signs of their stereotyping.

Some of the possible stereotypes are, 'Mentally handicapped people are children who will never grow up, or are sick, or are sub-human.

... children who will never grow up'

The reason for this view is that behaviour of mentally handicapped people, their understanding and emotional state are similar to that of children of the same mental age. Unfortunately this view may encourage those who deal with mentally handicapped people to maintain dependency in them, not allowing or encouraging the mentally handicapped person to make decisions for himself and not treating him with the same respect that is given to non-mentally handicapped adults. This attitude tends to ignore the person's view of himself as an adult. For example many adult mentally handicapped people, particularly the less handicapped, dislike playing with brightly coloured games and toys, seeing them as for children (see Ch. 13). Interestingly the same toys are acceptable if sombre colours are used. Being seen to have boy or girl-friends becomes more important from adolescence onwards. To ignore the existence of sexual feelings in all adults is to deny a very important aspect of their make-up. Treating the person as a child is liable to lead to expectations of the person which may cause conflict between what the mentally handicapped person's own needs are and the behaviour he is expected to display. Expression of sexual feeling is likely to result in disapproval by others or guilt or shame.

'... people who are sick'

Society's way of dealing with people who are mentally handicapped supports this view. To an observer it seems reasonable to accept that people who stay in hospital, in wards, who are looked after by doctors and nurses and are called patients must be sick. Patients are people who need looking after. Their own feelings about things in their lives according to the traditional medical model are seen as irrelevant to the way they are treated. The well-behaved 'patient' as seen by staff is one who does as he is told, who conforms to the rules and who does not cause trouble by going against the wishes of the staff. Where staff adhere to the medical model the result is likely to be what has been termed 'institutionalisation'.

'. . . people who are sub-human'

This stereotype of mentally handicapped people is that they do not experience the same appreciation for attractive surroundings as non-mentally handicapped people. They do not respond to attempts at conversation because they do not understand what is being said. Therefore there is no point in talking to them. They do not respond to persuasion, therefore there is no point in trying. The extreme of this view is in treating the more severely mentally handicapped individuals as inanimate objects. Examples of this attitude may be seen in dressing or bathing a person without establishing any sort of communication or in feeding a person while talking to other staff. In a minor way this behaviour may have been experienced by the reader in being served in a shop by an assistant who maintains her conversation with a colleague and treats you with total indifference. The effect on the severely mentally handicapped person of being treated with indifference is likely to be withdrawal. Indifference or unresponsiveness to overtures may in turn be interpreted as indicating absence of awareness in the mentally handicapped person and reinforce the treating of the person as an inanimate object.

RESIDENTIAL CULTURE

As the majority of care staff, particularly nurses, dealing with mentally handicapped people work in residential settings, knowledge of the effect of the social environment on the residents and on themselves and their colleagues is of particular importance.

For these staff the experience of the first contact with mentally handicapped residents is likely to result in 'culture shock'. It is as if the person has moved to another part of the world and found herself in a different culture. The unspoken rules of interaction with people are different from what the person has been brought up to expect. Rules such as how close you stand to someone to whom you are talking, the length of eye contact, the amount of physical contact may be different. Behaviours such as staring and following and touching may cause those new to the culture extreme social embarrassment, i.e. they may have difficulty in making the appropriate social responses. Such acts in our society may justifiably be seen as threatening yet within the institution they are likely to have entirely different meanings.

The new arrival is likely to adjust quickly to the new culture and conform to these and other modes of behaviour acceptable in the institution which may not necessarily be acceptable in the person's dealings with people outside of the institution. It is these modes of behaviour that were of concern to Goffman (1961) in his study of the social lives of hospital inmates. In his book *Asylums* he described the influence of the institution on the lives of the residents. Though his work was based on relationships in mental illness hospitals and prisons, much of what he wrote has enormous relevance for care staff for the mentally handicapped (Goffman, 1959).

Goffman described as 'total institution' the situation where people are cut off from the wider society for an appreciable period of time and where the institution deals with every aspect of their lives. He identified the central feature of total institution as being the breakdown of the boundaries of three spheres of life: sleep, play and work. All aspects of life are conducted in the same place in the immediate company of others and all within the same hierarchical and bureaucratic framework, e.g. the hospital or residential setting.

One process which he described as 'role dispossession' involves the resident no longer being able to present different concepts of self to different individuals and groups. In his life in the institution he sees the same people in the same situations day after day and so develops one definition of self. Goffman feels that it is one of our fundamental freedoms as individuals to be able to present and manipulate different concepts of self to others. Readers may think of their own experiences in the past week where they have presented different concepts of self at home, at work, having an evening out, and even within each of these situations many have presented several different concepts of self. Total institution denies these possibilities to its residents.

The degree of acceptance of a resident's one presentation of self by staff may be indicated by the surprise expressed by staff at the aspects of the resident's behaviour shown in unusual situations, e.g. on holidays or outings or seeing the resident in his own home. Here the individual is not constrained in his role as a resident but is able to present different aspects of himself to others.

Other characteristics of total institution include:

— all residents being treated alike and being required to do the same things together. This ranges from total uniformity at mealtimes regarding times of eating, food available, utensils used, procedures for serving (having communal tea with sugar and milk added before being brought to the table etc) to social interaction with staff.

— a split between staff and residents. In the lower dependency wards the chief function of staff is supervision ensuring that all residents do what is required of them. Residents are typically excluded from any decision-making concerning their future, their personal likes, dislikes, desires and needs not being considered in planning what is to happen to them.

The effect on the residents of total institution is institutionalisation. Institutionalised residents are people whose view of themselves is the same as the institution's view of them as patients. There is a loss of individuality.

Goffman referred to 'being stripped of one's identity kit', with the institution providing the standard replacement. For the mentally handicapped resident the situation is even worse in that mentally ill people and prisoners have already had an identity kit on arrival at the institution. The mentally handicapped person's experiences may only have been of institutional life and their 'identity kit' may consist solely of the institution's issue.

Burn-out

As well as adversely affecting residents many residential settings with their bureaucratic and hierarchical structure and incessant demands on the care staff are a fertile ground for the occurrence of 'burn-out'.

Burn-out may be described as physical and emotional exhaustion resulting from intense and intimate work with people over a period of time. It is characterised by feelings of defeat and despair and a loss of concern and feelings for residents. It is an attempt by the person to cope with stresses by distancing himself/herself from residents and colleagues (Maslach, 1976).

This distancing can be seen in terms of avoiding residents. Some care staff may openly ignore or reject the residents' attempts at communication. Others may 'hide' in the duty or staff rooms to avoid contact with them. Distancing may be achieved by ridiculing and denigrating residents by describing them in terms such as 'low grades', 'Bennys', wallies' and in making derogatory jokes about them with other staff. Another way used to distance residents is to intellectualise. This strategy helps defend the staff member against stressful situations by being abstract and analytical.

Burn-out is not the expression of some permanent psychological characteristic of an individual; rather it is the result of exposing the individual, any individual, to a particular working environment. Instead of branding a colleague or indeed oneself as innately uncaring or cruel one should look at the social and physical work environment for responsibility for these behaviours. Changing the work environment may bring about changes in the individual's behaviour.

The following are possible ways of minimising the adverse effects on the person of his work environment:

— recognition of the phenomenon of burn-out by managers, taking into consideration the staff member's likes, dislikes, interests and opinions in making any decision affecting her/him, e.g. moving staff from one area to another, making available the opportunity for staff to discuss their feelings about burn-out and facilitating the giving of advice and support preferably in group settings
— frequent variation in type of work and/or residents, e.g. allowing staff easy movement from high dependency areas to lower dependency areas
— frequent breaks from work to obtain different perspectives of their work, e.g. attending conferences, study days, visits to other establishments
— shorter periods exposed to the same situation, e.g. doing away with the 'long day' shift system
— greater involvement of all care staff including untrained staff in the organisation of their work and in decision-making.

SUMMARY

Terms used to describe people with low intelligence are prone to carry a strong evaluative component. The term most commonly used in Great Britain is 'mental handicap' which carries the least negative connotations. Categorising the mentally handicapped by assessing their degree of independence with regard to activities of everyday living is perhaps the most positive approach.

Historically, segregation of the mentally handicapped was the policy of treatment pursued by society but recently there has been a trend towards providing more community care. Despite the wide usage of the IQ, Stanford-Binet and Wechsler tests, there is no standard classification to determine the degree of handicap of an individual. Statistically the actual number of people who are mentally handicapped has not been accurately established.

In general, mentally handicapped people are still viewed according to long-established stereotype images and care staff may be responsible for reinforcing such attitudes. Institutional care can have an impact on both staff and residents. 'Total institution' occurs when there is no longer any differentiation between life, play and work. All aspects of life occur in the same location, in the immediate company of others and within the same hierarchical and bureaucratic framework. It can result in all residents being treated alike and being required to do the same things together with a consequent loss of individuality. For care staff, the onset of burn-out is a real possibility. Burn-out is a state of physical and emotional exhaustion resulting from intense and intimate work with others over a prolonged period of time. It can be prevented by positive and effective management which utilises individual skills and group support.

REFERENCES

Baddeley A D 1976 The psychology of memory. Harper & Row, London
Butler F 1951 Sterilization in the U.S.A.. American Journal of Mental Deficiency 56: 2
Conley R 1973 The economics of mental retardation. Johns Hopkins University Press, Baltimore
Darwin C 1880 Origin of species. John Murray, London
Department committee on sterilization 1934 Report. H.M.S.O, London
General Nursing Council for Scotland Circular 1980/8.
Goffman E 1959 The presentation of self in everyday life. Doubleday-Anchor, New York
Goffman E 1961 Asylums: Essays on the social situation of mental patients and other inmates. Penguin, Harmondsworth
Goodman N, Tizard J 1962 Prevalence of imbecility and idiocy among children. British Medical Journal 1: 216–219
Grossman H 1973 A manual on terminology and classification in mental retardation Series 2. American

Association on Mental Deficiency, Washington D.C.

Ingall R P 1978 Mental retardation. Wiley, New York

Kuchlick A, Blunden R 1974 The epidemiology of mental subnormality. In: Clarke A M, Clarke A D B (eds) Mental deficiency: the changing outlook. Methuen, London

Martindale A 1976 A case register as an information system in a development project for the mentally handicapped. British Journal of Mental Subnormality 20(2): 70–76

Maslach C 1976 Burned-out. Human Behaviour 5: 16–22

Millar G A 1956 The magical number seven, plus or minus two: some limits of our capacity for processing information. Psychological Review 63: 81–97.

Mittler P 1979 People not patients. Methuen, London

Osgood C E, Succi G S, Tannerbaum 1957 The measurement of meaning. University of Illinois Press, Urbana

Tredgold A F 1909 The feeble-minded — A social danger. Eugenics Review 1: 97–104

2

Eamon Shanley

Social causes of mental handicap

- Mild mental handicap most prevalent in social classes 4 and 5
- Class differential due to genetic factors or result of social environment
- Existing bias towards middle class culture in educational system and IQ tests
- Working class culture reinforces negative influence
- Social environment causes can be remedied

INTRODUCTION

People who deal with mentally handicapped people in hospitals or in large institutions tend to get a somewhat distorted concept of the prevalence of mental handicap. They may feel that the people they deal with constitute 'the mentally handicapped' and fail to appreciate that they are dealing with a very small percentage of mentally handicapped people who are moderately and severely mentally handicapped.

By far the largest number of mentally handicapped people are to be found in the mild category with considerably less in the moderate range and ever fewer in the severe and profound category. Of the 2–3% of people who are mentally handicapped almost 90% fall in the mild category with less than 4% falling into the severe and profound range. Of the mildly mentally handicapped people the majority live a relatively independent existence.

	% of mentally handicapped population
Mild	86.7
Moderate	10.0
Severe & profound	3.3

Richardson (1975)

The vast majority of those who score within the IQ range of mild mental handicap, unlike those who are moderately and severely mentally handicapped, come from one particular group of people in our society, namely the working class. (They are also referred to as Classes 4 and 5.) This group supplies a disproportionate percentage of people who are categorised as mildly mentally handicapped. In his revision of the Stanford-Binet scale McNemar (42) estimated that the average IQ score of children in Class 1 (professionals) was 116 while in Class 5 (unskilled) the average score was 96. This contrasts the situation in the more severe range of mental handicap where the whole range of classes is proportionately represented.

SOCIAL CLASSES

The category of Classes 4 and 5 is part of a system of socio-economic classification using such criteria as education, occupation and income. These criteria seem to correlate with such ill-defined factors as spending patterns, attitudes and with IQ scores. This system has been used by the Registrar General in the U.K. to identify, 'people whose social, cultural and recreational standards and behaviour are similar'. It must be admitted that there is frequent overlapping of characteristics between classes, and a degree of movement between the groups. Despite this, social class has become an accepted and convenient way of classifying groups in our society.

In the Registrar General's classification scheme the following divisions emerged using the main criterion of occupation:

Class	Occupation
1	Professional — doctors, lawyers, engineers
2	Retailers, farmers, nurses, teachers
3(i)	White collar workers (office workers)
3(ii)	Skilled manual (tradesmen)
4	Semi-skilled
5	Unskilled (labourers)

The term 'working class' refers approximately to Classes 4 and 5, i.e. semi-skilled and unskilled workers, while 'middle class' refers to the remainder.

An alternative means of classification was adopted by Marx in which he emphasised the political nature of class differences. He predicted that in a capitalist society the proletariat (the workers) would become increasingly united and revolt against the bourgeoisie (the owners of the means of production). In other words he saw two classes emerging and being in conflict with one another. He worked out an elaborate theory to support his views. However his predictions have not proved accurate and his interpretation of the term 'class' is inappropriate in this chapter, though awareness of differences in definition of the term 'class' is important. The question we are examining here and which sociologists, psychologists and educationalists have been trying to answer is why there is a significant difference in school performance and IQ scores between Classes 1 and 2, and Classes 4 and 5.

There are two main theories that attempt to account for this difference — the genetic theory and the sociological theory. The genetic theorists take the view that over a period of generations individuals with low intelligence tend to gravitate or drift into semi-skilled or unskilled occupations because they cannot cope with more intellectually demanding work. They tend to socialize with and marry people of similar background thus building up a poor genetic pool. The converse is true of highly intelligent people.

In contrast, the sociological theory identifies the social environment of the working class as being responsible for the poor performance in IQ tests and at school.

GENETIC PERSPECTIVE

Most evidence related to the inheritance of intelligence comes from two sources; firstly in studies correlating IQ scores between people of various degrees of genetic relationship, and secondly in studies showing racial differences in IQ scoring.

In the former the closeness of genetic relationships to similarities in IQ score is measured in terms of a correlation scale. This scale runs from +1 through to −1. The closer to +1 the correlation score lies, the higher the relationship between two events. For example, if a mother scores *low* on a test there is a good likelihood that the child will also score *low*. If the correlation score is 0, then there is just a *chance* relationship, i.e. the mother's score has *no relationship* with the child's score. If the correlation score is near −1 the relationship is negative, i.e. if the mother's score is *high*, there is a good likelihood that the child will score *low*.

Erlenmeyer-Kimling & Jarvik (1963) concluded that the closer the genetic relationship the more similar are the IQ scores. The average correlation between the IQs of parents and their natural children is .50; between parents and adopted children .25; between fraternal twins the correlation is .55; between identical twins reared apart (sharing the same genetic material but not the same environment) the correlation is .75; between identical twins the correlation is .90. These studies indicate a high degree of influence of genetic factors.

The second source of evidence supporting the genetic theory is from studies of racial differences in IQ scoring, in particular in studies of differences between blacks and whites. On average, black Americans score 10–15 points lower than white Americans. In Britain as well as in the U.S.A. the majority of blacks do comparatively poorly at school and end up in unskilled occupations. In fact in Britain 67% of the black work force are unskilled compared to 37% of the total work force who are unskilled (Smith, 1977).

One of the greatest proponents of the genetic theory, Jensen (1969), concluded that differences in IQ scores reflected real differences in levels of intellectual functioning between blacks and whites. His claims have been supported by Eysenck (1971) and Burt (1972). Although the latter's work has been largely discredited these studies have supported the view that differences in IQ scoring exist between blacks and whites, and they contend that these differences indicate a difference in intellectual ability. The view that blacks have

lower intelligence than whites has led to intense political and emotional debate. The main argument against the genetic theory concentrates on the inference that IQ scores reflect levels of intelligence of individuals from different cultures.

> As long as systematic differences remain in the conditions under which blacks and whites are raised (and as long as the effects of these differences cannot be reliably estimated) no valid conclusions can be drawn concerning innate differences in intelligence between races. (Hilgard et al, 1975)

Layzer (1974) concentrated his criticism on the methodology used by Jensen in making the comparison between blacks and whites. He concluded that:

> published analysis of IQ data provides no support whatever for Jensen's theory that inequalities in cognitive performance are due largely to genetic difference.

As with many debates of this kind where apparently contradictory views are expressed there seems a good case for the middle ground, i.e. that both genetic and social factors are important. The argument changes from an 'either or' debate to one in which the degree of importance of each of the factors is contested. In reviewing studies Scarr-Salapatek (1971) concluded that genetic factors account for between 60%–80% of the variance in IQ score while Jencks et al (1972) postulated that 45% of the variance is accounted for by genetic factors, 35% by environmental factors and the remainder (20%) by the correlation between the genes and the environment. While there is not very much that we can do regarding changing the genetic factors closer scrutiny of environmental causes may indicate ways of improving IQ scores.

SOCIAL ENVIRONMENT PERSPECTIVE

The heading 'social environment' has been used in preference to the terms 'cultural deprivation' or 'sub-cultural' handicap used by Forrest et al (1973). Both these terms, although useful in emphasising the different cultural influences of the social environment, have unacceptable connotations. Both imply that the group of people described are inferior, i.e. that they are a subordinate culture or that they have been deprived of culture. The latter view disregards the richness of 'working class' culture and both reflect a dominant bias by a 'superordinate' culture, i.e. by those doing the classifying (the 'middle class'). In order to overcome these possible objections the more general heading of 'social environment' is used.

Studies that blame the social environment for low IQ scores and poor school performances have concentrated on children whose social conditions have altered and who subsequently exhibited marked changes in IQ score.

Skeel & Dye (1939) cited a case where 13 children who had been moved from an orphanage with few staff to an institution where mildly mentally handicapped residents acted as mothers. Following this change the children had made gains in IQ score ranging from 7 points to 58 points. A control group of 12 children who remained in the orphanage actually showed a decline in IQ scores. As adults those who remained in the orphanage ended up in wards of institutions, mental hospitals and mental handicap hospitals. The children who had been moved from the orphanage became independent as adults and compared well with other non-institutionalised people, i.e. the general population.

Davis (1964) described a case where a child had spent the first 6 years of her life in an attic. On discovery her IQ was assessed at 25 yet 3 years later her IQ score was found to be within the normal range.

Kugel & Parsons (1967) in a 2-year investigation studied IQ changes that coincided with social environmental changes in children between 3 years and 6 years of age. The children studied had no apparent organic brain damage and had been diagnosed as moderately or mildly mentally handicapped. A special educational programme was implemented that involved changes in the children's home life and at their school. The result at the end of 2 years was large increases in IQ scores of up to 51 points.

Garber (1975) in recording aspects of the Milwaukee experiment reported major changes in IQ scores as a result of special programmes. One group of black children were given experiences aimed at developing their cognitive powers while another similar group of black children from the same background were not given any special programme (the control group). At the age of 7 years (the experiment had been running from shortly after birth) the average IQ of the former group was 106 and the score of the control group was 85.

One consistent finding in these and other studies into low IQ scores is the relationship between social class and IQ score.

There are two main interpretations of this finding. Firstly, actual deficiencies in cognitive functioning may result from the social environment of Classes 4 and 5. These deficiencies are measured by IQ scores and are reflected in poor school performance. The other view questions the assumption that poor scores on IQ tests and poor school performance reflect deficiencies in cognitive functioning. Proponents of this view, Cole & Bruner (1971), Ginsburg (1972) and Baratz (1970), argue that poor performance may reflect nothing more than the existence of sets of values, language codes and motivation that are different from those of the measuring dominant middle class culture. Socializing someone to the norms, values and attitudes of the dominant culture may merely improve their score at an IQ test and equip them to deal with the 'hidden curriculum' at school. (The hidden curriculum is a phrase used to describe the expectations of the educational establishment based on middle class values.) This view does not imply that cognitive deficiencies do not exist. Instead it emphasises the fact that bias in assessment of intellect exists against 'working class', resulting in a greater likelihood of working class people being considered mentally handicapped.

IDENTIFICATION OF CULTURAL DIFFERENCES

Patterns of Child-Parent Interaction

One of the earliest studies on the differences between working class child-parent interaction and that of the middle class was carried out by Hess & Shipman (1965). They concluded that middle class mothers tended to use a reasoning and person-orientated means of control. Unlike working class parents they did not depend on the power of authority and did not rely on their own position or role to exercise control. This difference in child-parent interaction was emphasised by Bernstein (Trudgill, 1974) who described two possible types of family structures. Firstly, in the positional family, mainly working class, the influence on decisions made depended on the formal status of each member of the family, i.e. it is not so important what is said but who it is that says it. The other type of family structure is the person-orientated family, mainly middle class, where greater credence is given to the individual and where there is much less adherence to the person's position in the family hierarchy. As a result, according to Hess & Shipman, the middle class child learns to depend on reason both in interpreting the disciplining by others and giving justification for his own behaviour, while the working class child learns to be passive and unquestioning.

More recently White & Watt (1973) compared the behaviour of mothers and found that middle class mothers tended to spend much more time interacting with their children, particularly in naming things and explaining about them. They also encouraged up to three times more activity than they discouraged. Working class mothers tended to be much more controlling and discouraged activity more than they encouraged.

Locus of control

Working class people are socialized to being accepting and passive, seeing no possibility of changing their circumstances (Battle & Rotter, 1963). They live in relative poverty, job insecurity and poor housing and feel that they have no control over their lives. This contrasts with the outlook of many middle class children who learn that they can change things in their life through their own initiative and have an awareness of the opportunities of doing so. In other words middle class people feel that the power to change things resides within themselves (internal locus of control) while working class people feel that events outside their influence control their lives (external locus of control).

Research into the effect on school performance of different locus of control showed that locus of control was a good predictor of later school success (Coleman et al, 1966). If a person feels that his own efforts have little influence on how well he gets on, then he is liable to put little effort into trying which in turn is liable to result in low achievement.

Sociolinguistics

According to the Whorfian theory, language determines the way we think (Whorf, 1956). In other words people with different language think differently. While Whorf's theory has been subjected to severe criticism it has become more accepted that language, while not determining the way we think, at least influences our thinking.

Bernstein (1967) examined the different types of language used by the working class and the middle class and postulated that the type of language may account for the differences in performance in school.

He identified two different codes of speech; the elaborated code used by the middle class and the restricted code used by the working class and also by the middle class. Restricted code involves simple sentence structure with a limited repertoire of structures and vocabulary. The subject matter of conversation is more concrete and less abstract than that of those who use elaborated code. The speaker is less explicit, depending on shared assumptions with the listener in the same way as between intimate friends where a single exclamation will instantly convey a wealth of meaning without further elaboration being necessary.

The implications for education of Bernstein's theory are that elaborated code is an important requirement for learning and those who only use restricted code cannot think as effectively as those with elaborated code and, consequently, are at a considerable disadvantage at school. The solution would seem that working class children should be taught elaborated code in order to improve their thinking capacity and also their school performance. Teaching programmes such as Operation Headstart implemented in the U.S.A. proved to be unsuccessful in attempting to improve the school performance of black children despite the many millions of dollars poured into it. The emphasis here was to teach these children to use Standard English (as distinct from Non-standard or Black English).

Another view of Bernstein's theory is that elaborated code is merely a social convention and in education it is demanded as the appropriate style of communication. Working class children are not necessarily any less intelligent; the only difference between middle class and working class children is that the working class way of communicating is not accepted by members of the dominant culture. Those students who use elaborated code tend to be more successful in our educational system and their arrival in positions of authority perpetuates the use of elaborated code in education. The solution to this problem would be to change attitudes towards working class speech and to develop a greater understanding of working class culture and ways of communicating.

Self-fulfilling prophecy

Rist (1970) described how the teacher's expectation influences her behaviour in class. In an all-black kindergarten the teacher assigned each child to one of three groups: fast learners, average learners, and slow learners on the basis of having taught them for 8 days.

Rist felt that this period of time was too short for an accurate assessment to be made. He observed that children designated fast learners were generally neat and clean while slow learners were untidy and often smelled of urine. Slow learners were more likely to have parents on state benefit. The teacher's behaviour towards the children varied according to the grouping she had made. For example the teacher stood closer to the fast learners (the slow learners were furthest from the front) and addressed her remarks to them rather than to the whole class. She involved the fast learners in classroom activities much more frequently than the slow learners in such things as projects and in demonstrations to the class. After a year the teacher commented that the slow learners did not have an idea about what was going on in the class and 'were off in a world all by themselves'. She felt that her teaching was not responsible for the poor performance of the slow learners but was due to their being 'low achievers'. In other words she felt that teaching the low achievers was of little use and responsibility for poor performance resided within the child and not within her. This attitude has been reflected in her classroom behaviour.

Rosenthal & Jacobson (1968) clearly demonstrated the effect of the teachers' expectation on the child's performance. They gave a class of children an IQ test to complete and informed the teachers that certain children were going to show marked improvement over the coming year. In actual fact the children named were selected at random and not on the basis of the IQ scores. A year later the IQ test was repeated. The children described as liable to show marked improvement actually did show significant improvement. The other children showed no change in IQ score.

CONCLUSION

Genetic factors seem to play an important part in determining the level of intellectual functioning of the individual. The main debate now centres on the relative influence these factors exerts. A useful way of viewing this issue is to see genetic factors as representing the individual's potential which can also be influenced by his social environment. If the person with good genetic potential for high level of intelligence experiences adverse social conditions as described in the studies of children in institutions, his potential is unlikely to be realised and he may end up functioning at the level of mild mental handicap. Conversely if a child with low potential experiences favourable social conditions, he is liable to go closer to his maximum potential which might be still below average intelligence. Otherwise he may function at the level of mild handicap.

The culture (working class or middle class) into which a person is born represents an important part of the social environment. It has been shown to influence IQ score and school performance. The view that working class culture is responsible for deficiencies in intellectual functioning is not clear cut. The low IQ score of the working class may be due to factors other than the person's level of intelligence, e.g. different values, different language codes, different motivational factors, and the bias of IQ tests and the educational system towards the middle class.

From a purely practical point of view there is nothing as yet that can be done to alleviate the genetic factors responsible for low intelligence. The area of sociological factors seems to be a bit more amenable to manipulation. The solution for the exponents of the 'no deficiency theory' is to alter the educational system to less middle class bias and to devise IQ tests that are culture free or, as California has done, to use different tests for different ethnic groups. Those who feel there is a deficiency in cognition would argue that further identification with and possibly emulation of the socialization patterns of the middle class for children of working class background may offer the best solution.

SUMMARY

Most mentally handicapped people fall into the category of 'mildly' mentally handicapped.

According to a socio-economic classification based on occupation, education and income, the prevalence of mild mental handicap is concentrated at the lower end of the scale in social classes 4 and 5 whereas severe handicap is more widely spread.

This class differential has been explained by genetic theory — the inheritance of intelligence — and social theory — the effect of the environment. Studies support the idea that class culture is responsible for school failure and low IQ scores and that a bias exists towards middle class culture. Additionally working class culture exerts a negative influence through less effective child/parent interaction, lack of locus of control, restricted use of language and the impact of self-fulfilling prophecy.

If deficiency in cognition exists caused by genetic factors, no improvement is possible. However, if the deficiency is caused by the social environment, then attention should be turned to improving individual components, e.g. the educational system, to alter any bias.

REFERENCES

Baratz S S, Baratz J C 1970 Early childhood intervention: The social science base of institutional racism. Harvard Educational Review 40: 29–50

Battle E S, Rotter J B 1963 Children's feelings of personal control as related to social class and ethnic group. Journal of Personality 31: 482–490

Bernstein B 1967 Social structure, language and learning. In: Dececco J P (ed) The psychology of language thought and instruction. Holt, Rinehart & Winston, New York

Burt C 1972 Inheritance of general intelligence. American Psychologist 27: 175–190

Cole M, Bruner J S 1971 Cultural differences and inferences about psychological processes. American Psychologist 26: 867–876

Coleman J S 1966 Equality of educational opportunity. U.S. Dept. of Health and Welfare

Davis K 1947 Final note on a case of extreme isolation. American Journal of Sociology 57: 432–457

Erlenmeyer-Kimling L, Jarvik L F 1963 Genetics and intelligence. A review. Science 142: 1477–1478

Eysenck H 1971 Race, intelligence and education. Temple Smith, London

Forrest A, Ritson B, Zealey A 1973 New perspectives in mental handicap. Churchill Livingstone, Edinburgh

Garber H L 1975 Intervention in infancy: A developmental approach. In: Begeb M J, Richardson

S A (eds) The mentally retarded and society: A social science perspective. University Park Press, Baltimore

Ginsburg H 1972 The myth of the deprived child. Prentice Hall, Englewood Cliffs, N.J.

Hess R D, Shipman V 1965 Early experience and socialization of cognitive modes in children. Child Development 36: 869

Hilgard E R, Atkinson R C 1975 Introduction to psychology. Harcourt Brace, New York, p 419

Ingall R P 1978 Mental retardation. Wiley, New York

Jencks C et al 1972 Inequality: A reassessment of the effect of family and schooling in America. Basic Books, New York

Jensen A R 1969 How much can we boost IQ and scholastic achievement? Harvard Educational Review 39: 1–123

Kugel R B, Parsons M H 1967 Children of deprivation. Washington: Children's Bureau Pub. No. 440. Welfare Administration DHEW

Labov W 1970 The study of nonstandard English. Urbana Illinois: National Council of Teachers of England

Layzer D 1974 Heritability analysis of I.Q. scores: Science or numerology? Science 183 (March 29th): 1259–1266

McNemar Q 1942 The revision of the Stanford-Binet scale. Houghton Mifflin, Boston

Richardson S A 1975 Reaction to mental subnormality. In: Begeb M J, Richardson S A (eds) The mental retardee and society: A social science perspective. University Park Press, Baltimore

Rist R C 1970 Students social class and teacher's expectations: The self-fulfilling prophecy in ghetto education. Harvard Educational Review 40: 411–451

Rosenthal R, Jacobson L 1968 Pygmalion in the classroom. Holt, Rinehart & Winston, New York

Scarr-Salapatek S 1971 Race, social class and IQ. Science 174 (Dec. 24th): 1285–1295

Skeels H M, Dye H B 1939 A study of the effects of differential stimulation on mentally retarded children. Proceedings & addresses of the AAMD 44 114–136

Smith D J 1977 Racial disadvantage in Britain. (The P.E.P. Report). Penguin, Harmondsworth

Trudgill P 1974 Sociolinguistics: an introduction. Penguin, Harmondsworth, p 51–56

White B L, Watt J C 1973 Experience and environment: Major influences on the development of the young child. Prentice Hall, Englewood Cliffs, N J

Whorf B L 1956 Language thought and reality. Wiley, M.I.T., New York

3

Biological and physical causes of mental handicap

- Autosomes, sex chromosomes and genes can give rise to abnormalities
- Classification of causation must enhance and not dictate care
- Care must be related to the needs of the individual
- Prenatal diagnosis of genetic conditions is increasingly possible
- Infection, nutrition and toxic agents during pregnancy and after birth are risk factors

INTRODUCTION

A knowledge of the causes of mental handicap is essential for all groups involved in the care of mentally handicapped people. It must be recognised, however, that only a small percentage of mentally handicapped people have identifiable causation factors or can be placed within a common grouping or syndrome.

A background knowledge of the causes of mental handicap can enable staff in hospital and community settings to provide the most appropriate care, to play a full role in the prevention of mental handicap at a primary and a secondary level, to help and support the families of mentally handicapped people and to give meaningful advice and counselling. A wider role in health education is also possible through an understanding of the principles of inheritance, the danger from infection, toxic agents and trauma in the causation of mental handicap.

An appreciation of the possible clinical features associated with a particular condition can be a useful guide to planning all aspects of care, as in Down's syndrome, where many physical and mental characteristics appear in almost all sufferers. However, caution must be exercised to prevent a 'label' given to mentally handicapped people becoming a further handicap. Care for each mentally handicapped person must be based on the needs revealed by an individual assessment. Assumptions about physical and intellectual deficits must never be made on the basis of causation factors or any other 'label' imposed on a person.

CHROMOSOMES AND GENES

Hereditary characteristics can be considered as being either chromosomal or genetic. The hereditary characteristics which are referred to as chromosomal result from the effect of an identifiable chromosome or part of a chromosome. Sex is determined by the effect of a chromosome.

Hereditary characteristics, such as eye colour, can be identified as being caused by the effect of one or more genes and so are referred to as genetic.

CHROMOSOMES

Contained within the nucleus of all human cells is a supply of genetic material, organised as strands, known as chromosomes. Humans have 46 chromosomes grouped in pairs: 22 pairs are referred to as autosomes and 1 pair as sex chromosomes. The autosomes are matched. In the female the sex chromosomes are matched and referred to as XX. In the male they are unmatched and referred to as XY.

By convention chromosomes are numbered from 1 to 23 according to the Denver System. The largest pair is number 1 and they are arranged by size to the smallest number 22. The sex chromosomes are pair 23. In an alternative system of classification several pairs of chromosomes are grouped, by size, under a letter, alphabetically from A to G. This facilitates the description of normal and abnormal karyotypes.

The sex cells (the ovum and the sperm) have 23 unpaired chromosomes, 1 chromosome from each pair. The fusion of the ovum and the sperm at conception forms the zygote which has 46 chromosomes. Each parent contributes 1 chromosome to each pair found in the offspring. As many as 50 chromosomal abnormalities have been identified although most are very rare.

Autosomal abnormalities

When abnormalities occur in the autosomes, both male and female clinical sufferers will be found. There are two main types of autosomal abnormality: numerical and structural.

Numerical

A numerical abnormality is where there is the loss or the gain of one or more chromosomes. The main abnormality of this type is the presence of an extra chromosome. It is usually the result of non-disjunction during meiosis.

Examples of autosomal trisomies are:

Down's syndrome — trisomy in pair 22:
Edward's syndrome — trisomy in pair 16 or 17 or 18.
Patau's syndrome — trisomy in pair 13 or 14 or 15.

Structural

Translocation. The transfer of a segment of a chromosome to a chromosome of another pair is a translocation. A balanced translocation carrier is generally physically and mentally normal. Such carriers are, however, at a high risk of producing a clinical sufferer who will have 46 complete chromosomes plus an extra segment. A monosomic fetus is nonviable.

A balanced carrier, male or female, would in theory have 1 chance in 3 of producing a normal non-carrier child, 1 chance in 3 of producing a balanced carrier who would be clinically normal, and 1 chance in 3 of producing a child with a clinical abnormality. The statistical risk of producing a child with an abnormality is much less than the theory suggests. A female carrier is at greater risk than a male carrier of passing on the abnormality.

Example of translocation is:

Down's syndrome — the extra chromosome segment may be attached to a member of one of the following pairs: 13, 15, 21, 22.
Deletion. Abnormalities occur when part of a chromosome is missing. Examples of deletion are:

Cri-du-chat syndrome — deletion of the short arm of a number 5 chromosome.
Wolf's syndrome — deletion of the short arm of a number 4 chromosome.

Mosaicism. In some individuals a percentage of cells have an abnormal chromosome count while the other cells have a normal chromosome count. The non-disjunction responsible for the mosaicism occurs after fertilisation during mitosis, unlike the abnormalities mentioned above which occur during meiosis. Mosaicism of both autosomes and sex chromones has been noted (Craft, 1979).
Examples of mosaicism are:

Down's syndrome — between 2 and 4% of Down's syndrome sufferers are mosaic (Richards, 1974).
Klinefelter's syndrome

Sex chromosome abnormalities

Non-disjunction of the sex chromosomes leads to a number of abnormalities. Basically 2 female and 2 male sex chromosome abnormalities are found:

Phenotype female
Turner's syndrome   Karyotype: XO.
Triple syndrome   Karyotype: XXX.
Phenotype male
Klinefelter's syndrome   Karyotype: XXY.
XYY syndrome   Karyotype: XYY.
Cases have been noted where more than one extra sex chromosome has been present, e.g. XXXX, XXXY (Craft, 1979).

CHROMOSOME ABNORMALITIES

Down's syndrome

Down's syndrome is probably the most well-known condition which results in mental handicap. It is often referred to as mongolism. Although first described by Langdon Down in 1866 it was not until 1959 that the condition was recognised as a chromosomal abnormality. Over the past few years there has been a slight decrease in the incidence of Down's syndrome as a result of antenatal diagnostic techniques and genetic counselling. However, the prevalence of Down's syndrome has increased as the life expectancy of sufferers has improved.

Amniocentesis
Amniocentesis is a procedure by which antenatal diagnosis of a large number of congenital abnormalities can be made. The procedure, normally carried out between the 15th and 20th week of pregnancy, involves the aspiration of liquor amnii from the amniotic sac. Technical considerations make it difficult to carry out the procedure earlier and if carried out later it could be impossible to offer termination for legal reasons.
10–20 ml of fluid is the usual volume aspirated. Centrifuging of the cells gives a quick determination of the sex of the fetus. Culturing cells for karyotyping takes at least 14 days and biochemical analysis as long as 30 days.
Amniocentesis enables identification of the sex of the unborn child, and the diagnosis of certain chromosomal abnormalities, such as Down's syndrome, cri-du-chat and the sex chromosome abnormalities. Elevation of levels of alphafetoprotein makes it possible to identify open neural tube defects such as anencephaly, meningomyelocele and spina bifida. Biochemical analysis enables diagnosis in utero of more than 60 autosomal and X linked recessive disorders, including:
  Galactosaemia
  Maple syrup disease
Various types of mucopolysaccharidosis such as:
  Hurler's syndrome
  Hunter's syndrome (X-linked)
Various types of gangliosidosis such as:
  Tay-Sachs disease

Table 3.1 Types of Down's syndrome (Richards, 1974)

Cause	% of sufferers
Trisomy 21	90+
Translocation	4–5
Mosaicism	2–4

Incidence of Down's syndrome

The overall incidence of Down's syndrome in populations of European origin is approximately 1:700 (Smith & Berg, 1976). Its prevalence is not related to any specific geographic location and it is found in all racial groups.

The incidence of trisomy 21 type of Down's syndrome increases with maternal age. For a mother under 20 years of age the risk is 1: 2300 and at 45 years of age 1: 40 (Siggers, 1978.) Half the children with trisomy 21 are born to mothers over 35 years of age (Siggers, 1978). Age is not significant with translocation mongolism and either parent can be the carrier.

Features and care

There is a large number of common features exhibited by those who suffer from Down's syndrome which makes them look very like each other and makes it possible for them to be identified visually. However, not all of the features will be seen in every case and those features exhibited will vary in degree in each individual. Care must therefore be taken when assessing the needs of Down's sufferers to

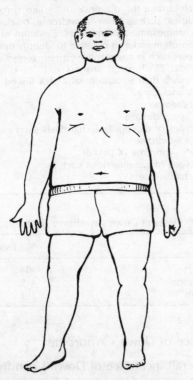

Fig. 3.1 Young adult male suffering from Down's syndrome.

take account of the wide range of physical and intellectual variation found within the syndrome. All those involved in the care of a person with Down's syndrome will find a knowledge of the features of the syndrome a helpful guide to care needs.

Head and brain. The head is small and round with a reduced cranial capacity (brady-cephaly). The brain is simple in structure and underweight. Intellectual deterioration occurs from middle age. Libido is reduced. Epilepsy and cerebral palsy are rare. Co-ordination is poor. During infancy and childhood they are slow for milestones and lag further behind as they grow older.

Hair tends to be dry, sparse and fine. Scalp and skin become dry and flaky. The face is flat as is the occiput. Ears are small with poorly developed lobes.

Skin and hair care is essential. Moisturising creams can be applied to the cheeks and exposed areas, and regular washing of the hair together with brushing and grooming should help to avoid problems with the hair and scalp. It is important to avoid the effects of uncared for skin and hair which can be visually unpleasant, as well as uncomfortable.

Eyes. The eyes are upward and outward slanting. Strabismus, nystagmus and cataract are common, as is an epicanthic fold on the inner aspect of the upper eyelid. The iris is often poorly developed and Brushfield's spots are to be found flecked through the iris. Chronic conjunctivitis and blepharitis are common due to a lack of lysozyme, an enzyme in tears which acts as an antiseptic. Poor sight is also a common problem. All eye infections must be detected quickly and never allowed to become chronic. Chemical agents such as 'artificial' tears can be helpful in some extreme cases.

Nose. The bridge of the nose is poorly developed which leads to mouth breathing. The risk of respiratory tract infection is high. Before the advent of antibiotics the development of serious respiratory tract infections led to few Down's sufferers surviving beyond early adulthood.

Mouth. The mouth is small with a high

Fig. 3.2 Down's syndrome facial characteristics.

narrow palate, whereas the tongue is large with horizontal fissures. As a result, the mouth tends to be open with the tongue protruding. It is possible, through training from an early age, for the tongue to be held in the mouth in a normal manner which improves the general appearance.

Teeth are late, abnormal in size, shape and alignment. Mouth breathing, the protruding tongue and an increased likelihood of dental decay make infection a problem. Care of teeth from an early age is therefore important, as is training of the muscles that control the tongue. Attention should also be paid to the diet. To overcome the problems of mouth breathing and poor teeth, a balanced diet must be presented in such a way that meat and other foods which could be hard to chew are consumed.

Heart. In the past respiratory infection and heart defects resulted in up to 50% of Down's sufferers dying by 5 years of age (Craft, 1979) but this is no longer the case.

Poor circulation in those with heart defects can be present and this will add to the problems with skin care already mentioned. The presence of a heart defect should not lead to overprotection as this in turn could result in understimulation of the cardiovascular system.

Body. The adult with Down's is usually small and broad in stature, rarely being more than 1.5 m tall. They are also hypotonic with joints with an abnormal range of movement. The abdomen tends to be protuberant with umbilical hernia being common. The hypotonia can lead to the adopting of abnormal postures. This is undesirable and planning of care should take account of this potential problem, and suitable exercises be carried out.

Hands and feet. The hands and feet are characteristic. The hands have a square palm with a transverse palmar crease and a wide gap between the thumb and second digit. Fingers are short and stumpy. A gap between the big toe and the second toe is common.

Fertility. Genitalia are underdeveloped. There are no recorded instances of a male sufferer fathering a child. In the few instances where female sufferers have had children, half the children were also Down's sufferers.

There is a wide range of intellectual ability in the Down's group. The majority have IQs of less than 50 and many are profoundly handicapped. Some can learn to read and write. Those with the mosaic type of Down's are least intellectually handicapped. The wide range of ability and the variety and degree of physical effect of the syndrome require individual assessment and the subsequent planning of care and training on an individual basis.

Care should extend beyond the person with Down's syndrome and include his family. The majority of Down's sufferers live at home with their family, and should continue to do so (Jay Committee, 1979).

The person with Down's syndrome is easily recognised. Every effort should be made to

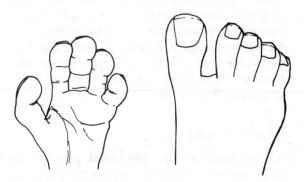

Fig. 3.3 Characteristic hand and feet appearance in Down's syndrome.

minimise the visual impact of the syndrome by taking account of those physical manifestations of the syndrome, such as the protruding tongue and open mouth, which have so stigmatised those with Down's. Attitudes are also important. An optimistic approach to care and training must not be limited by the labels, Down's syndrome and mongolism.

Cri-du-chat

Cri-du-chat, or cry of the cat, syndrome is an autosomal abnormality. There is a deletion of the short arm of one of the number 5 chromosomes. The condition is rare, with an incidence of 1: 50 000 (Niebuhr, 1971).

The cry is distinctive, a high pitched wailing like a cat, and in infancy this is diagnostic. Microcephaly is common. The eyes slant downward, the chin is small and the ears are low set. Characteristically sufferers are of small stature.

During the early months birth weight is low; there is a poor sucking reflex and a failure to thrive. Life expectancy, however, can be into adulthood.

Intellectual handicap is severe, and speech is limited. Approach to care must be individual, taking account of physical and intellectual characteristics.

SEX CHROMOSOME ABNORMALITIES

Only a proportion of people with sex chromosome abnormalities are mentally handicapped. XYY syndrome is not associated with mental handicap. A number of years ago XYY syndrome was linked with psychopathic and criminal behaviours but this link has been disproved (Noel et al, 1974).

Klinefelter's syndrome

In this condition the individual presents as male, but with sex chromosomes XXY. Such an individual is described as chromatin positive male. The incidence of the syndrome is approximately 1 in 1400 live births (Craft, 1979).

Many people with Klinefelter's are of normal intelligence and the majority, who are mentally handicapped, are in the mild and borderline groups. Just over 1% of mentally handicapped males suffer from Klinefelter's syndrome (Heaton-Ward, 1975).

Development until puberty appears normal, but at puberty it becomes evident that secondary sex characteristics are failing to develop. Testes are small or undescended, body hair is sparse and the body shape is feminine due to the distribution of fat. There is a tendency to breast development. Sufferers are infertile. Psychotic and personality problems are common. Secondary sex characteristics are promoted by giving male hormone, such as testosterone. Support and care are especially important during adolesence.

Turner's syndrome

Diminished secondary sex characteristics are a feature of Turner's syndrome. The individual presents as female but lacks ovarian tissue and sex hormones, is sterile and shows primary amenorrhoea. Other physical features include dwarfism, webbing of the neck and a low hairline at the back of the neck.

1:3300 live births are Turner's (Craft, 1979) with only 20% being mentally handicapped. Those who are mentally handicapped are often of low intellect. Oestrogen replacement therapy can help minimise the physical impact of the condition. As in all conditions care needs and subsequent treatment must be determined on the basis of individual assessment and not on the basis of the label.

Triple X syndrome

Triple X syndrome is fallaciously called superwoman. There are no physical characteristics which typify this group of women. They are found through the whole range of mental handicap and can be of normal intelligence. Skeletal and neurological problems are common and psychotic disorders are more frequent among women with triple X than in the normal female population. Incidence is thought to be about 1:1500 live births. There are reports of triple X women bearing normal children.

GENES

Genetically determined conditions can be considered under four headings:

Autosomal dominant inheritance
Autosomal recessive inheritance
Sex linked (X-linked) recessive inheritance
Polygenetic inheritance.

Mechanism and principles of autosomal dominant inheritance (Fig. 3.4)

1. There is a degree of manifestation, i.e. the condition is present to a greater or lesser extent in all cases.
2. There is variation in degree of manifestation over time.
3. A constant risk of 1 in 2 exists that the condition will be passed on.
4. Clinical sufferers can be of either sex.
5. Spontaneous mutations occur. The more serious the clinical impact of the condition, the higher will be the mutation rate.

Examples of autosomal dominant conditions are tuberous sclerosis (Epiloia), neurofibromatosis (Von Recklinghausen's disease), and Huntington's chorea.

Mechanism and principles of autosomal recessive inheritance (Fig. 3.5)

1. Both parents must carry the gene, but they do not suffer clinically.
2. Clinical sufferers can be of either sex.
3. A constant risk of 1 in 4 exists that carrier parents will have an offspring with the recessive condition.
4. A constant risk of 1 in 2 exists that carrier parents will have a carrier child, who will be normal.
5. A child with a rare recessive condition is more likely to be born if parents are related.

Examples of autosomal recessive conditions are phenylketonuria, galactosaemia and Tay-Sachs disease.

Mechanism and principles of sex linked (X-linked) recessive inheritance (Fig. 3.6)

1. Males suffer when they inherit the recessive gene on their X chromosome. There is a constant risk of 1 in 2 for the male child of a carrier mother suffering from the condition.

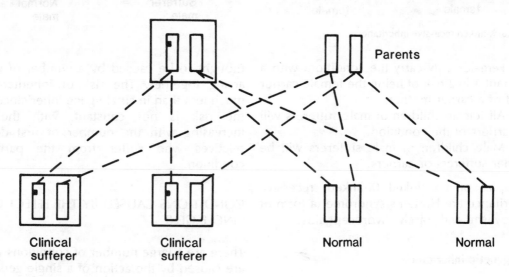

Parents

| Clinical sufferer | Clinical sufferer | Normal | Normal |

Fig. 3.4 Autosomal dominant inheritance.

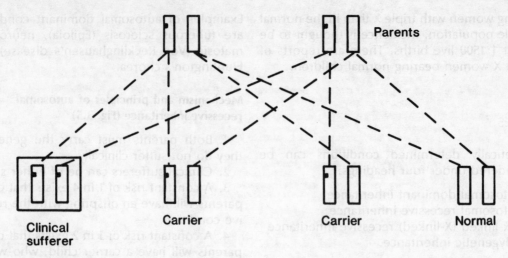

Fig. 3.5 Autosomal recessive inheritance.

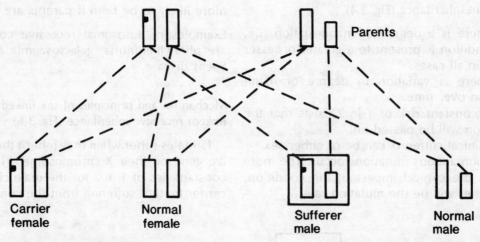

Fig. 3.6 X-linked recessive inheritance.

2. Females only carry the condition, with a constant 1 in 2 risk of being the female carrier child of a carrier mother.

3. All female children of male sufferers will be carriers of the condition.

4. Male children of male sufferers will be neither sufferers or carriers.

Examples of sex linked (X-linked) recessive inheritance are Hunter's syndrome (a form of gargoylism) and, rarely, hydrocephalus.

Polygenetic inheritance

A number of congenital conditions are thought to be caused by a number of genes acting together. The risk of inheritance is much less than in single gene inheritance, but the risk is not constant, with the risk increasing with the number of first degree relatives who suffer from the particular condition.

CONDITIONS CAUSED BY THE EFFECT OF A SINGLE GENE

There are a large number of conditions which are caused by the action of a single gene and which can result in mental handicap.

Autosomal dominant conditions

Tuberous sclerosis

Tuberous sclerosis, also called epiloia, is a rare condition caused by a gene of poor penetrance. The condition only rarely presents in its severest form but it is difficult to estimate the number of sufferers as many cases are so mild that physical and intellectual manifestations of the condition do not show. Incidence is thought to be about 1 in 50 000 (Kirman & Bicknell, 1975). When a person with the gene is mentally handicapped, usually severely affected, epilepsy and a facial rash are present giving three cardinal signs of the condition. The facial rash, adenoma sebaceum, which appears over the cheeks and the bridge of the nose, is described as a butterfly rash (Fig. 3.7). The rash is caused by an overgrowth of the sebaceous glands. 'Shagreen patches', found in the lumbrosacral region, are raised thickened areas of skin. They are found only in some cases.

Tumours are found in the muscle wall of the heart, kidneys and lungs. There are sclerotic nodules in the brain which often become calcified.

The child who is eventually diagnosed as having tuberous sclerosis would typically be slow for milestones, with the adenoma sebaceum becoming evident by 4 or 5 years of age.

Initially the facial rash appears like grains of rice under the skin, but in later life the rash can become red and unsightly.

Mental and physical deterioration may occur and when it does reassessment will be necessary along with an attempt to restore as many lost skills as possible. In this way the highest possible degree of independence can be maintained for as long as possible. Life expectancy in severe cases will be reduced.

Neurofibromatosis

Von Recklinghausen's disease is the other name given to this autosomal, dominantly-inherited condition in which about one-third of sufferers are mentally handicapped. Mental handicap is more likely when lesions are found in the brain. Skin tumours and café-au-lait patches are found on the surface of the body. The skin tumours are painless and can be present in vast numbers, many hundreds in severely affected people. Complications include epilepsy, cerebral palsy, deafness and blindness. Periodic deterioration tends to occur in sufferers resulting in or adding to physical and/or mental handicaps.

Autosomal recessive conditions

There are a large number of autosomal recessive disorders, many of which are associated with mental handicap. Many of these recessive disorders are metabolic.

Phenylketonuria

Phenylketonuria is one of the best known genetic conditions which if untreated can

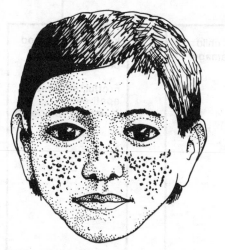

Fig. 3.7 Facial appearance of young adult with tuberous sclerosis.

Table 3.2 Autosomal recessive disorders

Phenylketonuria
Maple syrup disease
Galactosaemia
Tay-Sachs disease
Hurler's syndrome (a form of gargoylism)
Hepatolenticular disease (Wilson's)
Laurence-Moon-Biedl syndrome
Some cases of microcephaly, 'True microcephaly'
Niemann-Pick disease
Some cases of hypothyroidism

result in mental handicap and a number of associated problems. The overall incidence of the condition is about 1 in 10 000 with variations in different geographic areas. The condition is found most frequently in areas of mainland Britain with a high immigrant Irish population such as Liverpool and the industrial west of Scotland.

Phenylketonuria is a disorder of protein metabolism which can be detected by blood test. The Guthrie test is carried out routinely on all babies around the 5th–6th day of life,

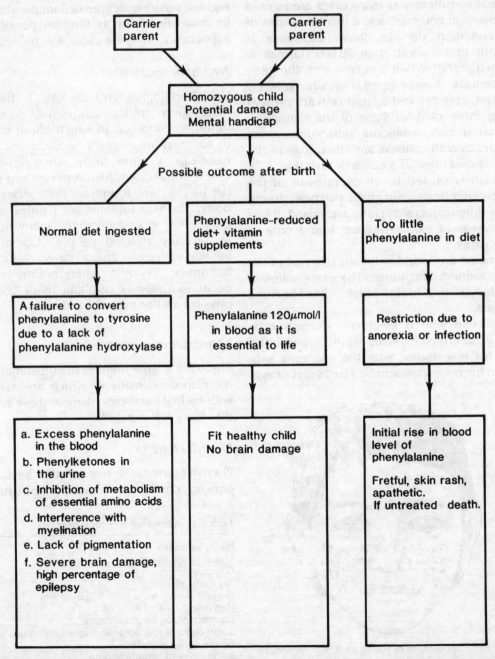

Fig. 3.8A Phenylketonuria's genetic progress

provided that milk has been ingested. If it is established that a baby is phenylketonuric, a phenylalanine-reduced diet must be commenced at once. It is necessary to include phenylalanine in the diet to meet nutritional requirements for normal physical and mental development.

Insufficient phenylalanine in the diet. When there is dietary restriction, caused by food fads or anorexia in infection, there is a breakdown of body protein (catabolism). Blood levels of phenylalanine will show an initial rise and urine testing will be positive for phenyl-ketones. There will be no lasting effect if corrected quickly, but if the situation becomes chronic the child will become fretful, fail to thrive, become apathetic and could die.

Untreated child. Blood levels of phenylala-nine rise and phenylketones appear in the urine. Phenylalanine is not converted to tyro-sine due to a lack of the enzyme phenylalanine hydroxylase. Vomiting and irritability in a child slow for milestones is characteristic. By the second half of the first year of life the child becomes hyperactive and brain damage is apparent. Tyrosine is a precursor for melanin and most sufferers show lack of pigmentation of eyes, hair and skin. Eczema is common as

are autistic features. There is resistance to cuddling and a tendency for self-mutilation. Many damaged sufferers are epileptic. The degree of mental handicap in the completely untreated cases is severe.

Well controlled phenylalanine-reduced diet. A blood level of phenylalanine maintained between 0.125–0.250 μmol will result in a fit healthy child. The phenylalanine-reduced diet is possible by giving protein substitutes and must be accompanied by vitamin supplements and tyrosine. Food products suitable for those on a phenylalanine-reduced diet include Albu-maid, Cymogran, Minafen and Lofenalac. The effectiveness of the diet is monitored by regular urine tests for phenylketones and blood tests to ensure correct levels of phenyl-anine. Problems in maintaining a child on the diet will include the capacity of parents to understand and cope with providing the appropriate diet. Food fads by the child will present difficulties in maintaining phenylala-nine levels as could alterations in health which could interfere with the child's metabolism. Exposure to inappropriate foods found lying about in the kitchen, or stolen from cupboards, or given by people who do not realise the danger, can cause dietary difficulties.

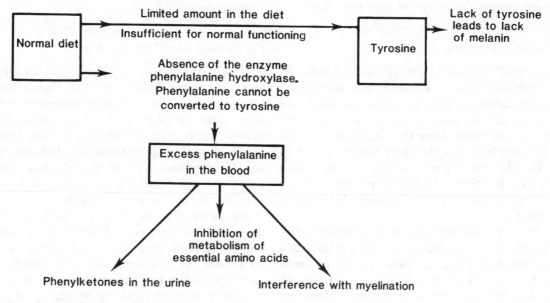

Fig. 3.8B Phenylalanine in the phenylketonuric.

There is considerable debate about when the diet can be stopped. It is thought best to continue dietary treatment after 8 years of age although a measure of relaxation can probably be tolerated (Smith et al, 1978). It is advisable for carrier mothers — and this includes successfully treated sufferers — to be on a phenylalanine-reduced diet prior to and during pregnancy (Lenke et al, 1980).

Galactosaemia

Galactosaemia is an autosomal recessive disorder of carbohydrate metabolism. It is a rare condition with an incidence of approximately 1 in 20 000 live births (Kirman & Bicknell, 1975). Brain damage can be prevented with a milk free diet. Prenatal diagnosis is possible. In galactosaemia there is a failure by the liver to convert galactose into glucose with the result that galactose builds up in the blood. The untreated infant presents as lethargic, with liver enlargement and jaundice in the first few weeks of life. There is a failure to thrive and progressive mental deterioration and the condition may be fatal. Treatment must be started as early as possible with the removal of dietary galactose. Galactomin and nutramigen are food products which are given to provide the appropriate milk free diet.

Hurler's syndrome (Fig. 3.9)

Abnormal storage of mucopolysaccharides in connective tissue is a feature of a number of degenerative conditions, many of which are autosomal recessive. Gargoylism is a name given to sufferers from the condition because of their physical appearance which is said to resemble the figures which project from Gothic Buildings. Hurler's syndrome is an example of an autosomal recessive form of the condition.

Although prenatal diagnosis is possible, the condition is not apparent at birth but becomes evident during the first year of life. The facial features are distinctive. The head is large with frontal bossing, the supra-orbital ridges are prominent and the bridge of the nose is

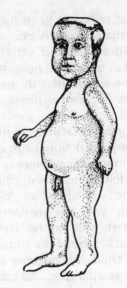

Fig. 3.9 Hurler's syndrome.

depressed. Eyebrows are coarse and hairy. Ears are low set and there is corneal clouding in the majority of cases. The teeth are irregular and are late in appearing. The neck is short and thick. Kyphosis, due to abnormal vertebral deposits, develops. The individual is short in stature as the limbs are relatively short. There is limited extension of the joints. Mental and physical deterioration leads to death in adolescence.

Cerebromacular degeneration

Tay-Sachs disease is an example of an autosomal recessive disorder of lipid metabolism. There are a number of lipid metabolism disorders under the general title of cerebromacular degeneration, also known as amaurotic family idiocy. Age of onset differentiates between the various manifestations of the disease. Nowadays the condition can be detected in the prenatal period by amniocentesis.

Tay-Sachs disease develops early in life, usually in the first year. There is progressive mental deterioration for which there is no treatment at present. As the condition develops in the early months mental deterioration is accompanied by spastic paralysis, blindness and convulsions. A 'cherry red spot' is found in the macula of the retina. Death occurs at about 2 years of age.

When the onset of the disease is delayed until the 6th or 7th year of life, death is likely to occur in the mid teens, the disease having followed a similar course to the early onset type. This late onset type is called Batten's disease.

Hepatolenticular (Wilson's disease) degeneration

Wilson's disease is a rare disorder of copper metabolism with excessive absorption of copper from the diet and a deficiency of copper-carrying protein in the blood called caeruloplasmin.

A failure to thrive and jaundice are followed, usually in adolescence or young adulthood, by mental deterioration. This is accompanied by involuntary choreiform movements and progressive difficulty in articulation and swallowing. There is also a tremor. Contractions and muscle wastage are found with rigidity in the muscles of the trunk, limbs and face. These are associated with copper deposits in the lenticular nuclei of the brain.

Copper is excreted in the urine and deposits are found in the outer margin of the cornea forming what are known as Kayser-Fleischer rings. Liver and kidney function are affected. A reduction of dietary copper and the use of chelating agents such as D-penicillamine can help reduce the physical and mental deterioration.

X-linked (sex linked) recessive conditions

A number of genetically determined conditions associated with mental handicap are inherited in an X (sex) linked manner. Males are affected, while females are carriers of the conditions.

X (sex) linked hydrocephalus

In sufferers of this rare form of hydrocephalus the aqueduct of Sylvius fails to develop fully and without surgical intervention cerebro-spinal fluid accumulates in the ventricles and brain damage can occur.

Hunter's syndrome

This is a form of mucopolysaccharidosis (gargoylism) which affects males. The condition is similar to Hurler's syndrome but with a much slower rate of physical and mental deterioration and sufferers usually survive into adulthood. There is no corneal clouding in Hunter's syndrome.

A non specific X-linked mental retardation with an incidence of 1.8 per 1000 males has become apparent in recent years (Herbst et al, 1980). Such a group of mentally handicapped males may help explain the larger number of males as compared with females in the mentally handicapped population. The indication that a male has a non specific X-linked form of mental handicap is the presence of megalotestes after puberty and a fragile site on the X chromosome, now detectable with improved laboratory techniques. The degree of mental handicap has been found to vary from borderline to profound, with the majority being moderate to severe.

Other specific conditions and syndromes

A large number of conditions, most of them very rare, with a suspected polygenetic origin, or with no known cause but with readily identifiable features, are associated with mental handicap.

Sturge-Weber syndrome

This syndrome, also known as naevoid amentia, is a rare condition, the cause of which is unknown. The condition is typified by a naevus of the face. Part or all of the territory of the trigeminal nerve is affected on one side of the face. The facial marking is referred to as a 'port wine stain' (Fig. 3.10). A meningeal angioma is found on the same side of the naevus. In some cases there may be calcification in the meningeal angioma and the cerebral cortex. Epilepsy is common as is spas-

Genetic counselling

Genetic counselling is a service to parents and potential parents. Risks of genetically inherited conditions can be given and such risks put into perspective. Knowledge of the possible birth of a child with a treatable genetic condition, e.g. PKU, can make early treatment possible and so avoid or minimise damage. A secondary purpose of genetic counselling is the reduction of the birth frequency of genetically determined conditions.

Genetic counselling is appropriate in a number of instances:

1. When a person suffering from a genetically inherited condition wishes to have a family.
2. In families with a member who has a recognised genetically inherited disease, especially if they are parents who already have a child with a genetically inherited condition.
3. Women who are pregnant, or are planning a family and who are over 35 years of age.
4. Women who have had multiple miscarriages.

A careful diagnosis of the condition which brings a person for genetic counselling must be made. This can be achieved with the help of cytogeneticists, biochemists, neuropathologists and, if the condition involves mental handicap, a team with a high level of expertise in the clinical aspects of mental handicap.

Increasing numbers of genetically inherited and congenital conditions can be diagnosed in utero, with the possibility of termination. Amniocentesis is an important prenatal diagnostic procedure. An accurate family tree in some cases can enable the mode of inheritance to be determined and risk established. An explanation of the facts of the disease must be given, with the inheritance pattern. Estimates of risk only reflect statistical probability.

Account must be taken of the person's ability to understand the facts presented. It must also be remembered that a person's attitudes, beliefs and hopes will influence the way they interpret the facts. The psychological and emotional turmoil must also be borne in mind. Counselling should be non-directive, but care must be taken to ensure that decisions made reflect realistically the alternatives available.

Genetic counselling can lead to a number of alternatives for people who wish to have a family or parents who wish to increase family size. It may be that assurance of minimal risk can be given. The choice will be influenced by the disease, the degree of risk of inheritance and the views and feelings of the person being counselled. Where prenatal diagnosis is possible, therapeutic abortion can be offered if tests indicate the fetus has inherited a genetic condition or is damaged in some detectable way. Sterilisation, contraception and adoption are alternatives which might be considered.

ticity. Hemiplegia occurs on the opposite side of the body to the facial marking. The degree of mental handicap can be severe. The effect on the sufferer of the visual impact of the condition must be taken into account by care staff.

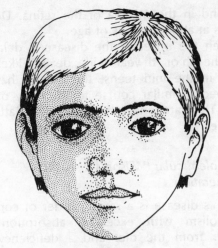

Fig. 3.10 Sturge-Weber syndrome.

Cornelia de Lange syndrome

In 1933 a Dutch paediatrician, Cornelia de Lange, described the syndrome, which has become known as Amsterdam dwarfism. The incidence of de Lange syndrome is said to be 1 in 40 000 (Berget et al, 1970). Cause is unknown.

Microcephaly, facial hair, confluent eyebrows, downward outward slanting eyes and mouth, small ears, small palate and irregular teeth typify the syndrome. The person is dwarfed with limb abnormalities and small hands and feet. Genitals are underdeveloped. In infancy feeding problems are common due to sucking difficulties. All sufferers are mentally handicapped and the degree of handicap can be very severe.

Hydrocephalus (Fig. 3.11)

Hydrocephalus is due to an increase of cerebral spinal fluid (CSF) within the skull, in the ventricles or in the sub-arachnoid space. A whole range of different processes can end in hydrocephalus, including congenital malformation which can cause a blockage to the pathways through which the CSF flows; the aqueduct of Sylvius is a common site for such blockage. Brain tumours and infections, such as meningitis and encephalitis, may end in hydrocephalus.

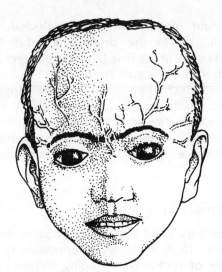

Fig. 3.11 Hydrocephalus.

As well as blockage of CSF pathways, over-production or a failure of absorption of CSF into the venous circulation can lead to an increase in the volume of CSF. A considerable increase in head size can occur without evident brain damage. However, if the damage to brain substance is severe with dilation of the ventricles, then the degree of mental handicap will be profound. As many as 40% of cases spontaneously arrest (Craft, 1979) but surgical intervention is necessary in unresolved cases. The excess fluid can be drained by the insertion of a ventriculo-atrial shunt; drainage into the peritoneal cavity is also possible.

The main visual feature of the condition is the grossly distended head. Spina bifida and hydrocephalus frequently occur together. When the skull has become distended it is thin and veins are dilated. Blindness and deafness are common, as is paralysis. Convulsion can occur and early death results in a considerable number of cases. Intellectual impairment may be a good deal less than initial visual assessment of the gross physical signs of the condition suggest, although severe mental impairment can be found.

Early detection and the advances in surgical treatment mean that no new cases of grossly distended skulls and accompanying severe

mental handicap should occur. Where a mentally handicapped person with hydrocephalus requires care intellectual capacity must not be underestimated as such underestimation can lead to secondary mental handicap caused by lack of appropriate stimulation and a failure to encourage the individual to reach his or her full potential.

Hypothyroidism (cretinism)

Cretinism, or more properly hypothyroidism, are the names given to a group of conditions caused by a deficiency of thyroxine, which is secreted by the thyroid gland. Cretinism can be caused by a number of different metabolic errors all of which result in a similar clinical picture. Several of the errors are thought to be caused by autosomal recessive genes. Incidence of the condition is around 1 in 4–6000 (Crafts, 1979). The problem is treatable with thyroxine, usually given orally, and treatment should be commenced as early as possible, within the first few months of life. Screening, making use of dried blood, is possible but as yet is not routine in the United Kingdom (dried blood from the heel prick used for the detection of phenylketonuria could be used).

The untreated case presents as a child with retarded growth who is apathetic, poor at feeding and sucking and a noisy breather due to an enlarged tongue which protrudes. The condition is characterised by a dwarfed stature, severe mental handicap and delayed acquisition of speech till 7 or 8 years of age. The skin is yellowish, loose and wrinkled with thickening of eyelids, nostrils, lips, hands and feet. Hair is usually scant. Puberty is late and external genitals fail to develop. Care of hair, scalp and skin is particularly necessary in cretinism, as is care to minimise the visual stigma of the condition.

NON-GENETIC CONDITIONS

Prenatal problems which can lead to brain damage

A number of causes of mental handicap operate during pregnancy. The causation factors are not as clear as in genetic causes but are very important, especially in the prevention of mental handicap.

Maternal infection

Examples of maternal infections which have been implicated as a cause of mental handicap include:

syphilis
toxoplasmosis
rubella (German measles)
cytomegalic-inclusion virus
herpes virus.

Congenital syphilis, resulting from maternal infection, is less common than in the past as a cause of mental handicap. Recently, however, there is evidence of an increase in incidence of syphilis (Scottish Health Statistics, 1980). Improved antenatal care and the use of antibiotics have reduced the number of mentally handicapped people damaged by the bacteria.

In untreated cases the mental and physical development of the child can be affected. Jaundice at birth is common. There is a failure to thrive and growth is stunted. There is a typical facial appearance: saddle back nose, opacities of the cornea, strabismus and nystagmus. Teeth are peg-shaped, especially the upper incisors. The effect on the central nervous system is variable as is the possible degree of mental mandicap. Epilepsy may also be present.

Rubella, also known as German measles, is the best known maternal infection which can be a cause of mental handicap. A number of other viruses have also been implicated in causing damage to the developing fetus, including mumps and poliomyelitis virus, and infections such as chicken pox. With rubella the danger time is during the first trimester. The earlier the infection strikes during pregnancy, the more severe will be the damage in affected cases, and the more extreme the degree of mental handicap. Subclinical infection can cause damage and so rubella in the

expectant mother can go undetected. The overall risk to the developing fetus from rubella virus in the first 16 weeks of pregnancy is about 21% (Heaton Ward, 1975).

Affected children show a wide range of defect. Problems include congenital heart lesions, deafness, blindness and microcephaly. Where mental handicap is a feature of the damage the degree varies from mild to severe.

Maternal nutrition

The unborn child is totally dependent on the mother. If there is an interruption to the supply of nutrients, including oxygen, over the placental barrier, the development of the fetus will be affected. Abnormal development of the placenta can be a cause of placental insufficiency. Cardiovascular disease in the mother can limit blood supply to the placenta, and severe diabetes mellitus in the mother puts the fetus at risk. There can be underdevelopment of the fetus in multiple pregnancy. Health education and good antenatal care can help minimise the impact of these problems when they arise.

Assault on the fetus by toxic agents

A number of toxic agents can cause injury to the developing fetus. In some instances the agents are ingested as with alcohol, smoking and drugs. In other instances exposure to such factors as radiation from X-ray and environmental pollutants has been implicated as a causation factor in certain cases of mental handicap.

Alcohol. The intake of alcohol during pregnancy is dangerous. It is impossible to give a precise amount of alcohol which has to be consumed to damage the fetus, but a recent report in the United States pointed out that any alcohol consumed during pregnancy can be harmful.

Damage to the fetus, by alcohol, can lead to fetal alcohol syndrome. In children of alcoholic mothers microcephaly has been noted, as has a failure to thrive. Motor performance has been found to be poorer. There may be as many as 75 000 women of child-bearing age in Britain who are alcoholics (Shaw, 1980). This presents a challenge to health professionals to educate and so help limit the impact of this damaging substance.

Smoking. A birth weight of less than 2500 kg is more likely when a woman smokes during pregnancy. Smoking in pregnancy has also been linked with an increased risk of abortion. It is thought that there is vasoconstriction in the placenta and an increased CO_2 in the blood and so a reduced oxygen carrying capacity. A lack of vitamin B_{12} is found as smoking depletes supplies of vitamin B_{12}. Cerebral palsy and mental handicap are more likely in children with a low birthweight (Kiely et al, 1981).

Drugs. A link between drugs ingested during pregnancy and fetal damage has been positively established in a number of instances, perhaps the most publicised case being thalidomide. Many other cases have been suspected, such as Debendox, though not yet proved. Only drugs prescribed should be taken during pregnancy to avoid all possible risk to the developing fetus.

Radiation. The effect of radiation from excessive use of X-ray during pregnancy has been found to cause damage to the fetus, especially if the radiation exposure is early in the pregnancy. Microcephaly in the children of women who were pregnant and were contaminated in the atomic bomb blasts in Japan was noted, as have been subsequent chromosomal abnormalities and mutant genes. Ultrasound screening techniques are increasingly used for diagnostic purposes during pregnancy and should reduce the potential damage caused in the past by use of X-ray.

A recognition of the effects of external influences on the developing fetus is essential. The provision of good antenatal care and increased health education can help reduce the impact of these influences and so reduce the risk of damage to the developing fetus.

Perinatal problems which can lead to brain damage

Prematurity and low birthweight

There is a link between prematurity, low birthweight and mental handicap. Smoking and the consumption of alcohol during pregnancy are important factors. Members of social class 5 show a disproportionately high incidence of having children with a low birthweight.

Good antenatal care is essential in minimising the number of low birthweight babies being born. The availability of intensive care facilities in obstetric areas can help reduce the effects associated with low birthweight (Kiely et al, 1981).

Jaundice of the newborn (*kernicterus*)

Jaundice in newborn babies is common and only presents a problem if severe. In severe cases staining of the brain substance with bile pigments can occur and so lead to brain damage. A degree of mental handicap can occur, but the bile pigment staining of the basal ganglia causes athetosis, a form of spasticity which involves involuntary movements of the limbs and speech problems. Athetosis should not lead to wrong assumptions about the mental level of the affected person. The uncontrolled movements and speech problems will not necessarily reflect the level of intellectual impairment.

Rhesus factor incompatibility can also result in brain damage due to the bile pigment staining. Again mental handicap can result, as can athetosis. Incompatibility occurs when a

Table 3.3 Conditions in which microcephaly is, or may, be found

'True microcephaly' (autosomal recessive inheritance)
Cornelia du Lange syndrome (Amsterdam dwarfism)
Bird headed dwarfism
Cri-du-chat syndrome
Phenylketonuria
Damage caused by maternal infection, e.g. rubella
Damage caused by radiation, usually early in a pregnancy

woman does not have the Rh factor in her blood. She is described as Rh negative, and she conceives a Rh positive child who has inherited the Rh factor from the father. A first child is not usually affected but at the birth of a first child, Rh positive blood from the child enters the mother's bloodstream and anti-bodies develop. It is only during a subsequent pregnancy that the antibody level increases sufficiently to pass through the placental barrier and begin to destroy the Rh positive blood of the fetus. At birth such a child will be jaundiced and brain damage could result if untreated. It is now possible to prevent the formation of these dangerous antibodies by injecting the Rh woman within 48 hours of delivery of a first child with anti-D gamma-globulin. If maternal immunization has occured or if the condition has not previously been diagnosed, exchange transfusion can be carried out in utero or immediately after birth.

Anoxia

If the brain is deprived of oxygen for 4–5 minutes, irreversible changes occur in the brain. There are a number of causes for oxygen deprivation in the perinatal period, which include:

    eclamptic fit
    prolonged second stage of labour
    coiling of the umbilical cord round the neck
      of the child
    reduction in respiration due to excessive
      maternal sedation
    severe respiratory infection in the immediate
      period after birth.

Parts of the brain most affected by oxygen deprivation are: cerebral cortex, cerebellum, hippacompus, basal ganglia. Administration of an atmosphere too rich in oxygen can be dangerous and can result in blindness (retro-lental fibroplasia).

Trauma

Other damage which can occur during the perinatal period includes:

excessive moulding of the head during delivery
instrument delivery
breech delivery.

Other disorders

In the immediate period after birth untreated hypocalcaemia and hypernatraemia in the child can result in brain damage.

Cerebral palsy and epilepsy as well as mental handicap can be the result of damage done during the perinatal period. The extent of the damage and the part or parts of the brain affected will determine the nature and the extent of the results of brain damage.

Monitoring the fetus is essential during labour. This can be done with the aid of ultra-sonic scan and other electronic monitoring equipment and enables early signs of fetal distress and so potential danger to the fetus to be detected. This, together with knowledge of fetal size and presentation and placental size and site, can reduce the risks of damage to the fetus.

Postnatal and developmental period

During development, before and after birth, the brain can be damaged and mental handi-cap and a number of associated conditions can result. In the period after birth a number of factors can cause brain damage.

Trauma

Severe assault to the head in an accident can cause brain damage, e.g. child being thrown through the windscreen of a motor car. Any accident where oxygen deprivation to the brain occurs, be it a blow to the head or drowning, can result in irreversible brain damage if the deprivation lasts more than 4–5 minutes.

Battered baby syndrome is the name given to a group of brain damaged children whose injuries are non-accidental in origin. The injuries are usually caused by a parent. The extent of the brain damage and the degree of mental handicap will depend on the extent of the injuries. Close monitoring of children at risk of such non-accidental injury is essential and will involve the co-operation of social workers, health visitors and GP's.

Nutrition

Nutritional factors can have an effect on the mental development of a child. Severe malnourishment in infancy has been shown to lead to poorer performance in school.

Those infants who are malnourished, either through ignorance or through the relative poverty of their parents, will also be in a high risk group for social and emotional deprivation.

Infection

Various infections in childhood carry the risk of brain damage as a complication and so mental handicap and associated handicaps will be manifested to some degree.

Gastroenteritis. This is especially dangerous in the very young. Dehydration can occur very quickly leading to brain haemorrhage which can result in permanent brain damage. The subsequent mental handicap can be severe.

Meningitis. Acute pyogenic and chronic granular meningitis can both lead to damage to the brain with resultant mental handicap. In recent years, however, improved health care has reduced the incidence of such infections and the complications which resulted from them.

Encephalitis. Following viral infections such as rubella, chickenpox and mumps, the brain substance can become infected. This is encephalitis. Post vaccination encephalitis is rare but has been noted following whooping cough and other vaccinations. While the incidence of encephalitis is rare the degree of mental handicap which results can be severe.

Malignant growth. Mental deterioration can occur in children with brain tumours. The handicaps experienced and the degree of these handicaps will depend on the parts of

the brain affected. Surgical intervention can help reduce damage and improve the quality of life for the child.

Toxic substances. As in the prenatal period toxic substances can damage the developing brain. Lead intoxication was fairly common in the past when water supply pipes were lead and when the base for paint contained lead. These sources of lead have been greatly reduced or eliminated. The danger of lead in motor vehicle exhaust fumes is being increasingly recognised as contributing to a degree of brain damage, expecially in urban areas (Yule et al, 1981).

Other materials, from industrial sources in particular, which are increasingly polluting the environment are being linked with brain damage. One example is the effect of mercury on a community in Japan where damage was traced to ingested mercury from fish.

Secondary mental handicap

Where it is established that a child is mentally handicapped, for whatever reason, parents and professionals involved in the care of the child must avoid further or secondary handicap.

To label or classify a child as suffering from Down's syndrome, for example, must not limit the expectations for that child. The degree of handicap of individuals with a specific condition will vary, in some cases, over the whole range of mental handicap. An optimistic dynamic approach to each child must be taken. Knowledge of particular features of a condition should be used as a tool to improve the prospects for the child and in no way inhibit stimulation and training and so development.

Suppositions about mental capacity must never be based on visual appraisal and superficial ability. Hydrocephalus or other conditions in which the stigma is obvious, and in some instances gross, need not be accompanied by severe mental handicap. Assessment must therefore be carried out objectively so that care and treatment can be aimed at the real needs of the individual. In all circumstances assets should be identified and built on.

CONCLUSION

Classification of mental handicap can be done in a number of ways, none of which is completely satisfactory. In all systems of classification there will be overlap.

Whatever system is used classification should never be the most important or over-riding factor for parents or care staff. Knowledge about causation and specific features should be known and used as a means of improving care and so quality of life, never inhibiting the life and development of the mentally handicapped person.

Mackay, in his report on the severely mentally handicapped population (those most needing care) in England, states that in over 80% of cases examined, causation of their condition was detectable. Of the detectable cases 55% were prenatal, 20% perinatal and 10% acquired during the developmental period. Identification of a specific cause or grouping by recognisable characteristics is not possible for so large a percentage of the mildly mentally handicapped.

SUMMARY

Hereditary characteristics which have resulted in mental handicap are the result of an abnormality occurring in the genetic make-up of the body in the autosomes, sex chromosomes or genes. Clinical features and prognosis of a particular condition should be used as an aid in planning care but should not impose rigid set patterns unresponsive to individual needs. Not all features of each syndrome or abnormality will be exhibited in every case and individual assessment must take account of the wide range of variation. With advances in technology and scientific investigation prenatal diagnosis of many genetic conditions is now possible.

Non-genetic causes of mental handicap stem from infection, nutrition and assault on the fetus from toxic agents such as alcohol, drugs and radiation. Damage can occur any time during pregnancy and after birth and may be unavoidable, but the provision of good antenatal care and health education is essential to reduce the effect of these risk factors.

Once it is established that a child is suffering from mental handicap, care staff and parents must ensure that secondary handicap does not result. This can be prevented by establishing from the outset what the individual needs of the child are and setting out to meet those needs objectively and realistically.

REFERENCES

Craft M (ed) 1979 Tredgold's mental retardation, 12th edn. Bailliere Tindall, London

Heaton-Ward W 1975 Mental subnormality, 4th edn. Wright, Bristol

Herbst D S 1980 Nonspecific X-linked mental retardation I: a review with information from 24 new families. American Journal of Medical Genetics 443–460

Jay Committee 1979 Report of committee of mental handicap nursing and care. HMSO, London

Kiely J L, Paneth N, Stein Z, Susser M 1981 Cerebral palsy and newborn care II: mortality and neurological impairment in low-birthweight infants. Developmental Medicine and Child Neurology 23: 650–659

Kirman B, Bicknell J 1975 Mental handicap. Churchill Livingstone, Edinburgh

Lenke R R, Levy H L 1980 Maternal phenylketonuria and phenylalaninemia: an international survey of the outcome of untreated and treated pregnancies. New England Journal of Medicine 303: 1202–1208

Mackay R I 1982 The causes of severe mental handicap.. Developmental Medicine and Child Neurology 24: 386–393

Niebuhr E 1971 The cat cry syndrome (5P-) in adolescents and adults. Journal of Mental Deficiency Research 15: 277–291

Noel B, Revil D 1974 Journal of Sex Research 10: 219

Richards B W 1974 Investigation of 142 mosaic mongols; Cytogenetic analysis and maternal age at brith. Journal of Mental Deficiency Research 18: 199

Scottish Health Statistics 1980 Syphilis. Table 3.10, p 31

Shaw S 1980 Women and alcohol. In: Camberwell Council on Alcoholism. Tavistock, London, ch 1, p 1–40

Siggers D C 1978 Prenatal diagnosis of genetic disease. Blackwell Scientific, Oxford

Smith et al 1978 Effects of stopping low-phenylalanine diet on intellectual progress of children with phenylketonuria. British Medical Journal 2: 723

Smith G F, Berg J M 1976 Down's anomaly. Churchill
   Livingstone, Edinburgh
Yule W, Lansdown R, Miller I B, Urbanowicz M-A 1981
   The relationship between blood lead concentrations,
   intelligence and attainment in a school population: A
   pilot study. Developmental Medicine and Child
   Neurology 23: 567–576

Kirk A 1978 Mike — a man with tuberous sclerosis.
   Nursing Mirror August 31: 24–25
Lees A J 1978 De Lange syndrome. Nursing Times August
   3: 1296–1298
Letham P A 1981 Batten's disease. Nursing Times January
   15: 101–106
Minns H 1976 A baby with trisomy E or 18. Nursing
   Times September 16: 1430–1433

FURTHER READING

Baraitser M 1981 Clinical genetics: Down's syndrome.
   Mental Handicap Bulletin 41
Crome L, Stern J 1972 Pathology of mental retardation,
   2nd edn. Churchill Livingstone, Edinburgh
Dowdell P 1981 Alcohol and pregnancy. A review of
   literature 1968–1980. Nursing Times October
   21: 1825–1829
Fitzsimmons J S 1980 A handbook of clinical genetics.
   Heinemann, London
Gath A 1978 Down's syndrome and the family. Academic
   Press, London
Gibson D 1978 Down's syndrome: The psychology of
   mongolism. Cambridge University Press, Cambridge
Heath R B, Griffiths P D, Kangro H O 1980
   Cytomegalovirus: Is it as bad as rubella. Action
   Magazine Summer: 16–19
McElkatton P R 1981 The fetal alcohol syndrome. Action
   Magazine Sept: 21–22
Meadow R 1979 The struggle for child survival. Nursing
   Mirror 149 (13): 34–35
Parkinson C E, Wallis S, Harvey D 1981 School
   achievement and behaviour of children who are small
   for dates at birth. Developmental Medicine and Child
   Neurology 23: 41–50
Schiener A P 1980 Perinatal asphyxia: Factors which
   predict developmental outcome. Developmental
   Medicine and Child Neurology 22: 102–104

Care studies

Cranston J A 1979 A Down's baby. Nursing Times
   October 18: 1792–1794
Dromgoole D 1977 Spina bifida cystica. Nursing Times
   March 24: 406–408
Goodwin R G 1977 Sturge Weber. Nursing Times
   October 6: 1544–1546
Hoyle A 1976 A family tragedy. Nursing Times October
   28: 1669–1671
England F 1979 Detection of non-accidental injury.
   Nursing Times October 25: 1858–1861
Kelly J 1979 Excess copper invades the body. Nursing
   Mirror February 22: 39–41

GLOSSARY

Autosome	A chromosome, other than the sex-chromosomes.
Chromosome	Rod-shaped bodies in the cell nucleus, which contain the heriditary units, the genes.
Congenital	Any abnormality which is present at birth.
Deletion	Where part of a chromosome is missing.
Gamete	A reproductive cell; the male is the sperm, the female the ovum. The gamete contains half the chromosomes and so half the genes of the parent.
Gene	The biological unit of genetic information which occupies a specific site on a chromosome.
Karyotype	The chromosomal make up of an individual. 46 XX for a normal female; 46 XY for a normal male.
Meiosis	The process of gamete formation.
Mitosis	The process of cell division and multiplication.
Mutation	An abrupt change in phenotype due to a change within a gene or a chromosome.
Non-disjunction	The failure of two members of a chromosome pair to separate during cell division. Both chromosomes will thus pass to the same daughter cell.
Phenotype	The outward visible expression of genetic material.
Sex chromosomes	The X and Y chromosomes that are involved in sex determination.
Sex linked	This refers to genes which are carried on the sex chromosomes.
Translocation	The transfer of all or part of a chromosome to a site on another chromosome.
Trisomy	The presence of three chromosomes instead of a pair.
Zygote	The fertilized ovum.

4

Frank Quinn

Associated conditions

- *Associated conditions can arise from damage to the brain and/or nervous system, resulting in physical and/or further mental impairment*
- *Detailed assessment should be made with referral to specialist services if necessary*
- *Accurate observation, recording and reporting by care staff are vital to successful outcome of treatment*
- *Mental illness — psychoses, neurotic and organic reactions — may be present in addition to mental handicap*
- *Abnormal behaviour can often be modified by establishing a channel of communication to create a link with reality*

INTRODUCTION

The aim of this chapter is to concentrate on the more common conditions associated with mental handicap. Many mentally handicapped residents suffer from multiple handicap and the aim of each establishment should be to ensure at least as good a quality of life for those in care, as for non-mentally handicapped people living in the community. They must provide specialist services as a significant number of residents have disabilities and impairments which require active treatment apart from their mental handicap. Management teams should ensure that the needs of each resident for specific treatment, aids and appliances, are carefully considered as part of the process of assessment and continuous review.

EPILEPSY

Epilepsy is one of the oldest conditions known to man. References are made to it in the Bible, and it was described in the writings of Hippocrates. The word 'epilepsy' is derived from the Greek, meaning 'a seizure'. It occurs when there is abnormal neuronal discharge, which is a sudden and unusual discharge of electrical energy in the brain. Within the brain are million of cells called neurones which discharge electrical energy. Sometimes these electrical discharges become erratic and this leads to altered mental and bodily function and may result in some kind of seizure, the visible result of such dysfunction.

Prevalence

The condition is more common in mentally handicapped people, and, like mental handicap, it is a symptom·and not a disease. It was reported (Corbett et al, 1975) that the more severe the brain damage, the more prevalent the epilepsy. The British Epileptic Association *Project Notes* (1975) state that the incidence of epilepsy is 1 in 200 of the population, i.e. 300 000 sufferers in the United Kingdom. A prevalence rate of 43% has been recorded in a hospital population of severely handicapped adults by Reid et al (1978a). Epilepsy is simply a symptom that needs interpretation. However, to many people epilepsy is greatly feared and linked in the public mind with the supernatural. The reaction of the ordinary person to epilepsy is often tinged with superstition, ignorance and mistaken beliefs.

Classification

Various attempts have been made to classify epilepsy with two major categories emerging: (1) generalised epilepsy and (2) partial epilepsy.

Generalised epilepsy. When the seizure involves most of the brain it is called generalised. It includes the grand mal or tonic/clonic type; petit mal and other forms of lapse attacks; akinetic or drop attacks; generalised myoclonic attacks and infantile spasms.

Partial epilepsy. The second category is so-called because the excess discharge of energy is localised to one area of the brain and partial seizures result. The most common type is called temporal lobe or psychomotor seizure, which takes the form of automatic behaviour. Another example is the Jacksonian or focal motor seizure which causes sudden, jerky movements of one part of the body.

Other ways of classifying epilepsy are: idiopathic and symptomatic epilepsy.

Idiopathic epilepsy. The word 'idiopathic' indicates that the condition has no known cause in relation to disease of the brain structure and such cases may have a hereditary link. Parents of children with epilepsy may worry about the inheritance aspect. They fear that the genetic make up of one or both parents may have caused the epilepsy to develop and they will be concerned that subsequent children may develop the condition. To discuss this question of heredity and epilepsy they should consult a genetic counsellor, who can advise on individual risks.

Symptomatic epilepsy. This indicates that there is a known cause of the condition. The cause may be within the brain, such as head injury, tumour, disease, e.g. meningitis, cerebral arteriosclerosis, and associated conditions such as phenylketonuria. The cause may be outwith the brain, such as anoxic disturbance, endocrine disorder (hypocalcaemia, hypoglycaemia), renal disease (uraemia), poisons and toxins (alcohol, lead, insecticides), and pregnancy (eclampsia).

Epileptic seizures may be precipitated by various factors depending on the person's seizure threshold. A seizure threshold is the point at which a seizure occurs. Individuals who have a low seizure threshold tend to develop seizures with less irritation than others. Precipitating factors include excessive fatigue, emotional upset (many are familiar with the saying 'I was so upset I nearly had a fit'), febrile illness and hyperventilation.

Types of seizures

Major/grand mal/tonic-clonic epilepsy

The onset may occur at any age. These seizures can be primary in origin or can result from secondary generalisation of a focal discharge. Characteristics of such seizures can be divided into various stages:

Stage 1 — Warning. Some people experience a warning of an impending seizure. The warning may take the form of prodromal symptoms hours before the event. Individuals may complain of a prodromal headache, a flash of light, feeling of numbness, tingling sensation, an unpleasant taste, smell, visual disturbance, vague feeling of fear, or may experience a change of mood. The prodrome is to be distinguished from the aura which precedes the grand mal fit by seconds or a few minutes. The aura is in itself a partial or focal fit, reflecting abnormal focal discharge in the brain, prior to secondary spread and generalisation (Marsden & Reynolds, 1982). The aura is experienced by some but not all people who suffer from grand mal seizures. Mentally handicapped people may be unable to indicate the presence of a warning.

Stage 2 — Cry. The convulsions may begin with the epileptic cry which occurs as a result of the sudden contraction of the respiratory muscles, which forces air out of the lungs through the vocal cords. This does not always occur and may be an uncommon occurrence.

Stage 3 — Tonic phase. The patient loses consciousness and becomes completely rigid and stiff. The muscles of the body contract and remain in tonic spasm for approximately 30–60 seconds. The pulse is imperceptible and cyanosis is evident as the respiratory muscles are rigid.

Stage 4 — Clonic phase. The rigidity is replaced by a period of intermittent, usually severe, generalised muscle contraction. The tongue may be bitten because of the contraction of the facial and jaw muscle. Urinary and faecal incontinence, and salivation from the mouth may occur. This phase may last for approximately 1–3 minutes.

Stage 5 — Recovery period. The involuntary jerking movements of the clonic phase die away gradually; a period of sleep often follows and may last for only a brief period but could last for hours. Following the seizure, patients are often drowsy, confused, complain of backache or headache and may vomit. Amnesia is usual. Occasionally a serious confusional episode may occur during which the patient may become extremely restless and commit acts of aggression, which he later cannot recall. This is called 'post-epileptic automatism'.

These five stages make up what is called the classical pattern which is subject to variation. However, loss of consciousness and convulsion always occur.

Minor or petit mal seizure

This condition mainly affects children, usually starting between 3 years of age and the teens. It consists of brief lapses of consciousness, thus stressing its short duration. Although the attacks last only a few seconds, they may become very frequent. This is called Pyknolepsy. During the attack the child will cease whatever he is doing and may drop what he is holding. He may stare ahead or roll his eyes upwards. He is unresponsive for a short spell and then continues what he was doing.

Focal epilepsy

This type of seizure is characterised by localised motor, sensory or combined phenomena in a specific area or focus of the brain. Two examples of focal epilepsy are:

Jacksonian epilepsy. It consists of muscular contractions in a localised area of the body, but the contractions may progress and spread and end in a full grand mal seizure.

Psychomotor/temporal lobe epilepsy. This type of epilepsy combines motor seizures with other symptoms, including a diverse variety of behavioural disturbances. Abnormal electrical discharge occurs in the temporal lobe which is a sensory area and causes disturbance in sensory experiences. It is characterised by the performance of automatic activities, altered consciousness, peculiar experiences of smell, taste, sight or hearing, and psychic symptoms, such as 'déjà vu' (a feeling of familiarity despite the fact that the experience is entirely new). Hallucinations, illusions and lack of contact with reality may occur. The patient is in a kind of dream-like state and he may appear confused, become extremely irritable and show destructive behaviour with violent tendencies, during which crimes may be committed. This is the so-called 'epileptic furor'. Occasionally he may wander away — the so-called 'epileptic fugue'.

Myoclonic epilepsy

The term 'myoclonic' refers to involuntary, irregular jerks of muscle groups which can be due to disorder in various parts of the nervous system. It can occur on its own, without evidence of any other central nervous system disease, or it can occur in association with major seizures.

Infantile spasms (West's syndrome: Salaam attacks)

This is a serious form of myoclonic epilepsy which is often seen as flexion spasms and tends to be more common on waking. It is linked to neurological abnormality which may be prenatal, e.g. tuberous sclerosis or phenyl-ketonuria; perinatal, resulting from anoxia at birth or haemorrhage; postnatal, e.g. cyto-megalic virus infection or viral encephalitis. The child commonly regresses in his developmental attainments with the onset of the spasms.

Lennox-Gastaut syndrome

This is a condition associated with a continu-ation of myoclonic absences, tonic and focal fits. Gordon (1976) reported that there is often evidence of mental handicap before the onset of the epilepsy.

In myoclonic encephalopathy of infants or 'the dancing eyes syndrome', a state of almost continuous myoclonus jerking occurs for long periods, affecting the limbs and eyes. There is no clinical evidence of abnormal electrical activity on electro-encephalogram.

Reflex epilepsy

There are a number of people who are abnor-mally sensitive to flickering lights. Jeavans & Harding (1975) reported that this may be induced by being close to a television set and both the frequency of the flicker and the intensity of the illumination may be vital factors. Flashing lights and noise effects in discotheques could well pose problems in this area.

Status epilepticus

This is the state whereby the patient has had a series of grand mal seizures following one another without the patient regaining consciousness between them, and is a medical emergency. Continuous seizures cause hypoxia, brain swelling, hyperpyrexia, and the patient may die if not treated quickly. Sudden with-drawal of anticonvulsant drugs may give rise to this serious situation. Quick and efficient therapy is essential to arrest the seizures.

Investigations

In the search to discover the cause of the epilepsy and the parts of the brain affected, various investigations are undertaken.

Physical and neurological examination

In determining the type of epilepsy involved a careful history must be obtained and a detailed account of each individual's attacks is essential. Reports are helpful, particularly if recorded immediately after a seizure, and completion of a questionnaire is useful. It is important to know the frequency and duration of attacks. Possible precipitating factors must be assessed as the treatment or removal of these may be possible. Muscular movements, reflexes, appreciation of sensations, eyesight and hearing will be examined by the doctor.

Neurological investigations including an electro-encephalogram (EEG) will be carried out. This machine records the electrical activity of the brain (Fig. 4.1). Electrodes are placed on the scalp and this gives information concerning basic rhythms and characteristics of these electrical waves. It is important to correlate the EEG results with the clinical picture presented by the patient because

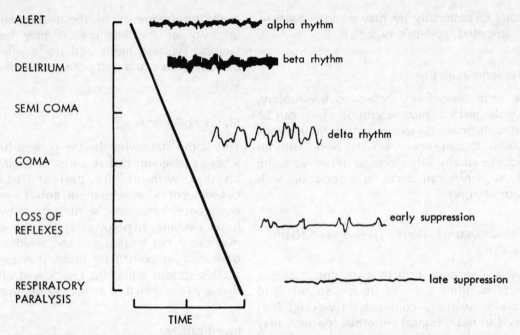

Fig. 4.1 Electrical activity of the brain during different levels of consciousness. (Reproduced from Roddie I C, Wallace W F M 1975 The physiology of disease. Lloyd-Luke Medical, London by kind permission of authors and publisher.)

many people show 'abnormal' EEG readings without any abnormal manifestation in behaviour. Examples of EEG normal and abnormal rhythms are shown in Figures 4.2 A & B. New developments, such as electro-encephalogram telemetry, where recordings are taken in a mobile patient over a period of time, and techniques whereby electro-encephalogram output is stored and analysed in an on-line computer, are very useful.

Radiology

Skull X-rays may reveal abnormalities of the bony skull and sometimes of the brain. Evidence of intracranial pressure or intracranial calcification may be apparent. Nowadays benefit can be obtained from detailed neuroradiological studies such as the use of computerised axial tomography (C.A.T. scan), in which a non-invasive technique allows detailed pictures of the brain to be produced.

Blood tests and urine analysis

Estimation of levels of glucose, calcium and

magnesium are important as seizures may be due to hypocalcaemia and hypoglycaemia. Inborn errors of metabolism may exist and could be the cause of seizures, especially in infants.

Lumbar puncture

This procedure may be helpful in excluding other conditions such as meningitis, encephalitis, subarachnoid haemorrhage or neurosyphilis, although it is not as commonly used as previously.

Psychological tests

Personality and intelligence testing are sometimes necessary in evaluating patients with epilepsy. The cause of the fits, the damage caused by the fits, and subsequently by drugs and other treatments may contribute to producing a degree of intellectual and behavioural impairment in some people suffering from epilepsy (Marsden & Reynolds, 1982).

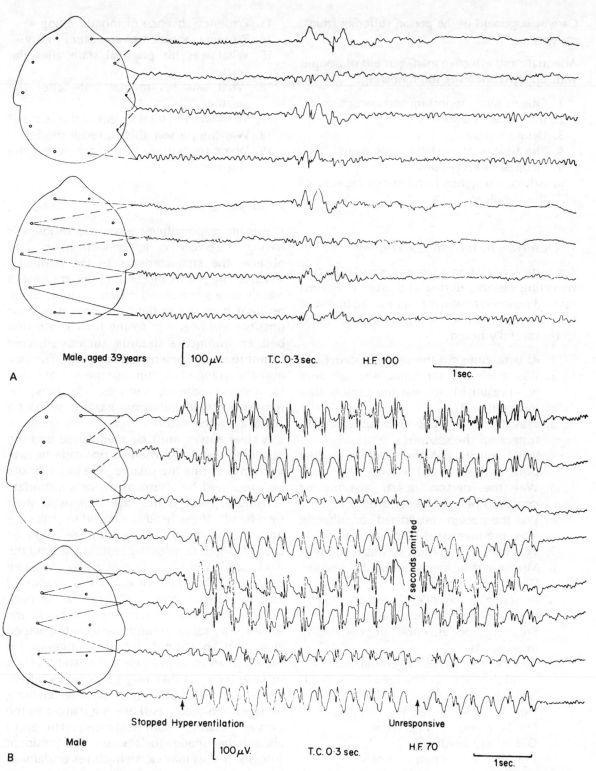

Male, aged 39 years   [100 μV.   T.C. 0·3 sec.   H.F. 100   1 sec.

A

Stopped Hyperventilation   Unresponsive   7 seconds omitted

Male   [100 μV.   T.C. 0·3 sec.   H.F. 70   1 sec.

B

Fig. 4.2 EEG rhythms. (A) Normal (B) Abnormal. (Reproduced from Clarke D 1982 Mentally handicapped people. Bailliere Tindall, London by kind permission of the publisher.)

Care/management of the person suffering from epilepsy

Adequate and effective management of people with epilepsy involves the following:

1. Observation, reporting and recording
2. Individual seizures
3. Drug therapy
4. The treatment of status epilepticus
5. Surgical intervention
6. Advice on general and social aspects of the handicap.

1. Observation, reporting, recording

Accurate observations, recording and effective reporting before, during and after a seizure assist diagnosis, treatment and management of the individual. The following matters will need to be carefully noted:

1. At what time did the seizure occur?
2. Was there any indication that an aura was present? If so, was the person able to describe it?
3. Was there anything that appeared to trigger off the seizure?
4. What activity was the involved in just prior to the seizure?
5. Was the person upset, anxious or confused before the seizure?
6. Was the person constipated, or suffering from pre-menstrual tension?
7. Was the onset gradual or was it sudden?
8. Muscular movements during the seizure: Did the person fall?
   Presence or absence of rigidity
      Was it bilateral/unilateral?
   Presence or absence of convulsive movements
      Were they localised/generalised?
      Did they start in one area and spread?
9. Did the person lose consciousness?
   How long did he remain unconscious?
   Did he respond to his name?
   Did he say anything?
10. Presence/absence of cyanosis
11. Was he incontinent of urine or faeces?
12. What pupillary changes were present?
13. Presence/absence of tongue biting
14. Presence/absence of any other injury
15. What was his physical state after the seizure?
16. What was his mental state after the seizure?
17. What was the total length of the seizure?
18. Was the person able to recall the fit?
19. Were any witnesses present during the seizure?

2. Individual seizures

The main responsibility when the resident is having a seizure is to prevent injury and observe the characteristics of the particular seizure. The points discussed here are related mainly to a generalised motor seizure. If the resident is in the upright position, it may be possible to lower him to the floor or on to a bed. Environmental hazards, such as adjacent furniture or equipment, are removed. Furnishings are arranged to minimise the risk of injury to residents during seizures. He must be removed immediately from hazards such as a roadway, water or fire.

A clear airway must be maintained and the resident's head is turned to one side in case he vomits during the seizure. The head should be supported by a firm pillow or appropriate substitute, such as the care staff using their own hands. If the head is allowed to strike the ground repeatedly, serious damage could be caused. Tight, constrictive clothing around the neck and waist is loosened to facilitate breathing. The angle of the jaw is supported and the tongue prevented from falling back into the pharynx, which would occlude the airway. Any saliva around the mouth is wiped away. Staff should not place their fingers in his mouth in an attempt to clear it of spittle, food or false teeth, as they may get severely bitten. There is no justification in placing anything between the teeth, as there is a danger of the person inhaling tooth fragments. No effort should be made to restrain the resident forcibly, as this may cause fractures or damage to soft tissues.

After the seizure, the resident may be left

where he is to recover if not in danger, or placed in bed and given longer to recover. The staff need to tell him that he has had a fit, his whereabouts, and that someone is there to care for and look after him. He may be confused, disorientated, and complain of headache and backache. If he has been incontinent he needs to be washed and a change of clothing provided; children and adults can get very upset if they wet or soil themselves. It should be emphasised that it is just part of the seizure. Protective clothing can save embarrassment.

In seizures characterised by disturbed behaviour, handle the resident with gentleness as he may lash out with resulting injury to himself or to you. The resident may become irritable, abusive, hostile or aggressive and be unable to keep control of himself. He may become very frightened if he senses that he is losing control. In such a situation the resident desperately needs someone who remains in control, understands and is capable of creating a quiet, accepting atmosphere which makes little or no demands on him.

As soon as possible after the seizure, the care staff must write down their observations. Details regarding the seizures must be discussed with the more able residents and difficulties which they may encounter with insensitive people, talked about. Many mentally handicapped people are unable to discuss their difficulties so this information must be carefully recorded in the resident's notes and on his Epileptic Chart (Fig. 4.3). All injuries must be recorded and, if necessary, an Accident Report must be formulated. The frequency, duration, character, timing and precipitating factors aid the doctor when making an accurate assessment, and contributes valuable and essential information for the staff when planning the individual's care programme.

3. Drug therapy

The aim of drug therapy is complete suppression of the fits, or at least reduction of severity and frequency without interfering

Month _____

Time of attack:

Date	Just after waking	During your day	Bedtime	During sleep
1				
2				
3				
4				
5				
6				
7				
8				
9				
10				
11				
12				
13				
14				
15				
16				
17				
18				
19				
20				
21				
22				
23				
24				
25				
26				
27				
28				
29				
30				
31				

Fig. 4.3 Epileptic chart.

with the developmental aspects of the resident's lifestyle. Drugs which control epilepsy are called anticonvulsants. The recent facility of being able to measure the blood levels of drugs is very important as it indicates the level which controls the seizures but does not produce unwanted effects. These drugs 'soothe' the nerve cells in the brain that may otherwise cause seizures. Unfortunately, they do not change the nature of the cells permanently. A detailed account of the mode of action of anticonvulsant drugs is given by Glaser et al (1980). Anticonvulsants may be used in combination to potentiate the effects of each other, e.g. phenobarbitone and ethosuximide. Like all drugs, anticonvulsants can produce unwelcome side-effects. Any withdrawal of drugs is done in a gradual manner. The care staff must monitor the effects of withdrawal on the person, looking for changes in behaviour, eating habits and withdrawal symptoms. Any changes must be reported and recorded accurately. Anticonvulsants may have a 'slowing' effect on some individuals and physical co-ordination may be affected. If this happens it should be discussed with others involved in dealing with that person as it may severely limit the mentally handicapped individual in his daily programme. Continued medication for 2–4 years is the generally accepted rule and it is important to avoid sudden withdrawal of medication at any time, and particularly during puberty.

Administration of drugs. The effect and side-effects of the drugs administered must be carefully recorded and immediately reported. Close supervision of the resident is important to ensure that the correct dose of the drug is taken at the correct time. Care staff must be aware that there is a wide variability in the rate of metabolism; people with slow metabolism may receive toxic doses of a drug and those with fast metabolism may be undertreated. Table 4.1 contains a number of anticonvulsant drugs currently in use, outlining the indication, average daily dose, and side-effects of each drug.

4. Treatment of status epilepticus

Status epilepticus is a medical emergency and it is vital to have an effective therapeutic regime available and to commence it immediately if the situation arises. The aim of treatment is to suppress the seizures as quickly as possible. A clear airway must be maintained by adequate positioning, oropharyngeal suction, inserting an airway and, if necessary, machine-assisted respiration. The patient needs careful observation as for any unconscious patient, preferably in an intensive care area. Urgent drug treatment is necessary. Medications used include diazepam which is given intravenously or rectally, but may be administered intramuscularly. Paraldehyde can be used by intramuscular injection, but it is painful, has an unpleasant smell and can cause sterile abscesses. The injection site should be massaged to promote absorption; alternatively it may be given slowly intravenously in normal saline. It may be administered rectally but the onset of action is slower. Clonazepam, chlormethiazole and thiopentone administered intravenously, are alternatives. Phenytoin sodium, by intravenous injection, is sometimes helpful and does not depress respiration. In prolonged convulsions it may be necessary to give general anaesthesia. Kemeny et al (1964) reported that the administration of nitrous oxide has been found to be useful. Oxygen may be administered to counter the effects of cerebral hypoxia. The nurse must assist with the administration of drugs and carefully observe the rate of intravenous infusion if this is the method chosen to administer the drug.

If convulsions continue, coma deepens, and pyrexia and hyperpyrexia develop. Respiratory depression and cardiac changes may occur in response to drugs and continuous seizures. Stress may develop in the kidneys and electrolyte imbalance may occur. As a result of these serious implications, fluid balance and serum electrolytes must be carefully checked and the blood urea estimated at frequent intervals. Constant monitoring of the vital signs is essential.

A safe, quiet and non-stimulating environment must be provided. Once the seizures are controlled an assessment of the patient and his drug therapy needs to be reviewed. It is important to determine why status epilepticus should have occurred at this particular time.

Modification of diet. A ketogenic diet which consists of a high fat and low carbohydrate intake may be employed in epilepsy when there is a poor response to anticonvulsant therapy. The diet is designed to make a change in the body's basic chemistry. In some people it has the effect of preventing seizures. The medium chain triglyceride (MCT) diet has been developed, which produces a ketogenic effect by adding a special oil to the diet. It allows a more palatable diet for the individual but diarrhoea and occasionally reduction in growth rate are its chief drawbacks. Occasionally its use has been very successful

Table 4.1 Commonly used drugs in epilepsy

Drug	Indication	Average daily dose	Side-effects	
carbamazepine (Tegretol)	Grand mal and focal seizures	Initial dose = 100 mg/day in children 200 mg/day in adults, then 20 mg/kg/day in 2 or 3 doses	Dizziness Blurred vision Skin rashes Stevens-Johnson syndrome	Possible teratogenicity
clonazepam (Rivotril)	Myoclonic status epilepticus	Oral: 0.01–0.02 mg/kg/day in children. 2.5–20 mg/day in adults	Drowsiness Dizziness Fatigue Hypotonia Ataxia Diplopia	
diazepam (Valium)	Status epilepticus Relieves anxiety	i.v. 0.15–0.25 mg/kg/day Oral: 4–20 mg/kg/day	Dizziness Drowsiness Ataxia Dysarthria Skin rashes	
ethosuximide (Zarontin)	Petit mal	20–60 mg/kg/day in children 200–500 mg/kg/day in adults (oral)	Drowsiness Nausea Vomiting Dizziness Ataxia	Possible mental changes Skin rashes Stevens-Johnson syndrome
nitrazepam (Mogadon)	Myoclonic infantile spasms	0.5–1.0 mg/kg/day (oral)	Drowsiness Ataxia Increased mucus in young	
phenobarbitone (Gardenal) (Luminal)	Grand mal seizures Status epilepticus	Under 6 yr 30 mg 1 or 2 times/day Over 6 yr 60–100 mg 1 or 2 times/day i.v. 20–30 mg per year of life to maximum of 250 mg (in adults); in children: maximum 150 mg	Drowsiness Giddiness Blurred vision Dysarthria Skin rashes General allergy Stevens-Johnson syndrome	
phenytoin (Epanutin)	Grand mal seizures Status epilepticus Psychomotor (temporal lobe) epilepsy	Oral: 500 mg/day i.v. 150–250 mg/day 50 mg (1 ml) per min.	Giddiness Dysarthria Ataxia Blurred vision Confusion Allergy Liver & bone damage Hypersensitivity Sickness	Gum hypertrophy Hirsutism Folate deficiency
primidone (Mysoline)	Grand mal seizures Psychomotor (temporal) lobe) epilepsy Myoclonic attacks	Under 6 yr 50–100 mg 2 to 4 times daily. Over 6 yr 100–250 mg 2 to 4 times daily.	Giddiness Skin rashes	
sodium valproate (Epilim)	Myoclonic grand mal seizures Petit mal seizures Psychomotor (temporal lobe) epilepsy	Children over 20 kg: 20–30 mg/kg/day Children under 20 kg: 20–50 mg/kg/day Adults: initial dose of 600 mg; add 200 mg every 3 days to 1000–1200 mg per day occasionally up to 2600 mg/day	Nausea Vomiting Diarrhoea Abdominal cramps Drowsiness Unsteadiness Hair loss Weight gain	

and the diet may merit more attention in the future (Hopkins, 1981).

5. Surgical intervention

Various surgical techniques have been devised in recent years, but before surgical intervention is considered, certain criteria must be fulfilled. Medical treatment must have completely failed and removal of local epileptogenic lesions must be expected to result in no unacceptable disabilities.

One of the more recent techniques is cerebellar stimulation. It has been shown that not only does electrical stimulation of the cerebellum inhibit normal cortical neuronal activity, but experimental cortical seizure discharges as well (Hopkins, 1981). The technique involves placing electrodes over the anterior and posterior surface of the cerebellum through posterior burr holes. These are activated at intervals by electromagnetic coupling through an antenna placed subcutaneously in the subclavicular region (Cooper, 1978). Cerebellar stimulation is a new approach to an age old problem and the future will allow assessment of the value of this technique as a treatment for intractable epilepsy.

In the case of temporal lobe epilepsy the sufferers who seem to respond best are those with a history of status epilepticus complicating a febrile illness in early life (Gordon, 1976). Symptomatic epilepsy may result from some conditions which are susceptible to surgical treatment. Removal of the problem could enhance the quality of life for the individual. However, brain surgery carries with it many risks and it is critically analysed by the neurosurgeon before any decisions are taken.

6. General and social aspects of care

A person who has seizures and is mentally handicapped should be treated first and foremost as a person, and then the disability seen only in relation to that person. Each one is unique and has to cope in his own way with his epilepsy. Advice and guidance may have to be given to help the sufferer structure his day and plan his activities. The disability should make as little difference as is reasonably possible. This means that the care staff should be prepared to allow the individual to take certain risks. No activity is wholly safe and the element of risk certainly adds zest to life. Certain activities, such as swimming, horse-riding, football, cricket, physical education, are to be encouraged with supervision. Taking precautions to minimise hazards allows the individual to experience these activities he would not otherwise experience. The wearing of a protective helmet gives added protection to those with difficulty in controlling attacks.

Occupational therapy. For the person living in residential centres or hospitals, occupational and industrial therapy departments allow him the opportunity to participate in 'work' situations. Success and a sense of achievement stimulates further effort. Positive reinforcement is a very necessary factor of care to prevent the individual from slipping into a disinterested and apathetic frame of mind. Every effort must be made to identify and encourage the potential he possesses, rather than emphasise what he cannot do.

The person living in the community needs assistance from the social worker or community mental handicap nurse when selecting appropriate accommodation and from the Disablement Resettlement Officer when finding employment. If he is unable to compete in the open labour market, he will be best served by employment in a sheltered workshop or Remploy Factory. He may be assisted to find employment through inclusion in the Register of Disabled People under the Disabled Persons Act.

Family's role. Epilepsy has implications not only for the person affected but also for family members. Family and friends may need to be educated in regard to their attitudes towards the individual's disability. If the individual is cared for at home, parents may need to guard against the tendency of neglecting the other family members, which can lead to resentment and feelings of neglect. They must also resist the acceptance of bad behaviour because of the epilepsy. Other children should be encouraged to talk and ask questions about the condition. They may have misconceptions about it and fears should be allayed that they might 'catch' the condition.

Overprotection and excessive attention can deprive the sufferer of necessary developmental experience. This can result from worry and anxiety, and uncertainties produced by family members may exacerbate the person's seizures. The approach of the family may depend on the degree of other handicaps the person may suffer from, and also on their own experiences and personalities.

Public attitudes. Very often individuals do not suffer as much from their seizures as from the problems created for them by society. The British Epilepsy Association does a great deal in educating the public regarding the condition. It provides identity cards stating that the individual suffers from epilepsy. The card ensures that if a seizure occurs outside the home, prompt and correct treatment can be given and his family informed.

Even so epilepsy may cause the person to feel different from others and this could cause rejection or reluctance to adhere to drug treatment. Further seizures could result and cause problems such as loss of employment. The side-effects of anticonvulsant drugs should be explained but the importance of continued treatment emphasised.

Driving regulations. The necessary legal restrictions regarding driving can cause problems if the person suffering from epilepsy wishes to drive. Eligibility to hold a driving licence in Great Britain is determined by the Road Traffic Act 1974. It allows licences to be granted to those with a history of epilepsy who satisfy certain conditions. For ordinary vehicles:

a. the applicant must have been free from epileptic attacks whilst awake for at least three years from the date when the licence is to have effect, and
b. the driving of a vehicle by the person is not likely to be a source of danger to the public.

The regulations pertaining to those who wish to drive heavy goods vehicles effectively bar anyone from holding a HGV licence if they have had a seizure of any type after the age of 3 years.

Proper management of epilepsy requires the co-operation of everyone involved with the person. Care staff must have a sympathetic and supportive attitude and help the person and his family to fulfil his potential and thereby foster independence.

CEREBRAL PALSY

The term cerebral palsy is used to describe varying disorders of posture and movement, which result from a defect occurring in the immature brain. The clinical picture varies considerably as the disorders present varying levels of muscle tone, involuntary movements and ataxia. Many cerebral palsied people, in addition to having to cope with the primary defect of motor control, experience secondary handicaps, such as intellectual defects, epilepsy, defects of hearing and vision, speech and emotional disruptions.

Causation

The condition may be inherited or arise from factors occurring before, during or after birth. Woods (1969) reported that it is estimated that 5–10% of cerebral palsy is inherited. In other cases brain cells may be damaged by anoxia, resulting from infectious diseases, or birth damage. Rubella can cause cerebral palsy in association with blindness, deafness and microcephaly. Chickenpox, cytomegalovirus infection and toxoplasmosis may affect the fetus and account for cerebral palsy in some people. Blood group incompatibility may cause athetosis, but this is rare nowadays due to advances in this field. Postnatal factors include meningitis, encephalitis and direct violence.

Classification

1. Spasticity

Damage to the cerebral motor cortex causes the most common type of cerebral palsy, with resulting rigidity of the limbs and an inability to relax the muscles. Damage to other areas of the brain may result in athetosis or ataxia. Hitchcock (1978) reported that it is estimated that 70% of cases show spasticity.

The extent and part of the body involved varies:

a. Hemiplegia — the arm and leg of one side of the body are affected.
b. Monoplegia — only one arm or leg is affected.
c. Paraplegia — both legs are affected.
d. Quadriplegia — all four limbs are affected.

2. Athetosis

Damage to the basal ganglia causes frequent involuntary movements which considerably interfere with normal movements of the body. Bowley (1969) reported that writhing movements occur, slurred speech may be in evidence and hearing defects occur in over 40% of this group. Hitchcock (1978) reported that approximately 10% of cerebral palsied people show athetosis.

3. Ataxia

Damage to the cerebellum results in poor body balance, unsteady gait and hand/eye co-ordination difficulties. According to Hitchcock (1978) approximately 10% of people suffering from cerebral palsy show ataxia.

4. Mixed types

Hitchcock (1978) reported that approximately 10% of cerebral palsied people present mixed forms of the above three types. Others may show different types of muscular tension, such as dystonia, hypotonia and hypertonia.

Care of the cerebral palsied individual

Adequate and appropriate treatment principles depend on detailed assessment which includes careful consideration of motor function, hearing, vision and communication tests, and psychological testing.

Assessment dictates the approach of care staff in care and management. It is vital to assess the abilities of the individual and compare these to the developmental norm expected of his age group. The acquisition of abnormal postures may prevent cerebral palsied people from acquiring certain skilled movements. The orderly development of motor patterns as in non-cerebral palsied individuals fails to take place. The handling of the cerebral palsied person when feeding, dressing, bathing, the way the person is spoken to and interacted with, must all become therapy. Cerebral palsy is a multi-faceted problem and involves the work of all disciplines; care staff work closely with a team of therapists in treatment and with parents. Treatment generally aims at improving co-ordination of posture and movement. The abnormal patterns of co-ordination must be stopped or changed, and all the basic movement patterns of head control, turning, sitting, kneeling, standing and balance, built up (see Ch. 9). Change of position both night and day is important in preventing pressure sores. A daily bath is important for skin care and presents an opportunity for carrying out passive exercises.

Feeding

One of the important basic skills is the ability to feed ourselves. We need to eat to live, but also, in our society, we must eat tidily and presentably if we are to be socially acceptable. Correct feeding patterns are important for the cerebral palsied person. He must learn to use tools, e.g. he should at least be able to manage a spoon, as finger-feeding is not socially acceptable as he gets older. Very often cerebral palsied people need specific help to overcome feeding difficulties. The ability to bring the hand to the mouth is basic in learning to feed oneself. It is also an important part in developing hand/eye co-ordination, so vital in later life for more complex motor skills. An inability to develop feeding patterns may cause difficulties with the development of speech.

Feeding a cerebral palsied person in the reclining position excludes him from his peer group at mealtimes and makes him less socially accepted. It also reinforces the extended position. All cerebral palsied individuals can be placed in an upright position for feeding. The extension spasm is prevented by fully flexing the hips and bringing the shoulders and arms forward. If he is too large to be held, he can be placed in a special chair that fits exactly, to allow full support for his thighs with his feet on a foot-rest. The aim is to sit the individual in a position as near normal as possible with minimum support. A harness and groin straps will aid positioning initially. Various aids are available to prevent the plate from slipping on the table.

The care staff will assist the less handicapped to learn to feed himself by sitting on his dominant side and guiding by supporting the elbow and correcting the angle as the hand nears the mouth. If the individual is unable to feed himself, the staff should allow him time to look and see the food he is eating; inform him when food is placed in his mouth so he can concentrate on it, thus preventing choking and startle reactions. Mealtimes are social occasions, people need time and must not be rushed. They need to be encouraged to take part. Food should be given in small amounts to prevent gag reflex. A wooden spoon should he used if the 'bite reflex' is severe. This reflex is stimulated by touching around the mouth and gums but can be reduced by stroking those areas during the day.

Pathological tongue thrust

Pathological tongue thrust, or reverse swallowing, can be associated with cerebral palsy. Thomson et al (1979) reported that observable tongue thrust in a 10-year-old mentally handicapped male was modified during mealtime using operant conditioning techniques. Their findings suggest that operant conditioning is an effective means of treating tongue thrust and associated problems and a desirable alternative to surgical or mechanical procedures.

Communication

The mentally handicapped person suffering from cerebral palsy often has great difficulty in communicating. The speech therapist aims to help the individual control the muscles of the lips, tongue and throat in order to learn correct movements. All opportunities to link speech with objects and activities must be taken. All spontaneous attempts at verbal imitation should be immediately rewarded by praise.

Music and rhythm

This can be integral part of the cerebral palsied person's learning programme. It allows the person to respond and channel inner feelings of joy, sadness, aggression, and tranquillity. Attempts at rhythmically moving to musical sounds aid co-ordination.

Physiotherapy

Following assessment, physiotherapy is concerned with improving balance and head/neck control, maintaining joint mobility, preventing contractures and deformities, the use of reflex-inhibiting posture and concentrating on the person's antigravity muscles. The care staff and physiotherapist should work very closely in relieving 'spasm'. This can be done at bath-time, as warm water relieves spasm or through the use of a pool which provides relaxation and greater freedom of movement. Another technique to relieve spasm is that of 'shaking' the limbs.

After relieving spasm, both active and passive exercises may be carried out. Various aids, e.g. 'standing frame' and 'walkiepen' are useful if aiming for independence. Balance is taught by reducing support, using the 'tailor sitting' position, and using a mirror which allows the person to see himself off-balance. Pony-riding is useful in developing balance and self-confidence. Temple Fay, a neurosurgeon in Philadelphia, recommends that cerebral palsied children be taught movement according to their development in evolution. Lower animals carried out basic movements of progression; similarly, they can be carried out by humans with cerebral cortex damage. This 'Temple Fay patterning' counteracts the assymetrical tonic neck reflex posture and can be used to unlock clenched fists and to correct ankles.

Paralytic dislocation of the hip

The incidence of this complication varies in the available literature. Matthews et al (1953) reported that they found hip dislocation in 2.6% of an ambulatory cerebral palsied group. Samilson et al (1972) reviewed 1013 institutionalised patients, most of whom were unable to walk, and found hip dislocation or subluxations in 28%. This condition can be prevented by surgery but Moreau et al (1979) found that surgical treatment for already dislocated hips is reserved in many cases for the neurologically mature and athetoid patient.

Surgery

Surgical intervention may be advocated in treatment. Orthopaedic surgery attempts to assist walking by lengthening the Achilles tendon, and stabilisation of joints may be achieved by arthrodesis. Neurosurgery, e.g. hemispherectomy, may alleviate associated epilepsy. Hitchcock (1978) reported that stereotactic surgery, which involves destruction of parts of the basal ganglia, may achieve a reduction in involuntary movement and alleviate articulation problems.

Drugs

Muscle relaxants, e.g. diazepam, may be used but large doses cause side-effects, such as drowsiness. Excess salivation may be reduced by drugs such as benzhexal. Associated epilepsy is controlled by anticonvulsants.

VISUAL HANDICAPS

The National Development Group for the Mentally Handicapped (1978) reported that 11.5% of children and 4% of adults in hospitals for the mentally handicapped are blind or almost blind; others have lesser degrees of visual impairments.

Types

Refractive errors

a. Myopia (near-sightedness). The individual cannot see clearly at a distance, because the light rays focus in the vitreous humour before reaching the retina. The problem is corrected by spectacles with concave lenses.

b. Hypermetropia (far-sightedness). The individual has difficulty seeing at close range because the light focuses behind the retina. The problem is corrected by spectacles with convex lenses.

c. Astigmatism This is caused by an irregularity in the curvature of the cornea or lens, giving rise to distortion and blurring of vision.

Eye movement defects

a. Strabismus (squint). This is caused by lack of co-ordination of eye muscles with the result that the eyes do not simultaneously focus on the same object. If the eye is turned inward, it is called convergent squint. If the eye is turned outward, it is called divergent squint. Treatment involves the use of eye patches, corrective spectacles, eye exercises and surgery to shorten or lengthen the muscle attachments to straighten the eye.

b. Nystagmus. This condition gives rise to involuntary rhythmic movements of the eyeballs. It can be associated with good vision but may be associated with retinal disease process producing defective vision.

Developmental defects

One of the most common developmental defects is cataract. A cataract is a clouding or opacity of the lens which blocks the normal passage of light rays through the pupil to the retina. This leads to blurring of vision and eventual loss of sight. Congenital cataract may occur in infants as a result of the mother contracting rubella in the first trimester of pregnancy. Surgery is the only satisfactory treatment for cateract.

Other disease or defects resulting in visual handicap. Injury, infection and other causes that affect the eye can result in visual defects such as partial sightedness or blindness. Common among these are diabetes, syphilis, keratitis and retrolental fibroplasia (Fleming, 1973). Any condition that affects the brain can damage the visual cortex and result in visual handicap. Anoxià may cause swelling in the brain and give rise to cortical blindness, e.g. after status epilepticus. Injury to the brain could result in bleeding and visual cortex damage. Excessive cerebrospinal fluid as occurs in hydrocephalus can cause direct compression and visual problems.

Implications

It is important for staff to appreciate the varying degrees and types of vision which visually handicapped people may possess and use their own abilities to help them to make the best use of this. This demands thorough understanding, knowledge and adequate preparation on the part of the staff with assistance from specialists.

The National Mobility Centre for the Blind and Regional Associations for the Blind offer advice and support in the use of simple mobility and other aids. Remarkable advances have been made in such electronic sensing aids for the blind as the sonic torch, monaural sonic glasses and the binaural sensory aid. These aids partially substitute for the information which sighted people receive through their eyes. They help blind people to become more mobile and help them to reach for objects and materials in their surroundings.

This stimulates the individual's interest, motivation and zest for life. Problems can emerge for the mentally handicapped person trying to learn how to use these aids. Patience, perseverance and time to practise are important to allow full advantage to be taken. The Royal National Institute for the Blind has a specialist advisory service for aids and appliances for visually handicapped people.

It is important that the environment in which the blind mentally handicapped resident lives is carefully planned. 'Landmarks' should be created and the arrangements in the area not changed too often. Address him by name and make your presence known. Let him hold your hand or arm. Continuous disturbing noises, e.g. television, can distract the blind person from listening and developing and co-ordinating other senses. The resident's curiosity should be encouraged by giving incentive for exploration.

Introduction to various occupations and activities should be made slowly and sensitively. Allow the person to explore, using his sense of touch, smell and taste. The visually handicapped may be cautious in their movement and need time and support to build up confidence. At meal-times allow him the opportunity to feel and smell his food, as well as eating it. The blind child must be taught all the things which the sighted child learns naturally by imitation. It is essential to give the blind mentally handicapped individual as many and as varied experiences of everyday conditions as possible. Staff should talk about the objects he handles and the sounds he hears in a way that he understands. They should express their feelings in their voices as well as in their words. The use of drama techniques can develop confidence, a sense of achievement and realisation of the blind individual's own potential and capabilities (Mumford, 1981).

HEARING IMPAIRMENTS

The National Development Group for the Mentally Handicapped (1978) highlighted that approximately 8% of children and 3% of adults in hospitals for the mentally handicapped have little or no hearing. Deafness is a problem for any age group and can come in varying degrees from simply being hard of hearing to being severely handicapped with deafness.

Types

Conduction deafness

This can result because of defects in the external auditory meatus or the middle ear. Defects may include impacted wax or foreign body blocking the canal, damage to the ear drum, such as scarring, thickening or perforation, and failure of the ossicles to transmit sound waves, such as fixing due to otosclerosis.

Sensorineural deafness

This arises because of damage to the cochlea in the inner ear or the auditory nerve. Some causes may include infectious diseases, meningitis, drug toxicity, blows to the head and degeneration of the eighth cranial nerve.

Central deafness

This results because of damage or underdevelopment of the areas of the brain involved in translating sounds. This deafness may be inherited or due to other causes such as infection, for example meningitis or drug toxicity.

Implications

Hearing is more difficult to assess than vision in the mentally handicapped; although a person appears to be responding to sound, he may still be suffering hearing loss. He may hear some sounds but not others, so he behaves as though he has normal hearing, when, in fact, he can only hear a limited range of sounds. A handicap such as deafness isolates the person and cuts him off from the experiences and opportunities that ordinary people take for granted and enjoy. Deafness is often overlooked because it is less obvious than other disabilities. It fails to gain the immediate sympathy that the more obvious blind individual can evoke.

Deafness affects the development and the maintenance of normal communication, i.e. understanding and use of speech. Early detection and continuous assessment are important. Without early detection and skilled intervention he may never acquire enough speech to achieve adequate social interaction. If a mentally handicapped child is also deaf, he may appear more handicapped than he really is, as he will have great difficulty learning from the environment.

Various testing procedures are used according to the maturation of the person and the suspected loss of hearing, and he should be referred to the Audiology Unit for appropriate testing. The need for accurate assessment is stressed because programming for the acoustically handicapped person may involve the provision of a hearing-aid.

Staff should be aware of the services available in the community and the requirements of the deaf mentally handicapped individual. They should ensure that comparable services are extended to residents in homes or hospitals. The Royal National Institute for the Deaf publishes leaflets to help care staff in their efforts to communicate with deaf people. If a resident has a hearing-aid it must be comfortable to wear, the battery checked regularly and the device labelled with the resident's name. Both staff and resident must understand how to use it most effectively. The speaker is advised to speak slowly and clearly to a hearing-aid user. Distractions should be avoided when speaking. If the hearing-aid breaks down, the resident must not be left without one. This would undermine his confidence, and possibly undo weeks of training. The resident should have a spare hearing-aid and facilities for a speedy repair should be available. Units should be equipped with various devices to facilitate conversation with a deaf resident, such as an electrical converser with microphone, amplifier and earphones.

For the mentally handicapped person who has failed to develop spoken language the use of non-verbal communication techniques as an alternative, or as a supplementary form of communication, is important. Makaton is commonly used in the United Kingdom (see Ch. 11). This system can be used to facilitate language, can help to develop understanding of lexical and expressive abilities, and is a medium of communication for those with restricted communication potential. A major requirement for its success is that those in contact with the handicapped person must use it if effective communication is to be achieved.

The management programme for any individual is designed to suit his handicaps and enables him to fulfil his potential most easily. The principles are based on an assessment of the person's disability and a defined set of aims of treatment. This should enable him to reach a more independent and fulfilling mode of life. Speak in a normal voice and inform the resident if he speaks too loudly when it is not necessary. This allows the resident to regain his normal modulation. Talk directly to the individual and in a clear voice but do not accentuate words. If the resident does not appear to understand what is being said, express it differently. Careful and continuous treatment with regular re-assessment of ability and aims is necessary to avoid the otherwise inevitable decline of potential.

STEREOTYPE BEHAVIOUR

This type of repetitious behaviour is characteristic of severely mentally handicapped individuals (Ingalls, 1978). It is ritualistic and has no apparent adaptive purpose. Common examples of stereotype behaviour include rocking, rolling of the head, jumping up and down, twirling of the fingers in front of the eyes, flapping of the arms, picking at oneself. Extreme forms include slapping of the face, banging of the head, biting of fingers or hands, and poking of the eyes.

Theories

Various theories have been suggested to explain this type of behaviour. It may be related to boredom or sensory deprivation. If severely mentally handicapped individuals live in institutions where they lack adequate stimulation in their environment, they resort to stereotype behaviour (Ingalls, 1978). Berkson & Mason (1964) give evidence of stereotype behaviour in chimpanzees who were deprived of the opportunity to interact with other chimpanzees. Forehand & Baumeister (1970) showed that with increased stimulation, the frequency of the stereotype behaviour decreased. Other theories include explanations that stereotype behaviour increases if the individual is frustrated (Hollis, 1971), deprived of the opportunity for adequate exercise (Levy, 1944) and is used as a reinforcement of the stereotype behaviour itself (Ingalls, 1978).

Behavioural approaches

The use of behavioural approaches in the modification of stereotype behaviour is a useful and valuable contribution to the management of severely mentally handicapped individuals displaying such behaviour. Young & Clements (1979) have indicated the importance of the behavioural approach in stereotype behaviour. However, in extreme forms of stereotype behaviour, it is very important to check that there is not in fact some clear reason, related, for example to skin irritation, or general irritation, in the area that is being injured. The choice of a particular approach is dependent upon the individual and his situation. The reasons why a child does what he does must be considered when choosing a means of management if a successful outcome is to be achieved (Cullen et al, 1977).

Various behavioural techniques are used in an attempt to modify stereotype behaviour, for example:

a. withdrawing of social rewards
b. rewarding alternatives to the problem behaviour. Robbins 1977 stressed the importance of differential reinforcement of other behaviour
c. over-correction

d. aversion — which must be administered under certain controlled conditions
e. time-out — which must be carefully monitored.

HYPERKINETIC SYNDROME

Hyperkinesis, overactivity, hyperactive behaviour are descriptive terms indicating patterns of abnormal behaviour in childhood. This condition of motor unrest can be a symptom of great suffering within the family, giving rise to pressure, stress and disarray in the home. The child, in his pursuit of constant lively attention, can, in some cases, cause the extinction of family life and lead to broken homes. The hyperkinetic syndrome is difficult to define. Doctors do not use the same criteria for diagnosis, making discussion on the topic of hyperkinetic behaviour difficult.

In our everyday existence it can be argued that restlessness is a symptom of boredom and detailed concentration results from challenge and interest. The pathological implications of over-activity can be seen in the field of psychiatry. Overactivity, associated with mood elevation, is a distressing and upsetting feature of mania; restless, violent, impulsive and unpredictable behaviour is a result of catatonic excitement in schizophrenia; restlessness and irrational behaviour often present themselves in delirium as a result of acute organic disorders.

Corbett et al (1975) reported that hyperkinesis may overlap epilepsy and is common in mentally handicapped people. In association with behaviour problems, perceptual and conceptual difficulties are likely to be encountered. The syndrome is characterised by:

1. Hyperactivity

The hyperactive child wanders about in a purposeless manner and appears to be unable to control the degree of reaction to a given situation. The channelling of this behaviour into socially acceptable pursuits is an aim of the care staff. Recreational and leisure pursuits, such as music, mime, drama and sporting activities, can be constructed as positive responses to frantic, aimless, noisy and destructive behaviour.

2. Distractibility

One interpretation of hyperkinetic behaviour sees the child as being unable to filter important and unimportant details in his environment. He is bombarded by the constant activity emerging from the surroundings; trivial background details emerge to compete for his attention. He perceives only parts of the whole situation and is sidetracked and distracted in an attempt to try to deal with all stimuli in his environment. Individual attention in small family units is considered essential in setting realistic goals that avoid frustration. Manipulation of the environment to effect learning is a responsibility of the caring staff.

3. Attention

A short attention span causes difficulty in concentration and interferes with learning programmes. From adequate assessment a clear understanding of what the child can do, can assist the care staff in planning potential and allowing for limitations. A quiet room is essential and distractions must be minimised, as excessive stimuli tend to make the child over-excited and impulsive. A planned sequence is desirable for any teaching programme as structure and concrete planning reduce the need for excess control. Toys, clothing and furniture should be strong and durable, as fragility invites destruction.

4. Impulsiveness

As people develop and mature, they progress to controlled behaviour from purely emotional functioning. As they progress they develop a checking mechanism that allows inhibition of impulses. The hyperkinetic is often unable to do this, and, consequently, overreacts emotionally. He is highly emotional and often behaves in a panic-type reaction.

5. Temper tantrums

Difficulty in perceiving the environment and paying attention can cause frustration in the child and he may react in an explosive outburst, such as a temper tantrum. Ignoring the incident may work; he learns that such behaviour does not produce what he wants. If it occurs in situations such as crowds of people, removal to a quiet situation is necessary. If the tantrum continues, the care staff can talk quietly to the child, embrace him showing him that he is still cared for and suggest some pleasant activity. It is important to remain calm and in control of emotions if such an incident arises.

6. Destructiveness

The child is often attracted by stimuli and is prone to touch many objects, over-explore, mishandle and cause breakages. He may be reluctant to let go of objects, manipulate them and cause them to become damaged. A patient and consistent approach is important in handling him. Attitudes towards him must be firm and supportive.

7. Aggressiveness

This child may be aggressive to siblings, parents and care staff without provocation. He needs help in constructing his behaviour boundaries. Care staff need to teach him what is, and what is not, acceptable. Rules regarding acceptable and non-acceptable behaviour give him security, and allow attainable behaviour goals to be set for him.

Treatment

Improvement in the behaviour of some severely disturbed children by the administration of amphetamine drugs has been widely described, particularly in the United States of America, but the long-term effects are debatable (Shaffer et al, 1977). In the 1950s researchers in Canada and in the United States gave serious consideration to diagnostic criteria, and stimulants, such as methyl phenidate, have been widely used. However, considerable objections have been raised about the use of amphetamines in view of problems with drug abuse. Winsberg et al (1972) reported that impramine, a tricyclic antidepressant, had received favourable mention in reducing over-activity.

Major tranquillisers, e.g. thioridazine from phenothiazine group and haloperidal from the butrophenazane group, are sometimes used in controlling the syndrome. Lithium carbonate is used by some doctors, especially if associated with mood disturbance, as in mania (Cantwell, 1977). As in epilepsy, the use of drugs for hyperkinesis is not to treat a specific illness, but to control symptoms. In recent years there has been extensive and optimistic literature on the use of operant conditioning techniques in the treatment of children with hyperkinesis. Christensen (1975) has advocated a token reinforcement programme as a viable alternative to the use of stimulant drugs in mentally handicapped people. Perhaps the best results could be obtained if the two methods of treatment were combined to help alleviate the problem.

Diet

There have been suggestions in recent years that hyperkinesis can be produced by food additives, such as tartrazine (Havard, 1973).

AUTISM

This disorder was first described by Kanner in 1943. He described the outstanding features as a lack of response to other people, a delay in the acquisition of speech and an insistence on the preservation of sameness in the environment. Between one-half to two-thirds of all autistic children are severely mentally handicapped with IQs below 50 (Carr, 1976).

Creek (1961) classified the behavioural

characteristics of autism into a nine-point scale and Clancy et al (1969) extended the scale, listing 14 behavioural symptoms indicative of the condition. He indicated that if seven or more of these were present, autism should be considered:

1. Stand-offish manner; communicates very little with other people; treats them as objects rather than people.
2. Great difficulty in mixing and playing with other children.
3. Strong resistance to any learning of new behaviour or skills.
4. Resists change in routine.
5. Acts as if deaf.
6. No eye contact.
7. Repetitive and sustained odd play.
8. Not cuddly as a baby.
9. Unusual attachment to particular objects.
10. Marked physical overactivity.
11. Spins objects, especially round ones.
12. Prefers to indicate needs by gesture.
13. Lack of fear about realistic dangers.
14. Laughs and giggles for no apparent reason.

Rutter (1970) formulated his four essential points:

1. Delayed and deviant language development which has certain defined features and is out of keeping with the child's intellectual level.
2. Impaired social development which has a number of special characteristics and is out of keeping with the child's intellectual level.
3. Insistence on sameness, as shown by stereotyped play patterns, abnormal preoccupations, or resistance to change.
4. Onset before the age of 30 months.

The autistic child, behaviourally, is characterized by extreme withdrawal and having little interest in people. He shows an inability to concentrate on anybody or anything. He cannot tolerate emotional demands and is unable to offer emotional response. In order to help him, care staff aim to communicate with him to build a relationship with him.

Contact is the foundation of a relationship and all use is made of any means available to do this. Withdrawn children may enjoy playing with or in water. They enjoy the texture and sound of sand trickling through their fingers; such activities create the opportunity to join in and play with the child. Rhythmical movements may offer the autistic child a satisfying outlet; rocking and swinging offer the communicator a chance to break through to his inner world. Music may elicit a response and offer the chance of singing a tune or playing a musical instrument.

These simple approaches allow the formation of a channel of communication. The child will avoid any situation that makes demands of him, so making use of his ritualistic mannerisms allows an opportunity to experience and share. We must create an environment that is undemanding for him and offers a warm and accepting climate. His eccentricities must be accepted and ideas of normality and reality offered. Close observation of his obsessional and bizarre behaviour will often indicate that he is telling us more by his actions than he could ever consciously communicate in words.

Care staff are the most important aid to communication for the autistic child. They communicate by word, gesture, eye contact and expression. Patience, understanding and good humour are essential assets in doing so. They are the child's link with reality; the bond between his fantasy world and the real world. They create the situations in the environment which allows the child to become more aware of himself and other people. His emergence into the real world is slow. He can quickly withdraw into his private world, but the aim is to extend his level of participation.

MENTAL ILLNESS SUPERIMPOSED ON MENTAL HANDICAP

Williams (1971) and the Department of Health and Social Security (1972) reported that psychiatric symptoms and illness are known to be common in hospitals for the mentally handicapped. Reid & Aungle (1974) described psychotic illness, both functional and organic, that occur in people with mental handicap. Goldberg et al (1970) established a method using the standardised psychiatric interview for use in community studies. Ballinger et al (1975) showed that the modified version of Goldberg's standardised interview for use with the mentally handicapped was valid, reliable and applicable. There is substantial research, but little published work relating to mental illness superimposed on mental handicap, although *The Psychiatry of Mental Handicap* (Reid, 1982) is a useful resource.

Affective psychoses

These are disorders where the primary disturbance is that of affect or mood. Mood is a term which refers to the existing emotional make-up which affects the person's total experience and outlook. The disorders consist of depression and mania. Both are usually classed together as manic-depressive disease of pathological origin. Any sequence of depression and mania can occur, but depression is more common than mania. Many residents have depression only, and even in cases that have both, depressive episodes are the more frequent. It may be that some unipolar cases represent as an entity distinct from bipolar cases. Unipolar affective disorders are disorders where the person has either mania or depression (one pole). Bipolar is where the person's mood is likely to swing from one extreme (mania) to the other extreme (depression) within a few months.

Manic-depressive psychoses associated with mental handicap have been studied over the years. Kraepelin in 1896 and 1902 indicated that 'imbecility may form the basis for the development of other psychoses, such as manic-depressive insanity'. Rohan (1936) in his description of 36 mentally handicapped people, some suffering from affective psychoses, indicated that accompanying delusions tended to be grandiose and expansive. Penrose (1941), Hayman (1939), Herskovitz & Plesset (1941) indicated that the more severely

mentally handicapped showed fewer typical features of psychoses. Prevalence rates for in-patient populations range from 6% found by Penrose in 1938, 1.2% by Reid in 1972 and 1.2% quoted by Heaton-Ward in 1977. This compares with 3–4 per thousand of the general population (Hamilton, 1980). In mentally handicapped out-patient populations, Neustadt (1928) found 8% and Craft (1958) quoted 6%. Corbett in 1979 carried out a detailed study of all mentally handicapped individuals over 15 years of age in Camberwell attending mental handicap services. He indicated a prevalence rate of 1.5% for bipolar affective psychoses on 31 December, 1971 and 2% for current depressive illness.

Depression

There are few people who have not experienced some state of depression. In some, the symptoms are trivial and disappear quickly; in others the symptoms persist and are so severe that they affect the person's abilities to cope.

Psychological features. The resident looks sad, preoccupied, self-concerned and tired. His facial expression is distressed, tormented and shows little or no emotion. Dysphoria is a feature. He loses interest and withdraws. Everything looks gloomy and hopeless. Psychomotor activity is inhibited — movement is slow and dragging; speech slow and monotonous; there is poverty of thought and lack of concentration. Diurnal variation and suicidal tendencies and delusions of guilt about his moral worth are experienced; hypochondriacal delusions regarding his bodily health; delusions of poverty pertaining to financial worries and paranoid delusions in relation to interpersonal relationships and social status. Hallucinations are rare but may be limited to reproaching voices; agitation and stupor when they occur cause added difficulties.

Physical features
1. Insomnia — variations of sleep disorder occur. It may be marked at the beginning, middle or latter part of the night.
2. Anorexia and loss of weight.

3. Constipation is common and may be linked to hypochondriasis.
4. Palpitations and tight feelings in the chest.
5. Amenorrhoea in women.
6. Progressive retardation leads to a depressive stupor with no response to stimuli.

Many mentally handicapped people have communicative difficulties and may lack the ability to describe a mood of depression; others would be completely unable to do so because of their intellectual capacity and/or lack of speech. Depressive symptoms may be masked behind a statement such as 'I'm very fed up' or acted out in aggressive or agitated states of behaviour. Kielholz et al (1973) indicate that the more handicapped the person, the more likely is his depressive illness to be 'masked'. Reid (1982) has indicated that disturbance of sleep, appetite, bowel habits, headaches, abdominal pain, hysterical fits, bizarre gaits and persistent attention-seeking hypochondria are common features.

The major caring problem in dealing with a person who is depressed is suicide. When a person is hopeless and desperate, he will consider it. Reid (1982) reported that suicide and attempted suicide are not unknown among people who are mentally handicapped. Often the suicide attempt is ineffective and may contain an element of plea, though all attempts should be treated very seriously.

Care and management of the depressed patient. Adequate assessment and diagnosis of the condition is an important feature in the mentally handicapped person as the condition may be masked. A depressed patient needs close observation and the care and management of a skilled, tolerant, sympathetic and understanding staff. By establishing a therapeutic relationship indicate to the patient that you appreciate his difficulties; understand his problems; are interested in what happens to him and that he can trust you. An environment should be created by care staff that allows for close observation (bearing in mind suicidal tendencies) and permits moderately stimulating surroundings. Ob-

servation must include knowing where he is, what he is doing and the mood he is in, and if he has any access to a means of injuring himself.

Drugs. Depressed patients may be prescribed antidepressant drugs which restore the abnormally depressed mood to, or towards, normal. It is the nurse's duty to administer these drugs in the correct dose, to the correct patient, at the correct time. There are two main groups:

1. *Tricyclic group*, e.g. imipramine or amitriptyline
2. *Mono-amine oxidase inhibitors* (MAOI), e.g. phenelzine

1. The tricyclic group appears to be safer and more widely used. Their pharmacological action is to increase the concentration of noradrenaline at the receptor site, inhibiting the re-uptake of released nor-adrenaline. They have an antidepressant effect, but usually only after 7–14 days. They also have some sedative effect, thus easing the agitation experienced in some depression. Side-effects include:

a. Those due to its effect on noradrenaline. It is potentiated or potentiates other drugs which increase the concentration of amines, hence there is a risk of hypertensive crisis, excitability and excess body temperature if they are combined with
   (i) mono-amine oxidase inhibitors
   (ii) amphetamines.
b. Those due to its anti-cholinergic or atropine-like properties, e.g. dry mouth, constipation, blurred vision, urinary retention, tachycardia, difficulty in micturition. Care must be taken in the elderly with benign prostatic hypertrophy and patients suffering from glaucoma, as these drugs can cause further increase in intra-ocular pressure.

Usually these drugs are well tolerated and Reid (1982) indicates that a dosage level of 100–200 mg per day of amitriptyline or imipramine, in divided doses, usually suffices.

2. The mono-amine oxidase inhibitors are

probably less frequently used because of more problematical side-effects. Their pharmacological action is to inhibit the enzyme monoamine oxidase which aids the breakdown of noradrenaline, causing an increase in the noradrenaline concentration at the nerve ending. These drugs produce an antidepressant effect which takes 2–4 weeks to have optimal effect.

Side-effects can arise as a result of an increase in amine concentration, e.g. the risk of a hypertensive crisis with a risk of subarachnoid haemorrhage and death. The patient complains of a severe throbbing headache and vomiting. This is especially likely where:

(i) the patient takes substances, e.g. amphetamines, adrenaline, isoprenaline, ephedrine, procaine, which liberate noradrenaline at the sympathetic nerve-endings.

(ii) if the patient takes foodstuffs rich in certain amines, e.g. cheese, wines, beer, yeast, Bovril and Marmite. They contain tyramine which is normally broken down by MAO in the liver, but in the absence of MAO it is absorbed into the bloodstream. It is essential to issue the patient with a card containing a list of foods to be omitted on it and kitchen staff notified.

(iii) the patient takes MAOI, in combination with tricylic antidepressants.

If the depression is severe, electroconvulsive therapy (ECT) may be prescribed as antidepressant drugs take a considerable time to act. Drugs may then be used to prevent a relapse. Reid (1982) indicates caution in using ECT in mentally handicapped people because of the high prevalence rate of structural brain abnormality, unless the indications are imperative.

Mania

Clinical features. Mania is the pathological elevation of mood with euphoric excitement which makes the patient exceptionally cheerful and optimistic. Behaviour is in a manner compatible with feelings. He is overactive and very restless; all inhibitions disappear. He is domineering, arrogant and rejects control. Irritability with quick temper and anger may suddenly manifest itself. Lability of affect with interchange of cheerfulness and suspicions and irritability occurs. He can be aggressive, destructive, tactless, and extravagant. He is easily distracted, has little concentration and is provocative. There is pressure of speech and flight of ideas. Delusions of grandeur and an attitude of superiority are in evidence. There is lack of insight with an impaired judgement and foresight.

Reid (1982) indicates that elevation of mood and over-activity may be poorly sustained in mentally handicapped people and some lability is common; restlessness may be severe. Components of the following may be in evidence: irritability; excitability; impulsiveness leading to assaultive behaviour; delusions and hallucinations appropriate to the mood, but often naive, grandiose and wish-fulfilling; hysterical symptoms; sexual disinhibition.

Care and management of the manic patient. The emphasis here is on the creation of a quiet, controlled and unstimulating environment. The care staff need a blend of patience, kindness, firmness, good humour, tolerance and tact in caring for this resident. Close observation is needed to protect the patient from exhaustion and from injury both to himself and others. Supervision of personal hygiene and close scrutiny of food and fluid intake, and channelling the patient's activities into non-aggressive and non-destructive behaviour are all important aspects of care.

Drugs. Major tranquillisers of the phenothiazine group, e.g. chlorpromazine, or of the butyrophenone group, e.g. haloperidol, are used in treatment of mania. They are readily absorbed and have a rapid onset of action; this allows a quick control of manic over-activity. Craft & Schiff (1980) indicate that they are well tolerated in mentally handicapped people, but side-effects may be more obvious because of the existing brain damage. The care staff must observe carefully for any side-effects. Dosage is measured against response and side-effects. Reid (1982) advises 100–400 mg of chlorpromazine per day in divided doses and haloperidol 5–15 mg per day in divided doses. Larger doses may be required in acute manic states, but as mania subsides the tolerance disappears.

Lithium carbonate is used in the treatment of mania but it takes 10 days before it acts. It is often combined with haloperidol or chlorpromazine in the early stages. Blood serum levels are checked every 5 days to ensure that the optimal therapeutic level of 0.6–1 mmol/l is not surpassed. The dose is varied according to the need of the individual, but the average daily divided dose of lithium is between 1000–1200 mg per day. Side-effects include: nausea, vomiting, diarrhoea, tremor of the hands, polyuria, polydipsia, weight gain, oedema, sleepiness, vertigo, dysarthria, and occasionally hypothyroid goitre.

Schizophrenia

This term describes a variety of psychotic disorders characterised by fragmentation of the mind with thought, perception, emotion and behaviour all effected.

Prevalence

Among mentally handicapped hospital residents Penrose (1938) reported 3%; Craft (1958) 4%; and Heaton-Ward (1977) 3.4%, suffering from schizophrenia. In the Camberwell survey of mentally handicapped adults in hospital and in the community Corbett (1979) reported a prevalence rate of 3.5%.

Clinical features

These include:

1. Thought disorder — thought blocking where the train of thought suddenly stops and a completely new one begins. Speech ranges from vague woolliness to incoherence with neologisms. Echolalia — repetition of the spoken word — occurs. Flight of ideas may be in evidence.
2. Delusions of a religious, paranoid, sexual or hypochondriacal nature occur and these are often weird and bizarre.
3. Hallucinations, especially auditory, can occur, but any type of hallucination, i.e. visual and, less commonly, tactile, olfactory, bodily, gustatory, may appear. Voices may be hostile, abusive, criticize, give orders, or reassure the patient. Noises and sounds that are associated with machines may be heard.
4. Abnormalities of affect; flattening of affect, emotional blunting with coldness and loss of finer feelings. Incongruity of affect — the emotional response is not appropriate to the topic.
5. Disturbance of volition; lack of drive and initiative; negativism. The patient withdraws from reality into a fantasy world. Reid (1982) reported that personality eccentricities and abnormalities can emerge.
6. Disturbance of movement with strange mannerisms, grimacing, posturing — called catatonia.
7. Disorders of behaviour — tics, disturbed unpredictable, destructive, impulsive and aggressive behaviour may manifest itself.

Types of schizophrenic reaction

1. *Simple.* It begins in late adolescence or early adult life, with insidious onset. There is a gradual deterioration with indifference, a shallowness of emotional response and loss of drive. Thought disorder is prominent; social deterioration occurs. Earl (1961) and Shapiro (1979) maintain that this type of schizophrenia is particularly common. Reid (1972) and Heaton-Ward (1977) state that it is impossible to identify such an ill-defined illness in mentally handicapped people.

2. *Hebephrenic.* Onset is between 15–25 years with insidious onset. Thought disorder, incongruity of affect, volitional disorder and disorganisation of the whole personality occurs.

3. *Catatonic.* Onset is between 15–40 years, with sudden onset. Features may include cata-

tonic stupor, in which the patient becomes completely withdrawn from outside stimulation and adopts strange postures, and catatonic excitement where the patient is very restless, impulsive, unpredictable and often violent. Echolalia, echopraxia, and rituals may occur.

4. *Paranoid.* Tends to occur later in life, after the age of 30 years but it can occur earlier. Persecutory delusions and auditory hallucinations are prominent. Disturbance of thinking, feeling and volition, and mannerisms may occur.

Care and management of the schizophrenic patient

Building up consistent and contructive interpersonal relationships with the schizophrenic resident is an important feature of care. In establishing such relationships it should be appreciated that this resident's interpretation of the external world is quite different from the normal individual's interpretation. His/her perception is disturbed. When we relate different events in our environment, they fall into an overall pattern. If an event is out of context, we go and investigate, or ignore its existence, hoping it will disappear. For the schizophrenic resident, events do not relate to each other as they should. The resident responds by withdrawing or responding aggressively. In either event he tries to limit contact with other people and events surrounding him.

The schizophrenic resident must live in an environment that is understanding, friendly, stimulating, and helpful, one which accepts his behaviour, however disturbed, while attempting to help him control and modify it. The atmosphere must be one that is best calculated to promote improvement. He needs to be helped to live in the real world and prevented from withdrawing into an isolated world preoccupied with fantasy. The care staff must be representatives of healthy reality and assist him to do real things with real people, in order to prevent further regression. They must not argue with him over his delusions or hallucinations but help the resident at the opportune time to see things in realistic terms rather than from his own distorted viewpoint.

Initially, the resident must be allowed to dictate the terms. The staff must make a constant, conscientious attempt to see his behaviour, however antisocial, disturbed or degraded, as representing an infantile attempt at communication. Unacceptable behaviour must be checked without conveying any sense of rejection to the resident. Patience, tact, and forbearance are necessary on the part of staff members. Very often the schizophrenic resident speaks in gestures, postures and expressions and staff must learn how to communicate in this particular language. He cannot be rushed or hurried into more mature patterns of behaviour. He needs time to try out and consolidate new relationships.

He needs to live a life which gives him the opportunity to use initiative and judgement and not conform passively to others. Institutional care must be geared to increasing his personal identity and degrees of responsibility, diminishing authoritarian attitudes among staff members, maintaining a stimulating environment, and creating an individual programme of care to prevent boredom and loneliness.

Recreational and occupational activities are vital aspects of the programme. A sense of achievement must be fostered. He should spend some part of each day at recreational and occupational tasks that are rewarding and fulfilling. Opportunities should be created for the channelling of unacceptable impulses, particularly aggressive ones. Activities must be carefully planned to benefit the resident and not be solitary ones whereby the resident can shelter behind routines which he uses to protect himself from involvement with other people. His activity needs to be stimulated and his chances of complete withdrawal made as few as possible. Creative activities such as music, art and mime have a therapeutic place in promoting recovery and in preventing deterioration. Psychotherapy with emotional support is valuable in aiding the resident to trust others and in learning to develop interpersonal relationships.

Constructive relationships can only be established after close contact with the resident. The staff must play an active part in his activities and not merely supervise the resident's daily programme. Any identification with the care staff, whereby the resident copies tasks or wishes to be of assistance is a constructive sign and this behaviour should be met with encouragement and warm approval. He must be given the opportunity to discard gradually the unhealthy defences he has developed. The delusional and hallucinatory world of the schizophrenic may convey to the resident that he is being poisoned. This can result in refusal of food. The staff need to find out what the resident's motive is for refusing food. He may reject food from some members of staff and accept it from others. If offered a selection of food, he may select some items. He may eat if the staff also eat the food. It may be necessary to allow him to prepare his own food, or to provide him with items which cannot be tampered with, such as tinned foods. The resident may only accept fluids, so frequent drinks of milk, Complan or other such foods will help to ensure adequate nourishment.

The resident may be urged by auditory hallucinations to act aggressively. An aggressive outburst is disturbing not only for the staff but also for the resident, as he is afraid of his own aggression; a relaxed friendly atmosphere where the resident feels secure and accepted is important. A satisfactory relationship allows anticipation of an aggressive outburst as each resident has his own way of showing tension. Mutual trust and respect are prerequisites to effective communication which is an essential when dealing with situations that anger the resident or that he perceives as hostile.

Drugs

The phenothiazine group of tranquillising drugs have been a major advance in controlling schizophrenic behaviour. Chlorpromazine and thioredazine are commonly used. The longer acting, injectable preparations, e.g. fluphenazine decanoate and flupenthixol have a useful role to play. Reid (1982) reported that butyrophenenes have also been used in the treatment of schizophrenia with varying success. The benefits of these and similar drugs are manifold. They create a calmness in the patient, a quiet atmosphere in the ward, and, consequently, a reduction in incidences of restraint. More constructive relationships can be developed and active treatment programmes instituted. While these drugs are extremely beneficial, staff must guard against the danger that patients are given unnecessary drugs in a desire to produce a tranquil ward, as this can over-tranquillise the patient and retard his progress. The use of tranquilliser drugs in the treatment of schizophrenia can cause unpleasant side-effects. These include skin photosensitivity, blood dyscrasias, liver disorders, dystonic reactions, parkinsonism, rigidity, akathisia and oculo-gyric crises. Tardive dyskinesias, consisting of bucco-linguomasticatory movements, are also a troublesome and persistent side-effect of phenothiazine treatment.

If the patient refuses his medication, gentle persuasion may succeed in encouraging him to take the drug. It should be explained that the medication is to help his symptoms. Care must be taken to ensure that the patient has, in fact, swallowed the tablets. If he refuses to take tablets, he may take an elixir of the drug. If not, the drug may need to be administered by injection.

Organic reactions

Organic reactions are found in those conditions characterised by some abnormality of structure or function of brain tissue. Structural brain pathology is common among mentally handicapped people (Reid, 1982). These reactions are conventionally divided into two groups, the acute form, called *delirium* and the chronic type called *dementia*. In the acute form, the symptoms are reversible if the underlying condition can be corrected. In the chronic group the conditions tend to be irreversible so that paramount damage to the central nervous system may result.

Delirium

This is usually a short-lived, reversible disorder of cerebral function; as the cause is treated, so the confusion tends to disappear. It is characterised by clouding of consciousness and; impairment of perception of the environment, with disorientation. His memory of recent events is impaired; illusions and hallucinations occur, with impulsive and disturbed behaviour. It is difficult to engage his attention; his concentration is impaired; he is apprehensive and restless. Physical symptoms, such as perspiration, dehydration, tachycardia, chest and renal complications may be in evidence and fits can occur. There is nothing distinctive about delirious reactions in mentally handicapped people. Many such people suffer from structural brain abnormality and it may be that, as a result, delirium is particularly readily provoked in them (Reid, 1982). The treatment of delirium is removal of the underlying cause. The restlessness may be treated by drugs such as chlorpromazine or chlormethiazole.

Care is aimed at preventing confusion in a familiar environment with familiar staff; orientation of the patient to his environment helps to reduce disorientation. Adequate diet with sufficient fluids and relief of constipation and urinary retention is essential. Nutritional and fluid balance needs to be carefully observed and accurately recorded.

Dementia

This syndrome is characterised by a rapid deterioration of the intellect due to degeneration of the brain cells. It is commonly associated with the extremes of life, namely childhood and old age.

Childhood disintegrative psychosis is the name given to childhood dementia, and disorders such as the lipidoses, i.e. Tay-Sachs disease, Niemann-Pick disease and Gaucher's disease; Huntington's chorea, Wilson's disease, congenital neurosyphilis and severe and uncontrolled epilepsy can be associated with this dementia.

Dementia tends to be more commonly associated with the elderly and is often called 'senile dementia'. Pre-senile dementias are a group of dementing illnesses occurring before the age of 60 years. They include: Alzheimer's disease, which is characterised by widespread involvement of the entire cortex with intellectual impairment predominating and epileptic fits a relatively early feature, and Pick's disease, in which a relative predominance of deterioration in the sphere of emotional integration and behaviour occurs. Reid & Aungle (1974) stated that the only uniquely distinctive feature about dementia in mentally handicapped people is the greatly increased liability of people with Down's syndrome to premature senile dementia. They reported that 25% of this population, aged 45 years or over, whom they studied in Strathmartine Hospital, Fife, showed clinical evidence of premature senile dementia.

Aetiology of dementia

1. Hereditary conditions, e.g. Huntington's chorea inherited as a Mendelian dominant.
2. Damage from injury.
3. Damage by poisoning: (a) by alcohol, (b) by lead and other heavy metals, such as manganese or antimony.
4. Damage from anoxia, particularly from carbon monoxide poisoning and asphyxia.
5. Damage from infection, e.g. following encephalitis or cerebrovascular syphilis.
6. Damage from metabolic error, e.g. vitamin B deficiency (beri-beri), or as a further, less direct complication of chronic alcoholism. A disturbance of protein metabolism secondary to chronic liver damage may produce a reversible type of dementia before the onset of hepatic coma.
7. Damage by neoplasms. These primary or secondary growths may be intra or extra cerebral.
8. Degenerative conditions, e.g. hypertension and arterio-sclerosis and atherosclerosis, with resulting arterial spasm.

Clinical features

Impairment of mental function affects all three

aspects of personality: intelligence, emotion and behaviour.

Deterioration of intelligence. Deterioration of intellect resulting in failure of recent memory is the most consistent disability. The patient may be unable to remember the nature or the place of his last meal, where he is living, the whereabouts, or even the death, of his closest relatives or friends. Remote memory may be relatively unaffected. There is failure of grasp and comprehension, disorientation and a reduction in problem-solving ability. Frequently, patients have no insight and maintain a fatuous and stereotyped social facade, with impoverishment of thought, excessive narrowing of interest, shallowness, and emotional lability. Eventually, speech becomes grossly affected, with expressive and receptive dysphasia.

Deterioration of emotional integration. Emotional lability, some secondary anxiety, depression, or agitation may be the reaction to the patient's subjective awareness of intellectual impairment. An associated uneasiness may find expression either as a hypochondriacal preoccupation on the one hand, or as a querulous evasion or suspicious hostility on the other. This may lead to their becoming increasingly isolated, self-concerned, rude, lonely; while ostensibly aggressive. Delusions of poverty and paranoid attitudes may be in evidence.

Deterioration of behaviour. This results as a consequence of intellectual and emotional deterioration. There is a progressive loss of self-help skills, with hygiene and personal appearance being neglected. Shameless and inappropriate behaviour may be painfully apparent. Sleep patterns may be affected and patients may confuse night and day.

Care and management of the patient with dementia

The pace of living needs to be geared to the patient's restricted capabilities. Establish a simple, fixed regime and routine in an environment which he knows best. Changes of environment can add to the confusion experienced by the patient who cannot orientate himself correctly, and this can cause further confusion. Tasks should be appropriate to the current ability of the patient and be as realisitic as possible. The patient will be happier if given a sense of purpose and his relatives may furnish information regarding his special interest. Simple, repetitive chores are useful. The patient must be treated with dignity, and every effort made to prevent shame, fear and anxiety. This patient is responsive to feelings in the environment so must not be spoken to impatiently or brusquely, or treated in an off-hand or intolerant manner. The tone of voice, abruptness of movement and the fleeting contacts are all registered by the patient at a mood level, even although coherent conversation is no longer possible. If the patient is treated in an uncivilised manner, he will resort to aggressiveness which is often shown in destructiveness and incontinence.

Care must be taken to avoid accidents, with the provision of non-slip floors and avoidance of hazards at floor level to prevent falls and possible fractures. Shoes and slippers must be well-fitting and laces securely tied. Simple entertainments to keep the patient as physically fit and mentally alert as is possible are an important feature in helping to delay deterioration. Every effort should be made to encourage and maintain independence in relation to dressing, undressing, and feeding. Attention must be paid to personal hygiene as the patient may show little interest in hygiene, appearance and clothing.

Eating habits may show remarkable deterioration to a socially unacceptable level. Intake of nourishment and fluids needs careful monitoring; the nature of this depends on his ability to feed himself and whether or not he has dentures. Care staff should see that dentures are kept clean and are well-fitting. Constipation is a common problem that may increase the patient's confusion and make him extremely irritable. This should be treated without recourse to drastic purging. Continence should be encouraged by regular visits to the toilet. Incontinence may be due to an inability to find the toilet in time, an inability to respond to the impulse to micturate, or have a neurological basis. Sleep is often a problem for the chronic psychotic patient. This can be helped by discouraging him from dozing or sleeping during the day, by giving a hot milky drink at night and having a warm bath before retiring.

The patient may hoard rubbish, and while this should be treated with tact and consideration, a weekly clear-out keeps the situation under control, as no amount of reasoning or persuasion will convince the patient to clear out his booty.

Drugs

Sedative drugs, especially the barbiturate group, cause confusion and can become drugs of habituation. Chloral hydrate, oxazepam or chlormethiazole appear to be more suitable drugs. It should also be remembered that the patient may be on drugs already for some underlying disorder which are causing confusion, e.g. anti-Parkinsonian drugs, chronic overdose with analgesics and digoxin, and some anti-depressant drugs. Diuretics and hypotensives may be causing postural hypotension with confusion and unsteadiness. Symptoms such as daytime restlessness, paranoid behaviour and aggressive tendencies may be controlled by the use of the phenothiazine group of major tranquillisers.

This patient needs constant care and observation to be adequately nourished, protected from danger, kept in touch with his environment and treated with dignity and respect.

Neurotic disorders/conduct disorders/ personality disorders

Neurotic disorders

This term is used for emotional disorders in mentally handicapped people of any age, in which a sense of reality is preserved. It includes states of disproportionate anxiety, panic and fear, phobias, hypochondriasis, unhappiness, depression, sensitivity, shyness and relationship problems, e.g. sibling jealousy (Reid, 1982). Mentally handicapped

people, like others, are exposed to stress, strain, anxiety and apprehension throughout their lives. Feelings of guilt, embarrassment and inadequacy felt by the family may be projected on to the handicapped member. This can result in rejection or overprotection. Difficulty in learning and coping with educational attainments can give rise to failure and stigma and be the subject of jokes and unfair comparisons with normal siblings and other children. Failure to grasp the real essence of his surroundings can cause the patient to misjudge social situations. Various studies show that mentally handicapped people do suffer from neurotic reactions often related to psychological difficulties emerging from such problems.

Rutter et al (1970) commented that intellectual retardation in children is associated with an increase in neurotic and conduct disorders. Reid (1980 B) noted that neurotic disorders could be diagnosed in mentally handicapped children down to the severe range of mental handicap. A team approach is indicated to try to isolate the significance of the symptoms and modify the situation for the patient. General support, encouragement, explanation and guidance are necessary for the patient when trying to cope with various everyday problems. He needs guidance in developing interests to direct his attention away from his preoccupations. Care should be taken to consider the patient's limitations and potential to avoid excess pressure in trying to achieve certain goals. The assistance of the psychologist is useful in defining behavioural treatment approaches which include various deconditioning procedures such as systematic desensitisation. Symptoms may be relieved by drugs such as the butyrophenone group, e.g. haloperidol or the benzodiazepine group, e.g. diazepam. Depressive features may respond to antidepressant drugs, e.g. phenelzine.

Conduct disorders

Socially unacceptable behaviour such as aggression, destruction and sexual misdemeanours, may be shown by mentally handicapped people. Inability and inconsistency in handling such conduct may create additional problems of antisocial behaviour, and psychopathy may emerge, in mildly handicapped individuals. Identifying and curtailing the factors which are reinforcing the conduct and substituting an alternative behavioural pattern is the treatment of choice.

Personality disorders

According to Reid (1982) there is an immense range of personality types in mentally handicapped people and there is no system of classification which can be regarded as acceptable, valid or reliable.

It ranges from abnormally shy and withdrawn behaviour to excessively friendly and forward approaches, easily provoked to aggression, excessively passive or prone to obstinacy. Treatment approaches include use of self as a therapeutic tool in a relationship that offers kindness, trust and understanding, but using firmness and flexibility as appropriate. Phenothiazine drugs are useful for aggressive and irritable behaviour.

Careful planning and structuring of interesting activities is important to avoid boredom and creation of tension. Behaviour approaches may be necessary for disruptive behaviour.

FORENSIC PSYCHIATRY AND MENTAL HANDICAP

The relationship between mental handicap and criminality is the subject of much debate and research (Woodward, 1955; Bluglass, 1966; Walker & McCabe, 1975). Many mentally handicapped people are all-trusting and gullible and may easily be manipulated. Because of this they may be easily led into petty crime, exploited, and be more liable to police apprehension. The police may charge the individual who may be completely incapable of defending himself while in custody and in dealing with police interrogation. Others may not be charged and sent home or direct to hospital. Courts may prefer to seek a

hospital disposal rather than face risks in sentencing the individual. Fox (1946) indicated that crimes of forgery were related to higher intelligence. Milner (1949) indicated that the incidence of sex offences was 25% among mentally handicapped adult criminals as compared with 3% among criminals in general.

Reid (1982) reported that it would seem there is no direct link between defectiveness of intelligence and crime beyond sexual offences and arson. Perhaps this results from the fact that the mentally handicapped male may have great difficulty securing a suitable sexual partner and have little awareness of the significance of socially appropriate sexual behaviour. As the emphasis nowadays is for community care for the mentally handicapped, it is imperative that a proper network of social support is developed and maintained, otherwise problems of anti-social behaviour, leading to criminality, may occur.

SUMMARY

Mental handicap is often found in association with other impairments. Factors which affect the development of the brain may interfere with bodily development. Damage to the nervous system can result in such conditions as epilepsy, hearing impairments, and autism.

Epilepsy may be controlled by anti-convulsant drugs. Regular monitoring of blood levels of these drugs is now standard practice with a regular review of the medication at least every 6 months. The role of the care staff relating to observation, recording and reporting is vitally important.

It is vital to ensure that mentally handicapped people, who also suffer from disorders like cerebral palsy, achieve their maximum potential, and that appropriate aids, appliances and expert help and advice are available.

Visual handicap is an acknowledged common condition in mentally handicapped people whereas hearing impairment is often neglected as it is difficult to assess. Although a person appears to respond to sound, he may still be suffering hearing loss and should be audiologically screened.

Abnormal behaviour may pose problems and require modification by drug treatment or operant conditioning techniques. Stereotype behaviour when it tends to occur in institutionalised mentally handicapped people is often self-destructive. Hyperkinesis is characterised by excessive motor activity, distractibility, poor concentration, impulsiveness, temper tantrums, and possible aggression to others. Autism is evident in early childhood. Autistic children are handicapped in language development and display no response to other people.

Mental illness may be superimposed on mental handicap. Psychoses, in which a drastic change in the person's personality occurs, can present itself in the form of affective disorders and schizophrenia. Delirium and dementia are the two main types of organic states; delirium presents in a dramatic and urgent way while dementia is a slow, insidious process. Neurotic disorders is a term for emotional disorders in mentally handicapped people of any age, in which reality is preserved.

The link between criminality and mental handicap is the subject of much debate and research. However, the understanding of the relationship remains somewhat unsophisticated and further research is required on the subject.

REFERENCES

Ballinger B R, Armstrong J, Presly A S et al 1975 Use of a standardised psychiatric interview in mentally handicapped patients. British Journal of Psychiatry 127: 540–544

Berkson G, Mason W 1964 Stereotype behaviour of chimpanzees: Relation to general arousal and alternative activities. Perceptual and Motor Skills 19: 635–652

Bluglass R S 1966 A psychiatric study of Scottish convicted prisoners. MD Thesis, University of St Andrews

Bowley A 1969 Psychological aspects: Cerebral palsy and the young child. Blencowe S.N (ed) E & S Livingstone, Edinburgh

British Epilepsy Association 1975 Project notes. BEA, London

Cantwell D P 177. Hyperkinetic syndrome. In: Rutter M, Herson L (eds) Child Psychiatry — Modern approaches. Blackwell Scientific, Oxford.

Carr J 1976 The severely retarded autistic child. In: Wing L (ed) Early childhood autism, 2nd edn. Pergamon Press, Oxford

Christensen D E 1975 Effects of combining methylphenidate and a classroom token system in modifying hyperactive behaviour. American Journal of Mental Deficiency 3: 266–276

Clancy H, Dugdale A, Rendle-Short J 1969. The diagnosis of infantile autism. Developmental Medicine and Child Neurology 11: 432–442

Cooper I S 1978 Some technical consideration of cerebellar stimulation. In: Cooper I S (ed) Cerebellar stimulation in man. Raven Press, New York, p 13

Corbett J A 1975. Aversion for the treatment of self injurious behaviour. Journal of Mental Deficiency Research 19: 79–95

Corbett J A 1979. Psychiatric morbidity and mental retardation. In: James F E, Snaith R P (eds) Psychiatric illness and mental handicap. Gaskell Press, London

Craft M J 1958. Mental disorders in the defective. Royal Institution, Starcross, Devon.

Craft M J, Schiff A A 1980. Psychiatric disturbance in mentally handicapped patients. British Journal of Psychiatry 137: 250–255

Creak M 1961 Schizophrenia syndrome in childhood. British Medical Journal 2: 889–890

Cullen C N, Hattersley J, Tennant L 1977 Behaviour modification — some implications of a radical behaviourist view. Bulletin of the British Psychological Society 30: 65–69

DHSS 1972 Census of mentally handicapped patients in hospital in England and Wales at the end of 1970. HMSO, London

Earl C J C 1961. Subnormal personalities. Bailliere Tindall, London

Forehand R, Baumeister A A 1970 The effects of auditory and visual stimulation on stereotype rocking behaviour and general activity of severe retardates. Journal of Clinical Psychology 26: 426–429

Fox V 1946 Intelligence, race and age as selective factors in crime. Journal of Criminal Law and Criminology 37: 141–152

Glaser G H, Penry J K, Woodbury D M (eds) 1980 Antiepileptic drugs: Mechanisms of action. Raven Press, New York

Goldberg D P, Cooper B, Eastwood M R et al 1970 A standardised psychiatric interview for use in community surveys. British Journal of Preventive and Social Medicine 24: 18–23

Gordon N 1976 Paediatric neurology for the clinician. Clinics in Developmental Medicine No. 59/60. Spastics International Medical Publications. Heinemann, London

Hamilton M (ed) 1980 Fish's outline of psychiatry. Wright, Bristol

Havard J 1973. School problems and allergies. Journal of Learning Disabilities 6: 492–494

Hayman M 1939 The interrelations of mental defect and mental disorder. Journal of Mental Sciences 85: 1183–1193

Heaton Ward A 1977 Psychosis in mental handicap. British Journal of Psychiatry 130: 525–533

Herskovitz H H, Plesset M R 1941 Psychoses in adult mental defectives. Psychiatric Quarterly 15: 574–588

Hitchcock E F 1978 Stereotactic surgery for cerebral palsy. Nursing Times 74 (50): 2064–2065

Hollis J H 1971 Body rocking: Effects of sound and reinforcement. American Journal of Mental Deficiency 75: 642–644

Hopkins A 1981 Epilepsy — The facts. Oxford University Press 5: 103–104

Ingalls R P 1978. Mental retardation — The changing outlook. Wiley, New York

Jeavons P M, Harding G F A 1975 Photosensitive epilepsy clinics. In: Developmental Medicine No. 56. S.I.M.P., Heinemann, London.

Kanner L 1943 Autistic disturbances of affective contact. Nervous Child 2: 217–250

Kemeny P, Hodosi J, Szanto I 1964 Control of prolonged convulsive seizures in childhood by administration of inhalation with nitrous oxide, N_2O. Annales Paediatrici 203: 77

Kielholz P (ed) 1973 Masked depression. Hans Huber, Bern

Kraepelin E 1896 Psychiatrie. Translated as: Clinical Psychiatry 1902 by Deferndorf A R, New York.

Levy D M 1944 On the problem of movement restraint. American Journal of Orthopsychiatry 14: 644–671

Marsden C D, Reynolds E H 1982

Matthews S S, Jones M H, Sperling S C 1953. Hip derangements seen in cerebral palsied children. American Journal of Physical Medicine 32: 213–221

Milner K O 1949. Delinquent types of mentally defective persons. Journal of Mental Science 95: 842–859

Moreau M, Drummond D S, Rogala E, Ashworth A, Porter T 1979 Natural history of the dislocated hip in spastic cerebral palsy. Developmental Medicine and Child Neurology 21: 749–753

Mumford D 1981 Drama with the blind adult. In: Lord G (ed) The arts and disability. Macdonald Publishers, Edinburgh

National Development Group for the Mentally Handicapped 1978. Helping mentally handicapped people in hospital. ch 6, p 63

Neustadt R 1928 Psychoses of defectives. Karger, Berlin

Penrose L S 1938 A clinical and genetic study of 1280 cases of mental defect. Special Report Series of Medical Research Council No. 229. HMSO, London.

Reid A J 1980B Psychiatric disorders in mentally handicapped children: A clinical and follow-up study.

Journal of Mental Deficiency Research 24: 287–298

Reid A H 1982 The psychiatry of mental handicap. Blackwell Scientific Oxford, ch 7, p 61–69

Reid A H, Aungle P G 1974. Dementia in ageing mental defectives: A clinical psychiatric study. Journal of Mental Deficiency Research 18: 15–23

Reid A H, Ballinger B R, Heather B B 1978a. Behavioural syndromes identified by cluster analysis in a sample of 100 severely and profoundly retarded adults. Psychological Medicine 8: 399–412

Rohan J C 1936. Mental disorder in the adult defective. Journal of Mental Science 82: 551–563

Rutter M 1970 Autistic children: Infancy to adulthood. Seminars in Psychiatry 2: 435–450

Samilson R L, Tsou P, Aamoth G, Green W M 1972. Dislocation and subluxation of the hip in cerebral palsy. Journal of Bone and Joint Surgery 54A: 863–872

Shaffer D 1977 Drug treatment in child psychiatry. In: Rutter M, Herson L Child psychiatry: Blackwell Scientific, Oxford

Shapiro A 1979 Psychiatric illness in the mentally handicapped: an historical survey. In: James F E, Snaith R P (eds) Psychiatric illness and mental handicap. Gaskell Press, London.

Thompson Jr G A, Iwata A, Poynter H 1979. Operant control of pathological tongue thrust in spastic cerebral palsy. Journal of Applied Behaviour Analysis 12(3): 325–333

Walker N, McCabe S 1973 Crime and insanity in England, vol. II. New Solutions and New Problems. University Press, Edinburgh

Williams C E 1971 A study of the patients in a group of mental subnormality hospitals. British Journal of Mental Subnormality 17: 29–41

Winsberg B, Bialer I, Kupietz S et al 1972 Effects of impramine and destroamphetamine on behaviour of neuro-psychiatrically impaired children. American Journal of Psychiatry 128: 1425–1431

Woods G E 1969 The Causes. In: Blencowe S M (ed) Cerebral palsy and the young child. E & S Livingstone, Edinburgh

Woodward M 1955 The role of low intelligence in delinquency. British Journal of Delinquency 5: 281–303

Young R, Clements J. 1979. The functional significance of complex hand movement stereotypes in the severely retarded. British Journal of Mental Subnormality 25: 79–87

5

Robert Paterson

Facilities and provisions

- Increasing trend towards community care with reduction of hospital ward populations
- Therapy can improve abilities necessary for everyday living, provide occupational and industrial skill and enhance recreational activities
- Residential provision within the community can create a home environment and help promote independence
- Voluntary agencies add to existing facilities and exert powerful influence as pressure groups
- Nurse's role in multi-disciplinary team is central and requires development of liaison skills

Historical development in Britain
Current National Health Service provision
  Psychiatry
  Medical services
  Psychology
  Physiotherapy
  Speech therapy
  Occupational therapy
  Industrial therapy
  Drama, music, art therapy
  Play therapy
  Recreational therapy
  Social work in hospitals
Community provision
Residential services outside NHS
  Children's homes
  Fostering
  Hostels
  Group homes
  Sheltered housing
  Lodgings
  Nursing and rest homes
Non-residential provision
  Adult Training Centres
Voluntary agencies
Financial and other provision
Types of care staff

HISTORICAL DEVELOPMENT IN BRITAIN

It is difficult to establish when the first efforts to care for the mentally handicapped took place as no distinction was made between the mentally handicapped and the mentally ill until fairly recent times. As a result both groups were cared for in the same situation. In addition life expectancy was much less than it is today for the entire population, so only the very fittest lived beyond what we now refer to as middle-age. Only the most physically fit mentally handicapped people survived to maturity and only then because of the close assistance and supervision of the family, so that the more severely mentally handicapped people did not present the same problem to society.

Some of the earliest efforts to organize care for the mentally handicapped were made by religious groups, orders or sects, e.g. the Hospital of St Mary of Bethlehem, founded in 1247. After the dissolution of the monasteries it was incorporated by Royal Charter for the reception of the insane, eventually becoming known as Bedlam.

During the 18th century, as life became more complex and social problems developed, it was more difficult for mentally handicapped people to survive in the community. Many of the physically able found their way to workhouses and prisons. For those born to families of means, there were the private

77

madhouses. These were institutions run for profit and conditions in these establishments varied widely from confinement in small rooms to special apartments with a special keeper.

The 18th century gave birth to a new social awareness towards the treatment of the insane. An Act of Parliament was passed in 1774 to regulate private institutions but enforcement was practically impossible and did not apply to 'public subscription' hospitals. After pressure by several societies and individuals, the County Asylums Act was passed in 1808 which paved the way for the development of hospitals to care for those suffering from a mental illness and handicap.

In 1845 the Lunatics Act distinguished between mental defectives and those of unsound mind which led to experiments in providing special schools and asylums. This development created the problem of distinguishing between the two groups, which led to the Idiots Act of 1886, permitting local authorities to build special institutions for idiots and imbeciles, but this was brought to an abrupt halt by the Lunacy Act of 1890 which stated 'lunatic means idiot or person of unsound mind'. This provided a way out for those local authorities reluctant to spend money on providing for the mentally deficient. The Charity Organisation Society took up the challenge in 1875, expounding the view that mentally deficient children could be trained and improved, so that they became less of a burden to their families and society.

In 1904 a Royal Commission was set up to 'investigate the existing methods of dealing with idiots and epileptics, with imbeciles, feeble minded or defective persons not certified under the lunacy laws'. The outcome of the Commission's report was the Mental Deficiency Act, 1913. This Act replaced the Lunacy Commission with a Board of Control, charged with making better provision for the mentally deficient. Mental deficiency was defined as 'a condition of arrested or incomplete development of mind, existing before the age of 18 years, whether arising from inherent causes, disease or injury'.

Under the Act, 'defectives' could be sent to an institution or placed under guardianship. However, legal measures were introduced which divorced the mental deficiency authorities from the general work of Public Health Departments. This hampered the social approach and caused the setting apart of the mentally deficient. New 'colonies' were created and not only was institutional care being developed by the authorities but at the same time they were accepting the responsibility for guardianship, teaching and supervision. Realisation began to grow that institutions could not cope with the problem alone and that community care was not only cheaper, but more beneficial to the individual.

This laid the foundation for a new approach which was hampered by the outbreak of war. Funds dried up and the mentally deficient became less of a priority within the Health Service. Due to the absorption of the hospitals into the National Health Service in 1948, these hospitals had now to compete for finance with hospitals catering for other areas of medicine.

In 1959, the Mental Health Act was passed (1960 Scotland), bestowing informal status on the majority of patients which allowed the less handicapped to leave the hospitals, and resulted in an increased concentration of the more highly dependent and multiply handicapped within the hospital. The Development Team for the Mentally Handicapped in their report 1976–77 stated that adults resident in hospital in 1969 numbered about 56 000, compared with 49 500 in 1976, a drop of 6500 in hospital over a 7-year period — a trend which has continued since.

In 1974 the National Health Service was reorganised and responsibility for the hospitals was passed to Regional Health Authorities (Health Boards in Scotland). Whether the hospitals for the mentally handicapped benefited from this it is hard to determine, but it could be speculated that some did and some did not, depending on the priorities of the Authorities involved.

CURRENT NATIONAL HEALTH SERVICE PROVISION

The greatest residential provision for mentally handicapped people by far is provided by National Health Service hospitals. In 1975 hospitals in England had 49 683 residents (National Development Group 1978). Great effort has been expended to reduce the population of the hospitals by programmed discharge into the community of many previously hospitalised clients. This has allowed the hospital management in many areas to reduce the overall hospital population and at the same time alter ward environments to a more compatible living situation. In these areas large wards have disappeared to make way for smaller living units that fit more readily into the category of 'home'. Personal space has been increased and subsequently more privacy is available to each resident which is more in line with the expectations of a 'normal' life. Life in hospital can never be described as normal, but by the creation of the new uncrowded environment, changing attitudes and the availability of Non-Contributory Invalidity Pension (NCIP) life in hospitals in most cases is now as 'normal' as possible. However, it has to be pointed out that some hospitals have made greater efforts than others to reach this situation whilst others had the advantage of design and more modern layout. Even today with the average design provision being for ward populations of 25–30 residents, architects and planners can end up by designing a hospital and not a home, ultimately causing the ward to display a clinical, rather than a domestic layout.

Many dormitories are now smaller, more private and more personal, allowing nurses and residents to use imagination in the creation of a homely atmosphere and by thoughtful, assisted use of the NCIP the resident can purchase personal items of clothing of his own choice as well as decorative items for his or her own personal living areas.

This approach has been advocated by the Hospital Advisory Service over a number of years, which has always criticised the lack of privacy and has encouraged individuality for each resident. This approach has also been strongly advocated by the National Development Group (1978) in their report *Helping Mentally Handicapped People in Hospital* and by the Development Team for the Mentally Handicapped in their first report (1976–1977).

The Hospital Advisory Service and the Scottish Hospital Advisory Service are groups consisting of medical, administrative and nursing personnel, established to visit and report on all long-stay hospitals in the country at regular intervals, to make recommendations on the environment and care offered by these hospitals. Unfortunately, they cannot enforce their recommendations, which many professionals regard as a disadvantage. Irrespective of this, these groups do have influence and have assisted greatly in the development of services for the mentally handicapped. Since the introduction of NCIP in 1975, hospital residents have had more of a say in their life-style, as they can now afford to purchase items for themselves, or save, and contribute towards their holidays, for example. This payment has opened up new horizons and opportunities to the mentally handicapped by giving them independent purchasing power.

In addition to the reduction in ward populations in many hospitals, there has also been a dramatic change in ward furnishings and fixtures. Stark wooden floors and enamel painted walls have been replaced by carpets and walls of various finishes and textures, adorned with pictures and posters, more in line with the average home environment. Only in very isolated cases do we encounter the traditional hospital tubular steel easy chairs which have been replaced elsewhere by more domestically designed furnishings. However as modern furnishings are more costly and not as solidly-built, breakage and replacement cost can be a serious drain on maintenance budgets. This factor has influenced the choice of furnishings and regularly the third or even fourth choice of furnishings has had to be accepted.

Whilst we have stressed the fact that the

ward is a home, it is also the organisational centre for residents' treatment programmes, e.g. physiotherapy, speech therapy, psychology etc. The medical input to the residents' care will be co-ordinated from ward level and it seems reasonable to assume that the ward nurses are perhaps in the best position to co-ordinate the services.

In recent years, more hospitals have been using a systematic nursing approach (process of nursing) and where implemented and used in conjunction with the recommendations of the other specialities by incorporating them into the 'process', it has enhanced the life of the residents involved by recognising each resident's individuality and needs. Irrespective of the 'process' it still seems reasonable that the nurse will assume the role of co-ordinator of care and the ward, the role of information centre (see Ch. 14).

Although the ward is the focal point of care for the hospitalised resident and the greatest part of his life is under the supervision and influence of the nurse, other provisions and services are available within the hospital.

Psychiatry

Each resident is by custom attached to a consultant psychiatrist's case load. The consultant has the overall responsibility for the care of the resident whilst in hospital, which not only includes his mental and physical wellbeing, but also the guaranteeing that the resident is treated in accordance with contents of the Mental Health Act.

In addition the consultant has the responsibility for all treatments that are prescribed for the resident. Unfortunately, there are fewer and fewer consultant psychiatrists willing to practise solely in the field of mental handicap today and this has led to part-time consultancies in the speciality. This has been identified and referred to in a paper produced by a working party of the Royal College of Psychiatrists' Mental Deficiency Section in Scotland in September 1983.

This paper identified the consultant's role as:

1. To assess, diagnose and treat in mentally handicapped children or adults psychological and concomitant neurological problems as part of a division of psychiatry in which there are also other whole or part-time psychiatrists with an interest in psychiatry or mental handicap in adults or children.
2. To advise teachers, social workers and others in adult training centres and schools on the mental health of mentally handicapped people.
3. To prescribe medication.
4. To organise and manage the intensive treatment unit, and clinics for psychiatrically and neurodevelopmentally disabled retarded persons.
5. To provide advice to families of mentally handicapped persons.
6. To co-ordinate medical and paramedical services for the mentally handicapped in a defined district.
7. With others, to collaborate in behavioural treatments, social skills training, linguistic and cognitive intervention.
8. To liaise with others to provide general advice on the natural history of behaviours in the mentally handicapped.

As can be seen from this list of factors, the psychiatrists identified a wide role for themselves as advisers, co-ordinators of care as well as medical overseers within the community. This view is not universally held but it cannot be denied that there is undoubtedly a weight of opinion in favour of this approach within medical circles.

Certainly today the consultant's role in the community differs from the role within the hospital. In the community setting the consultant does function as an adviser to parents/guardians and all other agencies caring for the mentally handicapped whilst in hospital, even where a multi-disciplinary approach is adopted, the consultant has the authority to insist that his instructions on care and approach are carried out. As an alternative to the above view it could be reasonably argued that there is no need for a consultant psychiatrist to be permanently involved in the care of the mentally handicapped. The alternative suggestion could be to refer specific residents who display psychiatric symptoms to the consultant psychiatrist in the same way as done for any other member of the public, the resident being registered locally with a general practitioner for his everyday health supervision. It could be anticipated that there would be two different schools of thought on this suggestion, and almost definite that the voices of the medical fraternity would be raised in dissent.

Medical services

General medical supervision in hospital is under the direction of doctors of varying levels of seniority and experience. It is quite common that these doctors have worked within the same hospital for a number of years and hence have come to know the residents on a very personal basis, leading in many circumstances to a better service for the resident. Again it is noticeable that younger doctors are not choosing to enter or stay in the field or mental handicap.

In 1981 a study of the ages of consultants in mental handicap based in Scottish hospitals (Fraser, 1981) demonstrated that the average age was 65 but this had fallen to 60 years in 1983.

It is becoming more common to contract GPs to hospitals to supervise the general medical care for the mentally handicapped. This service is often on a sessional basis and has its disadvantages, as well as advantages. It can cause delay in treatment on some occasions, e.g. weekends and evenings when the GP is the 'on-call' doctor, but most hospitals that employ this system have the machinery established to deal with the 'crisis'. This is an instance where the consultant must be satisfied with his back-up. On the other hand, who is a better person to deal with everyday maladies than the 'family doctor'? This system can work very well as long as there is continuity of doctors, indicating that where possible the same GP should attend the hospital from

group practices to allow the development of rapport between the doctor and the resident as well as with other professionals.

Other medical services are offered as the need arises by reference to the specialist consultant as for any other member of the public. Some of these specialities are — Surgery, Ear, Nose and Throat, General Medicine, Orthopaedics and so on, in fact any speciality as required.

Psychology

In recent years we have witnessed an increase in psychology services within the mental handicap hospital, perhaps due to developments in the field of behaviour modification and other behavioural techniques. Not so many years ago it was extremely difficult, if not impossible to acquire the assistance of a psychologist for the hospitalised resident. In recent years the move towards the team approach within hospitals has gained momentum and this has assisted the development of psychology services with the psychologist, psychiatrist and other professionals working in closer liaison with each other. This development has gained the speciality of psychology the recognition its skills deserve and we now have a situation where psychology services are more or less at hand when needed.

The psychology services are normally based within the mental handicap hospital, but have to serve a geographical area catering for the mentally handicapped in the domestic situation as well as in other community-based settings, e.g. hostels, sheltered workshops. In the hospital, the psychologist assesses all residents psychologically, as a matter of routine where the situation allows or on request from either medical or nursing staff. It is now the custom in most hospitals that all new admissions are psychologically assessed on admission. From these assessments, the psychologist can indicate how the resident could be developed in the field of social skills and it is also possible that behaviour patterns could be identified and recommendations made on how to eliminate socially unacceptable behaviours.

The psychologist's assistance should always be sought in the routine case conferences that are now a feature of the treatment and care of the mentally handicapped in most hospitals. In this situation, the need for re-assessments of the resident by the psychologist is an important feature of progressive care.

In addition to the assessment services, psychological techniques can be of great value when dealing with problems such as the resident with aggressive tendencies. The psychologist with the assistance of the medical and nursing staff may be able to construct a programme to correct this behaviour, but it must be emphasised that the success of this type of approach is dependent on the consistency and continuity of the approach. This aspect of the programme is invariably the responsibility of the nursing staff and therefore its success is dependent on the nursing team. Another service offered by the psychologist is the development of individual programmes to enable residents to maximise their social skills or develop new skills. This is done in conjunction with the nursing staff and success is dependent on the continuity of approach and regular reassessment of results. This type of approach lends itself to the 'Process of Nursing' as it deals with the needs of the individual. These programmes often cover areas such as feeding, hygiene, dressing, toileting or in fact, any of the areas of social skills that are absent or not fully developed or in need of refinement.

Physiotherapy

This is a service which has developed quite significantly over recent years and continued expansion is desirable. Physiotherapeutic techniques are of immense value to the immobile and the deformed, as they incorporate the use of special routines and exercises that prevent muscular contractures where none are present and relieve existing contracture. In addition to this preventative contribution, the physiotherapist's special skills can assist in the treatment of established conditions by assisting in the development of voluntary movement, with the eventual aim of self mobility. Such a goal is a long-term objective and success is more likely if treatment can be carried out at regular intervals with the cooperation of the whole nursing team and is not just dependent on the physiotherapist (see Ch. 9).

In the less active patient, physiotherapeutic techniques can be used to prevent respiratory problems by the use of special exercises and movements to assist in the prevention of pulmonary congestion, as an aid in feeding programmes, specific reflexes in the neck can be stimulated to help with the swallowing of food.

In many physiotherapy departments a hydrotherapy pool is a valuable addition to the range of treatments available. In the hands of the expert hydrotherapy can and does make immobile limbs mobile, decongests lungs and, in general, due to the buoyancy of water makes movement easier. It is worth trying to imagine how a person feels when limbs which cannot move unaided or have been confined to a wheelchair, move, be it ever so slightly, when in the hydrotherapy pool.

The beneficial effect of hydrotherapy is due to the elimination of gravity by the buoyancy of the water. When spastic limbs try to move in normal conditions, the effort involved increases the muscle tone, which in turn increases the spasticity. Water reduces the effort required for movement and makes the exercise more enjoyable. This widens the experience of the spastic person and enhances the development of balance and co-ordination. The fun component in hydrotherapy can never be overemphasised as this develops the person's confidence and from this confidence all other possible benefits can become a reality.

Speech therapy

This is another speciality that has recently become more accessible to the hospitalised resident. In the past, very few residents who had difficulties with speech had any hope of gaining the assistance and guidance of a speech therapist. Even today, there can be difficulties in getting the services of the speech therapist, as these services are often organised on an area basis and are therefore spread very thinly over the whole community including mental handicap hospitals. In addition services are offered on a sessional basis which means that the hospital or speech therapy staff have to decide who of the hospitalised residents should receive their assistance. As the speech therapist is involved with the patient on an intermittent basis, co-operation of nurses and care staff is essential to ensure most effective use of the therapy is achieved. After discussion with nurses, agreed programmes can be implemented. Training takes place during the person's day-to-day life and consistency is crucial to producing change. Co-operation through the multi-disciplinary approach will liberate more of the therapist's time to deal with other residents' needs.

In addition to assisting residents to vocalise and correcting faulty speech, the speech therapists are now deeply involved in the teaching of 'alternative communication systems', e.g. Blissymbolics, Makaton Voca-bulary and the Paget-Gorman Sign system. The most commonly used systems in the hospitals for the mentally handicapped are the Bliss and Makaton systems. However, it has been shown in practice that combinations of these systems can be successful, especially when adapted to individual resident's needs.

Blissymbolics is a system of simple symbols that can be adapted to the level of ability of the individual concerned (see p. 241). The system can be as simple or as complicated as can be competently used by the individual in question. Special boards of symbols have been designed to accommodate the needs of most individuals, and allow the individual to communicate by pointing to the appropriate symbol. The symbols are very basic and uncomplicated, so much so that they are easily deciphered by individuals who have never encountered the system before. It is recommended that in hospitals where this system is

a teaching aid, signs depicting the appropriate symbol should be used in practice, e.g. attached to doors of toilets, bathrooms etc., to encourage the use of the system by as many residents and staff as realistically possible. Care however must be taken to ensure that residents who can vocalise do not opt for the Bliss system rather than communicating by speech. This can be prevented and overcome by the insistence that speech, irrespective of crudity, is used in conjunction with the symbols (see Ch. 11).

The Makaton vocabulary is a system of hand signs and gestures. These signs are very simple and have been adapted from the American Sign Language and everyday signs and gestures that have come to be recognised as part of our culture. Where there was an absence of a commonly accepted sign, one was devised to meet the need, paying regard to the message it was meant to convey. This system is taught in different stages; the pupil progressing from one stage to the next only when competence is established in each stage. In residential settings where this system is used, all staff should be encouraged to learn this system to allow the individuals concerned to communicate freely outside their immediate environment. In many hospitals Makaton groups have been established and not surprisingly, due to the simplicity of the system, the use of Makaton has spread outside the groups to involve a fair percentage of staff and residents not directly in need of the system. In using the system, the spoken word must be used in conjunction with the sign to encourage vocalisation and discourage the development of a non-vocal community.

In addition to the development of speech and communication, the speech therapist can also be of great assistance in the development of feeding techniques with residents who are 'difficult feeders'. The therapist can advise and demonstrate to nursing staff techniques which can overcome the absence of tongue control or deformities of palate, e.g. tongue thrust and cleft palate. Tongue thrust is a condition where the resident immediately on presentation of food in the mouth, will thrust his tongue out of the mouth and consequently eject the food. The speech therapist has a valuable contribution to make with the feeding of this type of resident.

Occupational therapy

As its name suggests, this speciality deals with the provision of occupation for the residents. Traditionally, this meant the provision of some form of hand or craft work which could be executed by the resident, paying regard to his mental ability and manual dexterity. This took the form of rug-making, basket-work, collage, bead stringing, finger painting and a multitude of other simple pastimes. These occupations did not just consume time and amuse the resident, they also contributed to the development of some of the basic skills, such as colour discrimination, shape recognition and hand-eye co-ordination.

Today this speciality has expanded its scope so that it now also assists the resident to develop everyday skills such as cooking, dress-making and home maintenance. The occupational therapist is also trained to advise on 'aids to living' and can therefore suggest special pieces of equipment that could make life just a little bit easier for certain of the residents. As can be seen, there could be a situation where professional roles overlap, but this should not be a problem if the multi-disciplinary approach is adopted.

Industrial therapy

In the past when employment was more readily available in the community and before the change in the Mental Health Act of 1959 (1960 Scotland) that bestowed informal status on many of the more able residents, the purpose of this department was to prepare residents for work in a variety of settings from heavy industry to farm work. The residents were selected for their abilities and aptitudes, exposed to work situations and trained to function within these situations. In this era most hospitals had their own farm and this offered employment to many male residents, some of whom were eventually discharged to farm employment. In this same era, the hospitals had their own 'gardens' that produced vegetables for consumption by the hospitalised population; many of the residents were allocated work within the hospital as tradesmen, e.g. upholsterer, plumber, electrician, whilst the female residents were allocated laundry work, sewing room, and general domestic work.

Hospitals today do not have many residents with the abilities required for these pursuits. This has led in part to the disposal of the hospital farms and the run down to a more basic level of production in the gardening system. However, if suitable numbers of staff were available, the gardening system remains a valuable form of employment, but with the rundown of hospital staff numbers gardening schemes are no longer viable. If the Health Service was not so cost conscious, it is still realistic to suggest that farm work is still a valuable therapeutic outlet for the not so able resident, given adequate staffing levels to maintain the necessary supervision.

However, in recent years we have witnessed the dramatic increase in dependency levels of the hospitalised residents and the industrial therapy unit has had to adjust to meet the needs of today's hospitalised residents. Care has to be taken to ensure that the task allotted to the specific resident is within his capability. As some of the tasks can be of an 'industrial' nature, the safety factor must be a priority consideration when selecting residents for the 'job' and vice versa.

For the physically able occupations such as metalwork, welding, carpentry and concrete work (paving slabs etc.) are provided, while less robust residents, who have a fair degree of intellect, are engaged in soft-toy making, dressmaking and other forms of handicraft.

Many hospitals now undertake 'contract' work from various industrial/manufacturing firms, trading in the community. The range of work from this source is potentially endless and of varying degrees of simplicity or complexity, e.g. label stringing, toy assembly, toy packing, bundling pens, assembling pens, packing C.S.S.D. packs. These activities may involve the designing and use of a simple jig or template to allow the less able to perform the task. If twelve pens have to be placed in a box, for example, and it is beyond the ability of the resident to count to twelve, a board can be designed to facilitate the employment of this particular resident in this particular task. The board should have twelve clearly defined boxes drawn on its surface, each box clearly numbered. The resident places a pen in each square until each one accommodates a pen, the pens are now placed in the box, task completed. There are many different examples where a little ingenuity will facilitate occupation of the resident in an activity that would otherwise be denied him. The use of this type of board should not preclude teaching of numeracy.

However there are situations to be avoided in the Industrial Therapy Units:

1. exposure of residents to physical danger.
2. allotting tasks beyond residents' ability.
3. prolonged exposure of resident to repetitive tasks.
4. greater emphasis on meeting contract dates than on residents' welfare, i.e. 'driving' of residents to meet production demands of contract. Only contracts with a degree of flexibility should be accepted.
5. quality control — if the quality does not meet contractors' satisfaction the contract will be terminated. Staff within this unit should strive to assure this control.

Unfortunately opportunities to acquire 'contract' work are declining, mainly due to the present day recession in the manufacturing industry causing firms to retain some of these 'simple assembly' tasks for their own employees. Could the answer be to produce commodities for direct sale to the public? This could lead to self financing schemes. In many areas the initial steps have been taken to introduce these schemes in different forms, both from Adult Training Centres and from Industrial Units within the hospitals. Most of these schemes are in their infancy and the preliminary reports are encouraging.

Concrete products

This is a fairly common manufacturing process employed in many hospitals and Adult Training Centres today, but some establishments are now pricing their products at cost price plus 10%. The calculation of cost price is based on the cost of the raw materials plus a percentage for wastage in manufacture, heat and lighting and wages for clients/residents involved in the process. The 10% then is the profit margin which can be used imaginatively to develop the facilities in the Industrial Unit or augment the funds available for recreational purposes or purchase special items of equipment for the hospital/centre that would otherwise have been unavailable from the normal sources.

Gardening projects

Some establishments which have suitable facilities — greenhouses, cold frames — or can acquire these facilities are now raising garden plants for sale direct to the public on terms similar to those described in relation to the marketing of the concrete products. In some cases where vegetables are being grown, produce is sold to local traders who call to collect their requirements.

The early reports of these schemes are encouraging and could possibly be a replacement for the diminishing contract work. It should be noted that before embarking on a project designed to sell direct to the public, consultation with the local Traders' Association and the Local Trades' Council is advisable as both these organizations have vested interests in this type of project as it could affect the local traders and possibly have implications on employment. This is a very sensitive area and good public relations may be the key factor in the success of these schemes.

An example of the type of sanctions that may be imposed on the schemes and one that is widely adopted even in the sale of goods from the established Industrial Units, is that there should be no advertising of the schemes. Subsequently the schemes are dependent on word of mouth for their advertising and initial results indicate that this is not proving a drawback to their operation and success.

Drama, music and art therapy

These three specialities have recently become more popular and are more in evidence in today's hospitals. They all demand the residents' involvement, both physically and mentally.

Drama therapy. In drama, the resident is involved in role play to varying degrees, which encourages movement and if the therapist is aware of the resident's activity patterns, movement of limbs and muscles not willingly used by the resident can be incorporated into the drama. Movement plays a large part in this approach but encouragement in the use of imagination is also an important factor. The residents are encouraged to suggest a situation that they would like to 'act' through. The therapist's expertise comes into play by guiding or channelling the residents' imagination into physical activity, which can in turn be adapted to also provide a therapeutic effect on limbs that are spastic or otherwise impaired. Suggestions made by the residents can lead to full dramas being constructed stage by stage and eventually presented to an audience of their peers.

Music therapy is another form of therapeutic approach that can be devised to encourage movement, relaxation and participation. Encouragement can be given to residents to use muscles that they would not use in normal situations. Eurhythmics is a branch of music therapy that is designed to encourage the resident to move to specific musical cues. This form of therapy is not only of value to the physically active but can be devised to suit the needs of the chair-bound and otherwise physically limited resident. The value of music in relaxation is well recognised and can be used to good effect in the hospital for this purpose.

Music therapy can easily be combined with drama therapy to open up new channels for imaginative team work and role play.

Art therapy offers involvement to residents suffering from varying degrees of physical and mental handicap as it ranges from the refined creation to the crude finger painting of the profoundly handicapped or spastic resident. This speciality facilitates the use of imagination and has proved invaluable in causing the withdrawn resident to become more gregarious and socially active with peer groups. No hospital resident is unable, due to physical or mental handicap, to join in or be offered the opportunity of participating in art therapy.

Reaching the full potential of these three therapeutic activities is dependent on the enthusiasm of the therapists, the degree of cooperation offered and the available resident 'talent'.

Play therapy

The value of play is inestimable and provides an ideal vehicle for learning, development of movement and use of imagination. Many basic skills can be taught through the medium of play if the therapist or nurse uses ingenuity in developing the play situation around the skill to be taught, e.g. the selecting of similarly coloured cubes and building them into a tower. This assists in the development of colour recognition, perhaps basic numeracy and certainly hand/eye co-ordination. All these skills can be derived from one simple play situation, not to mention the fun in knocking the tower down again. Play situations can be developed in almost any situation in the life of the resident whilst in hospital, e.g. bathing, feeding, dressing etc. It can be very rewarding to witness developments in the residents' skills through the medium of play.

However, in many cases, play has to be taught and the nurse or therapist should make efforts to teach the resident to play as an individual and as group member, hopefully leading to the development of peer group co-operation and identification. Another commonly held misconception is that play is only for children; this is fallacious as the majority of adult residents willingly participate in play situations and sessions, especially of a competitive and team nature by the more able. This gives rise to further opportunities for nursing staff to construct learning around play situations. The importance of play cannot be overemphasised, particularly with the mentally handicapped and this recognition gave rise to the formation of the Toy Libraries Association. Most hospitals for the mentally handicapped now have their own toy library which provides toys of all types on a lending basis. The toys are normally selected by a committee of prefessionals and ideally the patients, for their educational qualities as well as for their basic play value.

This is only a brief outline of the basics of play, but more in depth information is contained in Chapter 12.

Recreational therapy

This service is organised to provide the recreational needs of all hospitalised residents and is usually staffed by nurses and occasionally by individuals who have special abilities or aptitudes, such as active sports persons or musicians. Ideally staff should be versatile outgoing individuals with a fertile imagination that is quick to develop or recognise potential recreational outlets. Ward-based staff should also seek to develop recreational programmes from the ward which involve residents in smaller numbers. Small group recreation can be provided by Darby & Joan Clubs, Senior Citizens' Clubs, Boy Scouts, Girl Guides, Concert Parties, Discos and 'Social Clubs'.

The recreational therapy department may also organise such activities as residents' holidays, day trips, theatre visits, sporting activities, horse riding and swimming. The scope is wide, but care has to be taken to ensure the activities meet the needs of the residents and not the staff. Recreational staff are of value in dealing with residents with specific problems, e.g. behaviourally disturbed. They can construct and offer basic recreational programmes in an attempt to divert the resi-

dent's attention to alternatives that will occupy his interest and prevent the onset of antisocial behaviour. This approach is normally made in conjunction with the psychologist and perhaps the drama, art or music therapist, as well as the regular nursing or care staff, illustrating the multi-disciplinary approach.

Social work in hospitals

Most hospitals now have a resident social worker or team of social workers who deal with a great variety of problems. Ideally, they visit relatives at home prior to planned admissions and compile a social profile on the family and prospective resident, follow up discharged residents, liaise with community social workers, seek out lodgings for potential discharges, and liaise with staff in hostels and adult training centres, seeking openings or placements for hospital-based residents. The social worker and the community mental handicap nurse will necessarily have to work in close liaison with each other to maximise their roles and prevent role overlap.

Further to the above, the social worker is heavily involved in the preparation of claims to Department of Health and Social Security for special allowances for specific residents, such as mobility allowance.

Chiropody and dentistry

These two services are available on a sessional basis to most mental handicap hospitals. They deal with all emergencies within their speciality as they arise and routinely inspect and treat all residents within the hospital at regular intervals.

Remedial gymnast

This speciality offers a service that develops, encourages and corrects movement by involving the residents in a series of specialised exercises. It also aims at encouraging and stimulating disinterested residents into physical activity, often accompanied with music. Nurses should familiarise themselves with the simple exercises under the guidance of the gymnast to ensure continuity of approach.

The potential range of services within the hospital is extensive, but it has to be stressed that it would be a very fortunate hospital indeed that had all these services available. Many of these services have arisen due to the fact that nurses failed to extend their skills to cover specific areas of care or indeed failed to recognise the potential breadth of their role. Nurses must now accept that they still have a part to play in most of these specialist areas by learning from the specialist, and, where possible carrying out the techniques of these specialities to ensure continuity of approach and facilitate permanent change where desired. The multi-disciplinary approach is necessary to ensure continuity and co-ordination of all agreed treatments/therapies for any specific resident.

COMMUNITY PROVISION FOR THE MENTALLY HANDICAPPED

Provision for children under 5 years of age

Let us first consider an extract of the report 'Fit for the Future' (Court Report) 1976, by quoting an extract from the summary on Chapter 14 dealing with the subject of handicap and health provision for children:

> Long stay residential accommodation should be provided for about 80 severely retarded children in each average sized district: not less than 40 of these places should be in local authority children's homes. This necessitates a major expansion in local authority provision.

It is sad to report that very few districts have established residential provision in line with this recommendation. By far the greatest percentage of residential places are provided within the National Health Service hospitals, and not by local authorities.

The child in its early months, if mental handicap is recognised, may be referred to a consultant psychiatrist in mental handicap. Extreme care has to be taken at this stage to ensure the parents are not 'frightened off' by the attention of too many 'specialists' offering advice and guidance on how to cope with the 'special child'. It is often wisest to leave the initial home support to the family GP and the health visitor. These professionals will assess the situation and at the correct time, advise the parents on the other services available to the child. Parents need to be handled with sensitivity and tact as they may be experiencing a grief reaction or guilt complex at one extreme and despair at the other. Faulty handling at this stage can cause parental rejection of the child, and possibly rejection of society and the assistance offered by society (see Ch. 13).

Some of the services that can be recommended are similar to those available at the hospital, e.g. psychiatry, psychology, community mental handicap nurse, audiometry, speech therapy. Care has to be taken not to flood the parental home with services or specialists; rather one person whether it is a health visitor, social worker or community mental handicap nurse should be seen as the key person. Co-operation between disciplines is extremely important.

Caring for the mentally handicapped child at home is very demanding and trying on the family and by necessity, provision should be made to allow the parents and other siblings a break from these demands if they so wish. There are various schemes in operation in different parts of the country to meet this need. Some hospitals have a number of beds for this purpose, similar provision is made by some local authorities within children's homes where available. Some areas maintain a list of families willing to foster mentally handicapped children on a short-term basis. In other areas, charitable organisations provide facilities to enable the provision of this type of service.

The Education (Handicapped Children) Act 1971 stated that all children, irrespective of the degree of mental handicap, should receive an 'education'. This removed the stigma of the label 'uneducable' from many of these children. but it is not every area that provides the full facility as advocated by the Act. Some local authorities make provision for special education for any child over the age of 2 years who is handicapped either physically or mentally. This has led to play-groups and nursery schools in most areas accepting mentally handicapped children into membership, enabling the child to learn alongside the other children. At this age the mentally handicapped child is readily accepted by the peer group. This approach facilitates imitation or mimicry and may encourage the child to develop further at this stage than originally anticipated. The degree of handicap, however, has a major influence on this possibility.

Education provision

At the age of 5 years, the child will enter the education system proper. The Education Act 1971 gave every child the legal entitlement to an education suitable to his needs. Some of the children, especially the more profoundly handicapped, may have to attend boarding schools. However, some authorities, lacking in the structural facilities, do provide a service whereby teachers attend the homes of the children to deliver their legal right to education and at the same time prevent the traumatic mother/child separation. This arose mainly from the recommendations contained in the 1978 Warnock Report which also advocated that the education of this special group need not stop at 16 years of age, but should continue beyond if it is going to prove advantageous to the 'child', now referred to as a 'young person'. This report also made recommendations on the training of teachers for this special field and we have witnessed a growth in numbers of teachers qualified to meet the challenge.

RESIDENTIAL SERVICES OUTSIDE NATIONAL HEALTH SERVICE HOSPITALS

Residential services within the community are sometimes provided to facilitate education or to provide family relief by temporary admission to a care setting. In the case of children, this may be in the form of hospital admission, children's home placement, nursery placement or temporary fostering. Residential provision by voluntary agencies will be discussed on pages 94–96.

Children's homes

Many local authorities who provide children's homes within their area now reserve a number of place for the mentally handicapped. Some offer long-term care, but it is more usual that they offer short-term care in special circumstances where family relief is required. The provision of this type of facility has expanded within the past decade but not always up to the desired level.

In the past, children's homes tended to be built, or existing large houses adapted, to accommodate 20–30 children. Now there is greater opportunity to treat the child as an individual in this setting and subsequently provision can be tailored to the individual child. Small group living is more easily accomplished here than in the clinical environment of the hospital.

More recently, we have witnessed the adventurous and encouraging move to the provision of residential accommodation in a truly domestic setting, by locating homes to house small groups of children in modern housing estates. The home, perhaps slightly modified to cater for the group and its special needs, accommodates 4–6 children plus 'live in' staff. Food and clothing are purchased from local shops and the food is prepared and cooked at home. Admittedly, some appliances such as washing machines, may be the industrial type, but great effort is made to keep the home as 'normal' or standard as possible.

Some of these homes do accommodate the profoundly physically and mentally handicapped and not just select groups. There can be problems in relation to the behaviourally disturbed, and sadly in some circumstances alternative provision has to be found. This is a desirable move to normalisation, but realistically, it can be argued that this provision cannot offer an alternative for a large percentage of hospitalised children due to profundity of handicap and behavioural problems, but perhaps it could prevent some of these children from being admitted to hospital initially.

Fostering

Fostering schemes are not confined to providing for children, as many adults who are mentally handicapped have been successfully fostered.

Children of all ages and degree of handicap have benefited from this scheme which tends to be on a short-term basis, but many children have been fostered for lengthy periods and some have been totally 'absorbed' into the surrogate family as an accepted and independent member of the family.

Local authorities advertise for families willing to foster this type of child and retain a list of these families for future reference. Great care is taken to match the child to the prospective foster family and vice-versa. The foster family receives the close support of the social work department, health visitor and all other appropriate back-up services, as well as receiving payment for this service plus an allowance calculated to meet the cost of maintaining the child. This may appear to be a mercenary type of service, but the careful screening of prospective foster families and regular supervision by the social worker minimises, if not eliminates, this risk and any that do slip through the net are soon identified. Many profoundly handicapped children have been successfully fostered for varying lengths of time in family crises and thus have avoided hospital admission. This service can also allow the parents of some mentally handicapped children to have a holiday which would otherwise have been denied, either due to lack of alternative or by the parents refusing to admit the child to hospital, even for such a short period.

Hostels

Hostels provide residential facilities of varying

levels of independence to people suffering from varying degrees of mental handicap. The trend has been towards accepting people with a greater degree of mental and physical handicap into residence. In the past only the more able were considered for hostel placement and this still prevails today in some areas, e.g. some local authorities insist that prospective clients should be fully continent.

Hostels provide self-contained living units allied to other self support facilities in service areas within the building, e.g. laundry facilities, kitchen facilities, T.V. lounge, games room etc. Some hostels are staffed and others unstaffed, according to the type of client being catered for. Most hostels today have staff in residence which seems to be a more realistic approach as mishaps can occur and the more able of the mentally handicapped are now in other forms of accommodation that provide for smaller group living and offer greater independence.

The hostel often offers the first stage of independent living within the community to previously hospitalised residents who have gone through a pre-discharge training programme. Alternatively, it can provide an alternative to hospital admission for the individual who has been cared for by the family but whose relatives are now elderly, infirm or hospitalised themselves and are therefore no longer able to cope.

The hostel is usually empty by day as its residents are at work or attending the local Adult Training Centre except at weekends or during holiday periods. Each client contributes financially to the upkeep of the hostel, either from earnings or government allowances, with the contribution scaled according to the resources of each client. As well as promoting independence, the hostel allows a greater exposure to mixed sex living than is possible in hospital.

Hostels are normally provided by the local authority but in some areas the National Health Service has established hostels whilst in other areas 'joint funding' by both authorities had provided this facility.

Group homes

Group homes can be under the supervision of either the local authority, the National Health Service or both. The most prevalent however is the local authority supervised home.

This system allows for a group of mentally handicapped adults ranging in number from 3–5 to live in a 'normal' situation. The residents of the home are commonly of the same sex, but there is a definite move to the mixed sex home. The single sex situation is more to meet the approval of society and immediate neighbourhood than a deliberate attempt to keep the sexes apart. It has now become the practice to consult local residents prior to establishing new group homes. This is not mandatory but is often carried out as a public relations exercise to prevent misunderstandings from arising.

This system allows a group to live in an ordinary setting — a house. Members of the group are selected for their compatibility and range of skills. 'Specialists' may be selected for the group, e.g. someone who is skilled in basic cookery. Consideration would also be given to selecting a person who is able and willing to do general housework and shopping, and where possible this person would also be the cook. The objective is the formation of a competent all-round group that is a viable independent unit. Problems can arise, however, when one member leaves and removes some of the group's skills.

Group homes can be formed from clients presently residing in either a community or hospital situation or a mix from both. In most cases the local social work department looks after the initial establishment and management of the home, with assistance from the community mental handicap nurse. If the home is to house a previously hospitalised group, potential members will have received a pre-discharge training in domestic and social skills aimed at preparing them for their new roles. The social work department in some areas provides a 'home-maker' in the initial stages to assist in the settling of the group and the establishment of a domestic routine. The home is financed from members' wages or social security payments, and it is fairly common for a social worker to supervise financial arrangements until the group becomes competent in budgeting.

Sheltered housing

In some areas groups of houses are set aside both for the mentally and physically handicapped. It is normal practice to provide this type of accommodation for the more able or socially competent of the mentally handicapped. The houses are usually adjacent to each other and are often supervised by a warden, either resident or living nearby. Residents often form a mini society and tend to assist each other more readily than is possible in the standard neighbourhood. These groups receive all the benefits and services as described earlier for other groups.

Opinions vary on the merits of this type of provision; some authorities suggest that this scheme creates mini ghettos of assorted handicapped individuals, whilst others insist that it affords independence and freedom of choice for the handicapped. Certainly if the scheme is well supervised and managed, group members can have a full exposure to the benefits of society, leaving their home to enter the mainstream of society as and when they wish. This type of scheme is given social work support to ensure that the quality of life does not fall.

Lodgings

This is a relatively new scheme whereby the local authority pays local boarding houses, hotels and private householders to provide full board or part board for selected mentally handicapped people. Some hospitals for the mentally handicapped also adopted this approach to enable the discharge of some of their more able residents. Although successful in some areas it was shown that in some locations, the mentally handicapped were being exploited by their landlords, whilst in other areas they were not truly discharged as they were 'sleeping out' then being 'bussed' back to the local hospital in the morning to spend their day there before returning to their 'digs' in the evening.

In Scotland, this practice has largely disappeared and where these schemes still operate they are closely supervised to ensure that exploitation does not occur. In some locations boarding houses and guest houses now devote their entire accommodation to the mentally handicapped, providing the full range of hotel services to their guests throughout the entire year.

Nursing and rest homes

Many of the more elderly of the mentally handicapped are now being catered for in either nursing or rest homes and are receiving the same care as offered to the elderly from the mainstream of society. It appears that elderly non-mentally handicapped people tend to accept the same age group of the mentally handicapped more readily than any other adult group in society. If this is the case, it is a sad reflection that the mentally handicapped have to wait for their twilight years to be accepted as an equal by their generation.

Placed in this type of residential accommodation, the mentally handicapped receive the range of services enjoyed by any other individual in a similar setting.

NON-RESIDENTIAL PROVISION

Adult Training Centres (ATC)

These centres cater for the adult mentally handicapped domiciled in a specific geographical area. Today the adult training centre is geared to provide the client with all aspects of social education. The centre is usually divided into four distinct areas:

1. Admission and assessment
2. Activity and development
3. Special care
4. Advanced work area.

1. Admission and assessment

The admission and assessment area receives clients from all locations and services caring for the mentally handicapped: from the home, school and hospital. They are assessed initially by the psychology services and thereafter by the centre staff by observing and evaluating the strengths and weaknesses of the client's performance on specially allocated tasks. The client can remain in this area for some considerable time until the staff are satisfied that they have a fair knowledge of the client's abilities. The client is now ready to proceed to the next area.

2. Activity and development

The activity and development area may continue with the programme commenced in the admission and assessment area or offer further exposure to educational skills both in the academic and social competence fields. This education could be in the area of self-help, group skills, social behaviour or by exposing the client to work activity in simple workshop settings.

This area also involves and educates the client in recreational, leisure activities. The task of organising recreational and cultural activities as well as the traditional club and social activities normally associated with the centre is also the responsibility of this area and every client is encouraged to participate. This is the main area of the centre and the majority of the clients will spend the bulk of their time in this area except when assigned to special projects in the advanced work area.

3. Special care areas

The special care area is used for the more profoundly handicapped client where the emphasis is placed on caring for the client and the teaching of the more basic skills. Here the care staff concentrate on the development of skills such as feeding, toileting, communication, mobility and correction of behaviour. In most centres individual programmes are developed for the client and these involve input from various different services such as psychology, speech therapy and physiotherapy. Involvement and training of the parent/guardian also takes place in this area, in an attempt to ensure continuity of approach at home.

As the client is home based, this area provides a facility for evaluating the physical condition of the client and enables speedy access to the medical facilities should the need arise. It also provides a focus for the parent/guardian to relay information, seek advice or generally gain the moral support so often denied people in this situation.

4. Advanced work area

The advanced work area provides a facility where the client is introduced to and taught some of the more advanced skills such as carpentry, metal work, welding, sewing machine operation, knitting machine operating, printing and toy making. This provides a realistic pre-work experience before the client moves on to employment in a sheltered workshop or enclave.

Sheltered workshops

These workshops provide employment on a variety of skill levels for clients with varying degrees of handicap, both physical and mental. This facility provides an area of experience that allows the client to gain a sense of achievement and fulfilment by contributing to a manufacturing process. In return for his efforts, the client is remunerated not according to production, but as a reward for effort and enthusiasm. Some local authorities provide this type of facility but by far the greatest supplier is Remploy Ltd, with somewhere in the region of 80 factories throughout the country. These factories, whether under the control of the local authority or Remploy, have to compete in the market place to sell their goods, and like every other manufacturing industry are feeling the effects of today's economic recession. Subsequently, these work-

shops have had to lay-off employees which in turn adds to the already existing immense problem of meeting the needs of the mentally handicapped in a modern society.

Parent groups

These self-help groups have many advantages for both parent and child. Many are affiliated to e.g. the National Society for Mentally Handicapped Children. Most have created their own facilities and by and large raise their own funds. The groups arrange activities for parents, mentally handicapped children and adults. The activities vary from one group to another but regularly include play-groups, swimming clubs and other sporting activities. Often they are in contact with other similar groups and organise joint activities and competitions.

Many parents are hesitant to join these groups but they should be encouraged to 'come and try' and the fact that they come in contact with families who have similar problems to their own can help the parent to accept the group. The group can provide a good source of information about local and national facilities as well as keeping the parent up-to-date with new developments.

Above all else these groups provide a means of mutual support and a sense of belonging to a group that accepts the situation for what it is. Much of the effort of these groups is directed towards self-help but they are an effective pressure group both at local and national level. Often these groups have good links with local health and social services departments. It would be wrong to assume that these groups are inward looking as they do have a valuable role within the broader community and raise their funds from the community by organising dances, discos, jumble sales and coffee mornings.

Gateway Clubs

These clubs are usually run by parent groups and other voluntary bodies. The groups are frequently sponsored by the National Society for Mentally Handicapped Children (NSMHC) and normally consist of junior and senior sections. The parents assisted by groups of volunteers, offer various activities including meeting and competing with other groups. The Gateway Club sponsors the Gateway Award Scheme, which is similar to the Duke of Edinburgh Award Scheme and many mentally handicapped people derive great pleasure from participating in this scheme and from attending the Gateway Clubs in general.

Enclave schemes

These schemes provide supervised special employment for small groups of mentally handicapped people. The size of these groups varies, but seldom exceeds 10 in number. These schemes are provided by the local authorities and employ the mentally handicapped in such activities as special gardening projects, park maintenance, street cleaning and other environmental schemes. The client is paid for his efforts and by this gains a sense of achievement.

VOLUNTARY AGENCIES

In addition to National Health Service and local authority provision, some voluntary agencies provide services for the mentally handicapped or contribute much-needed additional finance to existing services. Some organisations such as Mencap, Mind, National Society for Mentally Handicapped Children, Dr Barnardo's and the Cheshire Foundation provide residential facilities of differing types and design for the mentally handicapped.

The Spastics Society finances the running and maintenance of village type settings that accept the mentally handicapped as clients, e.g. Hansel village in Ayrshire. The client is resident in this setting on a more or less full-time basis, receiving care and education to return to the parental home by arrangement with the parents. The society also provides holiday facilities and relief for families who have a spastic member residing with the family.

The Dr Barnardo's organisation is now providing accommodation for mentally handicapped children in different areas of the country. They are purchasing houses in ordinary housing estates and accommodating mentally handicapped children within them. This type of scheme has been extended whereby several houses are purchased in the same vicinity with one becoming the administrative centre and the other houses organised and directed from it. Unless requiring special internal adaptation houses are left much as they are to provide a typical domestic setting or home for the children. The staff are organised on a group or family principle.

The National Association for Mental Health (MIND) and Campaign for the Mentally Handicapped tend to concentrate their efforts on the purchase and provision of houses suitable for using as group homes. Equally important is their crucial role nationally as pressure groups working on behalf of the mentally handicapped.

National Society for Mentally Handicapped Children (NSMHC) was founded in 1946 and one of its major roles is the support of local societies and the promotion of regional activities. It also offers a range of personal services such as counselling and advisory service to parents.

A recent innovation is its Trusteeship Scheme which helps reduce the anxiety of parents on the long-term future by ensuring that there will be someone to take a personal interest in the mentally handicapped person after the parents have died.

The society also runs holiday homes and residential courses for mentally handicapped teenagers as well as producing the magazine *Parents Voice* which helps parents keep up-to-date with the latest developments as well as containing topical and local information. Special courses and conferences are also organised by the society for professionals and it publishes its own journal and specialist books. As a national pressure group, it promotes the needs of the mentally handicapped and educates the public on the problems associated with mental handicap.

Camphill schools and village communities

This movement was founded in Scotland by Dr Karl Konig based upon the philosophy of Rudolph Steiner. The villages have a community of between 100 and 150 villagers and approximately the same number of staff or co-workers. There is no division between villager and co-worker who live and work together as equals.

The village has its hall, post office, store and is divided into several neighbourhoods, comprising of households in which between 3–10 villagers of both sexes live. Everyone contributes to the household budget and everyone is also expected to perform a full 5-day working week. The work is geared to self sufficiency, i.e. farming, market gardening and craftwork which is sold to raise much needed cash. There is a wide range of leisure and social activities centred on the village hall.

No wages are paid but everyone receives pocket money in relation to their individual needs. Relatives or social service departments are expected to supply larger items such as clothing, footwear and luxury items. No fees are charged and the communities are dependent on their own self sufficiency with income derived from produce and articles sold.

Although the village is self contained, there is contact with the wider community as the villagers are encouraged to go out to the local community and events are arranged within the village to attract the local community into the village.

The original concept has been modified from long-term care to one of rehabilitation and return to independent life within the community.

Camphill Houses have been established and run on the basis of equal partnership between the mentally handicapped people and the co-workers and aim to return the handicapped people to accommodation of their own in the community and provide a resource centre for those who have done so.

Cottage and rural exterprises (CARE)

The first CARE village was started in Devon in 1976 but there are now several villages established throughout England. All are in rural settings and have been developed around original farm buildings. Each takes up to 70 villagers and the minimum age of entry is 18 and all villagers must be supported by a local authority grant.

The villagers live in cottages with between eight and twelve others of both sexes, supervised over the full 24-hour period by house staff. Each village has one or more cottages, where supervision is reduced giving more responsibility to the villager in running the household. Personal privary has a high priority with each villager having his own room which he is expected to clean and maintain to acceptable standards.

Work within the village is of a rural nature including farmwork, market gardening, estate maintenance and traditional and modern craftwork. If possible, villagers are given suitable employment that they will enjoy doing, and will provide them with a sense of satisfaction and achievement. No wages are paid but everyone receives a standard rate of pocket money. Full recreational facilities are available but everyone is encouraged to develop individual leisure pursuits. Contact with the broader community is maintained and most villages are integrated with the local community and interchange is encouraged.

Home Farm Trust

Founded in 1962 by a group of parents, there are now several residential homes with more planned. The homes each provide about 30 places and offer 'care for life' and accommodate mentally handicapped people from the age of 16 years upwards.

L'arche

This is an international organisation founded in France in 1964 which has recently established communities in this country. The communities are small, for 20 or less, but have their own workshops and market gardens which provide a source of income but by no means covers the maintenance of the scheme which has to be met by voluntary donation and public subscription.

Elizabeth Fitzroy Homes

This Trust runs three small family style homes for mentally handicapped children and three homes for young adults, the finance being supplied from the Trust fund.

Riding for the Disabled Association

This association has a large number of groups throughout the country which provide horse and pony riding facilities for the disabled, including the mentally handicapped. The association was started for children, but is now extending in many areas to provide for adults.

Disabled Living Foundation

This organisation is concerned with the living environment of the disabled in all aspects including aids and equipment. They also concern themselves with clothing, housing, furniture design and physical recreation. Many specific studies have been directed into these areas, pamphlets published and booklets produced on an extensive range of help for the disabled; a free information service is also available.

Central Council for the Disabled

The primary concern of the Council is the improvement of State services for and public understanding of the physically handicapped of all levels of intellect. Campaigns have been organised by the Council, aimed at improving transport and toilet facilities, access to public buildings and other public amenities. the Council also provides other services including information and advice for the disabled and those caring for them.

Down's Babies Association

Founded especially for the parents of children with Down's syndrome, one of the Association's main aims is to provide practical advice and guidance to parents on the management of their child, and detailed guides to training are available from the association. As many of the volunteers involved with this association are Down's parents themselves, they have a full understanding of the problems and can provide an invaluable source of support.

Toy Libraries Association

This group aims to establish toy libraries throughout the country and put pressure on manufacturers and designers to produce toys and play equipment for handicapped children. The Association publishes a quarterly newsletter and useful booklets on the subject of play and choosing toys, organises exhibitions and courses as well as giving advice and help on setting up new toy libraries. The toy library itself provides a valuable meeting-place for parents and children.

The above groups are a selection of the various voluntary and self-help groups that provide services and support to mentally handicapped people and their families. Further information about these and other services is contained in the publication *Guide to National Associations for People in Need* produced by the Hertfordshire Library Service, County Hall, Herts.

FINANCIAL AND OTHER PROVISION FOR THE MENTALLY HANDICAPPED

Financial provision for the mentally handicapped can come from several government sources and in some areas special local provisions are also available.

Non-contributory invalidity pension (NCIP)

This is a pension payable to every mentally handicapped person in Britain over the age of 16 years. The pension need not be paid to its legal maximum, but can be reduced to a level that can be realistically utilised by the individual. The purpose of this pension was to allow the individual the opportunity to develop a degree of independence by giving purchasing power and personal choice, e.g. to save for holidays. Although the amount of pension has kept pace with inflation, it will never give total independence.

Some hospitals have allowed the joint purchasing by residents of items which would otherwise be beyond individual means. Other hospitals frown on this practice with the result that large bank balances can accrue to no-one's benefit.

Mobility allowance

This is available to people who suffer from varying degrees of imobility and must be used specifically by the individual on transport to facilitate greater access to society. A taxable allowance, it can be paid to people aged between 5 years and pension age, i.e. 65 for males, 60 for females.

To qualify for this allowance the person must be unable to walk or the quality of walking is so limited as to be considered as virtually unable to walk. Other factors taken into account are: exertion of walking may endanger life or lead to serious deterioration of health; the person is likely to remain unable to walk for at least 1 year and must be able to make use of the allowance. Consideration is also given to the manner of walk, the duration of ability to walk, and the speed and distance that can be safely walked without discomfort. When claiming for a mentally handicapped person, it is useful to supply supportive evidence from someone who knows the person well, e.g. family doctor, stating that benefit would be derived from the allowance. In some cases a medical examination is arranged before an allowance is paid.

Where the mentally handicapped person is resident at home or in local authority accommodation, the social worker will normally make the necessary claim and deal with the associated paperwork on behalf of the claimant. The National Development Team for the Mentally Handicapped Report (1976–1977) highlighted the fact that many residents of mental handicap hospitals who could be regarded as eligible, do not have claims made on their behalf by the hospital.

In hospitals where residents do receive the allowance, imaginative use has been made of it by utilising the monies for regular outings by taxi or bus. In some cases vehicles have been purchased to hire to groups of residents receiving this allowance. It has also facilitated more regular visiting by relatives and allowed the residents to benefit from outings and imaginative holidays.

Attendance allowance

This is a tax-free allowance paid to the family or the person caring for a person who is severely disabled, either physically or mentally, and has needed a lot of looking after for a period of 6 months, or more. Applications for this allowance are made for persons who meet the above criteria and are 2 years of age or over. There are two rates of allowance: one for those who require attention by day and by night and a lower rate for those who require attention either day or night. This payment has proved to be of tremendous value to affected families as it has allowed the hiring in some situations of additional help or the rewarding of individuals who assist in the care of the handicapped person on an ad hoc basis.

Supplementary benefits

Mentally handicapped people resident in the community, whether in the care of their family or in other forms of accommodation, may be eligible for a supplementary pension. This is payable if the person is over 16 years old, not in full-time work or their income is less than their requirements. Benefit may also be payable if the person is registered as disabled and in full-time work, but not receiving the full rate of pay and is therefore earning substantially less than other people who do the same sort of work.

If the person qualifies for supplementary benefit he will also be entitled to the following additional benefits:

a. Free prescriptions for all prescribed medicines plus elastic hosiery and wigs supplied from hospital out-patient departments.
b. Free dental treatment or reduced charges.
c. Free spectacles or reduced charges.
d. Free welfare milk and vitamins for handicapped children and those with approved child-minders, day nurseries and playgroups. Handicapped children aged 5–16 who are not registered as pupils at a school or special school are also entitled to free welfare milk.
e. Free school meals.
f. Hospital fares are payable if hospital attendance is required. If public transport is used the fares are reimbursed if the order book or exemption certificate is produced when the person attends for treatment.
g. Rent rebates and allowances are payable to those who cannot afford their full rent *except* for those who are receiving supplementary benefit.
h. Legal aid and advice for people in need of help from a solicitor or who may be involved in civil court cases.
i. Grants for extended education are also available though seldom called upon by mentally handicapped people. Nevertheless, these are available if needed on leaving school on the same terms as other students. A supplementary allowance may be paid to handicapped students who incur expenditure on the purchase of special equipment necessary for their studies because of their disability.

Family fund

The fund was set up to assist families with severely handicapped children under the age of 16 years. This assistance may be in the form of goods, equipment or a grant of money for some definite purpose that cannot be acquired from another benefit or source, e.g. transport problems, laundry equipment, unusual adaptations or aids. This fund is administered for the Government by the Joseph Rowntree Memorial Trust.

Other allowances

The mentally handicapped person or his family may also receive payments/allowances from other government sources.

Family Income Supplement is payable to families who have at least one child and the income is below a certain level. This applies to the man's income in the case of a couple and also to single parent families. Family Allowance is also payable for a mentally handicapped child as are all other benefits available to the standard family. In addition to this all other services are available to the mentally handicapped residing in the community such as dentistry, ophthalmology, chiropody etc.

Some local authorities have special transport schemes. The criteria applied to gain access to such schemes vary, but one commonly applied condition is that the person can board and alight from a bus unaided and can travel without attendant supervision.

STAFF CARING FOR MENTALLY HANDICAPPED PEOPLE

When the immense variety of provisions from both community and hospital sources are considered in conjunction with the number of different professions involved in the care of the mentally handicapped, it seems realistic to suggest that the method of care delivery could be simplified. The greatest number of people working with the mentally handicapped are at the point of care delivery whether this be in a health service or local authority provision. If it is accepted that the needs of the mentally handicapped are the same irrespective of their location, it seems anomalous that the staff who will deliver the care, i.e. nurses in the National Health Service and care staff in local authority provision, receive different forms of training. This anomaly was tackled by the Jay Committee in 1979 in their Report of the Committee of Enquiry into Mental Handicap Nursing and Care, and the findings created a furore when published. The Committee was not in entire agreement and dissent was voiced by an economist, a consultant psychiatrist and a trade unionist (who is also a qualified nurse) who served on the committee.

The Jay Report listed 47 main recommendations which were dependent on the acceptance of the committee's 'model of care'. This model dictates that each mentally handicapped person should have access to the full range of facilities available to the general public and specialist services only provided where the general services cannot cope with a special need. Mentally handicapped people in residential care should not be isolated from their neighbourhood or more importantly from their families. The care staff should be caring and compassionate, but also professionally trained to assist each mentally handicapped person to develop mentally, physically and emotionally. Residents should live in small family type groups, sharing experiences with the staff, making their own decisions and taking necessary risks.

Care staff numbers

Mentally handicapped people in residential care require individual attention from highly trained staff. Every aspect of life offers the opportunity to learn self-help skills but this is only possible if sufficient staff is available to capitalise on these opportunities. The mentally handicapped also need care from a semi-permanent group of familiar people. Calculations based on the above considerations indicate that there should be 60 000 residential care staff, half of whom should be qualified, the other half 'in-service' trained.

Training the staff

The Committee recommended that the residential care staff should share common residential training. The staff require to know about mental handicap, the needs of adults and children and the practical skills in the mental handicap and residential care aspects of the work. Thus the training must include theoretical and practical elements. In bringing all these factors together, a new training system was devised which had more in common with courses for residential care staff, promoted by the Central Council for Education and Training in Social Work (CCETSW) than with mental handicap nurse training. The Committee therefore recommended that CCETSW should promote mental handicap care training within the framework with certain modifications of the Certificate in Social Service (CSS).

Organising staff

The Committee recommended a common career structure for mental handicap residential care staff in the National Health Service and local authorities. Each unit should have staff with differing levels of experience and skills. Qualified staff are essential but there is a practical role for in-service trained basic care staff. The head of the unit should be a qualified care worker.

Financing the proposals

The Committee recommended that a special fund be established to meet some of the training costs because of the problems of both the National Health Service and local authorities in respect of funds available for the mental handicap services.

The Committee went on to state that if their recommendations were not accepted and implemented, the result would be that mentally handicapped people would continue to suffer the indignities of the past. Also highlighted was the possibility of another Committee of Enquiry in 10 or 20 years if the principles of community care were not adopted.

Finally and most importantly, the Committee stated that more resources were required but implementation would only require a *tiny* shift in priorities for public spending and hoped that the Government would find the determination to make this shift.

The reason for the furore was the recommendation that all future 'care staff' should be trained by the CCETSW. The Committee based this recommendation on the conclusion that this form of training was more appropriate to the care of the mentally handicapped than the syllabus employed in 1979 for nurse training. Since then the syllabus has been revised and has come a long way towards providing training that enables the nurse to care for the mentally handicapped in today's situation. The English syllabus has been revised to conform to a social model whilst the Scottish syllabus is still largely based on a medical model and is in need of revision to meet the criteria of modern care and training of mentally handicapped people.

Whilst the recommendations on nurse training were rejected out of hand by the majority of practising nurses, the model of care outlined in the report was almost universally accepted and is practised today in many different areas of the country. The Jay Committee advocated the rundown of the hospitals for the mentally handicapped and stated that previously hospitalised mentally handicapped people should be transferred to community settings. However, this was regarded as too idealistic and far too expensive to implement in the foreseeable future, but it did cause the nursing profession to take a closer look at its philosophies, aims and objectives, accepted practices and the adequacy of the training syllabus.

Some modifications in nursing practice have been accomplished but progress has been hampered by financial restrictions and lack of adaptable facilities. Nursing staff attitudes also proved a problem in creating change in some areas. Since the Jay Report there has been an increase in community provision for the mentally handicapped and more nurses find themselves working in a community setting as part of the multi-disciplinary approach.

The slow recognition that there could be areas of care and training common to both social work and nursing resulted in the production of yet another report on the training of nurses and care staff working with the mentally handicapped. This report, entitled 'Co-operation in Training', was called for by the General Nursing Councils and the Central Council for Education and Training in Social Work (1982).

Part 1 of this report dealt with qualifying training and calls on the supervisory bodies to declare their support for the principle of shared training and issue guidelines to assist those responsible for training schemes and also asks that the schemes should reflect the model of care. It recommended that all students should have the opportunity to learn in residential and service areas where the model of care has been adopted and that all RNMH (Registered Nurses for the Mentally Handicapped) students and CSS students have some shared training. It was further recommended that machinery be developed to monitor shared training and seek funds to support innovations in introducing shared training.

Part 2 made recommendations on 'post-basic training' with the main recommendation being that all staff ranging from the planners and policy makers to non-qualified care staff should have the benefit of education and orientation followed up by further training within their area of employment and across agency and professional boundaries on a shared basis.

Community mental handicap nurse

In recent years we have witnessed a move towards developing a comprehensive system of community care for all ages and categories of mentally handicapped people. This development has facilitated the discharge of hospitalised mentally handicapped people to residential accommodation within the community. The government's consultative document 'Care in the Community' (1981) stated that 'it is estimated that about 15 000 mentally handicapped people at present in hospital — about one-third of the total number — could be discharged immediately if appropriate services in the community were available'.

The steady increase in discharge programmes and the setting up of new community facilities by local authorities created the need for more nurses based in the community who were trained in the speciality of mental handicap, and the nurse has now become a common feature of the multi-disciplinary community team.

In some areas, the nurse is confined to National Health Service clients whilst in other areas she serves both local authority and National Health Service clients. Difficulties can ensue when residents are discharged from an NHS hospital as NHS staff may not be allowed to become involved with mentally handicapped people who are resident in the community and not in the care of the National Health Service or its agencies. Where local authories provide the hostels and group homes and accept the responsibilities for their maintenance and administration, National Health Service community nurses are forbidden access, in some geographical locations, to the premises. This is a ludicrous situation that is unfair to the ex-hospitalised person in particular, who is totally cut off and makes continuity of care impossible to achieve.

Tasks and services carried out by the community mental handicap nurse can vary according to geographical location but in general the nurse is deeply involved in the preparation of hospital residents for discharge, familiarising the resident with life outside the hospital, introducing the resident to the local facilities and services as well as acquainting the resident with the local geography. This can prove to be a lengthy association as often the nurse will continue to follow up discharged residents, e.g. ensuring that all is well and that they are coping with their new situation, supervising medication or the administration of depot drugs. In many instances the associ-

ation may take the shape of a friendship, with the nurse employing professional expertise in an unobtrusive way and if necessary correcting and advising the ex-resident on areas where improvements could be made. This is a skill that develops with experience and allows the nurse tactfully to correct and advise without denigrating or removing independence from the mentally handicapped person. If problems are identified by the nurse there should be easy access to the other support services that have the machinery to resolve the problems, e.g. social work department.

Invariably the nurse will be involved in any case conferences organised to discuss community-based mentally handicapped people that the nurse is familiar with. At these case conferences, normally organised by the social work department, all the services involved with the client are represented and problems are identified and recommendations made on possible solutions. It is likely that the community nurse will assume the major role in the supervision of the corrective measures and in educating the client on how to avoid recurrences of the specific problems.

The nurse may have to liaise with such agencies as general practitioners, health visitors, special schools, adult training centres, hostels, sheltered housing schemes, voluntary agencies, social work departments as well as providing an advisory, supportive service to parents and relatives caring for a mentally handicapped person at home. Easy access to special services such as psychology, speech therapy, physiotherapy and psychiatry is essential to discuss problems that may arise in relation to community based mentally handicapped people, and if necessary the nurse should have the right to refer the individual to the appropriate specialist for specific problems.

Another role bestowed on the nurse in certain areas is to work in close liaison with the consultant in mental handicap, receiving referrals, making domiciliary visits and follow-up visits on behalf of the consultant. Arising from this often develops a close rapport between the nurse and the family and subsequently places the nurse in a position to make valued judgments on many personal issues and problems of a more intimate nature than any other professional dealing with the family.

Obviously the nurse has an important role in the multi-disciplinary team if the service has been comprehensively established and therefore it is essential that an accurate method of documentation is established and conscientiously maintained. This is an area of nursing that readily lends itself to the process of nursing or an adaptation of this system.

The community nurse plays an extremely important part in the care of the mentally handicapped and expansion of the nurse's role in this area is anticipated.

CARE STAFF STRUCTURE IN DIFFERENT SETTINGS AND FACILITIES

National Health Service

Within the National Health Service the direct care staff are invariably nurses, either qualified or unqualified, whether the setting is within a hospital ward on in a National Health Service hostel within the community and it is worth considering the staff structure from the most senior level to the point of care delivery.

There is a variation in the senior management tiers between Scotland and England. The most senior level in England is referred to as a Region made up of different Areas. In Scotland, however, the senior level is referred to as an Area with no other tier between the Area and the hospital.

The most senior nurse in the English Region carries the title of Regional Nursing Officer, while the equivalent nurse in Scotland is entitled the Chief Area Nursing Officer (CANO). These nurses are responsible for all nursing services within a set geographical area and are responsible to the Regional Health Authority in England and to the Health Board in Scotland. In each Area in England there is a nurse manager responsible for nursing services within the Area. The nurses employed at these levels have a generic responsibility in that they are responsible for all nursing specialities within the region and area of their remit.

The senior nurse at hospital level is the Director of Nursing Services (DNS) and in most cases the hospital caters for individual specialities, so it follows that the director has nursing qualifications appropriate to the speciality of the hospital. In hospitals offering care for the mentally handicapped, it is usual that the Director possesses the Registered Nurse for Mentally Subnormal or Registered Nurse for Mental Defectives qualification. Both these qualifications have been superseded by the Registered Nurse for the Mentally Handicapped qualification. This rule of appropriate qualification normally holds throughout the other tiers in the structure in hospitals for the mentally handicapped.

The Director is responsible for the nursing services within the hospital, ensuring the quality of nursing is maintained, and developing the role of the nurse within the speciality. The Director is assisted by Senior Nurses who may have a specialist role within the hospital such as resident development or a general role as a nurse specialist/co-ordinator within a group of wards. This role is supportive to the charge nurses within these wards and carries the additional responsibility of co-ordinating all staff and resident activities/services within these wards.

At ward level a Charge Nurse is responsible for the supervision and direction of care within the ward, and this applies to the physical, mental and developmental needs of the residents located within the ward. The charge nurse is supported by staff nurses who are qualified Registered Nurses for the Mentally Handicapped and State Enrolled Nurses (Mental Handicap) in England (in Scotland Enrolled Nurses opt to practise in mental handicap). These nurses also have a responsibility for the supervision of the unqualified staff placed in the ward. The numbers of these grades of nurses available to the ward is dependent on the type of care offered in the ward. These nurses play a valuable role in the delivery of care, as their knowledge and training linked to their close contact with the residents facilitates accurate observation, and subsequently, leads to informed opinion enabling improvements in the care and training of the residents to be made.

Within each ward there are normally several nursing assistants, the number allocated being determined by the type of ward and the resident population of the ward. Although these assistants are untrained, they play a valuable role in the care of the residents, attributable to their past experience within the hospital and to the application of their natural common sense, supported by appropriate in-service training.

Many hospitals also employ technical instructors and trainers in the special departments such as the industrial unit, who also support the charge nurse if the unit is within the nursing remit.

Local authority

The senior person responsible for all aspects of social work within a local authority area is the Director of Social Work who is responsible for all residential, community and social services, within the area and is likely to possess the Certificate of Qualification in Social Work (CQSW). The Director is supported in his task by Assistant Directors of Social Work, the number varying according to geographical spread and population of the local authority area. These Assistant Directors usually possess the CQSW qualification.

It is customary that the Assistant Directors head teams of social workers in set geographical divisions of the area and are responsible to the Director for the social work carried out. These teams consist of varying numbers of professionals of differing levels of experience and qualification. Individual team members may have specific responsibilities within the team, e.g. 'the homeless' or the elderly. It is customary that the Assistant Director establishes these teams within his resources, to deal with the priorities within the area so that the social work structure will vary from area to area dependent on the make-up of the catchment population and social background of the area.

The Director may also be supported by other senior social workers, responsible for specific provisions or specialities such as residential services, mentally handicapped, employment training officer, elderly and the homeless. These specialists are responsible to the Director but liaise closely with the area teams on matters related to their speciality.

Role of the specialist in mental handicap

This person will be familiar with the hospital provision within the area, the mentally handicapped people resident in the community, either at home or in sheltered accommodation, as well as being fully aware of the availability of places in the Adult Training Centres and other situations where mentally handicapped people are employed.

It is essential that this person should be known to the staff in charge of all facilities available to mentally handicapped people and therefore provide a focus of information and liaison for professionals from these areas of service. Co-ordination of service is an important aspect of this role.

Within the residential facilities for mentally handicapped people there is normally an 'officer in charge' who reports to the Senior Social Worker responsible for the residential services within the area. This officer in charge will usually possess the CQSW but may alternatively possess the Certificate in Social Services (CSS) which is a qualification developed to train the person for the needs of a particular job as well as dealing with specific areas of care. The officer may be supported by varying numbers of care staff, depending on the type of care and client group resident within the establishment. The support team may consist of care assistants who possess the CSS qualification and others who are unqualified.

Some of the residential facilities provided by the local authorities have qualified nurses as the leader of the care team, whilst others have nurses within the support team. This blend of nurse and care assistant has proved successful in some areas and is now recognised as the desirable situation.

Adult Training Centres are staffed by a mixture of care assistants, qualified and unqualified, as well as technical instructors and trainers in the areas where occupational skills and craftwork are taught.

The staff structure in the different facilities caring for mentally handicapped people can consist of varying permutations of staff, both qualified and unqualified. As the professional background of the different staff groups contains common elements, it should be possible to create teams composed of different professional people possessing individual skills that complement the team as a whole. The prime objective is the establishment of a team that contains all the skills required by the client group to enable them to live a full and happy life.

It is hoped that the importance of the role of the direct care staff has become apparent to the reader. Nurses and care assistants are the key people in the care of the mentally handicapped, particularly in residential settings. They have the greatest contact, the closest relationships and the most intimate knowledge of their charges. It is only in working closely with direct care staff that other

professionals, e.g. psychiatrists, psychologists and teachers, can hope to achieve the goal of improving and maintaining the quality of life of mentally handicapped people.

REFERENCES

Baly M E 1973 Nursing and social change. Heinemann, London
Development Team for the Mentally Handicapped 1976–77 1st report. HMSO, London.
Fraser W 1981 Age of consultant psychiatrists practising in Mental Handicap in Scotland. Presented to Royal College of Psychiatrists Scottish Section. Reviewed 1983
GNC/CCETSW Joint Working Group 1982 Co-operation in training parts 1 and 2. GNC/CCETSW
HMSO 1981 Care in the community. HMSO, London
HMSO 1979 Committee of enquiry into mental handicap nursing and care (Jay Report). HMSO, London
HMSO 1978 Committee of enquiry into the education of handicapped children and young people (Warnock Report). HMSO, London
HMSO 1976 Fit for the future (Court Report). HMSO, London
HMSO 1971 Education (Handicapped Children) Act. HMSO, London
National Development Group for the Mentally Handicapped 1978 Helping Mentally Handicapped People in Hospital
Royal College of Psychiatrists Mental Deficiency Section in Scotland 1983. Consultant Psychiatrist role in treating Mentally Handicapped People.

6

Education

- *Playgroup provision may lack professional expertise to deal with problems of mentally handicapped children*
- *Education should be an enjoyable experience geared to individual ability*
- *Systematic approach to teaching involves identifying and evaluating each step to ensure child is coping*
- *Development of verbal skills more important than reading skills*
- *The usefulness of integration has yet to be decided*

INTRODUCTION

In our society there seems to be an inverse relationship between the rate of learning and the amount of education provided, i.e. the slowest learners get the least amount of education, whereas those who learn quickly continue in education longest. Fortunately, of late more attention has been given to the needs of the slow learners, though more help in terms of service and provisions is required to meet recommendations made in the Court (1976) and Warnock (1978) Reports.

PRESCHOOL EDUCATION

The main types of services available are playgroups and nursery schools. Many local authorities have established their own playgroup schemes, following the lead given by voluntary associations and parent groups which were instrumental in starting and maintaining the movement. Local authorities give financial support to voluntary schemes and usually parents pay a fee which covers the cost of wages, rent and equipment, and take an active part in its running. Playgroups usually cater for children between the ages of $2\frac{1}{2}$ and 5 years of age. Mentally handicapped children attend either the conventional playgroup or playgroups specially organised to cater for their needs. Although parental involvement is usually high, playgroups may lack the skills of trained teachers to facilitate optimal learning; they may lack the provision of the services of psychologists and other professionals and the permanency of staff with whom the children can form stable relationships.

Nursery schools run by the Education Department, on the other hand, do have trained teachers and have much easier access to services provided by the Education Department such as speech therapists, physiotherapists and remedial teachers. In addition the staff, being permanent, offer a greater opportunity for stable relationships with the children. Notwithstanding these stated advantages of the nursery schools, playgroups fulfil an important need for both children and parents and the degree of parental involvement may offset any advantages of the service offered by professionals.

SCHOOLS

At the beginning of the 1970s in the U.K. responsibility for educating all children including mentally handicapped children was given to the Department of Education and Science. Previously severely mentally handicapped children were considered ineducable and were excluded from the education system.

In England and Wales there are two types of special schools, namely schools for the educationally subnormal (severe) (ESNS) and schools for the educationally subnormal (mild) (ESNM). Children in the ESNS school range in age from 2–19 years. Here there may be a 'Special Care Unit' which caters for the most severely handicapped children who require intensive supervision that includes physical care. In addition mentally handicapped children may attend special observation classes, assessment units, special classes in conventional schools and conventional classes.

Care staff are most likely to have contact with the formal education system through the hospital school. These schools usually cater for the severely mentally handicapped and differ from ESNS schools only in that most pupils are hospital residents. Warnock (1978) recommended that nursing staff at the hospital be involved in the educational programmes devised for the children. It would seem important that the educational programmes be carried out during the day-to-day activities of the resident. However, there seems to be something illogical about a situation where nurses have to dress and feed a resident in order to get him to school on time so that he can learn to dress and feed himself! Two such systems working in isolation only work to the detriment of the resident.

SPECIAL EDUCATION METHODS

The approach of the educational psychologist Maria Montessori centred on the belief that educational establishments merely provide the environment that facilitates learning. Montessori contended that all children learn more effectively if allowed to work at their own pace in a way they enjoy. Providing them with the opportunity to learn rather than directing their learning is seen as the function of educationalists. Her idea of education being an enjoyable experience was revolutionary at a time when education was seen as a means of training or disciplining the mind. Many of her ideas have been incorporated into current practice of education though some techniques which concentrate on sense training have been discarded.

Piaget, like Montessori, emphasised the child's own ability to discover and learn for himself and de-emphasised the direct teaching role of teachers. He stressed that children learned by doing, that learning was not a passive experience in which knowledge was transferred from teacher to pupil. Children learned at their own pace with the role of the educationalist to provide a flexible learning environment that allowed each child to learn at his own rate.

While Piaget did not focus on any particular group of children in developing his theory, Kephart (1971) concentrated on brain damaged mentally handicapped children. He developed teaching techniques based on the assumption that development in motor skills and in perceptual discrimination preceded learning. He devised exercises to improve the development of motor skills by using beam balances, and trampolines, and exercises to develop perceptual skills by means of puzzles, identifying shapes and matching shapes.

Another technique to improve the training of motor and perceptual skills was designed by Doman & Delacata (Delacata, 1963). They developed a programme for brain injured children which took the child through his developmental stages (see Ch. 7, pp. 111–112). The principle seems to be somewhat similar to the basis governing Seguin's education method developed over 100 years ago which was an attempt to parallel what was then thought to be the sequence of physiological development. Doman & Delacata's regime is extremely demanding, for example, putting a child through the crawling sequence required four people to simulate exactly the movement of each limb in a naturally occurring pattern.

Many professionals believe these techniques designed to develop motor skills have received undue publicity with the result that expectations of many parents were raised to an unrealistic level. Research into claims have produced no convincing evidence of the efficiency of the techniques.

According to Mittler (1979) the mainstream teaching of mentally handicapped children has followed the educational pattern of non-mentally handicapped children. The special learning difficulties facing mentally handicapped children have not been taken into account. For example, whereas non-mentally handicapped children may benefit from free play activities, many mentally handicapped children need to have their play activities structured because of their inability to create, initiate or organise their play (Clarke & Clarke, 1974). Mittler recommended as a teaching method the approach of clearly defining the immediate aims in educating each child in small measurable steps. Working on the premise that all children can learn, the success or failure of the programme is seen to reside in the teacher and not the pupil. He suggests the following approach:

1. Assessment
2. Selection and analysis of task
3. Presentation of task
4. Evaluation.

Those care staff who are familiar with the nursing process will well recognise the similarity of these steps to the stages of Assessment, Planning, Implementation and Evaluation on which the nursing process is based (Ch. 14). This approach may be seen as offering nothing new to teachers and care staff who may consciously or unconsciously have been organising their activities in this way for years. Much of the initial adverse reaction towards the method used in the nursing process has been caused by the implicit criticism felt by staff of their existing way of dealing with residents and the amount of additional work in the form of paperwork demanded to achieve the same ends. Fortunately the nursing process is not seen as being written on a tablet of stone and is increasingly being interpreted as simply constituting a systematic approach that staff might use to provide more individualised care that can be tailored to suit the level of services available.

Assessment — this procedure may be carried out formally or informally. Formal methods involve the use of standard assessment forms and charts. Knowledge of their administration, scoring and interpretation may require the services of a psychologist, perhaps in an advisory capacity. The informal methods are those devised by the teacher herself to suit her needs. But whatever methods are used their function is the same — to identify those areas the pupil is having difficulty with. It is on the basis of this assessment that the programme for the child is planned.

Planning — this stage involves breaking down the skill to be learned into small steps so that the steps that make up the skill can be taught one at a time.

Implementation — various techniques may be employed in teaching a new skill or reducing undesirable behaviour. These have to be classified using terms such as reinforcement, prompting, fading and chaining (see Ch. 8).

Evaluation — having clearly identified the area of difficulty, and having planned and implemented a teaching programme based on a step-by-step approach, it should be comparatively easy to evaluate whether the individual objectives of the programme are met. If they have not been met, then breaking down the steps still further into much smaller steps or changing the techniques used may be effective.

COMMUNICATION SKILLS

Most mentally handicapped children have difficulties in reading. Two main approaches to teaching reading are used. The first approach concentrates on reading for the meaning of a word right from the start. Once a word is recognised, other words are taught. Then relationships between letters in the words are taught and how they make up the sounds of the words. The second approach reverses this pattern by first teaching the alphabet, then teaching the relationship between the letters and sounds, and finally the child reads the whole word. Despite the claims for success from both methods, Ingalls (1978) contends that individual children may best benefit from either one or other of these methods or indeed from another of the many approaches to reading advocated, i.e. some methods may be more effective with some children than others.

Perhaps more important for the mentally handicapped person than learning reading skills is developing his verbal skills. Apart from the 'talk' sessions in class to encourage verbal skills there are language programmes available such as the Peabody Language Development Kit. This consists of a programme of activity that can be carried out daily with groups of children. It concentrates on developing receptive and expressive verbal skills. Examples of activities include Brainstorming (naming all the animals you know), Vocabulary Building and

Storytelling. In this and many other programmes the development of verbal skills is seen as an important prerequisite for developing reading skills (see Ch. 11).

ARITHMETIC

Mentally handicapped people's level of arithmetical competence is usually on a par with their mental age but their understanding of the concepts involved is behind their mental age (Dunn, 1973). Teaching arithmetic is necessarily practically based with an emphasis initially on such basic concepts as longer-shorter, more-less, bigger-smaller etc. followed by details of money, time and measurements such as length and weight.

INTEGRATION

Since the Education Act (1981) of England and Wales, local authorities have a duty to educate children with special educational needs in ordinary schools if such placements cater for the children's special needs and do not interfere adversely with the educational requirements of the other children. Parents' wishes are taken into consideration in the decision to place a child. This Act in many cases has put into the statute books policies of local authorities that had been implemented for some time. Whether it effects an overall increased integration of mentally handicapped children into the mainstream of school will not be apparent for some years to come.

The whole question of integration has been long standing. The argument *for* integration is based on:

a. Mentally handicapped children vary among themselves in their ways of learning, so putting them together in a special class is an artificial grouping.
b. The social implications of attending a special school may result in the child being stigmatised.

c. Research has shown that mentally handicapped children fail to do any better in special classes (Wiegerink & Simeonsson, 1975.)

d. Other children in ordinary classes will get a better understanding of mental handicap and other disabilities.

The arguments *against* integration are:

a. Mentally handicapped children are likely to fall behind the rest of the class and be 'dropped' by the teacher.

b. Psychological harm caused by such things as being seen as slow or stupid and consistently failing in competition.

c. Special provisions, more individual attention and greater specialist expertise of personnel including teachers, speech therapists, physiotherapists and psychologists are more likely to be available in special schools.

d. Other children may be kept back by the slow learners.

There is no doubt that the arguments will continue and as yet it is not a simple choice between total integration and total segregation. Examples of degrees of integration described in the Warnock Report are special classes in ordinary school either full-time or part-time with varying amounts of time spent in ordinary classes. The introduction of a resource room to provide services for any children with learning difficulties is a feasible option. The resource room is staffed by specialists who deal with individual students or groups several times a week. Research by Wiegerink & Simeonsson (1975) has indicated that this system is more beneficial in the education of some children than special classes.

SUMMARY

The two chief preschool provisions are playgroups and nursery schools. Playgroups benefit from increased parental involvement but may lack professional guidance and facilities available in nursery schools. Two types of special schools are for the educationally subnormal child (severe) and the mildly handicapped child.

A recent approach to teaching people with learning difficulty is using a systematic method involving assessment, planning, action, and evaluation. This helps to relate teaching more directly to individual need.

Integration into mainstream education is not an either-or dilemma but is seen in terms of degrees of integration.

REFERENCES

Clarke A M, Clarke A D B 1974 (eds) Mental deficiency: the changing outlook. Wiley, New York

Delacato C H 1963 The diagnosis and treatment of speech and reading problems. Thomas, Springfield, Illinois

Department of Education and Science 1978 Special Educational Needs, Report of the Committee of Enquiry into the Education of Handicapped Children and Young People (Chairman: Mrs M. Warnock) Cmnd 7212. HMSO, London

Department of Health and Social Security 1976 Fit for the Future: Report of the Committee on Child Health Services (Chairman: Prof. S.D.M. Court) Cmnd 6684. HMSO, London

Dunn L M (ed) 1973 Exceptional children in the schools: Special education in transition. Rinehart & Winston, New York

Ingalls R P 1978 Mental retardation: the changing outlook. Wiley, New York

Kephart N C 1971 The slow learner in the classroom. Merrill, Columbus, Ohio

Mittler P 1979 People not patients. Methuen, London

Wiegerink R, Simeonsson R J 1975 Public schools. In: Wortis J (ed) Mental retardation, vol 7. Brunner/Mazel, New York

Eamon Shanley

7

Aspects of development

- The rate of motor development of each child will vary but the sequence remains the same
- Socialisation is effected chiefly by the two processes of discipline and modelling
- Attachment occurs with the main caregiver and is determined by the intensity of interaction between caregiver and child
- Mentally handicapped individuals learn by manipulating and exploring rather than being taught how to do things
- Mentally handicapped adolescents are unlikely to reach the formal operational stage of development

MOTOR DEVELOPMENT

A person's growth rate while influenced by extremes of circumstances is relatively resistant to a range of environmental factors. The individual's self regulatory processes will compensate for degrees of deviation, e.g., while the average birth weight is $3\frac{1}{2}$ kilos, premature babies weighing as little as 2 kilos usually catch up. Where extra stimulation of motor skills is given to children the advantage is short lived. In studies by Hilgard (1932) children were trained in tasks such as climbing and buttoning and initially became more proficient than untrained or minimally trained children. However these untrained children soon caught up. Where movement was restricted or understimulated as in the case of Apache Indian children their motor skills were still acquired at the appropriate ages. These children had been strapped to a cradle board all day long. Unfortunately many children in institutions in the past have been subjected to extremes of privation and their mental development has suffered as a consequence, although the effects on motor development have not been clearly identified.

Reflexes

Reflexes are used in the neurological examination of the newborn. Toft & Cohen (1968) outlined 48 reflexes used in clinical examination. Some reflexes persist for the person's life, e.g. breathing, whereas others are present only for a limited period after birth. Variations in intensity and in characteristics of reflexes may be indicative of neural defects. Examples of transitory reflexes are:

Moro reflex. This involves the rapid stretching outwards of arms followed by an inward embracing movement. It occurs as a reaction to loud noise or the lack of support and usually disappears after 2 months. Variations such as asymmetrical movement may be indicative of neural malfunction (see Ch. 9).

Grasp reflex. The placing of an object against the palm of the infant's hand triggers off this reflex. The infant's grasp can be strong enough to allow the child to be lifted into a sitting position. Again this reflex usually disappears after 2 months. Its persistence after this period may indicate a spastic form of cerebral palsy.

Rooting reflex. Touching the infant's cheek or corner of the mouth elicits the head turning in that direction. The discrimination between what is suckable and what is not is one of the examples given by Piaget in describing the earlier stages infants pass through before they develop object permanency.

Chronology

At birth most body systems are not fully functional. It is not simply a question of the infant learning to operate his body as a driver learns to drive a car. There are still bits of the car missing! For example, the digestive system is unable to cope with most of the available foodstuffs, so the infant's diet is necessarily restricted. The child's bone structures are incomplete, particularly the epiphyses, the teeth, which start erupting at approximately 6 months, and the fontanelles, the posterior closing at 3 months, the anterior at 2 years. An important system that is not fully functional is the nervous system. Myelinization, which insulates the nerve axons in the peripheral nervous system, takes several years to complete.

While individuals may vary as to when stages of development are reached, the sequence remains the same. From birth onwards the child's movement becomes less gross and random and becomes more co-ordinated and purposeful. By 2 months he starts to lift his head and chest. By 3–4 months he is capable of turning his head and reaching for things. He starts to leave a strictly liquid diet and he eats soft food. At 4 months he plays with his fingers and toes. From 4–5 months he is able to turn over and make crawling movements. At 6–7 months he begins to chew and cut first teeth. 7 months sees the child sitting up unaided and at 8 months he begins to master the ability to pick up objects using thumb and finger. From 9–10 months he starts crawling and is capable of pulling himself erect. At about 1 year old he starts to walk (Fig. 7.1).

Between the ages of 1–2 years one of the child's main achievements is in learning to walk. Walking is initially performed with a wide base (feet far apart) and involves erratic movements. Gradually the child brings his feet together and the steps become regular. At 18 months the 'hurried walk' develops, which involves always having one foot on the ground at any one time. Running involves having both feet off the ground at a stage in the cycle of movement. (You might like to check the difference between running and walking yourself.) Most children cannot run until after 4 years of age.

The 2-year-old still needs to monitor his feet visually to avoid obstacles, but this monitoring disappears by the end of the third year. The 2-year-old has not yet developed other motor skills such as hopping, climbing, and catching and throwing balls. (Tests of child development frequently include setting the child such tasks.) He will, however, be able to co-ordinate his movements sufficiently to be able to feed himself using forks and spoons, after a fashion. By the age of 3 years most infants are toilet trained, i.e. have control over their bowels and bladder. Acquisition of control depends on the degree of mental handicap, the degree of maturation of sphincter muscles, the child's sex (girls achieve bladder control earlier) and the attitude of parent or

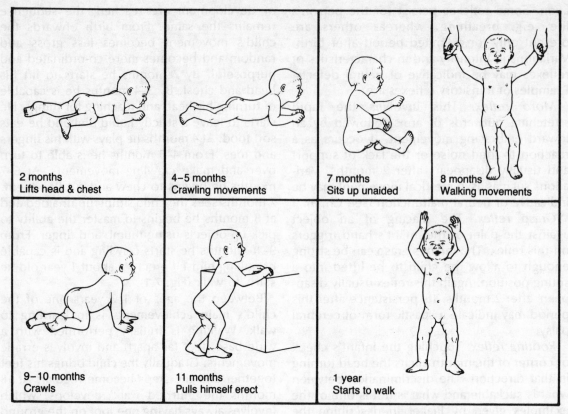

2 months Lifts head & chest	4–5 months Crawling movements	7 months Sits up unaided	8 months Walking movements
9–10 months Crawls	11 months Pulls himself erect	1 year Starts to walk	

Fig. 7.1 Progress towards standing position.

caregiver. Delay in or absence of control is likely to be the result of several of these factors simultaneously affecting the child.

Middle childhood from between 6–7 years of age to 11 or 12 is a time of involvement in games and sporting activities. Having mastered the co-ordination of muscles and balance, this period involves the refinement of fine movement such as writing and of gross movement used in sport.

Drawing and writing

One important area of motor co-ordination is in drawing and writing. The child's development in this area follows a set pattern. Initially the child starts making apparently random marks with a crayon or pencil. At about the age of 4 years the child gives meanings to his marks. He may refer to a squiggle as a fire

engine or later call the same squiggle an aeroplane. Later the child starts drawing his lines more purposefully into circles or other enclosing shapes. The next stage involves the child making drawings that have some semblance to the object represented, though it may only be apparent to the child. Gradually the drawings become more and more organised. Through the earlier stages, particularly, adults should avoid directing children in their drawings and avoid quizzing them on what they have drawn. This is because the child's free expression and development are likely to be inhibited if he feels he can only draw things he can justify to others.

Sensory-motor training

Since the time of Sequin (1866) various theorists have devised techniques for achieving greater motor co-ordination in children. Strauss & Lehinen (1947), Borsch (1965), Delacato (1963) and Kaphart (1971) have concentrated on sensory-motor training. The basis of their training techniques is that development of the child passes through definite stages, each one being necessary before the child passes on to the next stage. Development of motor skills is seen as preceding all others (see Ch. 6).

SOCIALISATION

Socialisation is a process whereby an individual becomes a responsible member of society. Successful socialisation involves the person conforming to the rules of society, many of which are incorporated into law. However, there is not simply one set of rules that a person must learn and adhere to. What we call society is made up of many different subgroups with their own and differing sets of rules. For a person to be successfully socialised, he must conform to the rules of each of a number of groups showing behaviour appropriate to each group while conforming to the general rules of society. It is an important function of care staff to socialise residents into not only their immediate situation, i.e. as residents, but also into the wider rules of society. Unfortunately successful socialisation into the culture of the hospital or residence may inhibit socialisation to the culture outside the residence.

One of the first groups a child experiences is the family. Rules governing family interaction may differ from rules of other groups. For example the degree of acceptable physical contact and rights and duties are clearly different from other rules involving relationships with friends. As the child grows older he becomes part of other groups. Mentally handicapped children may have particular difficulty in learning the rules of new groups they encounter, particularly if they continue to behave according to the rules of a previous group they have been familiar with.

Development of social behaviour

From birth, a child makes social contact by various means such as crying, gazing, smiling, babbling and imitating. These behaviours are strongly influenced by the responses they elicit in others. For example, responding to babbling by smiling, caressing and talking has been shown to increase the amount of babbling by the infant (Haugan & McIntire, 1972). Similarly, smiling is increased when they are smiled at, talked to and picked up, and is decreased when they are no longer receiving attention (Brossard & Decarie, 1969). Bloom (1975) has demonstrated that infants need social stimulation in order to develop normal social behaviour. When an infant is rarely smiled at, talked to or picked up as may happen in institutions and in some homes, the effects may be permanent and may result in mental handicap (see Ch. 2). Studies by Cross & Harlow (1965) on monkeys show that permanent damage is caused by social privation.

Attachment

Infants up to the age of 7 months are relatively indiscriminate in their interaction with others and do not react differently to familiar people and strangers. At about 7 months there develops a tendency for the infant to become attached to one individual usually the mother or main caregiver.

The earlier view of this attachment was that it was a phenomenon which occurs between the infant and its biological mother. This belief reinforced the view that a woman's place was in the home and her absence from the child's side would be detrimental to its development. Bowlby (1973) inadvertently gave credence to this view by describing this phenomennon as 'maternal deprivation' meaning the child has been deprived of its mother and its development would suffer accordingly. Later the idea of the importance of the biological mother was questioned and the view developed that the length of time spent with the infant was the most crucial element. The person with whom the child formed the attachment could be the biological mother or could be any other person, male or female with whom the child had spent the longest period of time. While appearing a more reasonable view, most recent studies have shown that it does not satisfactorily account for the attachment phenomenon. For example, in the kibbutzim, where infants spend much more time with the same nursery staff they do not form attachment with these individuals but with their parents with whom they interact evenings and on the Sabbath. It is now felt that it is not so much the amount of time spent with the infant but the intensity of interaction that is important.

There are two major characteristics associated with the attachment phenomenon of interest to care staff: stranger anxiety and seperation anxiety.

Stranger anxiety

This is a reaction of the child to the presence of a stranger. It occurs after attachment has occurred and appears particularly strongly from 1 year to 18 months. The degree of anxiety is affected by:

(i) the child's previous experience of people. If the child feels secure in his dealings with a variety of people then the degree of anxiety will be low.

(ii) the person's approach. Where a person with whom the child is unfamiliar allows the child to become accustomed to him before making any direct overtures to the child the degree of anxiety is low (Decarie, 1974). Allowing the child to make the first move is likely to avoid the occurrence of anxiety.

(iii) the situation. If a child is in unfamiliar surroundings then there is a greater likelihood of him experiencing anxiety at the approach of a stranger (Rheingold & Eckerman, 1973). Evidence of this process may be experienced by care staff who may find that being accepted by the child in his home does not necessarily mean that the child will accept the person in a strange setting, e.g. hospital, or vice versa.

(iv) Proximity of the mother. This has a strong bearing on how the child deals with strangers (Moss et al, 1969). Morgan et al (1969) showed that children in the presence of strangers will tolerate their attachment figure being very specific distances away from them. Infants became more distressed at the approach of a stranger when their mothers were only 1.2 m away, than when they were on their mothers' laps.

Separation anxiety

Separation anxiety tends to overlap with the occurrence of stranger anxiety and is most obvious between 13 months and 18 months. When the child is separated from his attachment figure he is likely to go through a series of stages. (These stages may be seen to parallel somewhat the grieving process of adults.)

The first stage is protest, where the child will frantically search for the attachment figure, crying and being generally upset. During the second stage, as the separation continues, despair is likely to occur, followed by indifference and apathy, with the child losing interest in his surroundings and withdrawing. Separation anxiety can be lessened by the child maintaining contact with familiar things, e.g. toys, familiar people and surroundings. When reunited, the child may show total indifference to the attachment figure, who may feel that it is a punishment for abandoning the child. Later, when the child does start responding emotionally to them, he is likely to be demanding and clinging for some time.

Factors affecting socialisation

Socialisation is effected by two main processes: discipline and modelling. The chief agents of socialisation in a residential setting are the care staff, whether they are consciously trying to influence the residents or not.

Discipline

There are three major aspects involved, i.e. consistency in applying discipline, instructive rather than punitive discipline, and behaviour-directed rather than person-directed discipline.

Consistency. Where there is no consistency in exercising discipline, the person will sometimes get rewarded for the same behaviour for which at other times he is punished, e.g. a resident who makes a gesture of defiance after being told off may be rewarded by the expression of amusement by a member of care staff whereas at other times, he gets punished for the same behaviour. If the getting of rewards or punishment is not dependent on the resident's behaviour, but on the mood of the care staff or 'shift' that is on duty at the time, the resident will come to see that his own behaviour has little relevance to whether he gets rewarded or punished. The result of this inconsistency is that over a period of time, the resident will fail to develop internal locus of control. This means that he will fail to develop consistent rules of behaviour in himself and will depend instead on factors outside himself, e.g. fear of being caught, rather than developing an internal sense of what is right and wrong (Lefcourt, 1976).

Instructive vs punitive discipline. The manner in which discipline is administered influences socialisation. Where discipline is carried out in a punitive way based on coercion, by means of punishment or withholding things the person likes, the person is likely to react in one of two ways: he may become cowed and very conforming, or he may react in kind, i.e. become aggressive, short tempered and violent. Hoffman (1975) described two types of punishments commonly used in exercising discipline.

Punitive discipline can be actual or threatened, physical or deprivational. It can be used to threaten or withdraw or withhold things the person wants, e.g. 'Stop throwing stones or I'll wallop you'. Another form of punitive discipline is psychological, i.e. to ignore the person deliberately, refuse to talk or listen to him, to give him the 'cold shoulder',

threaten to leave or, in the case of a child, to give him away. Where the first type of punishment is used, children develop a poor sense of right and wrong and depend on outside authorities to guide their behaviour. They develop an external locus of control (Forehand et al, 1976). While the second type of punishment does not have such a severe effect on children it still does not result in a child developing as strong a sense of right and wrong as in instructive discipline.

Instructive discipline is based on the premis that people, including very young children, can be reasoned with. In instructive discipline it is explained to the person why his behaviour is inappropriate, so he can understand why he should stop or change it, e.g. 'Stop throwing stones or you'll hurt someone'. Giving children reasons results in the development of a strong sense of right and wrong and a reliance on their own sense of morality to guide their behaviour (internal locus of control) rather than the fear of getting caught.

Focus of discipline. Discipline is usually directed at one of two sources. It may be directed at the person's behaviour or at the person who has broken the rules. The different ways may be seen in the case of a child breaking a window. Person-directed behaviour would result in the child being told: 'You're a bad girl for doing that.' Constantly referring to the child as 'bad' or 'naughty' may cause the child to feel that she, as a person, is bad, that it is a fact about her. Discipline directed at the person's behaviour is reflected in the statement: 'That was a bad thing to do.' In this way the child may learn to regard certain types of behaviour as bad but not that she is an inherently bad person (Ginott, 1965).

Modelling

Modelling is a process where a person takes on the behaviour of another person. There are four major factors that influence the degree to which a person models himself on another.

Availability. When the child, or indeed the adult, has access to the person both in a physical and in a psychological sense, e.g. knowing his attitudes, what his likes and dislikes are, modelling is more likely to occur then if the person is physically unavailable or psychologically distant. Accordingly, where staff experience burn-out (see Ch. 1) or are not available for any other reason, their influence on the resident's behaviour through this process is minimal, and the resident is likely to seek another person to model on.

Warmth. Studies have shown that a person's long-term influence as a model is affected by the degree of warmth between him/her and the child (Hetherington & Frankie, 1967). Care staff who have poor emotional ties with residents are unlikely to be used as models by the residents.

Model status. Where a person has high status in the resident's eyes, modelling on that person is more likely, for example, where the resident considers another resident or staff member who excels in a certain area, e.g. in sport, to be high status the resident is likely to model himself on other aspects of the person's behaviour in relation to sport.

Reinforcement. When modelling, e.g. adopting and expressing the same views as the model, receives approval, this behaviour is likely to be repeated.

Interaction of social and constitutional factors

Socialisation is a major factor in influencing a person's behaviour, though not the only one. The debate between the relative influences of constitutional characteristics and the socialisation process has not been resolved yet. What is accepted is that both play a part in the development of an individual. An example of the interaction of the two factors may illustrate their interrelationship. Adult males and females differ in behaviour, and the difference has been traced to the time of birth. From this time each sex is treated differently. Male children are handled less, are touched less and talked to less than females. The reason may be that female children are more responsive to attention and it is easier to elicit vocalisation. This may cause the mothers to behave differ-

ently to the children which in turn will cause infants to react differently. From this example it can be seen that not only is there a close interaction between the differences in inherited sex characteristics and the way the two sexes are treated, but also that the infant is not a passive partner in his relationships with other people. Right from birth he plays an active part in influencing the behaviour of others. A mentally handicapped child who is a 'good' baby, i.e. undemanding, may receive less stimulation than a non-handicapped child. Consequently his development may be further adversely affected.

Effect of social experience

All through childhood and adult life, people who are mentally handicapped are likely to have different social experiences from other people even within the same family (see Ch. 13). Characteristics seen as typical of mentally handicapped people may have less to do with the level of intellectual functioning than their common social experiences. Attitudes and behaviour of others towards the individual may result in social isolation or rejection. In addition the mentally handicapped person is likely to be stigmatised which reinforces the image of himself as being different from everybody else (see Ch. 2).

COGNITIVE DEVELOPMENT

Children's reasoning is not simply an immature version of adults' reasoning as it follows a quite definite set of rules that is often foreign to the adult mind. Adults' reasoning may be equally foreign to the child. Explanations given to the child on causality are not always understood — why his arm will not work, why he is not living at home, why staff close to him leave. As the child's reasoning is not the same as adults', the child's behaviour may be seen as illogical and his remarks dismissed as irrelevant. What adult would think that the moon followed her around?

Who would believe that everything that moves is alive or that inanimate objects such as trees and the sun have feelings and intentions? What adult would believe that getting sick was a punishment for past deeds? Children go through stages of development where they hold such beliefs. Care staff cannot assume that what is reasonable to them is necessarily seen as reasonable by the child and conversely what is reasonable to the child may be seen as illogical by the adult.

Piaget's theory of cognitive development

According to Piaget, an infant is born with two characteristics: reflexes, e.g. Moro, startle, sucking, and tendencies. There are two main tendencies. Firstly, there is the tendency for infant's psychological structures to develop from simple to complex, i.e. an organisational tendency. Secondly the individual tends to adjust to his environment (adaptation). The individual adapts to his environment by means of his existing structure (assimilation) and by accommodation in which the person's psychological structures are changed in response to the environment. For example, if the reader has reached a certain level of intellectual functioning, then the meaning of this section on 'cognitive development' may be assimilated into her existing structure, without any change in her psychological structures taking place. If on the other hand, the person has not quite reached this level of understanding, reading this section may result in changes in her psychological structures and consequently in her way of thinking, not only about cognitive development but in her general way of understanding. In other words, the process of accommodation describes the person's tendency to change in response to the environment, just as say, the shape of an amoeba changes to ingest food (Fig. 7.2). In assimilation, the food is transformed into a state where the amoeba can digest by means of its available body functions. In the same way the meaning of this section can be assimilated into the readers' existing psychological structures.

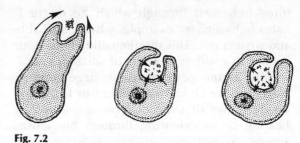

Fig. 7.2

Stages of development

There are four main stages of cognitive development:

1. Sensory-motor (birth–2 yr) — involves developments in the child's use of his senses and in muscular co-ordination.
2. Pre-operational (2–7 yr) — the child's mental ability is limited in that he cannot perform certain mental operations which he can easily do at later stages.
3. Concrete operational (7–11 yr) — the child can perform certain mental operations that are not as abstract as in the formal stage.
4. Formal operational (11 yr onwards) — the word formal refers to the logic a person uses in solving problems.

Sensory-motor (0–2 yr)

At birth, the child cannot think and cannot act on the environment other than through his reflexes. Gradually through the processes of accommodation and assimilation, reflexes are changed into psychological structures, e.g. the child from birth, in exercising his sucking reflex, will suck any object that happens to touch his cheek or mouth (Fig. 7.3). This reflex of indiscriminate sucking changes through the child's experience and he will stop sucking at the majority of objects. In other words, the child develops from a stage of having no way of acting on the world other than through his reflexes to developing psychological struc-

Reflexes $\xrightarrow[\text{Accommodation}]{\text{Assimilation}}$ Psychological structures

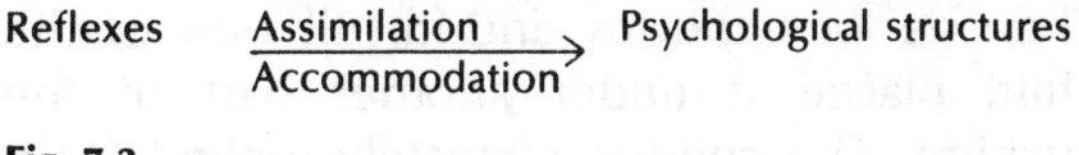

Fig. 7.3

tures (schemes) through which he discriminates between, for example, what is suckable and what is not. This discriminating behaviour applies to a widening range of situations.

Early in the sensory-motor stage nothing exists for the child independent of his acting on it. Things that the child is not seeing or hearing or experiencing through his senses simply do not exist. When a 5-month-old child drops a toy he has been playing with out of his pram, he immediately loses interest in it and behaves as if it has ceased to exist. He is not upset or surprised and will not start looking for it. The world of the child is for the first few months a collection of unconnected experiences, sights, sounds and tactile sensations. However the unconnected aspects of the child's experiences diminish with a repertoire of schemes (modified reflexes) building up around objects with which the child increasingly interacts. A major result of the repeated application of different schemes, e.g. touching, seeing and hearing, about the same object may be illustrated as follows. As the mother is leaving the room the child is applying two schemes to her — seeing and hearing. Unlike the earlier stage of development where out of sight was out of mind, the child at the age of 6–8 months watches, albeit momentarily, the place where his mother was standing before turning his attention to something more immediate. What is of great significance is that for a brief moment the child is aware of something to which he is not applying his schemes. The child at the age of 6–8 months is starting to show object permanency.

Up to the age of 1 year the child's awareness of objects is still tied, though to a lesser degree, to his own actions, i.e. he knows only those things he is experiencing through his senses. To demonstrate this characteristic, Piaget (1955) hid a toy under a cushion while his 10-month-old daughter watched. He hid it twice in succession in the same place. The child looked for it and found it each time. Then he took the toy and in full view of the child placed it under another part of the cushion. The child immediately looked for it in the previous hiding place! This example serves to illustrate that the child's understanding of the toy was still tied to her own actions. The toy did not have an existence independent of the child acting on it. The child simply repeated an action that had resulted in her getting the toy previously.

Before a child can develop an awareness of things that are not present he must have a symbol in mind to represent that object or event. Until the development of object permanency the infant has no symbol to represent the absent object. Therefore he cannot 'think' about it when it is not there. With the development of object permanency he develops symbols for absent objects such as his mother.

Piaget (1951) described how his 6-month-old child swung his legs immediately after seeing his toy parrot which could swivel on its perch. To the child this imitative movement was associated with the parrot, so it occurred only in the presence of the parrot. Later, however, this imitative movement occurred when the parrot was not present. Piaget described this as deferred imitation. According to Piaget the next stage was when this deferred imitation became abbreviated, i.e. to become almost like shorthand and the final stage is when instead of acting out the movement the child does it mentally (internalisation) (Fig. 7.4).

Imitation ⟶ Deferred imitation ⟶ Symbol

Fig. 7.4

By the end of the sensory-motor stage the infant has developed from an organism just able to exercise his reflexes and has reached the point where he has a degree of understanding of time, space, and objects. He can also represent symbolically objects and events which he is not immediately experiencing.

Pre-operational stage of development (2–7 yr)

This stage is characterised by the child's centration, i.e. he cannot deal with several aspects of a situation simultaneously. The inability to consider several dimensions at the same time is illustrated by the characteristic solutions presented by children to particular types of problems. The tasks set for the children have been classified as conservation tasks, e.g. testing the child's ability to discover that a quantity remains the same despite a change in its appearance, i.e. the quantity is conserved.

In the conservation of numbers task the child is shown one line of six spoons and one line of six forks, spaced evenly over the same distance (Fig. 7.5). It is confirmed that he accepts that there is the same number of spoons as forks. As he watches, the spoons are moved closer together and he is again asked 'Are there more spoons than forks?' At this stage of development he is likely to say that there are more forks and will point out that the fork line is longer!

In the conservation of mass task the child is presented with two balls of plasticine which the child accepts as containing the same amounts (Fig. 7.6). One of them, in full view of the child, is rolled out into a sausage shape. The child is asked which shape has the most plasticine. At the pre-operational stage the child usually selects the sausage shape saying, 'There's more 'cause it's longer.'

In the conservation of continuous quantity

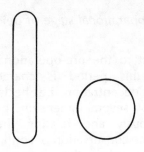

Fig. 7.6 Conservation of mass.

(liquid) the child is presented with two identical glass tumblers each filled with equal amounts of water (Fig. 7.7). The child on confirming that there is the same amount of water in each tumbler witnesses the pouring of one tumbler into a taller, thinner glass. The child will state, at this stage, that there is more water in the third receptacle despite the fact that he has seen no water being added or taken away.

In each of these examples the child selected only one dimension, e.g. height of the water level and ignored other aspects such as width in making his judgement. Furthermore he ignored the act of pouring, i.e. he concentrated on static states and not on the changes. Selection of one dimension and concentration on static states are the main characteristics of his thinking during this period. A third characteristic of pre-operational thinking is described as ego-centrism — the child assumes everyone sees things as he does which, can make communication very difficult.

Fig. 7.5 Conservation of numbers.

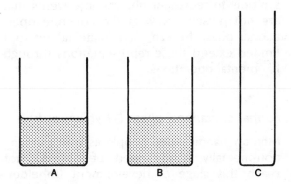

Fig. 7.7 Conservation of continuous quantity. (liquid)

Concrete operational stage of development (7–11 yr)

In contrast to the pre-operational stage the child at this period is characterised by increasing decentration, i.e. he is capable of focusing on several dimensions of a situation simultaneously and relating these dimensions. In the conservation of continuous quantity he recognises that amounts are equal when one column of liquid is at the same time taller but narrower than a second column. The concrete operational child is also attuned to change. He is aware of transformation, i.e. the act of pouring the liquid or rolling the ball into a sausage shape.

The child acquires what Piaget calls concrete operations, i.e. internalised actions that permit the child to do in his head what he would have to accomplish through real action. An example of the difference in way of thinking between pre-operational and concrete operational children is shown in the following study. Piaget (1952) presented 5-year-olds and 7-year-olds with six sticks in a row and asked them to take the same number from another pile of sticks. The 5-year-old children solved the problem by placing their sticks beside the sample matching them one to one. The 7-year-old children merely counted out six sticks from the pile i.e. they performed the tasks mentally. (Both could count to six so this was not a major constraint on the 5 year olds.)

From the state when knowledge of the environment is tied to the child's action in the sensory-motor period the child develops symbols to represent objects and events that are not present. Now at the concrete operational phase he can manipulate (albeit to a limited extent) these representations through his mental operations.

Formal operational phase (11 yr onwards)

Mentaly handicapped people as well as many non-mentally handicapped people do not reach this stage of development (Inhelder, 1968). The ability to perform operations reaches its developmental peak at the formal stage. Here the reality becomes secondary to possibility and the individual at this stage is concerned with how things might be and not just how things are. The development of more elaborate operations can be seen in the adolescent's tendency to become involved in abstract and theoretical matters postulating hypotheses about what might occur. He philosophises on social, political and religious matters and is likely to entertain radical views. This may be interpreted as the individual's tendency to exercise existing psychological structures. Just as in the sensory-motor phase where the sucking schemes are exercised, here he exercises his formal operations.

There are several important points to bear in mind throughout all four stages: firstly, the stages are sequential, i.e. the child cannot skip a stage but passes through them in the given order; secondly, the ages given are only approximate; thirdly, individuals do not always function at their optimal level, but perform at a lower level for much of their time.

Implications for the nurse

In the long-term care of children the nurse's role not only involves the care and management of the children but also the important task of educating them. In the case of children under 2 years of age and severely mentally handicapped individuals education involves encouraging a variety of sensations and movements. Particularly with severely mentally handicapped persons the nurse has to teach them to manipulate and play with objects in their environment. It is only through these sensory-motor activities that the person will develop the ability for thought.

Of the person's sensory-motor activities, play has a central role in his development. Usually play is initiated by the mother, often as a game such as peek-a-boo. Gradually the person will take a more active part in initiating and controlling play: in the early stages by gaze aversion or by directing it at the parent;

later by producing sounds and by body movements. In dealing with the severely mentally handicapped person it is important for the nurse to recognise and develop cues given by the person in attempting to influence her. In many cases the cues that initially may have been given out have been ignored and through time due to lack of reinforcement have faded and are now very difficult to re-establish (see Ch. 10). To develop cues one approach is to present the person with a structured play situation where little is demanded or indeed expected from him, and very gradually decrease the structured nature of the situation as the person initiates more of the interaction.

The beginning of the pre-operational stage is characterised by the development of language (sentence formation). However the child's understanding of words may be very different from that of adults. Here difficulties may arise if the nurse relies on language as the sole means of teaching. Unless the person actually carries out the task being taught understanding is unlikely to occur. The most important single proposition that the nurse can derive from Piaget's work is that children and mentally handicapped individuals learn by manipulating and exploring things not being 'taught' how to do them. The nurse must realise that she is not there to impart knowledge but to facilitate the interaction of the person with his environment.

Unfortunately there are no easy rules or procedures for the nurse to use in order to understand the person. What is needed chiefly is an awareness of the different nature of intelligence, an appreciation of the child's own system of logic and an avoidance of the assumption that what is true or customary for the adult is also true for the child. The nurse should not view the child or mentally handicapped person as an immature version of an adult or as an organism progressing along a stepping stone sequence of items on an adaptive behaviour scale or as a static point on an IQ scale but as an individual possessing unique ways of thinking.

ADOLESCENCE

Adolescence is a time of change in an individual and the degree of change may vary widely. For example, in a person with Laurence-Moon-Biedl syndrome who is also severely mentally handicapped there is little change physiologically or psychologically, whereas a person who is mildly mentally handicapped may experience marked physical and emotional changes. There are however unlikely to be any changes in intellectual functioning from the concrete operational level to formal operational stage in any mentally handicapped person. According to Inhelder (1968) it is not only mildly mentally handicapped people who cannot function at least occasionally at this level — many non-mentally handicapped people also fail to do so.

Physical changes

Males

The onset of adolescence is marked by changes in sexual characteristics. Secondary sexual characteristics include growth at adolescence. This occurs from the periphery inwards contrasting the characteristic growth in children where growth occurs centrally and progresses outwards. In young children the head and trunk are disproportionately larger than the extremities, whereas in early adolescence the often clumsy and ungainly appearance of a youth may be accounted for by the rapid growth of his extremities, i.e. hands and feet, in relation to the more central parts of his body. Pubic hair at first downy later becomes pigmented and takes on the person's characteristic hair colour. Other secondary sexual changes include the growth of facial hair, sebaceous and sweat glands and deepening of the voice. This may jump from deep bass to a high-pitched squeak much to the embarrassment of the speaker. Changes in primary sexual characteristics include the increase in size of penis when erect, an increase in size of testes and scrotum and the ability to produce sperm. This ability to produce sperm usually occurs about a year after the onset of puberty. Both the primary sexual characteristics and the secondary sexual characteristics are the result of the secretion of hormones, gonadotrophin (produced by the pituitary) and testosterone (produced by the testes).

In Klinefelter's syndrome when there is an additional chromosome, development of the testes is arrested; lack or absence of testosterone may result in the development of female characteristics such as enlargement of breasts. Delayed or absent male sexual characteristics may also be caused by an undescended testis or by both testes failing to descend.

Females

Puberty starts approximately 2 years earlier in females than in males. This is characterised by enlargement of breasts, rounding of hips and the growth of pubic hair. There is an increase in size of uterus and vagina, labia and clitoris. Ovulation occurs approximately 1 year after the onset of menstruation. In Turner's syndrome where there is a chromosomal abnormality (XO) there is a failure of the ovaries to develop.

Body image

This refers to the person's perception of his own body, which involves a large degree of evaluation. Both males and females compare themselves with the stereotype ideals. In our culture for men it is the tall, muscular male with a particular facial appearance seen in films and television shows as the hero. For females it is particular facial features and a body with quite specific measurements of certain parts, i.e. bust, waist and hips, seen in magazines, films and television. The person's degree of contentment with his body may depend on how close to the ideal he comes. For many mentally handicapped adolescents, particularly mildly handicapped, their evaluation of their bodies may be greatly influenced

by these ideal stereotypes. For those less susceptible to cultural values their perception of their body is likely to be of little importance to them. In general, women's body image seems to be of greater importance than men's because of the emphasis on female bodies in our culture.

Cognitive changes

In a non-mentally handicapped adolescent there may be a change in thinking ability. This is not to say that a non-mentally handicapped adolescent always functions at this higher level of thinking, i.e. formal operational level. Instead it may be that his level of thinking may characteristically operate at the concrete operational level with occasional involvement of his higher thought processes. In the mildly mentally handicapped, adolescent thinking does not extend beyond the concrete operational level where thinking focuses on reality, whereas for many non-mentally handicapped adolescents who can function at the formal operational level reality becomes secondary to possibility. They see how things might be instead of seeing how things are. They are likely to become preoccupied in questioning value systems, social structures and spiritual issues.

For many mentally handicapped people adolescence may be a time of confusion about the physical changes that are happening to them. In being helped to come to terms with these changes and the associated moral problems, awareness of the different system of reasoning used by adolescents of different mental ages is essential for staff to help them deal with these changes.

Emotional changes

For many, adolescence is a time of the experiencing of extremes of emotion; of irrepressible joy and inconsolable sadness and loss; of gregariousness and loneliness; of altruism and self-centredness; of insatiable curiosity and boredom; of confidence and self doubt. According to Erikson (1963) the central concern for adolescents is to develop 'a sense of one's own identity'. In developing one's own identity, trying on different hats is characteristic of adolescent behaviour; behaving as the confident man about town may contrast with the self doubting clumsy youth. How others see him is very important. In social situations, particularly in early adolescence, the person may feel as if he is on the stage, assuming that everyone else is watching him and evaluating his performance. Informing him that most other adolescents in the room are also on the stage will do nothing to reduce his egocentrism. Erikson felt that it was important for the adolescent to develop a feeling of consistency and stability of the self over time and situations. The role playing and the preoccupation with self reflects this need. The emotional changes as well as the physical and cognitive changes experienced by the adolescent may prove an obstacle to establishing this feeling of self consistency.

Sex behaviour

In the general population the frequency of sex before marriage for male adolescents has not changed very much, whereas among females it has increased substantially. This is not to imply that sexual permissiveness is not associated with love and affection. It may mean that the act of intercourse is included in the range of intimate behaviour between couples. Despite the increase in public discussion of sexual issues there is a strong private moral code which may inhibit the discussion of sexual issues.

Causes of concern or anxiety

Any development seen as a variation from the person's view of normal may cause anxiety. For women the size of breasts, being overweight or underweight, skin blemishes, ability to have children may be a source of worry, while for men facial hair, muscular development, size of penis, attractiveness to women may cause anxiety.

The following may be the focus of concern for adolescents to:

Menstruation (periods) — depending on the quality of information received, the person's reaction to the onset of menstruation may range from acceptance to the extreme of believing they are going to die.

Erection ('hard on') — a person has the capacity for erection and for pleasurable sensations from infancy. The experiencing of erotic sensations becomes more frequent in adolescence and a person at this time is likely to be aroused by a wide variety of stimuli not all overtly sexual, e.g. anxiety, warmth, etc.

Ejaculation ('coming') — ejaculation occurs about a year after the onset of puberty. It may be the result of intercourse, masturbation or nocturnal emission ('wet dreams'). Nocturnal emission occurs most frequently when there is no other sexual outlet, and may not be accompanied by overtly erotic dreams.

Masturbation ('wanking') — masturbation has a history of strong disapproval in the western world. The view that masturbation was not only morally wrong but also bad for your health was supported by religious groups and the medical profession. Earlier in this century the Surgeon General in the USA warned that masturbation could cause such diseases as cancer, heart disease or insanity. Here in Britain it was felt that someone who masturbated would merely run the risk of going blind! Religious groups quoted the Bible in support of their view that masturbation was sinful. Indeed the reference to masturbation in Genesis 38:9 led to the name of the perpetrator being given to the act in Victorian times, namely, Onanism. The current view is that the act of masturbation is not detrimental in itself. Kinsey (1953) felt that masturbation may help later adjustment to heterosexual relationships particularly in some women. What may be most damaging to the person is the accompanying reaction of anxiety, guilt or depression.

In a residential setting, particularly in hospitals due to the lack of privacy, it is not uncommon to come across residents masturbating. Staff reactions to this may vary in extreme — some may find this behaviour shocking and unacceptable, take immediate action to stop it and try to prevent it happening again, by increasing supervision, for example; others may accept this behaviour as normal and quietly leave the dormitory.

Which response is right? What is the responsibility of the care staff in this situation? In our particular culture there are unwritten rules which govern our sexual behaviour. Masturbation, though not approved of, is tolerated if carried out without any attention being drawn to the fact that it does occur, i.e. in private. In public this behaviour is totally unacceptable. We as non-residents have learned this rule through our socialisation.

Homosexual behaviour. In institutions where access to the opposite sex is limited the prevalence of homosexual behaviour is higher than among the general population. West (1967) cited incidences of the acquisition of homosexual behaviour in previously heterosexual males in prisons. Kolanzynska-Carr (1970) found that the length of stay in a single sex environment during adolescence was important for the development of homosexual behaviour in males. Kinsey et al (1948) in their survey of the general population found that 4–5% of men were exclusively homosexual. Of the remainder over 20% had one or more incidental homosexual experience. Feldman & MacCulloch (1980) have suggested that the prevalence among women is similar to males. Although in many cultures homosexual relationships are acceptable, in our culture it is considered unacceptable behaviour. Homosexual behaviour among residents may present considerable moral professional and personal difficulties to staff members.

Staff responsibilities

Mentally handicapped residents are at a disadvantage in that often the culture they are exposed to does not offer the same type of socialisation as we in the general culture have experienced. While they are socialised into one culture they are judged by the norms of another. In addition, in the different culture of the residence there may be problems such as having little room for privacy, and the fact that adults (staff) they have contact with are unlikely to talk about sexual matters unless responsibility for educating residents has been formally given to them. These factors exacerbate the situation. For staff to help mentally handicapped adolescents to understand and deal with their developing sexuality they must first come to terms with their own attitudes and feelings. Even in the less contentious area of discussing the mechanics of sex the words used by staff may reflect their own inhibitions. One method commonly used to deal with the issue is to distance the subject and avoid any uncomfortable feelings by using 'correct' or medical terms. Unfortunately using such safe words as ejaculation, scrotum, testicles, vagina instead of the words, albeit slang, with which the person is familiar, is likely to inhibit free communication between the resident and the member of staff. On the other hand using 'dirty' words may equally inhibit communication if the member of staff is embarrassed about it. Group discussions with other staff members may help the staff to come to terms with talking about sexual matters competently and comfortably. The policy of avoiding the subject adopted by many staff is itself detrimental to the development of residents, and in the experience of the author constitutes the most common way of dealing with any matters of a sexual nature that arise.

The more severely mentally handicapped resident's experience of sexual pleasure may be only in terms of masturbation, while others less handicapped are capable of giving and obtaining satisfaction with a partner. Sex education for them is important not only to avoid the possibility of unwanted pregnancy or of being exploited, but to enhance the quality of their lives. Love, affection and companionship of a close relationship are not the sole prerogative of non-mentally handicapped people. Ignorance and distorted views of sex could very easily undermine the development of such a relationship.

SUMMARY

Development of motor skills is relatively resistant to a range of environmental factors. While the rate of motor development may vary from child to child, the sequence remains the same including the development of drawing and writing skills. Some theorists maintain that continual progress through the sequence is necessary and that completion of one stage is necessary before starting the next.

Socialisation is a process whereby an individual becomes a responsible member of society, but adaptation is necessary to the various subgroups that make up society. From birth a child initiates and responds to communication and attachment occurs with the main caregiver. Successful socialisation, however, is effected by two main processes of discipline and modelling, and in a residential setting care staff will be the chief agents of these processes. All through childhood and adult life, mentally handicapped individuals experience different reactions from family, friends and others. Characteristics seen as typical of mentally handicapped people may have less to do with the level of intelligence than their common social experiences.

A child's reasoning follows its own set of rules and over time this will change. By means of assimilation and accommodation, psychological structures develop. Piaget described four main stages of cognitive development: sensory-motor (0–2 yr), pre-operational (2–7 yr), concrete operational (7–11 yr) and formal operational (11 yr+).

During the sensory-motor stage the child develops object permanency and gains a rudimentary idea of time and space. During the pre-operational stage the child can only deal with single dimension and, as shown in the conservation tasks, concentrates on static states and not on the changes. During the concrete operational stage the child is capable of focusing on several dimensions of a situation simultaneously and can relate these dimensions. He can do in his head what he would previously have had to accomplish through action. The formal operational stage is when reality takes second place to possibility. Mentally handicapped people as well as many non-mentally handicapped people do not reach this final stage of development.

Care staff should take account of the stage of development the child has reached and modify their actions accordingly. Mentally handicapped children and adults learn by manipulating and exploring things rather than being taught how to do them. Adolescence is a difficult time for any individual because of the physical and emotional changes that occur. Along with the development of primary and secondary sexual characteristics, the person's perception of his own body assumes great importance and comparison is made to a stereotype ideal.

Cognitive level in the mentally handicapped adolescent will not extend beyond the concrete operational level to the formal operational level as in many non-mentally handicapped people. Thinking remains focused on reality and they are concerned with how things are.

One important aspect of emotional change involves the adolescent developing his own identity, so self becomes the individual's main preoccupation. Establishing a sexual identity will also be an important consideration and physical changes may give cause for concern and require sympathetic counselling. In the residential setting, sexual matters may create particular problems due to lack of privacy and staff must come to terms with their own attitudes in order to help residents deal with sexual feelings. Avoiding the subject altogether may be detrimental and sex education should be included as part of the teaching programme.

REFERENCES

Barsch R 1965 A morigenic curriculum. State Dept of Instruction, Madison, Wisconsin
Bloom K 1975 Social elicitation of vocal behaviour. Journal of Experimental Child Psychology 20: 51–58

Bowlby J 1973 Attachment and loss. Vol II Separation. Basic Books, New York

Brossard L M, Decarie T G 1969 Comparative reinforcing effect of light stimulation on the smiling response of infants. Journal of Child Psychology and Psychiatry 9: 51–60

Cross H A, Harlow H F 1965 Prolonged and progressive effects of partial isolation on the behaviour of Macaque monkeys. Journal of Experimental Personality Research 1: 39–49

Decarie T G 1974 The infant's reaction to strangers. International Universities Press, New York

Delacato C H 1963 The diagnosis and treatment of speech and reading problems. Thomas, Springfield, Illinois

Erikson E H 1963 Childhood and society, 2nd edn. Norton, New York

Feldman M P, McCulloch M T 1980 Human sexual behaviour. Wiley, London

Forehand R, Roberts M W, Doleys D N, Hobbs S A, Reisick P A 1976 An examination of disciplinary procedures with children. Journal of Experimental Psychology 2: 109–120

Ginott H 1965 Between parent and child. Macmillan, New York

Haugan G M, McIntire R W 1972 Comparisons of vocal imitation, tactile stimulation and food reinforcers for infant vocalisation. Developmental Psychology 6: 201–209

Hetherington E M, Frankie G 1967 Effects of parental dominance, warmth and conflict on imitation in children. Journal of Personality and Social Psychology 6: 119–125

Hilgarde J R 1932 Learning and motivation in preschool children. Journal of Genetic Psychology 41: 36–56

Hoffman J 1975 Moral internalisation, parental power and the nature of parent-child interaction. Developmental Psychology 11: 228–239

Inhelder B 1968 The diagnosis of reasoning in the mentally retarded. Day, New York

Kaphart N 1971 The slow learner in the classroom. Merrill, Columbus, Ohio

Kinsey A C, Pomeroy W B, Martin C E 1948 Sexual behaviour in the human male. Saunders, Philadelphia

Kinsey A C, Pomeroy W B, Martin C E, Gebhard P N 1953 Sexual behaviour in the human female. Saunders, Philadelphia

Kolanzynska-Carr A 1970 Unpublished PhD thesis, University of Birmingham

Lefcourt H M 1976 Locus of control. Current trends in theory and research. Erlbaum, New York.

Morgan G A, Ricciuti H N 1969 Infants' responses to strangers during the first year. In: Foss B M (ed) Determinants of infants' behaviour, vol 4. Methuen, London

Moss H A, Robson K S, Pederson F 1969 Determinants of maternal stimulation of infants and consequences of treatment for later reaction to strangers. Developmental Psychology 1: 239–246

Piaget J 1951 Play, dreams and imitation in childhood. Heinemann, London

Piaget J 1952 The origin of intelligence in children. International Universities Press, New York

Piaget J 1955 The construction of reality. Routledge and Kegan Paul, London

Piaget J, Szeminska A 1952 The child's conception of numbers. Routledge and Kegan Paul, London

Rheingold H L, Eckerman C O 1973 Fear of the stranger: A critical examination. In: Reese H W (ed) Advances in child development and behaviour, vol 8. Academic Press, New York

Sequin E 1966 Idiocy and its treatment by the physiological method. Brandow, Albany, New York

Strauss A A, Lehtinen L E 1947 Psychopathology and education of the brain injured child. Grune and Stratton, New York

Toft C T, Cohen H J 1967 Neonatal and infant reflexology. In: Helmuth T (ed) Exceptional infant vol 1. Special Child Publications, Seattle

West D J 1967 Homosexuality, 3rd edn. Duckworth, London

8

Behaviour change

Mary Boyle

- Behaviour must be identified, defined and looked at in relation to the environmental setting
- Positive reinforcement always accompanies techniques for teaching new behaviour
- Unwanted behaviour should be reduced by differential reinforcement before resort is made to punishment techniques
- Clear and precise records should be maintained at all times
- Programmes should be reviewed on a regular basis to assess what has been achieved and to set future targets

Introduction
Staff training
The groundwork
    Learning theory
    Observation and measurement of behaviour
    Recording methods
    Functional analysis
Teaching new skills
    Positive reinforcement
    Types of reinforcers
    Delivery of reinforcement
    Negative reinforcement
    Additional teaching techniques
    Imitation, generalisation and discrimination
    What to teach
Reducing unwanted behaviours
    Differential reinforcement of other behaviour
    Extinction
    Punishment
    Ethical issues
Putting it all together
    The goal planning system
    Early intervention
    Staff behaviour
Summary

INTRODUCTION

It is an aspect of the use of language that words and terms come to convey more or less than was originally intended. The term 'behaviour modification' for many has come to mean only a particular set of techniques which can be employed in changing the behaviour of an individual. Consequently, there has been an over-emphasis on concepts of behaviour control with the exclusion of that process of 'behaviour analysis' which necessarily precedes and encompasses any programme or change. MacKrell et al (1980) suggest that this fundamental theoretical confusion has resulted in a 'cook book' approach to behaviour modification. It may also have been a major contributing factor to the development of a widespread (but not universal) equivocation towards the practice of this subject. Most of us are familiar with statements such as:

> 'We've tried behaviour modification and it doesn't work.'

> or

> 'Behaviour modification isn't used in this ward, most of the children are well behaved.'

Such anecdotal evidence would seem to suggest a certain resistance towards behavioural methods — an attitude which is difficult to explain and understand. Why is behaviour modification often dismissed as ineffective? Is there a basic flaw in the principles, or could

127

it be that low staffing levels inhibit efficient practice? The answer could be that staff of all disciplines in institutions frequently see as appropriate referrals for behaviour modification those people who exhibit behaviour which, in many cases, does little more than annoy or interfere with routine. Could this be because staff and management priorities dictate treatment goals, or is it due to the purely functional mechanism of an institution in which one group of people is in control of another group? It seems that there are certain factors of particular significance in creating and sustaining the conditions whereby (at present) the practice of behaviour modification falls below its true potential. Two important areas which merit closer examination are staff training conditions, and what the term 'behaviour modification' has come to mean.

STAFF TRAINING

In May 1974 every hospital in Britain known to have psychiatric beds was contacted and asked whether any behaviour modification procedures were being carried out in their area. The contact was made by a Joint Working Party set up to formulate ethical guidelines for the conduct of behaviour modification programmes. Later that same year, the 115 hospitals who replied in the affirmative were again contacted and asked to give details of certain aspects of behaviour modification practice. On the subject of staff training the published report (Zangwill, 1980) states:

> One third of all hospitals contacted gave some details of staff training . . . less than one in fourteen of all hospitals indicated the existence of a clearly thought out training scheme.

Considering the widespread practice of behaviour modification and the related ethical issues, this seems rather an exposed position for hospital staff to be in.

A number of external training bodies, such as the British Institute of Mental Handicap (BIMH) in Kidderminster and Hilda Lewis House in London, run short courses designed to give an overview of the general principles involved in changing behaviour. Although these courses are a useful extension of in-service education, they rely heavily on continued training and support being available on the return to the place of employment. If this support is not given, or is inadequate, course participants often have to choose between 'going it alone' with limited information, or settling back into their pre-course routine.

For qualified nursing staff who wish to specialise in the practice of behaviour change, the picture, although improving, is poor. The National Boards for England (ENB) and for Scotland (SNB) do organise post qualification courses in behaviourist methods for registered nurses, but the output of these courses is relatively small. To date the ENB course has produced 66 graduates and the SNB course only 39 graduates. It would appear that qualified nurses are not pushing their training establishments to organise more courses. Mental handicap nurses are constantly exposed to literature which tells them that their role is one of 'educator' and that training methods derived from the behaviourist school of thought are the most appropriate and effective methods to use with slow learners. The places available on the courses are not sufficient to meet the needs of qualified nurses in every hospital in Britain practising behaviour change methods. Hospital in-service education departments go some way to meeting this need, although the small numbers of nurses completing specialist training courses would suggest that most hospitals do not have an appropriately qualified nurse to teach the subject, and therefore rely heavily on psychology staff or, occasionally, medical staff.

Cullen & Woods (1981) raise another important aspect of training, the fact that most training programmes are evaluated in terms of the changes in staff behaviour, attitudes, and the ability to use terminology. Few studies have evaluated staff training in terms of positive changes in residents' behaviour. One consequence of this is the widespread use of behaviour modification 'jargon'.

WHAT HAS THE TERM BEHAVIOUR MODIFICATION COME TO MEAN?

Too infrequently one hears discussion or comment on behaviour modification referring to the analysis of behaviour, i.e. the identification of relationships between observed behaviour and events in the immediate environment. The title 'behaviour modification' has become widely identified with certain techniques, e.g. time-out, backward chaining, reinforcement, without enough emphasis being placed on the groundwork which has to be completed before these techniques can be employed successfully. Failure to identify 'the sufficient and necessary causes for a particular response to occur and persist' (Evans, 1971) is the most common reason for the 'failure' of behaviour modification programmes. How has this situation come about? Inadequate provision for training is one obvious reason that has already been suggested. The continued use of terminology which often succeeds in obscuring, rather than clarifying, the basic philosophy of behaviour modification has added to the general confusion and misinterpretation of the subject. According to the Zangwill report quoted earlier:' . . . the term behaviour modification itself gave rise to difficulty since it was open to varied interpretation.'

The most disheartening (and the most common) of these varied interpretations is that behaviour modification is something to be 'called in' when a problem arises and not as a method of increasing personal skills. For example, it is not commonly seen as an effective educational tool in the care of the elderly mentally handicapped person, something which can help to increase independence, alleviate boredom and generally improve their quality of life. Nor is it used to its full potential with those people who have been given the label 'severely sub-normal'. Often we hear

how effective behaviour change programmes can be with this group of people, but these training schemes tend to deal, in the main, with aspects of self care such as toileting and feeding. Little mention is made of the suitability of behaviour modification as a teaching method for increasing play skills (Carr, 1980) or as an efficient technique for training imitation (Bandura, 1969), a pre-requisite skill of play and a behaviour which many severely handicapped children do not have in their repertoire. Developmental models, such as the Portage Guide to Early Education are excellent media for the use of behaviour modification in the most positive way.

Words and terms will always be open to interpretation, but an attempt can be made to reduce such interpretations to a level which is not too destructive. It is necessary for teachers and practitioners of behaviour modification to keep terminology to a minimum, always to describe exactly what is meant when terms are used in relation to 'techniques' and to emphasise the need for a firm grasp of the basic philosophy before any programme to alter behaviour is attempted.

THE GROUNDWORK

Learning Theory

> It has been said that there are as many learning theories as there are psychologists.
>
> (Williams, 1980)

The one learning theory which has been frequently applied to helping mentally handicapped people is associated with the American Harvard psychologist, Professor B. F. Skinner (1953). Originally called operant conditioning, to differentiate it from Pavlov's classical conditioning (Hilgard & Atkinson, 1975), it is now seen as a set of principles, both of analysis and techniques, which can be used to explain how behaviour is learned and, consequently, how it can be changed.

To understand operant conditioning better, it is helpful to distinguish between two types of behaviour which Skinner called respondent and operant behaviour. Respondent behaviour is concerned with behaviour which is considered to be involuntary or 'reflex', e.g. eye blinks and knee jerks. This particular type of behaviour responds to the environment in which it occurs. Operant behaviour, in contrast produces some direct effect; it operates on the environment, e.g. walking, smiling and switching on a television set.

The fact that operant behaviour can be conditioned or learned is demonstrated under laboratory conditions, by carrying out the now famous 'Skinner Box' experiment:

A rat deprived of food for a specific period of time is placed in a box which is bare except for a small food dish, above which is a protruding bar (a small light bulb above the bar can be turned on at the discretion of the experimenter). While moving about the box, the rat will, by chance, occasionally press the bar. This is the way in which the rat has a direct effect (or operates) on his environment, before any learning takes place. The experimenter then attaches a device which will drop a pellet of food into the dish as the lever is pressed. The rat eats and soon presses the bar again. The food rewards, or reinforces, bar pressing and the rate at which this behaviour occurs increases dramatically. If the food dispenser is disconnected, so that the bar pressing no longer delivers food, the frequency of bar-pressing behaviour will decrease. That is to say, according to the consequence of bar pressing, the response either increases or decreases.

The importance of this theory lies in its practical applications to teaching. The principles by which we all learn can be applied to people who have special learning difficulties, not in an essentially different way but in a more systematic and planned way than is usual in everyday life.

Kirman & Bicknell (1975) present the Skinnerian theory in point form:

1. As a result of performing a piece of behaviour in a particular situation something will always happen to a person.

Example A

Behaviour   Johnny throws rubber duck out of bath.

Consequence Mother picks it up and gives it back to him.

Example B

Behaviour   Johnny throws rubber duck out of bath.

Consequence Mother ignores this behaviour and carries on as if nothing had happened.

2. The result can be pleasant (a reward) or unpleasant (a punishment).

Example

If Johnny's mother returns the duck laughing or feigning surprise, this could be rewarding to Johnny. Alternatively, if she ignores the throwing behaviour, Johnny may find this unpleasant or, more strongly, may feel that he is being punished for throwing by not getting his duck back.

3. Through observation of how the person reacts in the same situation over time, it can be seen how the experience has been enjoyed. From these observations the most effective rewards for that person can be discerned.

Example

The next time Johnny is being bathed by his mother, he will be more likely to throw out the duck if what happened the last time, as a consequence of throwing, was rewarding to him.

(*Note.* Another child may find having the duck returned very unrewarding, even unpleasant, if, for instance, he did not want the duck in the bath beside him.)

4. Learning is therefore ended by rewarding behaviour that is desirable, and refusing rewards for other behaviour.

However, before we can begin to help a person to learn something new, we must identify what he already does, what his strengths and weaknesses are. This necessitates developing our observational skills.

Observation and measurement of behaviour

The first principle of what has become known as behaviour modification is that all behaviour is observable and recordable. People can agree more readily over observed behaviour. If we, instead, describe a person by their feelings or emotions, we would be less likely to agree. This lack of agreement arises because we are trying to describe something that we cannot observe directly, something that is in the mind of the person we are looking at. Allyon et al (1965) carried out an experiment of a middle-aged, institutionalised, schizophrenic woman who was successfully trained to hold a broom, using behaviour modification techniques with cigarettes as reinforcer. Although broom-handling had been selected quite arbitrarily, two psychiatrists, unaware of the experiment, placed great emphasis on this aspect of her behaviour when invited to observe her : 'the broom represents . . . some essential perceptual element in her field of consciousness' and 'a ritualistic procedure, a magical action.' Hoch (1971) pointed out that normally the choice of activity would not be as meaningless as broom-handling but agreed that behaviour must be interpreted with caution. A behaviourist, in stark contrast, would have recorded the observation as 'the woman held a broom in an upright position, while walking, standing, smoking.'

Inaccurate observations are inevitable when individuals are left to their own devices when carrying out observations. A number of techniques can be employed to overcome this, the first one being *identification* of the behaviour you are interested in.

Example

Parent	'Lucy is awful!'
Therapist	'What does she do that is awful?'
Parent	'Everything!'

Before we can think of changing Lucy's 'awful' behaviour, we have to identify or define it. We must ask: 'how is Lucy awful? In what ways?' Only by doing this can we begin to define the behaviour which is being displayed. The next thing to do is to look at what is happening around Lucy when she behaves in this way: are there any factors which are contributing to her behaviour? If, for instance, on closer questioning we find that the most common feature of Lucy's 'awful' behaviour is 'throwing objects about the room', then we would want to know: what type of objects? at what times during the day? are there any 'triggering' factors and, very importantly, what happens to Lucy as a consequence of throwing things about?

The therapist, whether this be nurse, parent, psychologist or whoever, is interested in understanding the behaviour in relation to the environmental in which it occurs. Identifying a 'functional relationship' between a specific behaviour and its controlling factors is fundamental to the behaviour change process.

The A B C of behaviour

Behaviour change occurs when certain consequences are contingent upon the behaviour in question. A contingency refers to the relationship between a behaviour and the events which follow the behaviour (sometimes events which precede the behaviour are also specified by a contingency).

Example

| Behaviour | Lucy picks up an ornament and throws it across the room. |
| Consequence | Mother leaves 'what she is doing, goes up to Lucy and tells her off. |

If Lucy's mother always switches her attention from what she is doing to Lucy every time throwing occurs, we would say that maternal attention was *contingent* on Lucy's throwing behaviour.

Most programmes designed to change behaviour do so by altering the contingencies which surround the behaviour.

A method designed to help identify contingent relationships is the 'three term contin-

A	B	C
ANTECEDENT	BEHAVIOUR	CONSEQUENCE
Note carefully events associated with each of the person's responses, i.e. what happens IMMEDIATELY BEFORE the behaviour occurs.	Provide a careful description of the person's behaviour	Note what happens IMMEDIATELY AFTER the response

Fig. 8.1 Functional analysis.

		A	B	C
Date	Time	ANTECEDENT	BEHAVIOUR	CONSEQUENCE
21.9.81	3.15pm	Nurse Smith walked into Dining-room	Johnny banged left side of head with fist	Nurse Smith picked up Johnny and cuddled him

Fig. 8.2 Functional analysis of Johnny's head-banging behaviour.

gency system' (Skinner, 1953; Bijou et al, 1969), commonly referred to as the 'A B C of behaviour'. This system provides the information necessary to carry out an analysis of the relationship between the behaviour and the environment in which it is occurring, i.e. a *functional analysis* (Figs 8.1 & 8.2).

The layout of the form can be altered to suit the situation. The most important thing to remember is not to record wishes or wants, *only* what is happening.

Example

Incorrect — Sally was delighted to hold the cat.

Correct — Sally smiled as she held the cat.

After you have defined what behaviour you are interested in and looked at it in relation to the environment, you are then ready to observe it directly. This involves measuring how often or for how long the behaviour occurs and recording this information accurately on an appropriate data sheet or form. The measure

of behaviour prior to any change process is referred to as a *baseline* rate or behaviour. The following section describes the observational methods most commonly used for collecting data before, during and after intervention.

Recording methods

Continuous recording can be time-consuming. The observer is required to write down everything that happens. Not only is this impractical, it is also physically impossible, inevitably leading to inaccurate records. The use of video can, to some extent, avoid the inaccuracies of continuous recording, but the benefits of using audio-visual aids are diminished by both the number of manpower hours required to transcribe the tape on to a record sheet and the financial considerations.

Event recording calls for the observer to answer the question 'What event am I interested in?' (tantrums, head bangs), then to count every time the event occurs (Fig. 8.3).

This can be expressed as a frequency count

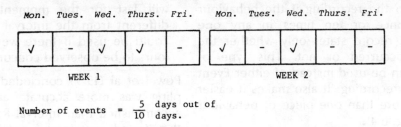

Number of events = $\frac{5}{10}$ days out of days.

Fig. 8.3 Event recording of Sarah's attendance at school.

by saying that Sarah was in 50% of full attendance:

i.e. $\frac{\text{No. of events}}{\text{No. observations}} = \frac{5}{10} \times \frac{100}{1} = 50\%$

Advantages of this method are that it is accurate and fast, a tick can be recorded as soon as the event takes place (a mechanical counter can be used for behaviours that occur at a high rate). One disadvantage is that behaviours like sitting or playing, which exist over a period of time, are not well recorded in this manner.

Duration recording is concerned with how long a time a behaviour lasts. For instance, we would use the duration method to record how long a child spends thumb-sucking. A stop watch is useful for this type of observation, but, if not available, an ordinary watch or clock will do.

Example
Using Duration recording, Andy was observed for thumb-sucking behaviour over a period of one hour. The time spent engaged in this particular behaviour was recorded as 45 minutes. This would be expressed as follows:

$\frac{\text{Duration of behaviour}}{\text{Duration of observation}} = \frac{45 \text{ min}}{60 \text{ min}} \times \frac{100}{1}$

$= 75\%$

Thumb-sucking occurred for 75% of the observational period. (*Note*. For efficiency in duration recording, a cumulative stop-watch can be used.)

Interval recording allows the observer to record whether or not the behaviour happened during a specific interval of time: 5 minutes; 15 minutes; 1 hour; 1 day. It would make no

Number of Intervals to be Observed

(Each number represents an interval of time, e.g. if each was ½-hour interval, total observation period would be 5 hours)

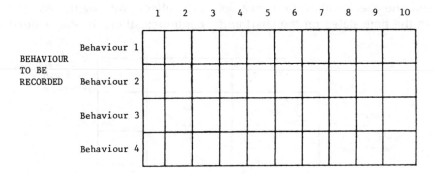

Fig. 8.4 Interval recording form.

difference to the recording if the behaviour happened once or ten times in any one interval, the record states only whether the behaviour occurred or not. This type of recording can be used instead of either Event or Duration recording. It also makes it easier to record more than one piece of behaviour at a time (Fig. 8.4).

Example

Let us assume that Jack's teacher intends to use the Interval method to record his swearing and wandering about class. She has decided to observe these behaviours for part of the morning, 10.30 a.m.–11.30 a.m. This time span would be divided into equal intervals (e.g. 5 minutes, ½-hour), and the teacher would note whether the behaviours occurred at all during each interval (Fig. 8.5).

This method demands a great deal of concentration from the observer. It is usual to allow some time for recording between intervals, e.g. 5 minutes of observing followed by 3 or 4 minutes of recording.

Time sampling is similar to interval recording in as much as the period under observation is divided into intervals, but in this case the observer records whether the behaviour is happening at one particular *moment of time*, usually at the end of the interval.

Example

Jane's mother has decided to use time sampling to assess Jane's readiness for a toilet-training programme. Every half hour she will check her daughter's pants and record a tick under wet or dry on the appropriate form. The check will occur as near as possible to the time stated on the chart and will last for the moment only. This is different from the interval method, which could be used if there were other behaviours to be observed concurrently (Fig. 8.6).

Powel et al (1977) concluded that time sampling was more accurate and more easily accomplished than Interval Recording, which they found contained a number of errors, a view reiterated by Murphy (1978).

For both Time and Interval Sampling, two people, observing the same behaviour, can calculate the reliability of their observations using this formula:

$$\frac{\text{No. of agreements}}{\text{No. of observations}} \times \frac{100}{1}$$

In Figure 8.7 there are nine intervals in which the two observers agree in what they record, i.e. if throwing behaviour did or did not occur during each of the ten intervals. The agreement of *reliability* of this observation period is:

$$\frac{9}{10} \times \frac{100}{1} = 90\%$$

Yule (1980) suggests that reliability measures in excess of 80% can be considered usable.

The above recording methods are used to obtain a measure of the operant level of behaviour before any change programme begins. The record of behaviour at this stage is referred to as a baseline, and keeping a record of the baseline rate of behaviour enables us to judge whether the behaviour change programme which follows is having the effect we want. As the programme continues, there is still a need for constant

	1	2	3	4	5	No.of intervals of 5 mins. each
Swearing	√	–	√	√	–	
Out of Seat	–	–	–	√	–	

Fig. 8.5 Swearing and 'out of seat' behaviour in classroom.

Date	Time	Wet	Dry
4.11.81	8 am	√	
	8.30		√
	9.00		√
	9.30		√
	10.00	√	

Fig. 8.6 Time sampling record of Jane's incontinence.

recording of observations. This data can be compared with the baseline data, alerting the therapist immediately to changes which are required in the training programme. Information collected using observational methods before, during and after training can be transferred into graph form for easy reading (Fig. 8.8).

It is important to choose a recording system which fits reasonably well into the daily routine. Home-made forms are easy to draw up and once some practice is gained in observational skills, collection of data becomes almost second nature. The value of keeping adequate and accurate records cannot be stressed too strongly. Without such records, both the therapist and the recipient are very vulnerable. Scientifically, record-keeping is an integral part of the behaviour change process. Ethically, it is essential to the credibility of the therapist and to the safeguards of the recipient.

TEACHING NEW SKILLS

Positive reinforcement

The ABC system has already been mentioned as a way of looking at behaviour, and will now be considered in relation to teaching some

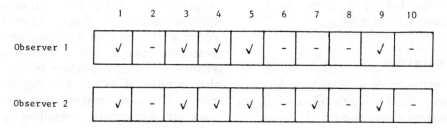

Fig. 8.7 Interval recording of throwing behaviour

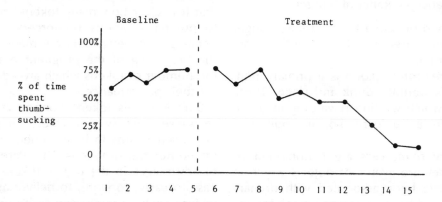

Fig. 8.8 Record of thumb-sucking behaviour. Time is always recorded along the horizontal axis; this can be days, hours or sessions. The vertical axis is concerned with the observed behaviour. The main point to remember about graphs is labelling. Each axis must be clearly labelled and the graph should have a title.

new behaviour, for example finger feeding in a very young child:

Example

Antecedent	Behaviour	Consequence
Bowl of food presented to child	Child lifts food to mouth with fingers	Food arrives in child's mouth

In this case food being in the child's mouth is contingent upon food being lifted to the mouth using the fingers. If the child finds the food rewarding it is likely that the behaviour which precedes it will increase, i.e. the behaviour of finger feeding will be strengthened or *reinforced*.

A consequence of behaviour which increases the likelihood of that behaviour occurring in the future is called a positive reinforcer. Therefore, in the above example if finger feeding increases it can be said that the child is being positively reinforced for finger feeding. Additional reinforcers which may strengthen the behaviour even more are smiles and praise from adults.

Types of reinforcers

We are all exposed daily to various forms of reinforcement. Food is highly reinforcing, and the ABC sequence involved is:

Antecedent — Hunger
Behaviour — Eating
Consequence — Relief of hunger.

The likelihood of eating the next time hunger strikes is increased by the rewarding consequence it has.

Primary reinforcer. Food is a primary reinforcer, as is warmth, drink and sleep. These are things which we find rewarding in themselves — they are unlearned or unconditioned reinforcers.

Secondary reinforcers are conditioned or learned. They are events or objects which in the past have been associated with primary reinforcers and have now taken on reinforcing properties of their own. One common example of this type of reinforcer is money. It is something which, when it follows a behaviour (usually work) increases the likelihood of that behaviour occurring in the future. It is not in itself reinforcing (the paper of the notes and metal of the coins are useless), but it is reinforcing in the types of things it can buy. This process of association is referred to as *pairing*. When a primary reinforcer is paired with a neutral event, that event should become reinforcing.

Example

Johnny's teacher is trying to increase his attention span. She tells him that for every 3 minutes that he attends to the task in front of him a tick will be put beside his name on the blackboard and he will receive a toffee. After a period of pairing these events the tick itself becomes reinforcing and the primary reinforcer can be gradually removed.

This example is one variation of the *token* system. Tokens are secondary or generalised reinforcers. They take the form of ticks, stars or plastic discs which are used as rewards for specific behaviours. When an individual or an entire unit is run on a reinforcement system based on tokens, this is known as a token economy. Tokens function in the same way that money does in a national economic system. They are earned and used to purchase back-up reinforcers, including goods and services, such as food, consumables, activities and privileges. The rate of exchange of tokens for back-up reinforcers must be specified so that it is clear how many tokens are required to purchase various reinforcers. The target behaviour or behaviours are made explicit at the beginning of the programme along with the number of tokens which are administered for their performance.

Built into this token economy is usually a *response cost* system where inappropriate behaviour results in being 'fined' a predetermined number of tokens. There are a number of advantages in the use of tokens: they are easy to carry, to store, to deliver and allow a wider variety of reinforcers to be used. Activities or outings which cannot be delivered immediately and contingently on a particular behaviour can be represented by a token which is exchanged for the original reinforcer at a convenient time. Some disadvantages in their use are seen with the more handicapped person, who may have difficulties holding or storing his tokens. It is also quite time-consuming to teach the use of tokens to this type of person, although studies have shown that it is feasible. Another problem associated with tokens is stealing. This can be controlled, to an extent, through a coding system, but can still present difficulties in the form of squab-bling or bad feeling.

Social reinforcer. Attention, smiles, cuddles and praise are all forms of social reinforce-ment. They are readily available in the environ-ment and it has been argued that these should be the first choice of reinforcers when begin-ning a behaviour modification programme. Social reinforcers have often been included in the category of secondary reinforcers, the assumption being that the young child finds them reinforcing because of their pairing with primary reinforcers, especially food. Hemsley & Carr (1980) suggest that social reinforcers should perhaps be in a category on their own. They mention work with young infants which has shown that social stimuli may cause a response without any previous pairing with primary reinforcers.

Note. There have been objections to the use of primary reinforcers such as sweets, because of their contribution to dental decay. When possible, fruit should be substituted. One other objection is that to give food, in particular sweets in the case of children, is bribery. This argument will be discussed along with the ethical implications of behaviour modification (pp. 145–6).

Delivery of reinforcement

The person who is being reinforced must be in no doubt as to why they are being reinforced.

Example
Sara has just used her potty, a behaviour which her parents are trying to encourage.

She proudly presents it to her mother who is busily ironing. As her mother glances at the potty she also notices a newly ironed blouse which has fallen to the floor. Quickly she turns and picks it up saying 'Good girl Sara. Well done!' When she turns back to Sara she finds an empty potty and a wet patch on the carpet.

Using the ABC system to do a functional analysis of this example, it would look like this:
A — Child presents full potty to mother.
B — Child empties contents on to floor.
C — Mother praises child.

Maternal approval in this case is contingent upon the undesirable behaviour of emptying the potty on the floor. As parental approval is usually a very strong reward for young chil-dren, it could be said that Sara's mother has just reinforced her daughter for this particular behaviour. It is even more important to pay close attention to how reinforcement is deliv-ered when working with people who already have learning difficulties. The delivery should be:

Clear— It should be said enthusiasti-cally, loud enough to be heard and accompanied by eye contact.

Contingent — It must *immediately* follow the behaviour you are interested in.

Consistent— When trying to establish a new behaviour reinforcement must be delivered *every time* the behaviour occurs, i.e. a con-tinuous schedule of reinforce-ment.

Schedules of reinforcement

Reinforcement can either be given on a continuous schedule, as mentioned above, or on an intermittent basis. Intermittent sched-ules are discussed in terms of being ratio schedules, concerned with number, or interval schedules, concerned with time. For example, a child on a ratio schedule receives reinforcement for every third or fifth brick he stacks correctly; while on an interval schedule the child might be reinforced for every 8 or 12 seconds that he is working with bricks. These schedules are used to fade out reinforcement gradually and maintain newly acquired behaviours at a high frequency. For a more detailed account of the schedules see Kazdin (1975) or Yule & Carr (1980).

Satiation and Deprivation

When a reinforcer is used too often or in too great a quantity, it loses its effect. When a person becomes satiated by a reinforcer the training programme begins to fail. It is advisable to bear this in mind at the beginning of any programme and to have alternatives available. Another way to reduce the possibility of satiation is to make sure that the reinforcer is only available at certain times, i.e. when training is in progress. Deprivation of a reinforcer increases its potency. However, great care must be taken to ensure that people are never deprived or their rights or basic needs.

Negative reinforcement

The use of negative reinforcement in the field of mental handicap is limited. It is mentioned here only because of the confusion which the term provokes. Many people equate negative reinforcement with punishment for doing something 'bad'. It does, in fact, increase behaviour. In this respect it is similar to positive reinforcement and differs from punishment, which aims at decreasing behaviours. In negative reinforcement the desired behaviour is followed immediately by the removal of an unpleasant stimulus — negative reinforcement is 'taking away something bad'. An example from everyday experience is a person's behaviour when it is raining heavily. Getting wet is aversive to most people. As soon as an umbrella is put up the aversive circumstances are avoided. Thus, the act of putting up an umbrella is (negatively) reinforced by the removal of the sensation of being wet.

Additional teaching techniques

People with learning difficulties may require some extra help to be able to do certain things on their own. Positive reinforcement is not always enough to teach or establish new ways of behaving. Often additional ways of teaching have to be used as well.

Prompting and fading

Prompting is basically a way of helping a person to do something which they find difficult. It can take three forms:

Physical prompt — Give manual guidance, e.g. holding someone's hand and helping them to pick up an object.

Gestural prompt — Indicate the behaviour you want, e.g. by pointing.

Verbal prompt — Give an instruction, e.g. 'pull up your trousers'.

When using prompts begin with maximum help then gradually reduce the amount of help being given until the prompts have been faded completely.

Example

Each mealtime, over a period of 3 days, Nurse Smart placed Simon's hands around his cup, covered them with her own and guided the cup to his mouth while giving the instruction 'Simon, lift your cup.' She praised him and allowed him to take his favourite drink from the cup. By the 4th day of training, Simon was lifting his cup with just a touch from the nurse's fingers. On the 5th day she tried pointing, first to the cup on the table, then to Simon's mouth, giving the verbal instruction. When Simon managed to lift his cup, Nurse Smart was very enthusiastic in her praise and made sure Simon heard her tell the other nurses of his success. At the end of the week Simon was lifting his cup without any help when given the command 'Simon, lift your cup.'

Nurse Smart began by 'physically prompting' the behaviour which she wanted to train (the target behaviour). She then faded her prompts until she was only just touching Simon's hand. In fading further she made use of gestural prompts by pointing to the cup and indicating where it should go. Eventually, the verbal prompt (which had been built in since the beginning) was sufficient to cue Simon to lift his cup. Note that at all times Simon was reinforced for correct behaviour, even when he was not performing this on his own.

Chaining behaviours together

Drinking and eating are skills that many of us take for granted. They are also good examples of responses requiring the co-ordination of several bits of behaviour, e.g. picking up and holding a spoon, filling it with food and placing the food in the mouth. Some mentally handicapped people may not have this complete chain in their behaviour repertoire, but can make certain responses compatible with it, such as picking up the spoon. Zeilder & Jervey (1968) taught a 15-year-old profoundly handicapped girl to feed herself using a method of chaining small pieces of behaviour together. At first she required total assistance during meals and by the end of the project she ate without help. Self-feeding was established by working backwards through the chain comprising loading the spoon and taking food from it. The teaching steps were as follows:

Step 1 — Moving spoon to mouth from directly in front of lips.

Step 2 — Moving spoon from bowl to mouth.

Step 3 — Loading spoon with food.

As the last step of this chain, 'putting spoon into mouth' is the first thing to be taught, the method is known as *backward chaining*. Moore & Carr (1976) used a backward chaining technique to teach a 15½-year-old severely mentally handicapped boy to put on his vest, pants and socks. They used five stages to teach putting on the vest:

Stage 1 Vest put over child's head, arms put through armholes and vest pulled down to rib level; child to complete.

Stage 2 Vest put over child's head, one arm pulled through armhole. Child to put other arm through armhole and pull vest down.

Stage 3 Vest put over child's head.

Stage 4 Vest handed to child rolled up and ready to go over his head.

Stage 5 Vest handed to child.

The chain can include as many or as few steps as the trainer feels is necessary, depending upon the existing skills of the person to be taught. Chaining is used in conjunction with positive reinforcement and prompting. If the target behaviour is not achieved in the set time, or the programme is very obviously failing, this could be an indication that the steps in the chain are too large. It must also be remembered that it could be an indication that there was insufficient reinforcement or inadequate prompting. Keeping accurate records of all training sessions will help identify the cause of failure.

Shaping

This is a procedure which relies on 'catching' a behaviour similar to that which is the target behaviour and reinforcing it until it is well established. Reinforcement is then only given for a behaviour which is even more similar to the target behaviour and so on. It is a process reinforcing successive approximations to the behaviour to be trained.

Example

Target behaviour	Sitting on seat.
Behaviour resembling target behaviour	Standing beside seat.
Next approximation to target behaviour	Standing in front of seat.
Next approximation to target behaviour	Sitting on edge of seat.

The person being taught to sit on the seat would initially be reinforced for standing beside it, then only when standing in front of it and so on until the target behaviour was reached. One advantage of this method is that it is useful when prompting is impossible, e.g. in a child who does not tolerate physical contact. The disadvantages are that it is slow and difficult to use for complex behaviours.

Imitation, generalisation and discrimination

Imitation. Children begin learning new behaviours through imitation, at a very young age (around 8–9 months). It is a very efficient method of teaching and should be the first choice of technique in any behaviour modification programme. However, a number of people who are severely mentally handicapped have great difficulty in imitating. In these cases it may be helpful to teach them imitation skills using the methods described earlier: *prompting* the response, *fading* the prompts and *reinforcing* the resulting response. Large motor movements should be taught first, such as hands on head. The trainer models the action and gives the command 'do this'. If the other person responds correctly he is reinforced immediately, if not a prompt is given according to the degree of help required, then the response is reinforced. Teaching imitative skills can be time consuming and not, initially, particularly rewarding for the trainer. It often requires two people, one to be the model and one to prompt the person who is being taught. This is another disadvantage as it means drawing in extra staff to help out. The one major reason for teaching imitation, particularly in children, is that it may be helpful in speeding up their learning generally. Skills in play, language and self-help may develop more quickly if some time is spent teaching imitation to the mentally handicapped child.

Generalisation. When a behaviour that is performed in one situation is also performed in another it can be said that generalisation has occurred. For example, if a child learns to use the toilet at home and continues to use the toilet when at school, he has generalised his learning of toilet behaviour from one situation to another. Generalisation occurs readily as children learn new behaviours and for this reason is often taken for granted when dealing with mentally handicapped people, both children and adults alike. A handicapped person may learn a piece of behaviour and perform it extremely well, but the behaviour may be confined to one situation, with one object and with one person. For example, a person who is learning social skills may find that he can now ask Nurse A if she would like to dance within the confines of the day room in Ward 4. When he is in a disco with his friend he finds it impossible to speak to any of the females. If it is necessary for a person to exhibit a skill in a setting other than that in which it was trained then generalisation must be included as part of the programme. The skill must be taught in the presence of other people, in different situations. Generalisation problems can be minimised if the behaviour is taught in as natural a setting as possible; feeding at mealtimes in a dining room; dressing in the morning, etc.

Discrimination. Sometimes a behaviour occurs which in itself is very appropriate, but is unacceptable because of the time and place of its occurrence. For example, it is appropriate to take off your clothes at bedtime, but not in the middle of a supermarket. Or, it is appropriate to kiss people you are well acquainted with, but not strangers in the street. In such cases, it would be helpful to train the person to discriminate between the appropriate and the inappropriate situations and to behave accordingly. To do this, the two (or more) situations must be made as different as possible and reinforcement must only follow the behaviour which is performed in the appropriate situation.

Example

Gelfand & Hartmann (1975) give a hypothetical example of training discriminative behaviour in a child who laughs and jokes with his friend during class. They suggest that the child might wear some distinctive and attractive 'article of apparel,' (perhaps a special badge) for the time when he is expected to be quiet and attentive, and then have the article removed when he is free to talk with his friends. The badge would act as a cue to make one situation different from the other. When he was working quietly in the class the teacher would continually reinforce him for this appropriate behaviour.

What to teach

Establishing where to begin with training programmes can present problems, the major one being the differentiation between the needs of the person being considered and the needs of the others involved in the intervention. It is essential to set goals which will have primary benefit to the individual. Sometimes goals are set which are too advanced from the present skill level. Developmental charts and systems of teaching can be of great help in determining 'what is to be taught'. They can be used to collect baseline information on the present level of skill a person has and suggest the next appropriate skill level. For the more competent trainees, social skills inventories are useful. There are also good arguments for using assessment tools such as the American Adaptive Behaviour Scale (ABS), but only if these are being used for the purpose of identifying areas where the person being assessed can increase his independence and quality of life, rather than for the purpose of categorising them on an assessment scale.

Once the general goal has been decided upon, e.g. dressing, simple cooking or play, it has to be broken down into a series of small steps or target behaviours. Each of these is taught separately and within a specified period of time. Some of the developmental systems actually break the behaviours down on the checklist, so a large part of the work is already done. When working with severely or profoundly handicapped people it may be necessary to break these target behaviours down even further. Each small step is then taught using the techniques mentioned earlier, positive reinforcement in conjunction with prompting, chaining or any of the others. Records of training sessions must be kept

accurately as this helps to evaluate the effectiveness of the training programme.

REDUCING UNWANTED BEHAVIOUR

Differential reinforcement of other behaviour (DRO)

As already seen reinforcement is used to increase behaviour. In behaviour modification programmes where the object is to reduce or decrease unwanted behaviour, it is often seen as inappropriate to use reinforcement, hence punishment techniques are employed because they decrease the frequency of the behaviour directly. However, an 'undesirable' response can often be eliminated or decreased by reinforcing any other behaviour which occurs, i.e. applying reinforcement in a *differential* manner. This procedure is much more effective when the behaviour chosen to be reinforced is incompatible with the behaviour to be reduced, e.g. silence is a behaviour which is incompatible with screaming, therefore in a DRO programme designed to reduce screaming, short periods of quietness may be reinforced. If the reinforcer is potent enough, the quiet behaviour will increase and the incompatible behaviour of screaming will be reduced. As with all behaviour modification programmes, a complete functional analysis must precede the training programme. The reinforcer maintaining the unwanted behaviour must be identified and if possible applied to the incompatible behaviour (Fig. 8.9).

If this analysis shows the same contingencies on a number of occasions it could correctly be assumed that screaming is being reinforced by a particular nurse. Using a DRO procedure, the consequences could be changed so that every time Peter is engaging in

Antecedent	Behaviour	Consequence
Nurse X walks into room.	Peter begins to scream loudly.	Nurse X picks Peter up and cuddles him.

Fig. 8.9 Functional analysis of Peter's screaming behaviour.

a behaviour incompatible with screaming (quiet, talking, etc.), he receives reinforcement, i.e. Nurse X picks him up and gives him a cuddle. The effect of this process would be encourage behaviours which are more appropriate than screaming.

A description of a very intensive DRO programme to reduce persistent emesis is given by McCoull & Gardiner (1979):

A 12-year-old profoundly handicapped boy was admitted in a state of undernourishment. Although a volvulus of the stomach had been treated 3 years before, full investigations revealed no physical cause of vomiting. As antiemetics were ineffective it was concluded that the behaviour had become, 'dependent upon and was maintained by reinforcement contingencies'. The DRO programme was applied mainly during the hour after a meal and began with reinforcement by praise and cheek-stroking, then a primary reinforcer and verbal praise contingent upon non-vomiting behaviour.

During the first week of the programme the rate of emesis halved and continued to fall steadily. As the boy's weight increased, the reinforcement was faded effectively. After completing the programme, 2 years later, the boy was reported to be 'physically mature and healthy', have learned to dress and undress himself, to co-operate in play activities and generally to have increased in independence and quality of life (McCoull & Gardiner, 1979).

The DRO procedure is relatively straightforward and has been said to be the most acceptable way of reducing 'problem' behaviours. Having said this, it must still be treated as a powerful method of changing behaviour and consequently subjected to the same 'ethical' considerations as other procedures. It is often used in conjunction with a technique called *extinction*.

Extinction

It is possible to reduce the frequency of a behaviour by not presenting contingent rein-

| Before extinction procedure | | |
A	B	C
Nurse X walks into room.	Peter begins to scream.	Nurse X picks him up and cuddles him.

| During extinction procedure | | |
A	B	C
As above.	As above.	Nurse X ignores Peter's screams and carries on with whatever she intends to do.

Fig. 8.10

forcement. Extinction refers to the process whereby a reinforcer, which was previously available, is withheld (Fig. 8.10).

In the use of the extinction technique the reinforcing consequence is no longer presented; instead, Nurse X acts as if the screaming behaviour has not occurred. In other words, she is withholding reinforcement which was previously available to Peter. If the procedure is working, an initial increase in the behaviour concerned will be observed. This is known as an *extinction burst* and is followed by a dramatic decrease in the frequency of the behaviour. Usually the procedure is paired with DRO, e.g. a child who repeatedly swears in class might be ignored when he swears (extinction) and praised for any verbal behaviour other than swearing (DRO).

Extinction may be impossible to use in cases of self stimulatory behaviour where reinforcement is by internal stimulus. Also, when the behaviour to be reduced involves aggression to others or to the child himself, extinction is impossible and unwise because of the initial increase in the rate of the behaviour.

Punishment

Both extinction and DRO rely on the fact that reinforcement increases behaviour and therefore, by withholding or redirecting reinforcement, behaviours can be reduced.

Punishment is the opposite of reinforcement. It is a consequence of behaviour which reduces the future probability of that behaviour. When punishment is applied contingently upon a certain behaviour, that behaviour will be less likely to occur. For maximum effect, it must be delivered in the same manner as reinforcement — *clearly, contingently and consistently.*

Types of punishment procedures

Time-out from positive reinforcement (Leitenberg, 1965) commonly referred to as 'time-out,' thus obscuring the most important aspect of the technique. The term refers to a period of time where reinforcement is not available. Either the reinforcement itself is removed (*instant 'time-out'*) or the person is removed from the source of reinforcement (*isolation 'time-out'*). If the situation in which a behaviour occurs is not reinforcing, then the technique of time-out from positive reinforcement will have *no* effect. It differs from extinction in that the reinforcer is there, and then is removed for a short period (in extinction the reinforcer is withheld completely). It is similar to extinction only in the fact that it can often be paired with DRO.

Isolation 'time-out'

Jean, a 28-year-old severely handicapped woman, is reported to be 'disruptive' in the ward where she lives. This behaviour takes the form of high-pitched screaming and has an unsettling effect on the other residents. A programme aimed at reducing her screaming behaviour, using the procedure of 'time-out', begins in the ward. When Jean screams she is to be taken immediately out of the dayroom and into the dormitory area. After a predetermined time she is to be brought back to the dayroom. This procedure is to be carried out every time Jean screams. After 3 days ward staff report that Jean's screaming behaviour has increased.

In the example there is no mention of baseline data being collected, or of a functional analysis being carried out. The procedure of 'time-out' has been applied to a behaviour in a 'cook-book' fashion with no thought to the element of positive reinforcement. Obviously, the dayroom was not a reinforcing place for Jean. When she was removed, her screaming did not reduce (as it would have done if time-out was effective); in fact, the opposite happened. Being put into the dormitory (a consequence of screaming) seemed to increase the behaviour. It could therefore be said that in this case, the procedure used was not 'time-out' but was, in fact, seclusion.

Thorpe (1980), in his article concerning the misuse of the terms 'time-out' and 'seclusion' states that the concept of 'time-out' is not appropriate unless certain requirements have been satisfied, including: 'the careful definition and identification of the behaviour under investigation, a behavioural analysis of what is maintaining the behaviour, and the facilities for monitoring the effects of the 'time-out' intervention for the person under training.' He goes on to say that, if these requirements are not met, the procedure of isolating a person is an example of seclusion and, 'it is unwise to name it otherwise'.

A more commonly used form of the technique is instant 'time-out'.

Instant 'time-out'

Barbara's parents and teachers report that she has started to use her fingers instead of her knife and fork at meal-times. They have observed her very carefully and both parties feel that it is 'laziness' on Barbara's part. If this behaviour is allowed to continue, she will be kept at the 'baby' table during school meal-times and it is felt that some of her other skills may deteriorate. After the unsuccessful application of other techniques (DRO, prompting), it is decided to try Instant 'time-out'. Whenever Barbara began to finger feed she was told: 'No', and her plate or food removed for a period of 10 seconds. The plate was then returned and she was prompted to use her knife and fork and praised for doing so (DRO).

Note that other ways of increasing Barbara's use of her knife and fork were tried first.

'Time-out' would not be used unless all positive methods had failed. Even then, when using both instant and isolation 'time-out' ethical guidelines must be referred to and all parties involved must be informed fully and give consent for the programme to begin.

Instant time-out from positive reinforcement involves removing the reinforcer itself.

Isolation time-out from positive reinforcement requires that the person be removed from the source of reinforcement.

Overcorrection

Similarly to 'time-out', overcorrection has become a blanket term. In practice it consists of two components — restitution and positive practice. Restitution involves restoring the environment to the state it was in before a particular behaviour occurred (e.g. picking up jigsaw pieces which have been thrown) and normally includes the over-correcting of environmental disturbances (e.g. more pieces than were actually thrown should be picked up). Positive practice, on the other hand, requires repeating behaviours which are seen as more appropriate or which should have occurred instead (e.g. completing three jigsaws correctly). When possible, both components should be applied contingently upon the occurrence of the behaviour to be reduced. Physical guidance can be used where there is a reluctance to co-operate or where there is confusion about what behaviour is expected.

Example 1
Azrin & Armstrong (1973) incorporated the overcorrection procedure into a feeding programme with profoundly handicapped adults. Spilling of food resulted in the 'students' cleaning the table. Throwing of utensils or food was also immediately corrected by the person responsible rather than removing him from the dining room (restitution). In addition, correct forms of the behaviour were practised. For example, if food was spilt from an overflowing spoon,

several practice trials in loading very small amounts of food onto the spoon were given (positive practice). If the 'student' seemed to be having difficulty at any stage, manual guidance was used to help him through the procedure.

Note. Reinforcement is never used *during* overcorrection but should be delivered when appropriate behaviour occurs at other times.

Example 2
The same technique was used in a programme concerned with toilet training (Azrin & Foxx, 1971). If a 'student' urinated on the floor or wet his pants, he was required to mop up the floor or wash out his pants (restitution). He was then taken to the toilet area and sat on the toilet on several occasions (positive practice). The technique of overcorrection was not used on its own, but, as always, in conjunction with reward programmes for appropriate behaviour.

Murphy (1978) states that, 'there is some confusion over the meaning of the term (overcorrection), its general applicability and its mode of action'. She is particularly concerned with the 'cookbook' application of the technique to certain 'undesirable' forms of behaviour and points out that it should only be used after completion of a proper functional analysis. In her recommendations concerning the future use of the term, she also suggests: 'it be accepted that overcorrection is a punishment technique requiring careful ethical consideration before use and preferably concurrent positive reinforcement programmes when in clinical use.' Claims regarding the positive 'educational nature' of overcorrection are attacked by Murphy and she recommends that these claims be dropped, at least until formal data appears 'to support the contention'.

Other forms of punishment procedures

There are a variety of terms associated in the literature with punishment. Kazdin (1975, pp. 146–171) gives a detailed appreciation of these. One particular form must be mentioned here, if only because it would be noticeable by its absence. Aversion therapy, involving physical restraint or electric shocks contingent upon a particular behaviour, has been one of the most controversial areas of concern in the use of behaviour modification techniques. Corbett (1975) considers that 'no informed discussion of the ethical issues is possible' without first considering the evidence for the 'efficacy and justification' for this particular form of treatment. It is not appropriate to detail the efficacy and justification here, but Corbett's review of the evidence is recommended for further reading.

Ethical issues

The behaviour of everyone who interacts socially is controlled in some way. Agents of this control include employers, parents, peers and spouses. Whether they mean to or not, these agents provide consequences or fail to provide consequences for behaviour. As discussed earlier, presenting consequences (e.g. reinforcement or punishment) or failing to present them (extinction) influence behaviour. Therefore our behaviour is always modified whether or not a particular programme has been designed for this purpose. The ethical concern does not appear to be with the science per se, but rather with the purposes for which the science is used and the people who will have the power to exert control.

In an attempt to reduce some of this concern, the Zangwill Committee produced a report formulating ethical guidelines for the conduct of programmes of behaviour modification in the National Health Service. As the report is available from HMSO and the details of the guidelines can be read at any library, it has been decided here to look at a review of the report rather than the report itself.

In his review, Yule (1982) agrees with one of the major statements of the report, that the goals of behaviour modification are socially determined and that value judgements are 'inevitably involved'. He then argues:' — but so too they are in deciding to use drugs, psychoanalysis, ECT, psychosurgery or even letting well alone'. He suggests that the committee should have broadened their terms of reference to enquire into all treatments which aim to modify the behaviour of National Health patients. Readers of the paper are urged to be concerned with the extent to which choice between alternative therapies is determined by reference to the evidence of efficiency of treatment, reminding us that behaviour therapy 'has been demonstrated to be more effective than other interventions for a variety of problems'. His concluding remark on the ethical principle is that therapists should always employ 'that intervention which is least restrictive, least intrusive and most effective in a particular case, as indicated by current empirical evidence'.

In addition to the Zangwill Committee there are a number of bodies who have produced ethical guidelines for practitioners of behaviour modification; for example, the British Association for Behavioural Psychotherapy (BABP, 1980), the American Association for the Advancement of Behaviour Therapy (AABT, 1977) and ethics committees run by local health authorities. Gelfand and Hartmann (1975) have drawn up a list of questions which the therapist must answer affirmatively if the rights and welfare of the client and his caretakers are to be protected. They are as follows:

1. *Caretaker Permission.* Did you obtain the appropriate care agent's fully informed consent to carry out the proposed modification programme? Did the caretakers understand that they could withdraw (in the case of a child) participation at any time?

2. *School* or *Treatment Agency Permission.* If the programme is to be carried out at a school or institution, did the responsible officials give their fully informed consent?

3. *Child/Client Consent.* If appropriate in terms of age and abilities, did the client also give fully informed consent? Does he understand that he can withdraw at any time?

4. *Consensus.* Is there agreement among

those responsible for the client's welfare that the anticipated behaviour change is desirable?

5. *Treatment Methods.* Will positive methods be used to modify the target behaviour?

6. *Aversive Procedures.* Are these to be used only after Positive Methods were tried and failed? Are they to be accompanied by Positive consequences of desired behaviour? Does the potential benefit to the client clearly outweigh any discomfort he might experience?

7. *Protection of Rights.* Are the client's legal rights protected? Does he have access to an adequate diet, comfortable and safe surroundings, exercise, education and recreation?

8. *Right to Effective Treatment.* Is the client receiving the most effective treatment currently available for his particular behavioural problem?

PUTTING IT ALL TOGETHER

The goal-planning system

The principle of using a simple training document has been developed in America over the past 10 years. The aim has been to produce a single sheet covering relevant aspects of the residents' needs, so that the people who are concerned with their welfare can, where possible, in conjunction with the resident, come to agreement in respect of the important areas that should be covered, and thereafter can follow the same precise pattern of intervention.

Houts & Scott (1973) are the people responsible for initiating one such system, Goal Planning. They suggest that four strategies are necessary for successful practice:

1. *Involve the client*
a. Treat the client the way that you would like to be treated. Put yourself in his shoes and try to feel what he feels.
b. The client's likes and wants should be part of each goal that is set.
c. As much as possible, the client should participate in setting goals.
d. Always explain the goals to the client.

2. *Use the client's strengths to set goals which help his needs*
a. Make a list of the client's strengths — what he can do, what he likes to do, and other people who are willing to help.
b. Make a list of his needs — possible goal areas.
c. Review the strength list to see how his strengths can be used to help with his needs.

3. *Use small steps to reach the goal*
a. Try to make each step something you can achieve in a few days to a week.
b. Each step should be mastered before going on to the next.
c. If you aren't making progress, it's probably because your steps aren't small enough.

4. *State clearly who will do what, and when*
a. Describe what the client will do or how he will be acting when the goal is achieved.
b. Make some person or persons responsible for helping the client achieve each step.
c. Always have a target date for the step you are working on. (This can be changed.)
d. Spell out clearly what is to be done so that a new person could read the plan and know what to do.

Bonham (1980) has described an extremely efficient way of completing the 'single training form'; the following is an outline of his method.

Both sides of the sheet designated 'The Goal Planning Sheet' are used. Side One is concerned with the client's descriptive data including such information as his abilities, suggested interventions needed and any necessary procedures to be carried out before those interventions can be made (see Fig. 8.11). Side Two is used to describe the type of intervention, who will carry it out, and how (see Fig. 8.12). Thus, one side presents definitive data on the aims and abilities of the person being considered, and from this a series of programmes are developed based on carefully considered goals.

SIDE 1 OF THE GOAL PLANNING FORM

```
NAME:    JANE THOMSON              FILE NO._____    SHEET NO.____

D.O.B. _____             WARD/ADDRESS_____

DATE    30.7.81 _____             _____


PRESENT AT DISCUSSION:
```

STRENGTHS	AIMS
Likes bright colours Likes disco music Likes swimming Can wash and dry face and hands independently Is friendly with Mrs Wood, who lives next door Co-operates with Mother Likes adult attention	To brush teeth independently To tie shoelaces independently To have friends her own age To colour match To have new glasses To have review of anti-convulsant drugs
MATTERS ARISING	**ACTION TAKEN**
Charge Nurse will contact optician for appointment re eye test. Dr A. will take blood sample phenytoin level and report to Charge Nurse.	Appointment made for 10.7.81. Blood sample sent off on 1.9.81 – now awaiting result.

Fig. 8.11 Side 1 of the goal planning form.

Side One

Strengths

The word 'strengths' has been selected to emphasise that this section of the sheet is concerned with the positive aspects of the person's behaviour. This section should list all of the major achievements of the person and the type of things he likes doing, or spend regular time doing. Strengths can be separated between: 'strengths as abilities', 'strengths as likes' and 'strengths as common activities'.

Strengths as abilities. It is not possible to list all of the person's abilities; highlights must be

SIDE 2 OF THE GOAL PLANNING FORM

```
NAME:  JANE THOMSON    DATE_____    WARD_____    FILE NO. _____

_____

GOAL/STEP                PROCEDURE                           DATE
                                                             ACHIEVED
_____

Will brush teeth in      After breakfast, tea and supper,
imitation of Mother,     Jane's mother will take her to
three times per day.     the bathroom.  She will have one
                         toothbrush with toothpaste on for
                         herself and one for Jane. After
                         saying, 'Jane, brush your teeth',
                         Mrs Thomson will model the action.
                         If Jane copies her, she will
                         praise her enthusiastically and
                         record a tick in Jane's homework
                         book.  If she does not copy, Mrs
                         Thomson will take Jane's hand
                         and help her to brush, praise
                         her and record a cross in the
                         book.
```

Fig. 8.12 Side 2 of the goal planning form.

selected, covering the more outstanding features of the person. For example, if the person was moderately handicapped it would not be unusual for him to be able to dress, undress and wash himself. If these are normally occurring, a simple statement, 'is capable of independent personal hygiene and care' would be sufficient to cover all these areas. In fact, some abilities such as walking and feeding would be accepted as present without being written in such a case. Alternatively, the fact that he travels by bus may be more outstanding, and so should be stated 'can travel independently by bus on familiar routes'.

Important features of that person's functioning should be picked out covering such questions as: is he capable of feeding himself? is he able to count money? is he capable of independent travel? Abilities will vary markedly according to the level of handicap of the person. A profile should then be established which delineates the high points of the person's strengths (see Fig. 8.11).

Strengths as likes. Sweets, cigarettes, going for walks, watching T.V. may be listed in this section if they are important reinforcers for that person. The principle of seeing strengths as likes is to develop an idea as to the form of activity or item which could be used to encourage appropriate changes in the person. Listing 'strengths as likes' is done to seek reinforcers which will be relevant in setting up the subsequent programmes.

Strengths as common activities. The Premack Principle is the theory behind listing strengths as common activities. For example, if a child runs around frequently (perhaps described as hyperactive), then he may be encouraged to sit quietly for a short period by being given the reward of being allowed to run around freely after he has done this. Conversely, a person who chooses to sit sleeping in a chair or likes to go to bed for long periods in the day can be encouraged to activity with the reward of that period of inactivity. It is, therefore, clear that any commonly occurring regular activity can be used as a potential reinforcer, and so should be listed as a strength.

Aims

The aims section of the 'Goal Planning Sheet' covers an agreed list of maintenance procedures and/or possible changes related to the person being considered. Maintenance procedures are those needed for the continued health and wellbeing of the person, e.g. to ensure adequate liquid intake in a profoundly handicapped person, or that a diabetic is given the appropriate injections of insulin each day. Any procedure which is considered outside the normal routines of the area should not be included as a maintenance procedure.

The possible changes are those changes which are considered relevant to improve the person and his lifestyle. All changes that could be executed before the subsequent review should be included, together with proposed long-term aims.

Each aim should be assigned a number according to its importance and then sequentially arranged. This number is also written alongside the training or maintenance procedures on Side two of the sheet. This acts to clarify which aim is covered by the programmes written. An aim should be stated in terms which define the desired end point of the treatment period, e.g. if the aim is to get the person to tie his shoelaces by himself, it is better written: 'Tommy will tie his shoelaces independently' rather than: 'To get Tommy to tie his shoelaces independently'.

All aims describe a state which it is hoped to reach: the state that a person would be at when they have completed the period of training.

Matters arising

This section caters for questions which arise which cannot be answered immediately, dealing with issues like medication, physiotherapy, assessment and consultation of people outside the meeting. Each matter arising should be designated to a particular person, and they should be named on the document (e.g. 'Mrs Murray will assess Jane's reading ability').

Action taken

After Mrs Murray has assessed Jane, she gives her report to the programme co-ordinator so that it can be written into this section of the form (Fig. 8.11).

Side Two

The aims have been listed according to their priorities on Side One. On Side Two, the highest priorities are formulated into an appropriate procedure. The principle that must always be observed is that the goals (or steps towards a goal) should be achieved by the time of the next review. All goals and steps must be written in simple form and defined in measurable terms. The purpose of clearly defined statements is to make certain that a record will show any improvements or change in the aimed-for activities. The procedures should be witten next to the appropriate goal/step and each procedure should be a clear, concise description of the behavioural programme. This will enable any other person who has to take over the programme to follow the same procedure as has previously been in operation.

Bonham suggests that the Goal Planning Sheet be completed at a meeting called by those people delegated to the care of the person under consideration. In a hospital, he feels this would most suitably be a Charge Nurse, whilst in an Adult Training Centre or hostel, a Manager, or Deputy Manager, would be charged with this first step. He goes on to say that those present at such a meeting should be the person himself, his parents and all of the staff concerned with the person, including professional advisory staff when necessary. For example, if there is any question or problems of mobility, a physiotherapist may be requested to be present, or a medical practitioner where there is any direct medical problem.

The Goal Planning System can be an effective tool in the care of the handicapped person. It is systematic and, if guidelines are followed, easy to operate. Perhaps one of its more attractive features is that it concentrates on the positive aspects of behaviour and uses these to develop and encourage new skills. As far as implementation is concerned, staff shortage may appear to be a problem, as the system involves organising one meeting to discuss each person. However, in considering this problem, Houts & Scott advise staff to '. . . begin in small steps, one person at a time . . .'; they offer further encouragement by stating that '. . . by developing strengths of clients they will need less care'. This could be taken a step further by suggesting that staff would be more free to concentrate on wider aspects of care and, perhaps more importantly, the handicapped person would have a greater part to play in a decision-making process which is going to affect his style of life.

This particular system produces all the relevant information on one single sheet which can either be substituted for or incorporated into the Nursing Process file. Another system which makes this provision is the Portage Guide (Shearer & Shearer, 1972), which will be discussed in the following section. Although originally designed for use with parents of pre-school children living at home this early intervention system can be adapted for use with adults and some residents in institutions.

Early intervention

There are a number of advantages in training parents to be behaviour change agents. Firstly, the problem of how to generalise new behaviours does not occur, because learning is taking place in the child's natural environment. Secondly, the 'therapist' is always on hand to make use of spontaneous learning situations, and thirdly, the new behaviours will be likely to be maintained at a high level due to the continued presence of naturally occurring reinforcers (parents). Basinger & Watson (1974) developed this line of thought and produced their Parent Training Technology System (PTTS), which provides a method for training parents in behavioural procedures.

In Britain in 1971, the Government White Paper, Better Services for the Mentally handicapped recognised the fact that parents required practical guidance on how best to help their handicapped child, indicating that we may be embarking upon a new way of looking at care and training of the handicapped, one which had already taken firm roots in the U.S.A. The Warnock Report (1978) stressed the need for early intervention, but did not detail how such a system could be implemented. It did, however, suggest that a 'named person' should be responsible for contact between service agencies and the parents of children with special needs. The report stated that for pre-school children the health visitor should automatically assume this role, an assumption challenged by Mittler (1978), who questioned the existing provision for an 'intensive programme of in-service training', which he felt would be required for health visitors. He indicated that the report might have expanded on the relationship of the health visitor to the District handicap teams and the Child Development Centres proposed by the Court Committee. A number of areas have attempted to develop this relationship — Northumbria, South Glamorgan, Wessex — by making use of a programmed learning system with parents of mentally handicapped children referred by health visitors or other agencies. One such learning system is the Portage Guide to Early Education.

The Portage Guide

This project was first funded in 1969 by the American Bureau of Education for the handicapped, and was originally designed for use with parents of pre-school mentally handicapped children in the rural area of Wisconsin, taking its name from the town of Portage. This system makes use of a 'home advisor' (named person) who visits families once per week, setting goals and preparing training programmes for children who are developmentally delayed. In 1972, the experimental edition was published and, after an evaluation of replication sites, the revised edition was produced in 1976.

Staff of the project were not satisfied with the range of curriculum material already in use and decided to develop their own. They designed a Guide to Early Education, which came in three parts:

1. Developmentally sequential *checklist* covering development stages from birth to 6 years in the areas of cognition, language, self help, motor and socialisation. The titles of each stage are stated behaviourally and the checklist is colour-coded and numbered.
2. *Card file*, which is colour-coded and numbered to correspond with the checklist. Each card contains teaching suggestions related to the behaviours stated on the checklist.
3. *Manual of Instruction*, which includes specific directions for completing the checklist and use of the cards. An outline of how to carry out a task analysis and state behavioural objectives is given, and there are also short sections on reinforcement, types of aid (prompts) and certain behavioural procedures.

On using Portage firstly, a checklist is completed for each child to pinpoint the behaviours exhibited in the five developmental areas (baseline data). This serves as an informal assessment and is often paired with a standardised developmental measure. Clements et al (1980) chose to use the Griffith Mental Development Scales, while Shearer & Shearer report the use of varied assessment tools; Alpen & Boll (1969), the Cattell Infant Scale (Cattell, 1940); the Peabody Picture Vocabulary Tests (Dunn, 1965) and the Slossen Intelligence Tests for Children and Adults (Slossen, 1963).

After the checklist has been completed, the home advisor, in conjunction with the parents, plans a curriculum for the child, following which a system of weekly visiting begins. During each visit a goal(s) is set which can be achieved in a week. The home advisor demonstrates the appropriate teaching procedure, then asks the parent to model the activity. An 'Activity Chart' is left in the home, giving detailed instructions about the task to be taught and the method for recording the child's performance each day (Fig. 8.13).

In the original project four certified Special Education teachers and three 'para-professionals' were employed and trained to serve as 'home teachers'. The inservice training included instruction in child development, assessment techniques and behaviour modification techniques. In the South Glamorgan project the two home teachers employed were nursery nurses who worked under the supervision of clinical psychologists. After the research phase, the availability of the service was extended to the whole county of South Glamorgan. In their conclusions, Clements et al identified some areas of the project requiring investigation:

1. Evaluation of the need for *weekly* visiting — less regular visits would allow the home teacher to support larger caseloads and to include children with a single handicap, e.g. physical, sensory and language handicapped children.
2. Training of parents for the role of 'home teacher'; several families are reported to have succeeded in this with the support of existing home teachers.
3. The contribution of parents' groups among those receiving the service. A survey has indicated that some parents like this idea and a study has been designed to evaluate the effectiveness of such groups.

Among users of the Portage System it seems to be generally agreed that the section on language could be improved upon. In the revised language section there is now greater provision made for the more handicapped

```
                          ACTIVITY CHART

CHECKLIST NUMBER    _____      ATTAINED    _____

CHILD'S NAME        _____      NOT ATTAINED _____

HOME TEACHER'S NAME _____
                                    B                                P
                                    A                                O
                                    S                                S
                                    E                                T
                                    L                                E
                                    I                                L
                                    N                                I
                                    E                                N
                                                                     E
BEHAVIOUR TO BE TAUGHT:
                                    4
State the behavioural objective


BEHAVIOUR TO BE RECORDED:           3

State number of times per day
the child is required to
practise the task (e.g. four        2
times per day)


                                    1  _____

                                       Mon. Tues. Wed. Thurs. Fri. Sat. Sun. Mon.


DIRECTIONS:


STATE:   1.  Where to work if it is important.

         2.  Who will carry out the training, and exactly how they
             will do this.

         3.  What the reinforcement is, and how to deliver it.

         4.  Type of prompts (or aid) to be used.

         5.  What to do if the child fails (correction procedure).

         6.  How to record the sessions on the graph.
```

Fig. 8.13

person but as with some of the other developmental sections, the gap between steps is still too great. If, however, the home teacher has a good grounding in the behavioural approach to training, the complete system can be used, as stated in its title, as a *guide* to curriculum planning and aim-setting.

The Activity Chart itself can be adapted to suit the type of records kept in a ward/unit situation and the system fits in well with the Goal Planning approach, offering developmentally sequential target behaviours which can be used as goals and providing teaching suggestions which can be incorporated into the procedure section or the Goal Planning Sheet. In Edinburgh, a small research project proved the value of this system with institutionalised adult mental handicapped people (Kennedy, 1978).

There are a number of formal systems which can be used as vehicles for behaviour change. Establishments such as the British Institute for Mental Handicap and the Hester Adrian Centre are constantly producing literature based on current research. Chris Cullen from the Hester Adrian Centre is currently directing a DHSS research project which is evaluating the effect of the nursing process on resident behaviour in a mental handicap setting. Whatever the system or choice, there is one point which is worth noting, as Bernie & Fordyce (1973) put it:

> It is well to remember that behaviour is behaviour, whether it be that of a patient or a nurse.

Successful programme implementation requires that reinforcement contingencies be applied to staff behaviour as well as to the behaviour of those in their care. It is not enough to supply theoretical information on new methods; motivation and encouragement are necessary during the early stages until results become obvious and, in themselves, prove to be reinforcing. In some instances staff reinforcement works against establishing learning environments. For example, let us consider this hypothetical situation which could exist on any high dependency children's ward.

On this particular ward the majority of children go to bed wearing nappies, which are changed on regular 'bed rounds' by staff on night duty. It has been decided that a small number of children should be wakened and toileted at specific times during the night. What are the reinforcers for staff? It may be that the workload is quite a bit lighter if staff do not toilet the children. If they do waken them, slippers have to be found, dressing gowns put on, children guided to the toilets, hands washed, etc. Rewards for staff are difficult to identify. A reduction in the number of wet beds may spring to mind as rewarding, but this could be achieved with less effort, i.e. by keeping the children in nappies. Increased independence for the child will probably not be obvious at the start of the programme, therefore positive feedback for staff may be missing. Unless this can be provided at a different level, for example, from nursing management, staff may, in fact, be reinforced for changing the children in bed, the contingency being a lighter or less time-consuming workload.

Cullen & Woods (1980) identified the need in long-term wards somehow to persuade direct-core staff to behave differently because what they and, to a lesser degree, other 'professionals' do has 'a profound effect on residents' behaviour'. They put forward 'room management' as one useful solution to the 'lack of staff' argument often used when programme implementation is mentioned. One person (the room manager) assumes responsibility for the group of residents, ensuring that suitable materials are available, prompting residents to use materials and encouraging those already engaged in a task. The remaining staff work on invidual training sessions which are more structured (see also Porterfield & Blunden, 1978).

Cullen & Woods do not offer answers to the issue of changing staff behaviour, but what they do suggest is that assets already present could be built on, e.g.

— Developing the use of the Nursing Process which has much in common with the behavioural approach.
— Closer attention to organisational factors which could increase the number of opportunities to engage in appropriate behaviour (e.g. minor changes in the physical environment).
— More attention by behavioural researchers into staff selection, e.g. why do certain staff behave in a therapeutic way even in the absence of change in the residents' behaviour, or when no unpleasant consequence will be applied to them if they fail to exhibit this behaviour?

SUMMARY

Observation and analysis or behaviour

— Identify the behaviour you are interested in
— Look at the behaviour in relation to the environment in which it occurs i.e. carry out a *functional analysis*.
— Employ the appropriate recording method to collect a baseline of the frequency or the behaviour.
— Using the same recording method continually evaluate the change process.
— Keep clear and precise records at all times.

Teaching new behaviours

— *Positive reinforcement* is the most common technique. Remember that this can be either *primary, secondary* or *social* and must be delivered *contingently*.
— Additional teaching techniques are
  prompting
  fading
  chaining
  shaping
— Remember the importance of *imitation*, use it as the first choice when selecting technique. It is quick and efficient.
— Build *generalisation* into every programme. This prevents problems at a later date.
— Ask *why* the behaviour is to be changed. Will it be for the ultimate benefit of the client?
— Obtain informed consent, if possible from the client himself or from parents/caretakers.

Reducing excess behaviours

— Collect data on the Baseline rate of behaviour and carry out a proper Functional Analysis or a reasonable period of time.
— Decide who will take responsibility and choose an appropriately qualified person to carry out the treatment programme.
— Try positive approaches first, particularly Differential Reinforcement. Only if these fail should punishment techniques be used, and then only in conjunction with positive techniques.
— Record all treatment sessions accurately and evaluate the programme continually.
— Remember to check informed consent and if necessary consult with the appropriate ethics committee.

Programme implementation

— Call a meeting of the relevant people to discuss the change process. Remember to include, wherever possible, the person being considered and/or his nearest relative, plus any staff who will be involved in the programme.
— Try to build on existing skills that the person has.
— Attempt to identify staff reinforcers; e.g. what will encourage them to continue the programme.
— Review the programme on a regular basis, for example, set a target behaviour to be attained by a particular time, a month hence, two months, or whatever time span is decided upon.
— Keep precise and easily available records at all stages at the change process.

REFERENCES

Allyon T, Haughton E, Hughes H B 1965 Interpretation of symptoms: fact or fiction? Behaviour Research and Therapy 3: 1–17
Alpern G, Boll T 1969 Developmental skill age inventory. Unpublished manuscript, Indiana University Medical Centre, United States
American Association of Behaviour Therapy 1977 Ethical issues for human services. Behaviour Therapy 8: 763–764
American Association on Mental Deficiency 1974 Adaptive behaviour scale for children and adults (1974 revision). American Association on Mental Deficiency, Washington.
Azrin N M, Armstrong P M 1973 The 'Mini-meal' — A method for teaching eating skills to the profoundly retarded. Mental Retardation 11: 9–13
Azrin N H, Foxx R M 1971 A rapid method of toilet-training the institutionalised retarded. Journal of Applied Behavioural Analysis 4: 89–99
Bandura A 1969 Principles of behaviour modification. Holt, Rinehart and Winston, New York
Basinger, Watson, 1974 Parent training technology. Mental Retardation 12: 3–10

Bernie R, Fordyce W E 1973 Behaviour modification and the nursing process. Mosby, St Louis

Bijou S W, Peterson R F, Harris F R, Allen K E, Johnston M S 1969 Methodology for experimental studies of young children in natural settings. Psychological Record 19: 117–210

Bonham K 1980 Guidelines to the goal-planning system. Unpublished.

British Association of Behavioural Psychotherapy 1980 Guidelines for good practice

Carr J 1980 Helping your handicapped child. Penguin, Harmondsworth

Cattell P 1940 Cattell infant scale. The Psychological Corporation, New York

Clements J C, Bidder R T Gardner S, Bryant G, Grey O P 1980 A Home-advisory Service for pre-school children with developmental delays. Child: Care, Health and Development 6: 25–33

Corbett J 1975 Aversion for the treatment of self-injurious behaviour. Journal of Mental Deficiency Research 19: 79–94

Cullen C, Woods P 1981 Determinants of staff behaviour on long-term wards. In press

Dunn L M 1965 Peabody Picture Vocabulary Test. American Guidance Service, Minneapolis, Minnesota.

Evans I M 1971 Theoretical and experimental aspects of the Behaviour Modification approach to autistic children. In:Rutter M (ed) Infantile autism: concepts, characteristics and treatment. Churchill Livingstone, Edinburgh

Gelfand D M, Hartmann D P 1975 Child behaviour — analysis and therapy. Pergamon General Psychology series. Pergamon Press, Inc., New York

Hemsley R, Carr J Ways of increasing Behaviour-Reinforcement. In: Yule W, Carr J (eds) Behaviour modification for the mentally handicapped, Croom Helm, London p 33–47

Hilgard E, Atkinson R 1975 An introduction to psychology. Harcourt Brace, p 195–200

Hoch E L 1971 Experimental contributions to clinical psychology. Brooks-Cole, Montary

Houts P S, Scott R A 1975 Goal Planning with developmentally Disabled persons.

Kazdin A E 1975 Behaviour modification in applied settings. Dorsey Press, Homewood, Illinois

Kennedy E P 1979 An application of the Portage teaching programme in an institutional setting. Master of Philosophy Thesis, Edinburgh University

Kirman B, Bicknell J 1975 Mental handicap. Churchill Livingstone, Edinburgh

Leitenberg H 1965 Psychological Bulletin 64: 428–444

McCoull K, Gardiner S 1979 'Good boy, Hugh, clean mouth'. Nursing Mirror, December: 37–39

MacKrell K, Todgood R, Stanley B 1980 Behaviour Modification: technique or analysis? Apex 8(2): 62–63

Mittler P 1978 Needs of the under-fives. Special Education: Forward Trends 5(3): 12–13

Moore P, Carr J 1976 Behaviour modification programme. Nursing Times Occasional Paper. 2 September.

Murphy G H 1978 Overcorrection: A critique. Journal of Mental Deficiency Research 22: 161–173

Murphy G, Goodall E 1978 Measurement error in direct observation: A comparison of recording methods. Behaviour Research and Therapy 18(2): 147–150

Porterfield J, Blunden R 1978 Establishing an activity period and individual skills training within a day setting for profoundly mentally handicapped adults. Journal of Practical Approaches to Developmental Handicap 2(3): 10–25

Powel J, Martindale B, Kulps Martindale A, Bauman R 1977 Taking a closer look: time-sampling and measurement error. Journal of Applied Behavioural Analysis 10: 325–332

Schaffer H R, Emerson P E 1964 The development of social attachment in infancy. Monograph of Social Research in Child Development 29: Serial No. 94

Schrag P, Divoky D 1981 The myth of the hyperactive child and other means of child control. Penguin, Harmondsworth

Shearer M S, Shearer D E 1972 The Portage Project: a model for early childhood education. Exceptional Children 39: 210–217

Skinner B F 1953 Science and human behaviour. Macmillan, New York

Slossen R 1963 Slossen intelligence test for children and adults. Slossen Educational Corporation, New York

Thorpe J G 1980 Time-out or seclusion. Nursing Times April: 604

Williams C 1980 A programme for the mentally handicapped. Nursing 19: 838–839

Yule W, Carr J 1980 Behaviour modification for the mentally handicapped. Croom Helm, London

Zangwill O L (Chairman) 1980 Behaviour Modification: Report of a Joint Working Party to formulate Ethical Guidelines for the conduct of Programmes of Behaviour Modification in the National Health Service: A Consultation Document with suggested Guidelines. HMSO, London.

Zeilder M D, Jervey S S 1968 Development of behaviour: self-feeding. Journal of Consulting and Clinical Psychology 32(2): 164–168

GLOSSARY

Backward chaining	The final step in a chain of behaviours is taught first, as in dressing. This is the opposite to Forward Chaining, in which teaching begins with the first step.
Baseline	Record of the rate of behaviour *before* training begins. The baseline recording is used to evaluate the effect of the training programme.
Behaviour	Any response or activity of an individual which can be seen and measured.
Behaviour modification	The systematic use of principles and procedures derived from Learning Theory, particularly Reinforcement Theory, in a teaching situation.
Chaining	Teaching a behaviour in a series of small steps to form a chain.
Contingency	The relationship between a behaviour and the events (consequences) which follow that behaviour.

Continuous reinforcement	A schedule of reinforcement in which a behaviour is reinforced every time it occurs.
Deprivation	The deliberate withholding of a specific reward to increase its reinforcing properties, e.g. a particular toy may be locked away and used only during training sessions.
Differential reinforcement of other behaviour (DRO)	Reinforcement occurs only when the person is not performing the target behaviour. Behaviours other than the target behaviour are reinforced. The effect of this procedure is to *decrease* the target behaviour.
Discrimination	Control of behaviour by Discriminative Stimuli (see below). Responding differently in the presence of different signals. For example, a child who has been toilet trained on a blue potty may refuse to use a yellow one. The blue potty is the signal for toilet behaviour and its subsequent reward.
Discriminative stimulus (S^D)	A signal that a certain behaviour will be reinforced. This is a result of the pairing of the S^D and the reinforcer so that the behaviour is reinforced in the presence of the S^D. For example, a certain nurse may become an S^D because she always responds angrily to a child who swears. In this case, if the child is reinforced by her annoyance, seeing her could be the 'signal' to him that swearing behaviour will be reinforced.
Extinction	Non-presentation of reinforcement. A behaviour which was previously followed by a reinforcing consequence is no longer reinforced and therefore weakens.
Extinction burst	An increase in the frequency and intensity of a behaviour at the beginning of an extinction programme. This is one indication that the procedure is having an effect.
Fading	Gradually reducing the amount of help (prompts) being given.
Fixed interval	Schedule of reinforcement under which a specified behaviour is only reinforced following a *fixed interval of time* since the previous reinforcement, e.g. every 3 minutes.
Fixed ratio	Schedule of reinforcement under which reinforcement is presented following a specified number of responses, e.g. after every fourth brick is stacked.

Functional analysis	Method of analysing the relationship between a behaviour and the environment in which it occurs.
Generalisation	A behaviour which is performed in one situation will also be performed in another, e.g. a child who has learned to use a knife and fork at home will also do so when at school, in a restaurant or when visiting friends.
Instant time-out (From Positive Reinforcement)	Removal of a positive reinforcer for a specified period of time, e.g. taking away a toy from a child who is scratching others, removing a spoon which is being used to bang the table rather to eat with. The reinforcer is always returned after a short period and the person prompted to behave appropriately.
Intermittent reinforcement	General term for schedules of reinforcement where the behaviour is not reinforced every time it occurs, only certain responses are reinforced. Very effective in strengthening behaviour.
Imitation/modelling	Copying what another person (a model) does. Sometimes referred to as Observational Learning, this technique is the quickest way to teach new behaviours.
Isolation time-out (From Positive Reinforcement)	Removal of the person from the source of reinforcement. This can be outside the door of a room, into a corner or into a special 'Time-out' room. After a specified period of time, the person is returned to the source of reinforcement and prompted to behave appropriately.
Negative reinforcement	The process by which a behaviour is strengthened or increases when a negative reinforcer is removed. For instance, you might turn down the sound on a loud television — the loud sound would be the negative reinforcer; turning down the sound would be reinforced by its removal. Negative reinforcement is 'taking away' something that is 'bad' or that you don't like.
Negative reinforcer	An aversive event (e.g. getting wet) which, when removed, increases the frequency of the behaviour which caused its removal (e.g. putting up an umbrella).
Overcorrection	A punishment technique consisting of two parts. *Restitution*: Restoring the environment to the condition it

	was in before the behaviour occurred. *Positive practice*: Practising correct forms of the behaviour.
Positive reinforcer	An event which, when it follows a behaviour, increases the chance of that behaviour occurring in the future.
Premack principle	This principle states that where an individual freely engages in any pair of behaviours, the more frequent one will reinforce the less frequent one, e.g. a hyperactive child may be reinforced for sitting for short periods by allowing him to run about contingent upon sitting behaviour.
Primary reinforcer	Generally considered to be something which is in itself rewarding, i.e. not learned. Examples are food, drink, sex, warmth and sleep.
Prompting	Changing the setting to make the behaviour more likely to occur. This can be by giving *physical assistance*, gesturing, or by verbal direction.
Punishment	An event which, when it follows a behaviour, *reduces* the likelihood of that behaviour occurring in the future. Punishment is the *opposite* of reinforcement.
Response cost	A punishment procedure where there is a 'penalty' or 'fine' contingent upon a specified behaviour. Usually paired with a token system of reinforcement.
Satiation	When a reward has been available for such an extended period, or in such great quantities that it is no longer effective as a positive reinforcer, satiation is said to have occurred.
Secondary reinforcement	Something which has become reinforcing through association with primary reinforcers (pairing). Money is a good example of secondary reinforcement.
Schedule of reinforcement	The rule denoting which responses orhow many responses will receive reinforcement.
Shaping	A method of teaching new behaviours by reinforcing behaviours which are *similar* to that which you are trying to develop. Begin with a behaviour that already exists and only reinforce variations in it that are near to the target behaviour (sometimes these variations are referred to as *successive approximations*).
Target behaviour	The behaviour to be altered or changed during a behaviour modification programme.
Time sampling	Observing and recording a person's behaviour only at the end of a particular predetermined interval of time, e.g. checking a child's pants, to see if they are wet or dry, on every half-hour.
Token economy	Reinforcement system based on the earning and exchange of tokens. These can be plastic discs, points, etc. They are earned for predetermined behaviours and exchanged for back-up reinforcers at a convenient time.

9

Physical aspects of care of the profoundly multiply handicapped

- Profoundly mentally handicapped people have exceptional needs determined by the nature and extent of their additional handicaps
- Providing effective care requires taking into account the person's individuality and his social, emotional and recreational needs
- Total care is unlikely to be achieved through a task allocation system
- Helping with activities of daily living can act as a means of providing essential care on an individual basis
- Consistency of care may help promote familiarity and contribute to provoking a response

Introduction
Care of the profoundly mentally handicapped
Development of care for the profoundly multiply
 handicapped
Basic concepts of care
Approaches to developing good practical care
 skills
The nursing process
Additional and associated handicaps
Helping the profoundly multiply handicapped
 person with the activities of living
 Adequate respiratory performance
 Adequate nutritional state
 Elimination
 Beneficial postures, positions and movements
 Rest and sleep
 Suitable clothing and helping with dressing
 Personal hygiene and skin care
 Dangers in the environment
 Recreation and occupation
 Learning
Summary

INTRODUCTION

Modern trends in mental handicap care have emphasised the need to move away from the 'medical model' of care where the handicapped person was viewed as a 'patient' whose primary need was for care and treatment. It had also been thought that a suitable place for the provision of this care was in a ward of a mental handicap hospital. Increasingly mental handicap has been viewed as essentially a social and educational problem which requires a change in both the emphasis of care given and in the location and type of residential care facilities provided. While most people would accept this proposition it must be remembered that there are some mentally handicapped people who require a considerable amount of direct care and assistance 24 hours per day.

These mentally handicapped people are usually those who are classified as the most severely and profoundly mentally handicapped and who may also have additional superimposed handicaps. Many of these people are cared for at home by their families often with little or no outside help, or are living in overcrowded and understaffed wards or units in mental handicap hospitals or other residential care facilities where standards of care can fluctuate widely.

It is neither possible nor desirable to discuss physical aspects of care as if these exist in isolation from other equally important aspects of care. Indeed, the essence of providing truly effective physical care is in giving the care with thought and regard for the many closely inter-related aspects of the person's total needs. While it is recognised that all mentally handi-capped people may present with potential or actual physical problems, it is necessary within the confines of a chapter to discuss physical care as it applies to those mentally handi-capped people who require this care most urgently.

CARE OF THE PROFOUNDLY MENTALLY HANDICAPPED

This group of people constitutes only a rela-tively small part of those whom we call mentally handicapped. Exact incidence or prevalence statistics for the profoundly handi-capped are extremely difficult to find due mainly to the unfortunate habit of researchers who include both the profoundly and severely mentally handicapped together and quote figures for their combined incidence or preva-lence. Most researchers agree that the inci-dence of profound mental handicap is less than 1 per 1000 of the general population. Craft (1979) cites an incidence of 0.5 per 1000 while Innes et al (1978) cite an incidence of 0.9 per 1000. However, due to the nature, extent and severity of their handicaps the profoundly handicapped require the utmost in thoughtful attention and care from their caregivers, on whom they may be totally dependent.

It is not possible to find an official classifi-cation of the profoundly multiply handi-capped. The World Health Organization and the American Association of Mental Deficiency define profound mental handicap as the most severe level of mental handicap and include IQ scores that fall 5.3 or more standard devi-ations below the mean. An IQ of below 20 is usually quoted (see Ch. 1). In addition to this level of profound mental handicap, there

could be additional serious handicaps which will hamper the person's development.

Sontag et al (1973) attempted to define the profoundly multiply handicapped person in terms of his behaviour:

... students who are not toilet trained; aggress towards others; do not attend to even the most pronounced social stimuli; self mutilate; rumi-nate; self-stimulate; do not walk, speak, hear or see; manifest durable and intense temper tantrums; are not under even the most rudimen-tary forms of verbal control; do not imitate; manifest minimally controlled seizures; and/or have extremely brittle medical existencies.

One or more of the following features are often found in the profoundly multiply handi-capped person:

1. has no speech at all;
2. makes no attempt at self help skills, e.g. feeding, dressing, washing;
3. is doubly incontinent: not toilet trained at all;
4. has serious sensory deficits, e.g. impaired sight, hearing or tactile sense;
5. has severe physical handicaps, which usually result in a serious degree of immobility;
6. does not engage in any constructive play with any objects;
7. seems not to understand any attempt at communication;
8. apparently lacks recognition of familiar people;
9. shows little or no reaction to even the most pronounced social stimuli.

While such profoundly multiply handi-capped people constitute a small percentage of the overall handicapped population it seems likely that their numbers will increase in years to come.

Several trends may serve to bring about this increase. Improvements in obstetric care and neonatology may result in more very severely handicapped babies surviving through infancy (Drillen, 1958; Holt, 1970). However, in a recent study of cerebral palsy and care of the new-born by Parneth et al (1981) there was found to be a sharp reduction in the frequency of neurological impairment in low birthweight infants during the 1950s and 1960s. In the 1960s and 1970s the same researchers found 'a sharp reduction in neonatal mortality and probably a moderate rise in the prevalance of neurological impairment'. They summarise their findings:

> Such evidence as we have suggests that the declining morbidity may not be keeping pace with the recent declines in mortality: thus, although more healthy survivors will result from newborn intensive care, a modest increase in the prevalence of handicap may also ensue.

The creation of 'special care' units within mental handicap hospitals should also improve standards of care and consequently raise the life expectancy of many profoundly multiply handicapped children.

A more controversial factor has been the rise of the 'right to life' movement, and in particular its efforts to prosecute hospital staff who might otherwise have 'allowed to die' the most severely handicapped babies out of concern for their future quality of life. Hospital staff may now feel compelled to revive vigorously and resuscitate in all cases for fear of litigation.

DEVELOPMENT OF CARE FOR THE PROFOUNDLY MULTIPLY HANDICAPPED

The profoundly multiply handicapped have for many years been among the most neglected and forgotten of society's handicapped people. It is not difficult to see why this may be so. The picture of a profoundly multiply handicapped person is not an immediately optimistic one, and in the past it was often thought that their deficits and problems were too severe to even begin to tackle.

Cleland (1979) quotes Tredgold, one of the 20th century's leading authorities on mental handicap, who wrote regarding the profoundly handicapped:

> They have eyes but they see not; ears but they hear not; they have no intelligence and no consciousness of pleasure of pain; in fact their mental state is one of entire negation.

When faced with the birth of a child with profound multiple handicaps, parents were often told to take the child home and look after it as though it were a normal baby. Many parents subsequently reported that their child was 'very good' and 'no trouble to look after'.

Educational facilities for these children were rare prior to the 1970 Education Act as were special education courses to prepare teachers to work with people with profound multiple handicaps. Facilities for people with profound mental handicap within our mental handicap hospitals were either poor or non-existent. It was common practice for these people to be placed in wards which were not orientated to cater for their very special needs. In this setting they would become the ward's 'babies' but were extremely unlikely to receive the loving attention and physical and social interaction that any baby could expect. The alternative was that they could find themselves in a ward with some 20–30 other profoundly mentally handicapped people. Age ranges in these wards could range from infants to adults in their 20s and 30s who had not been able to move on to more suitable areas because of the reluctance of these areas to accept people with their degree of handicaps.

Care staff often had extremely low expectations of the abilities and feelings of the profoundly handicapped person. Staffing levels and facilities were often inadequate to meet the handicapped person's needs. The inadequacy of the training which these staff received rendered them almost incapable of improving the abilities and enriching the lives of these people (Oswin, 1978).

These and other shortcomings in institutional care can hardly be viewed as surprising when we consider the historically low levels of financial allocation to the care of profoundly mentally handicapped people and the lack of professional and research interest shown in this group (Oswin, 1978, Swartz, 1979).

Wards for people with profound mental handicap seem to have been denied extra funds on the grounds that other groups of patients would appreciate the improved surroundings more and that the profoundly mentally handicapped patients would not notice any improvement in their conditions.

> Samuel with an IQ of about 10 is so severely deficient that any other information about him becomes relatively meaningless; it matters comparatively little how stimulating his environment is, for example, although of course the attitudes of those about him and the quality of his medical care effect his behaviour to some extent. (Robinson & Robinson, 1965)

The paucity of research and other material regarding the profoundly mental handicapped published before the late 1960s and early '70s has been recognised (Penfold, 1977; Cleland, 1979). With so little interest shown by the academic and professional communities in the care of the profoundly mental handicapped it is not suprising that care staff directly involved could find little research to help them to improve the daily life of the handicapped person.

There have however been some improvements in the care of the profoundly mentally handicapped since the beginning of the 1970s. The Education Act (Handicapped Children) 1970 said that every child should receive appropriate education provided by the Local Education Authority. There has also been an increase in the numbers of teachers with special training geared to the needs of the most severely handicapped (Stevens, 1976).

Within education there has also been a great increase in the level of interest and research regarding educational provisions for the profoundly mentally handicapped child and of even greater importance, in how the child learns, what his learning difficulties are, and how these can best be overcome. The work of individual educationalists such as Mildred Stevens, and research organisations such as the Hester Adrian Research Centre for the study of learning processes in the mentally handicapped which is based within the University of Manchester, have been especially useful.

Within mental handicap hospitals the quality of care for profoundly mentally handicapped people remains erratic. In *Better Services for the Mentally Handicapped* (1971) the Govern-

ment reiterated its view that the profoundly multiply handicapped require permanent hospital care because they 'require treatment or training under specialist medical supervision or constant nursing care.' Yet Oswin (1978) in her study found that it was this group of handicapped people who found themselves at the very end of the pecking order when it came to receiving these specialist services, and who often received the poorest quality care. However, as hospitals come to recognise the special needs of the profoundly multiply handicapped and cater for these within special care units with a full range of facilities, care staff and multidisciplinary support staff, we can hope that the quality of care for the handicapped person will improve.

BASIC CONCEPTS OF CARE

The profoundly multiply handicapped person has the same basic needs and rights as the non-handicapped person. The profoundly multiply handicapped child especially requires the warmth, sensitive handling, play and high level of social interaction that a non-handicapped infant or child would receive from his parents. However, the profoundly multiply handicapped also have exceptional needs which are determined by the nature and extent of their additional handicaps (Table 9.1). It is essential to understand that these multiple problems are closely interrelated. For instance, if we try to plan the care for a person whose skin is in danger of breaking down, we would consider nutritional aspects of his diet, especially his level of protein intake. This however leads us to consider his feeding capabilities and food preferences. If we then consider the problems related to good positioning for feeding then we also have to consider aspects of moving perhaps severely spastic joints and muscles.

We also have to consider his position. Is he being left in the same position for too long? Is care being taken when changing his position so that his skin is not 'dragged'? What about

Table 9.1 Common health problems affecting profoundly multiply handicapped people

Congenital abnormalities

Orthopaedic problems	Hip dislocation, talipes, scoliosis
Neurological impairment	Epilepsy, cerebral palsy, spina bifida, hydrocephalus, microcephaly
Sensory deficits	Hearing loss, visual defects, perceptual problems

Problems associated with immobility

Orthopaedic problems	Contractures, deformities
Skin problems	Pressure sores or decubitus ulcers, rashes and sores due to incontinence
Respiratory problems	Upper respiratory tract infections, hypostatic pneumonia, inhalation pneumonia
Urinary tract disorders	Urinary tract infections, formation of calculi or 'stones'

Other problems

Feeding problems	Bite reflex, tongue thrust, bulbar paralysis, over/under nutrition
Problems of elimination	Incontinence of urine and faeces, constipation
Dental problems	Caries, malocclusion, poor oral clearance, enamel deficiencies
Communication problems	No speech or language, unable to make meaningful gestures (see also Sensory deficits above)
Behavioural problems	Screaming attacks, self-injurious behaviour

his hygiene needs? If he is incontinent, is he being changed and washed regularly? If the person cannot speak or gesture, how will we know if his skin is causing him discomfort? How and when will we observe his skin and what will we look for?

We can now see that facets of care are not isolated but are all interrelated to form the network of total care. The effect of these multiple handicaps superimposed upon an existing profound level of mental handicap means that this person is almost totally dependent on his caregivers for the effective performance of all of the activities of his daily living, e.g. moving, eating, communicating, and for the overall quality of his lifestyle. It is essential that those care staff working with the profoundly multiply handicapped have a sense of optimism regarding the possibilities for improvements in the abilities of those people in their care. They must make themselves

aware of the person's assets and capabilities, however minimal these may appear to be.

It is a common reaction among care staff when first shown around a special care unit for the profoundly handicapped to feel immense sorrow and sadness at the extent of the handicaps which the people suffer from. 'What on earth can you do with them?' is often the first question to be asked.

While it is important for care staff to have a sound knowledge of the nature and extent of the person's handicaps and the implications of these for that person's daily living, it is a mistake to concentrate too much on the person's problems to the exclusion of their assets, however limited. This can lead to feelings of pessimism and defeatism among caregivers, who may subsequently develop low expectations of the abilities of the people in their care and of their own abilities as caregivers (Moores & Grant, 1977; Oswin, 1978). This atmosphere of hopelessness is one which is familiar to many staff working in mental handicap hospitals.

These wards are characterised by an adherence to routine. 'Because we have always done it this way' is the usual justification for thoughtless and unimaginative patterns of care. Suggestions and ideas from new staff are dismissed without discussion. 'We have tried it all before and it just does not work' is a familiar attempt to justify this type of inactivity. Where this atmosphere of pessimism prevails, it is not surprising that the bare minimum of interaction between the profoundly multiply handicapped person and his caregivers takes place. (Wright et al, 1974; Balla, 1976; Oswin, 1978). The work in this atmosphere characteristically involves only those most basic activities necessary to maintain 'life', such as dressing, feeding and toileting.

To make matters worse, it is almost certain that these tasks will be carried out as quickly as possible 'to get ahead of the routine' and with the minimum of interaction occurring between the care staff and the person on the receiving end of this care. It is clear that both the caregivers and the people in their care pay a high price in terms of lack of professional fulfillment and poor quality of life, for this atmosphere of hopelessness and low expectations. It is important to understand however that these care staff are not bad or evil people who purposely set out to harm or neglect the mentally handicapped. They are reacting in a perfectly natural way to the situation that they find themselves in at work and can only draw on their own work backgrounds and experiences. There are many very powerful forces which operate in any institution, be it a hospital, prison, school or bank which make it very difficult for a person not to 'fit in' and work in the way which the others work, thus perpetuating practices which may have gone largely unchanged for many years. This is especially true if the senior administration of the institution support the practices of the ward or unit (Goffman, 1961).

APPROACHES TO DEVELOPING GOOD PRACTICAL CARE SKILLS

For many years now, conscientious and imaginative care staff have realised that providing effective care for profoundly multiply handicapped people involves more than performing a 'wash, feed and change' routine upon people; a routine which takes no account of the person's individuality or other social, emotional, and recreational needs. It may seem to be stating the obvious to say that to provide a high standard of care is to be aware of and to cater for the profoundly multiply handicapped person's total range of needs. However, the obvious can often be forgotten or overlooked in the day-to-day life of a busy ward or unit.

This concept of providing total care should not be new to nurses. In the early 1960s the eminent American nurse, Virginia Henderson, encompassed this concept within her definition of nursing. She wrote that:

> The unique function of the nurse is to assist the individual, sick or well, in the performance of those activities contributing to health or to its recovery or to a peaceful death, that he or she would perform unaided had he the strength, will,

or knowledge. And to do this in such a way as to help him achieve independence as rapidly as possible (Henderson, 1969).

To provide a framework for identifying these activities contributing to health — or activities of living — she listed 14 components of basic nursing care:

1. Helping patient with respiration;
2. Helping patient with eating and drinking;
3. Helping patient with elimination;
4. Helping patient maintain desirable posture in walking, sitting and lying: and helping him with moving from one position to another;
5. Helping patient rest and sleep;
6. Helping patient with selection of clothing, with dressing and undressing;
7. Helping patient maintain body temperature within normal range;
8. Helping patient keep body clean and well groomed and protect skin;
9. Helping patient avoid dangers in the environment; and protecting others from any potential danger from the patient, such as infection or violence;
10. Helping patient communicate with others — to express his needs and feelings;
11. Helping patient practise his religion or conform to his concept of right and wrong;
12. Helping patient with work or productive occupation;
13. Helping patient with recreational activities;
14. Helping patient learn.

These were slightly modified by Roper et al (1980). While these activities of living may not be exhaustive they do provide a useful framework within which to plan and organise the daily care and activities of the profoundly multiply handicapped person.

THE NURSING PROCESS

Mention should also be made of the nursing process as being a potentially effective way of organising effective care. Although called the *nursing* process its application is not the sole prerogative of nurses. The basic philosophy and stages of the process can be applied by any care staff; indeed some care staff may already use a similar process when operating training or behaviour modification programmes (McFarlane & Castledine, 1982).

A detailed description of the theory and practice of the nursing process cannot be given within this chapter, but the basic stages of the nursing process can be stated.

1. Assessment

Initial and regular periodic assessments are undertaken to ascertain each person's level of functioning. These pinpoint specific problem areas and also assets and abilities, however limited. Assessments are completed by each member of the multidisciplinary team who is working with the handicapped person and these are kept in the person's file or case notes in order that the various members of the team are aware of each other's treatment aims and approaches.

Assessment however should not be carried out for its own sake. It must form a basis for action.

2. Planning

If care is to be given effectively then it has to be planned. It will inevitably be unsuccessful and confusing for the handicapped person if different care staff are following different approaches and have different aims.

Overall care can be planned at case conferences and team meetings which are attended by all those who are working with the handicapped person. Daily patterns of care and adaptations due to changes in the handicapped person's performance are then agreed by the staff of the ward or unit before each shift commences.

Each caregiver should be given an up-to-date report on each handicapped person in her care before she begins to work with them.

3. Implementation

The largest part of the care staff's day will involve actually working with the handicapped person, in giving care. It is important that some thought goes into how this care can best be organised.

Within nursing the traditional system of giving care has involved 'task allocation', whereby one nurse will get people up, another nurse will give people breakfast, and another nurse will dress people. This system has several major disadvantages. For the handicapped person there is little consistency of care. He is being attended to by several care staff, each of whom may have a different approach. For the profoundly multiply handicapped person task allocation is even more unsuitable. Due to the severity of his various handicaps he will find it extremely difficult to establish communication and rapport with his caregivers. This is made all the more difficult if he is having to relate to more care staff than is necessary.

'Task allocation' is also an unsatisfactory system of caregiving for the care staff themselves. Instead of staff seeing and caring for each person as an individual with specific problems and assets, they tend to view the work of the ward or unit as being simply a series of tasks to be performed upon a mass of homogeneous people. It is possible that task allocation will result in low morale and lack of professional satisfaction among care staff.

A much more satisfactory system of giving care is for care staff to be given responsibility for the total care of a group of residents. This means that there is increased consistency of care for the handicapped person. There is an increased likelihood of his achieving a rapport with a regular caregiver whom he can get to know and vice versa. There is the opportunity for the care staff to see 'their' group of residents as being individuals with a wide range of needs, rather than as being bodies which need to be bathed or fed and changed.

Communication and exchange of ideas is also more likely where a group allocation system is operating. Other care staff and team members know exactly who is responsible for the care of which handicapped person and therefore who to approach with any suggestions or to ask any advice.

4. Evaluation

It is very important that we are constantly evaluating the success or lack of success that we have when working with the handicapped person. Resources of both people and facilities tend to be scarce and must be used effectively. The most elaborate training programme or expensive educational toy is of no use if it does not achieve its aim with the particular handicapped person for whom it is used. 'If it does not work, stop trying and attempt something else' is a wise maxim, provided that people do not disregard the last three words.

There is an ever present danger here that care staff may give up too soon with a particular programme or activity which is then never repeated because it has come to be believed that 'we have tried that and it does not work.' If we accept that mentally handicapped people have difficulty in learning and profoundly mentally handicapped people have profound difficulty in learning we realise that teaching even the simplest response may take a long time. It is also inadvisable to accept a first response as indicative of the person's ability to learn the new skill. It is never an accurate indication.

5. Adaptation

This is the last stage of the process but an important one, which calls for the ability to think around a problem. If a programme or activity seems to be failing it should not be abandoned immediately. Perhaps there is some adaptation or alteration which could be made to the equipment, or method or timing involved in the programme which might improve its chances of success. It may be easier and more effective to modify a programme in the light of experience gained

than to abandon it and perhaps have to start again from scratch later on.

ADDITIONAL AND ASSOCIATED HANDICAPS

In addition to the serious neurological damage suffered by profoundly multiply handicapped people it is commonly found that other vital functions have also been impaired. These associated handicaps will now be discussed.

Cerebral palsy (see Ch. 4)

Cerebral palsy can be defined as a 'group of non-progressive disorders of the brain causing impairment of motor function in children.' It should be noted that it is not a single disease entity. As these disorders are non-progressive, unlike progressive neurological disorders such as the leukodystrophies or lipid storage disorders, the child does not deteriorate and inevitably die at an early age.

The disorder of cerebral palsy is manifested by impaired motor function, i.e. the child will be unable to control certain muscle groups to perform the wide range of motor movements, and to adopt the many postures and positions which the non-handicapped person will be capable of.

Causes. Many factors have been implicated as being causes of cerebral palsy. Prenatal factors include hereditary or genetic influences, prenatal infections, anoxia, rhesus incompatibility and metabolic disturbances. Natal factors include trauma, prolonged and difficult labour, vitamin K deficiency and prematurity. Postnatal factors include infections, trauma, anoxia, tumours and vascular accidents.

The highest incidence of cerebral palsy occurs in the prenatal and natal periods, and during this time prematurity is the most prominent factor. Due to advances in knowledge and neonatal care facilities, causative factors such as rhesus incompatibility are very rarely seen. However, this progress may be offset by increases in causative factors such as prematurity, multiple births and trauma (O'Reilly & Walentynowicz, 1981).

Classification

Cerebral palsy can be classified in several ways. It can be classified according to clinical type:

Spasticity. This is the most common type of cerebral palsy, affecting approximately 75% of children. In spasticity there is damage to the motor cortex of the brain or/and to the descending motor nerve pathways The characteristic feature of spasticity is an increase in muscle tone — hypertonicity. This results in severe stiffness, especially in the limbs. There is a marked resistance to any attempt to move the limbs and an inability to relax the spastic muscles.

Athetosis. This condition is thought to arise from damage to the basal ganglia, which lie deep within the brain and are thought to be responsible for co-ordinating purposeful movements. The characteristic feature of athetosis is that the person displays unco-ordinated writhing movements of his limbs, face and tongue. These uncontrolled movements tend to become worse when the person is attempting a deliberate movement or during periods of excitement.

Ataxia. In ataxia it is the cerebellum which is the part of the brain affected. The cerebellum is responsible for monitoring incoming sensory information and is also involved in maintaining balance and equilibrium. A person suffering from ataxia will have very poor body balance and may stumble and lurch when attempting to walk. Hand-eye co-ordination is also poor.

Mixed and Others. Other rarer forms of cerebral palsy exist such as rigidity, atonia, tremor and mixed types.

Occasionally a the type of cerebral palsy will be described in terms of the involvement of the various parts of his body. The suffix 'plegia' is used to indicate the presence of paralysis which means the loss of sensation and power of movement of a part of the body

Table 9.2

Type of paralysis	Effect
Monoplegia	One limb is affected.
Paraplegia	The lower half of the body is affected, usually a flaccid paralysis due to a spinal lesion.
Diplegia	The lower limbs are usually affected and accompanied by spasticity.
Hemiplegia	One side of the body is affected.
Quadriplegia or Tetraplegia	All four limbs are affected.

as a result of interference with the nerve supply. Prefixes are added to indicate the extent and location of the paralysis (see Table 9.2).

With any classification of cerebral palsy, however, it is vital for care staff to understand that there is a very wide diversity of severity, and that no two people suffering from cerebral palsy will display identical features.

Speech problems

Speech problems are often found in people with cerebral palsy (see Ch. 4) and may be due to articulation defects resulting from paralysis which affects the muscles of the lips, tongue, larynx and pharynx. These problems may be made worse due to the limited language directed toward the severely handicapped (Wehman, 1979). Indeed the profoundly multiply handicapped person may well have no speech or language and be unable to make any vocal gestures to express his wishes, likes or dislikes.

Visual defects

A wide variety of visual defects is found in cerebral palsied people. These can range from fairly minor abnormalities such as strabismus and nystagmus through to partial or complete blindness. It has been estimated that in wards for profoundly multiply handicapped people the incidence of complete blindness may be as high as 11% (Warburg, 1977).

Epilepsy

Epilepsy is a common accompaniment of profound multiple handicap (see Ch. 4). The types of epilepsy found will vary and may include major, minor, myoclonic and Lennox-Gastau types of seizures.

Hearing losses

Various degrees of hearing loss are common among people with profound mental handicap (see Ch. 4); ranging from a relatively mild high or low tone deafness to complete deafness. The profoundly multiply handicapped person has special problems in this area as they may be unable to co-operate in the more usual audiometric tests for hearing.

Other forms of hearing loss can be considered as a focus for nursing intervention related to hearing. Otitis media is an infection of the structures of the middle ear which is responsible for a great deal of partial hearing loss in children. Another common cause of impaired hearing is an obstructive build-up of cerumen or wax within the external ear.

Dental problems

The profoundly multiply handicapped person will require the same routine dental treatment as the non-handicapped person, such as regular check-ups, fillings and extractions. Special dental problems may be due to such factors as tooth enamel deficiencies and bruxism or tooth grinding. Poor oral clearance could also present problems. The person may have paralysis affecting his oral region which prevents him from clearing food debris from between his teeth and gums with his tongue. This increases the need for effective oral hygiene to be carried out by care staff.

Upper respiratory tract infections

Many profoundly multiply handicapped people have problems in maintaining an efficient respiratory pattern with consequent adequate exchange of oxygen and carbon dioxide. This may be due to paralysis of the muscles of respiration or to some physical deformity affecting the thorax such as a kyphosis, lordosis, or asymmetrical chest moulding.

Immobility could also impair respiratory function. It is still the case that some profoundly handicapped people may be kept lying on their backs for large parts of the day either as 'bed patients' or dressed but lying on the floor on mats or bean bags. This practice places the person in danger of developing a chest infection or hypostatic pneumonia with subsequent infection of the secretions of the respiratory tract or, more dramatically, as a result of the inhalation of saliva, regurgitated food or vomit. Particular attention should be paid to this aspect of care as most common cause of death among profoundly handicapped people is from respiratory disorders (Chaney et al, 1979).

Physical deformities

The person with cerebral palsy is very much at risk from developing secondary deformities. These deformities can either be fixed or unfixed. An unfixed deformity is an abnormal position of a joint or joints which can be corrected either passively or actively. A fixed deformity cannot be corrected by these means.

Contractures. If a person's limbs are kept in the same position for a long period of time, e.g. sitting in a wheelchair or lying in bed, the muscle fibres surrounding the joints atrophy and shorten. They then become progressively more resistant to movement and eventually the joint becomes fixed in one position and no movement is possible.

Windswept hips. This deformity involves difficulties in adduction, flexion and medial rotation of the hip. When the person lies on his back he is unable to bring his legs to the midline, instead they lie to one side. This position can often lead to dislocation of the hip on the side of the adducted leg (Fulford & Brown, 1976) (Fig. 9.1).

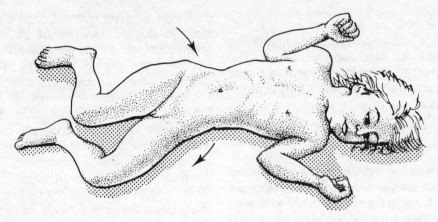

Fig. 9.1 Windswept hips.

Spinal deformities. Deformities of the spine are also frequently found. Most commonly these are:

Scoliosis — a sideways curvature of the spine (Fig. 9.2A).

Kyphosis — a flexion deformity of the spine; the person's spine protrudes at his back (Fig. 9.2B).

Lordosis — an extension deformity of the spine, usually found in the lumbar region. The person's spine curves towards the front (Fig. 9.2C).

Kypho-scoliosis — a combination of a kyphosis and a scoliosis (Fig. 9.2D).

Prevalence rates of deformities are very difficult to obtain but in a small study of 20 children with cerebral palsy, Fulford & Brown (1976) found that: 19 had plagiocephaly; 18 had facial asymmetry; 17 had asymmetrical chest moulding; 15 had a scoliosis; 19 had 'windswept hips' with asymmetrical passive hip movements.

HELPING THE PROFOUNDLY MULTIPLY HANDICAPPED PERSON WITH THE ACTIVITIES OF LIVING

Helping the person maintain adequate respiratory performance

The profoundly handicapped person who suffers from a serious degree of immobility has many problems in maintaining an adequate oxygenation process. The main factors conspiring to impair oxygenation are: (a) a reduction in blood volume and red cell mass which alters the oxygen carrying capacity of the blood; (b) venous stasis which decreases cardiac output thus reducing the oxygen transport process to the body's tissues.

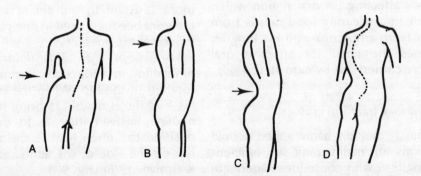

Fig. 9.2 Spinal deformities.

Chest and lung expansion is often impaired due to paralysis or other damage to nervous pathways. This results in very shallow breathing patterns with consequent lack of movement of respiratory secretions. Normally mucus in the respiratory tract is swept outward by ciliary action. When a person stands upright and moves normally the mucus lines the bronchioles evenly and drains by force of gravity. However, when a person is immobile and lying in the supine position the mucus in the bronchioles tends to pool in the lower areas, and the upper parts of the bronchioles tend to dry out. The diameter of the bronchioles also tends to be reduced in the supine position. This mucus can eventually form a plug which blocks the bronchioles causing a hypostatic pneumonia. The static pools of mucus also provide an excellent medium for the growth of bacteria and the development of chest infections.

Additional factors can also make the person prone to respiratory problems. Bulbar palsy or paralysis, which involves paralysis of the lips, tongue, larynx and pharynx, impairs coughing and swallowing mechanisms. As a result of serious problems with feeding, regurgitation and choking with subsequent inhalation of food is common, and can result in an inhalation pneumonia. Occasionally the handicapped person will have increased production of saliva and secretions which he may have difficulty in swallowing due to an impaired swallow reflex. This hypersecretion may be a result of drug side-effects, e.g. nitrazepam (Mogadon). If the handicapped person has to wear a supportive body brace because of lack of postural control, this may impede his chest and lung expansion and consequent respiratory function.

It is clear from the preceding passages that the handicapped person's posture and position are very important in preventing or minimising respiratory problems. As a general principle the supine or flat position is to be avoided for the profoundly multiply handicapped person. Lying the person flat on his back is dangerous, as this could lead to a fatal choking accident should the person regurgitate food or vomit and inhale the product. The upright position is used wherever possible, and where the person is to be moved to provide a variety of different positions throughout the day a side lying position is used. This position allows secretions to run freely from the mouth should the person have difficulty in swallowing. While in this position a pillow or rolled blanket is placed at the person's back to prevent him from rolling on to his back.

The handicapped person can also be helped to perform a range of movements and exercise which will help to reduce the stasis of respiratory secretions.

However, despite good preventative care, the profoundly multiply handicapped person may still develop a chest infection. Care staff should be aware of the signs and symptoms which would indicate the presence of a chest infection in order that prompt treatment can be initiated:

Dyspnoea — difficulty in breathing.
Pyrexia — an increase in body temperature.
A cough which may produce expectorated mucus.
Noisy respirations — the person's chest may sound 'bubbly' when breathing.
Anorexia — the person may be unwilling to eat as well as he does normally.
Malaise — the person may be listless and lethargic and may also experience a degree of chest pain.
Colour change — the person may be very pale, or in cases where breathing is extremely difficult the person may have a bluish colour (cyanosis).

Medical treatment of these infections will usually involve the prescription of an antibiotic. Initially this may be a broad spectrum antibiotic but could be changed to an antibiotic with a more specific action when the causative organism of the chest infection is identified. The easiest way for the handicapped person to take these medicines is usually in liquid suspension form. Although these suspensions may appear to be pleasantly flavoured and coloured, they often taste unpleasant and the handicapped person may need a lot of encouragement to take them. A pleasantly flavoured drink to follow these medicines helps remove any unpleasant after-taste.

Nursing management of the person's chest infection involves careful upright positioning of the person to minimise the obstruction of the respiratory passages with mucus. Postural drainage can help to clear the respiratory tract of mucus. The person is placed over a wedge in a prone lying position with head downwards in order that secretions can drain out on to a pad. The assistance and advice of a physio-therapist can be obtained regarding how to percuss the person's thorax in order to loosen secretions. The handicapped person may occasionally require to have excessive secretions removed from his respiratory tract by the use of naso-pharyngeal and/or oral suction (see Box 9.1).

Helping the person achieve and maintain an adequate nutritional state

One of the most basic skills which we all learn is how to feed ourselves. This is an obvious nutritional necessity, but also the ability to feed in an efficient and tidy manner is demanded by society if we are to be socially acceptable. This area of feeding however is one where the profoundly multiply handi-capped person is almost certainly going to experience great difficulty. Indeed, many of these people are unable to feed themsleves and are completely dependent upon their care staff to ensure that their nutritional needs are met.

Development of normal feeding patterns

Sucking. Sucking is a reflex mechanism which is present at birth or shortly afterwards. It is an important survival mechanism. Sucking is achieved by closing the lips around the nipple or teat to prevent the intake of air instead of liquid. To suck efficiently there must be a negative pressure inside the mouth in order to draw in the liquid. This is achieved by tight closure of the lips around the teat or

Box 9.1   Naso/oro pharyngeal suction

Definition
This procedure involves removing excess secretions from the respiratory tract by means of a catheter connected to a suction machine.

Rationale for carrying out this procedure
To help maintain a clear airway by removing excess secretions thus making it easier for the person to breathe through his mouth and/or nose and trachea.

A second reason may be to obtain a specimen of the secretions for diagnostic purposes.

Objectives
To maintain a clear airway to ensure adequate respiratory performance. To relieve any discomfort or distress which the person may be experiencing as a result of congestion of his respiratory tract by excess secretions. To make it easier for the person to carry out other activities involving his upper respiratory tract such as feeding.

Equipment required
A portable suction machine or a wall suction pipe if available.
A Y-connector.
Disposable suction catheters of the appropriate F gauge for the person. (This may be from 14–18 Fg for adults and from 8–18 Fg for children).
Yankauer or mini-yankauer suction catheter.
A small container of water.
K Y Jelly.
Clean disposable gloves.
Disposal bag for used equipment.

Technique
Infection can be transmitted to the person so the caregiver washes her hands thoroughly and puts on the clean disposable gloves.

The person's head is elevated and turned to one side. This helps secretions to drain from the pharynx. It also straightens the line of the person's airway thus making is easier to insert the catheter.

Dip the tip of the catheter into the water and apply a little of the lubricant jelly to the tip. This makes it less uncomfortable when the catheter is being inserted.

The catheter can then be inserted gently through each nostril in turn. To prevent trauma to the delicate linings of the respiratory tract, the catheter should never be forced, nor should suction be applied when inserting it.

After its insertion, the catheter is gently rotated and withdrawn simultaneously. Suction is achieved by closing the remaining leg of the Y-connector with a finger while withdrawing the catheter.

As the airway is obstructed during suctioning, do not prolong each suction action for more than 15–20 seconds.

Observations are made as to the amount, consistency, colour and odour of the secretions which were aspirated. After this procedure, which can be very distressing, the person is left comfortable, perhaps with a favourite toy or with someone to tell him a story.

Soon after the procedure an evaluation can be made to ascertain whether the objectives of the exercise have been successfully achieved.

---

nipple and by the back of the tongue raising to the soft palate to prevent air entering the mouth from the nose.

Swallowing. This is another reflex mechanism, which is stimulated by the bolus of food touching the back of the throat. Although swallowing is automatic the ability to chew and form the food into a bolus and pass it to the back of the throat is not.

Biting and chewing These abilities develop with the introduction of more solid food into the child's diet and with the emergence and growth of the first teeth. Unlike sucking and swallowing, biting and chewing are skills which the child must learn.

Head control. The head is the first part of the body which the child learns to control. This is an essential part of the development of feeding if good hand-eye co-ordination is to be achieved. This will enable the child to bring food to his mouth using his hands. The non-handicapped child is able to eat using a spoon with fairly little spillage by about 2 years of age.

Drinking. Initially baby sucks from the breast or a bottle. By around 9 months he may drink from a feeding cup with a mouthpiece. At around 15 months he may drink from an ordinary cup but rather messily, but by 18 months–2 years he will be drinking from an ordinary cup with little spillage as his lip closure has improved greatly.

Feeding problems affecting the profoundly multiply handicapped person

The person may be very floppy (hypotonic) and have little or no postural control, especially head control. In cases of severe spasticity the person may adopt a characteristic position of hyperextension where the whole body is stretched out in extension. In this position it is almost impossible to feed the person properly. The predominantly spastic person is also prone to episodes of abnormal reflex activity. For instance when the person's mouth opens, this causes his head and arms to extend, his back to arch and his legs to stretch out in extension.

Another abnormal reflex pattern which interferes with feeding is the asymmetrical tonic neck reflex (ATNR) (Fig. 9.3). In ATNR when one arm is flexed the other one is extended and the head turns towards the extended arm, which again makes face-to-face feeding impossible and also prevents the person from being able to bring his hands to his mouth.

The person may have such severe neurological damage that he possesses only infantile sucking and swallowing reflexes and will be unable to progress to biting and chewing. If, on the other hand, the person exhibits a strong sucking pattern, then tongue thrust may be common. Here the tongue tends to push food out of the mouth rather than gathering it and forcing it backwards. This can lead to most of the person's meal ending up in his feeder or lap.

A bite reflex is another serious feeding problem which affects many profoundly multiply handicapped people. When the

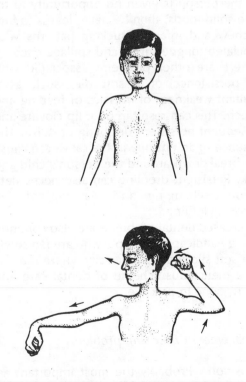

Fig. 9.3 Asymmetric tonic neck reflex. The arrows show the resultant movements when one arm is flexed.

person's lips or gums are touched (especially with a metal spoon) the person clamps his mouth shut tightly. This means that food cannot be put into the mouth or that the person will be biting hard on to a spoon until the spasm ends. This can be a very painful and unpleasant experience for the handicapped person. Try biting on a large ball of silver paper to get some idea of how this might feel!

Bulbar palsy or paralysis, resulting in damage to an area of the midbrain called the medulla oblongata, affects the muscles of the lips, tongue, larynx and pharynx. This makes co-ordination of these structures, which is so essential for effective chewing and swallowing, almost totally absent.

The handicapped person may also have physical abnormalities affecting his oral region such as an abnormally high palate, unusually large tongue or dental malocclusion. A cleft lip or palate may also be present in very young children who have not yet had these abnormalities surgically repaired.

If the person is given no opportunity to try more solid foods, then he never learns to bite or chew and infantile sucking patterns with associated tongue thrust and spillage occur.

There are other problems associated with the persistence of a soft diet such as a resultant weakness of muscles of feeding and speech. This can result in poor lip closure and consequent persistent dribbling of saliva. The presence of an enzyme in the saliva can cause skin breakdown around the person's chin and neck. Persistent drooling can also necessitate frequent changing and washing of the person's clothing.

Increased dental problems are also common among handicapped people who are fed solely on a soft sticky diet, especially where there is not a meticulous scheme of dental care and oral hygiene in practice.

Management of feeding problems

Position. Probably the most important aspect of developing good feeding technique is the person's position. Inexperienced care staff often attempt to feed a handicapped person by tilting the person's head backwards or by lying the person on his back. They may explain that this will make the person swallow their food more easily and cause less mess due to food spilling from the person's mouth.

In fact this practice is potentially dangerous and should be discouraged. Firstly to recline the person in a flat lying position severely limits the field of vision and sensory experience. It also perpetuates the outstretched extensor position which should be counteracted. The most urgent consideration however is that of safety. The person is very likely to gag or to choke while feeding if he is fed in a reclining position. This is a common cause of inhalation pneumonia and consequent death among profoundly multiply handicapped people, may of whom have impaired cough and swallow reflexes. To appreciate just how difficult it is to feed in this position, lie on your back and try to drink from a cup with a spout or a bottle.

The basis of a good position for feeding is that the person is sitting upright. This is something which can be achieved even with the most severely physically handicapped. The person should be seated in a comfortable and properly fitting chair. This means that his hips should be flexed and his bottom should be well to the back of the chair. A groin strap can be used to stop the person from going into the extensor position and perhaps sliding off o the chair. A good upright position can also be achieved when the person is sitting in a wheelchair.

For the young child an excellent feeding position is for the child to sit facing the feeder on his lap with his hips flexed and legs astride the feeders. The child's back and shoulders can be supported by a pillow laid against the edge of a table (Fig. 9.4)

Whichever position is chosen it is important that the feeder sits in front of the person to feed him. This face-to-face feeding is especially important with the sighted person who may learn actions such as opening his mouth by watching and copying the actions of the feeder.

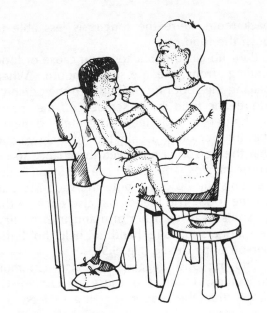

Fig. 9.4 Feeding against a table.

Preparation of food

A well-balanced diet includes adequate fats, carbohydrates, protein and vitamins plus other nutrients such as calcium, iron, thiamine and riboflavine.

Several important aspects of nutrition are considered when planning nutrition for the profoundly multiply handicapped person. If, for example, the person is confined to a wheelchair and is either totally immobile or has very reduced mobility then his energy requirements will consequently be reduced.

The person may be obese, which will make his physical management more difficult, although much more common among profoundly multiply handicapped people is being underweight for height. This is especially common in people with severe cerebral palsy and those who have very difficult feeding problems. Care staff will recognise the characteristic features which accompany this state of undernutrition such as diminished growth, poor skin lustre, tendency towards developing constipation, listlessness and reduced activity. This undernutrition can be extremely difficult to overcome even with intensive effort from the entire care team.

This person's diet may have to be radically altered to consist of perhaps several small snacks per day rather than two or three main meals. Foods high in calories and protein can be chosen with the help of a dietitian or nutritionist. These may be everyday foods such as carbohydrates and starches or special preparations such as 'Hycal' drinks.

Vitamin and iron preparations may have to be included as a diet supplement for the profoundly multiply handicapped person. These can be given in an easily taken liquid drops form such as Abidec multivitamins.

When ordering food or planning meals for the profoundly multiply handicapped person it is important to ensure the provision of a good dietary pattern which will meet the person's requirements for all nutrients. This can sometimes be difficult when care staff have to rely on a large hospital kitchen which by its very nature is involved in mass catering. A more individualised and improved standard of food can often be achieved for residents by involving the catering manager or dietitian in discussions and the planning of the management of the handicapped person's feeding problems and special nutritional needs.

The actual manner in which the food is prepared will depend on the feeding capabilities of the handicapped person. The most severely impaired people may require to have all meals liquidised and pureed. They may be able at a later stage to progress to more solid foods. There is a tendency for care staff to underestimate the ability of the person to progress to eating more solid foods. It is undesirable for the handicapped person to be kept on a liquidised diet and not be given the chance to learn to bite and chew more solid foods. This progression, however, is best made gradually, for instance from liquidised to mashed or minced food and then to solid foods. This progression may not be possible for all profoundly multiply handicapped people but we cannot tell who will be capable unless we try in a planned and systematic way.

Another important aspect of food preparation is that the person's likes and dislikes are respected. It occasionally surprises care staff that a person who is thought to be incapable of almost any mental functioning can indicate a like or dislike of a particular food. The person's relatives are more likely to know of any food dislikes or preferences and their advice can be sought here. It would be petty and harsh for care staff to force this person to eat food which he shows that he dislikes or to deprive him of a particular favourite food on the grounds that you are 'pandering to his food fads'.

The amount of food which is served is also important. The profoundly multiply handicapped person may require less food because of his lower level of physical activity. As a general rule it is better to serve frequent small meals rather than one or two large three course servings. When offered too much food at one sitting the person is more likely to vomit or regurgitate the meal. Frequent small meals also offer more opportunities to practise developing good feeding patterns.

Overcoming specific feeding difficulties

These problems such as tongue thrust and bite reflex are very difficult to overcome, especially in older people where they have become firmly established as 'bad habits'.

Bite reflex is stimulated by touching the sensitive area around the mouth and gums, and is often increased by the use of metal spoons which can be avoided. The use of metal spoons can also cause traumatic damage to the person's teeth and gums. An unbreakable plastic or polythene spoon is preferable when feeding a handicapped person with a strong bite reflex. Occasionally stroking the person's mouth and gums prior to mealtimes can help to desensitise this area.

Tongue thrust is very difficult to overcome. It may be possible to counteract it by placing the small spoonful of food on the front of the person's tongue as it is being put into his mouth. His lips can then be helped to close over the spoon. The most widely used method of overcoming tongue thrust is for the feeder to place alternate spoonfuls of food into the rear side of the person's mouth between his back teeth. Here the tongue is less able to push the food out.

Poor lip closure is a common cause of food spilling from the person's mouth. When placing the spoonful of food into the person's mouth the food is not scraped off the spoon by the person's top teeth. This method means that the person is usually fed from above and that the person is not given the chance to try to use his lips. The feeder can gently push the person's top lip down onto the spoon to pull off the food. The feeder can also encircle the person's head with her arm and use the first two fingers of one hand to help hold the person's lips closed (Fig. 9.5).

Choking and gagging are also common difficulties. Often the cause of choking is simply that the feeder is trying to feed the person too quickly. When feeding the multiply handicapped person it is necessary to feed at the person's own rate. Speeding this process up will result in a great deal of spilled and dribbled food plus an increased chance that the person will choke or vomit. The person may occasionally choke or gag if there are lumps in his food to which he is unaccustomed. For this reason, new and more solid foods are introduced gradually. Another very common cause of choking and gagging is that the feeder has tilted the person's head too far backwards while feeding him. This practice is dangerous (Fig. 9.6).

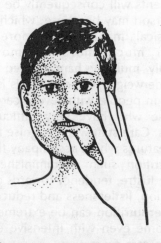

Fig. 9.5 Lip closure when feeding.

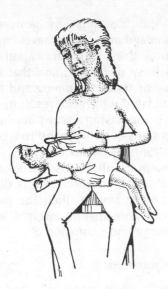

Fig. 9.6 Dangerous practice — feeding child tilted backwards.

Fig. 9.7 Heimlich manoeuvre.

Care staff are encouraged to learn an effective way of helping the person who is clearly choking during a meal. The most favoured method is the Heimlich manoeuvre (Richards, 1977). The caregiver stands behind the choking person, puts both hands firmly under his diaphragm and pushes upwards. This forces air from the lungs upwards thus dislodging any food or foreign bodies trapped in the person's glottis (Fig. 9.7). If there is any object or particle of food visible in the person's mouth this can be hooked out with a finger.

The person may have difficulty in chewing and swallowing, especially if he suffers from a bulbar paralysis. Chewing can be encouraged by offering the person pieces of toast, biscuit or apple to chew on. This will be extremely difficult for the person and instant success should not be expected. The feeder can help the person to chew by gently manipulating the person's jaw in chewing motions (Fig. 9.8).

Occasionally the person may have difficulty in swallowing. He may retain a mouthful of food for an extremely long time without swallowing or may have a very unco-ordinated swallowing mechanism. The feeder can help to stimulate the person's swallow reflex by

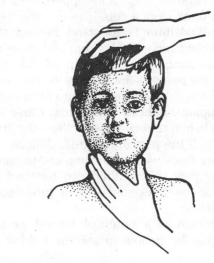

Fig. 9.8 Helping child to chew.

gently stroking under the person's chin. The head must remain forward however as a reclining head position makes swallowing very difficult (Fig. 9.9).

Drinking efficiently can pose extreme problems. It is important to maintain the person in an upright position as drinking is even more difficult and dangerous for the person if he is tipped backwards or lying down. Feeding cups with spouts are often used to give drinks to multiply handicapped people but are rarely

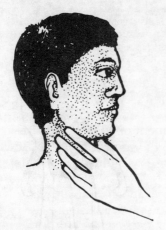

Fig. 9.9 Stroking chin/neck to assist swallowing.

used properly. They are not intended for pouring fluid into the open mouth of the person from a height of several inches. This will not improve the handicapped person's ability to drink from a cup.

A good position is to stand behind the person while supporting his chin and lower lip with your hand. Place the rim of the cup between the person's lips and tip the cup until the person is able to take fluid into his mouth. Avoid tipping his head backwards. Close his lips to help him to retain and swallow the fluid (Fig. 9.10). If the person has great difficulty in swallowing fluids without choking and gagging, then a slightly thicker fluid can be tried or drinks can be thickened with a proprietary thickener.

Dehydration is a potential hazard as the person may be unable to ask for a drink or even to indicate thirst by gesture. Neurological damage may even have impaired his sensation of thirst. Also the caregiver who is having a busy day may think that drinks are too messy or time consuming and may 'leave them until later' which can result in the handicapped person having a very poor fluid intake. Common signs of dehydration to watch out for are dry tongue, wrinkled skin, decreased urinary output with an associated increase in the urine's concentration. If this dehydration becomes more severe, then the person may suffer from constipation, weight loss, anorexia, lethargy and confusion.

Special equipment

There are a great many aids and pieces of special equipment which may be of use to some profoundly multiply handicapped people. Cutlery can be specially manufactured or ordinary cutlery can be adapted by adding built-up handles. Plates and bowls are better if they have a wide base. They are then less easily tipped over. A high side helps with scooping out food. Non slip mats help stabilise bowls and plates. Two-handled mugs promote bi-manual activity and are more stable.

Specialist advice on equipment and aids and appliances can be obtained from:

The Spastics Society
12 Park Crescent
London W1N 4EQ
or
The Disabled Living Foundation
346 Kensington High Street
London W14 8NS

Some general considerations

For most people mealtimes are a social occasion. Their purpose is not simply to ingest food and drink but to enjoy the food and conversation. For the profoundly multiply handicapped person living in institutional care, however, these events are rarely enjoyed. Indeed Maureen Oswin (1978) described mealtimes in wards for profoundly

Fig. 9.10 Helping with drinking.

multiply handicapped children as being 'the crisis of feeding'.

Mealtimes were viewed by care staff as occasions when the ward routine could easily be hindered. Food would often arrive late or in an unsatisfactory condition from the kitchen and might have to be returned. The children's meals could be delayed and 'run in' to staff meal breaks. Perhaps one or two care staff could be left to organise and feed 20 or more children with very severe feeding problems. They often had to cope with shortages in essential equipment such as bibs, plastic spoons and other aids. If mealtimes were not completed within a certain time care staff also risked being criticised by other therapists for not having the children ready for school or physiotherapy in time.

Clearly this overall atmosphere of mealtimes being a chore which must be accomplished as quickly as possible is against everyone's best interests. It creates tension among care staff who worry about getting the people ready in time. They also worry about their own abilities to feed those people with serious feeding problems but for inappropriate reasons. Often, they are not concerned about feeding the person correctly and paying careful attention to his specific problems and nutritional needs, but instead are worrying about whether they can get the food inside the person as quickly as other staff can. Failure to do this can lead to the caregiver being viewed as less than capable of feeding 'difficult' people. This rush to complete mealtimes does not benefit the handicapped person and reduces mealtimes to the level of mere refuelling stops.

Thoughtful, basic care can make all the difference to feeding technique. Try not to put spoonfuls of food into the mouth of an un-suspecting person who has had no prior warn-ing of its arrival. The person may well be trying to cope with food already in his mouth or be about to swallow or cough or sneeze when, unannounced, the next heaped spoonful is in-serted. Non-handicapped people do not eat meals at breakneck speed and in a stony silence. We ought not to expect the profoundly

multiply handicapped person to do this for the sake of keeping ahead of the routine.

Establishing good feeding patterns is im-portant for the multiply handicapped person. It is not only important from a purely nutri-tional point of view but because good feeding patterns are important for the possible future development of speech and also in the devel-opment of good sitting postures, and co-ordination. Mealtimes are also potentially very valuable sessions between the caregiver and the handicapped person where communi-cation can be established.

The management of feeding problems is a good example of an area where multidisciplin-ary co-operation is essential if progress is to be made. The advice of a physiotherapist would be helpful regarding the most suitable feeding positions for people with various de-grees of physical handicap, e.g. the severely spastic or very floppy person. The physio-therapist can also advise on positions and techniques which will help to counteract undesirable reflexes such as extensor and asym-metrical tonic neck reflex.

The advice of a speech therapist may be sought regarding actual feeding techniques which will help overcome problems such as tongue thrust and bite reflex and help to es-tablish proper patterns of eating and drinking. If it is thought that the handicapped person will be able to make some progress with self-feeding, then an occupational therapist could provide specialist advice on the most suitable feeding aids for that individual such as special cutlery, plates and mugs and where necessary demonstrate their proper use.

Helping the person with elimination

The processes of eliminating waste products from the body are essential to health and indeed for life itself. However, topics such as urination and defaecation are not regarded as topics of general conversation even among nurses and other care staff. Perhaps for this reason and because of the unpleasantness associated with dealing with incontinence the whole area of helping the person with elimination has traditionally been allocated a very low priority by care staff. Indeed the daily management of elimination is often left to the most junior or untrained care staff. It is likely that the great majority of profoundly multiply handicapped people will be incontinent of both urine and faeces. Due to the severity of their neurological impairment and the extent of their additional handicaps it is likely that these handicapped people would be unable to benefit from a toilet training programme.

Our aims in the management of elimination include the following:

1. To ensure that the person is kept as clean and dry as possible.
2. To prevent secondary problems due to elimination difficulties such as constipation, urinary tract infection, faecal impaction or skin breakdown.
3. To carry out toileting procedures with due regard for the person's right to privacy and physical comfort
4. To keep the handicapped person's environment as pleasant and odour free as possible.

Urinary incontinence

It is very important that the incontinent person is checked at frequent intervals thoughout the day to ascertain whether he is dry or wet. If he is wet then he is changed immediately.

The normal pH of urine is between 5.5 and 7 which is acidic. If urine is left for a length of time it will react with bacteria on the body and become alkaline. This is the cause of the characteristic 'ammonia' smell of a wet nappy which has not been changed for a long time. In either its acidic or alkaline state urine can rapidly cause skin irritation and breakdown, even to the extent of causing a urine 'burn' which is similar in appearance to any burn caused by corrosive chemicals such as acids or alkalis. It is important therefore when changing the person that the skin around his perineal area be carefully cleaned with soap and water and dried afterwards, with special care being taken to dry the skin folds around the groin. A barrier cream such as zinc and castor oil can be used to protect the skin.

Each ward or unit will have its own preference as to whether to use terry towelling nappies, disposables or some other proprietary incontinence pads. The decision as to which to use may be influenced by cost and availability and efficiency of laundry services. There seems to be little difference in the effectiveness of the various methods. It is important however that the pad or nappy is put on correctly. A close fitting nappy will prevent serious leakage of urine or faeces and may also deny access to any handicapped person who tends to smear faeces. Disposable nappy liners are also useful in helping to keep harmful urine from contact with the skin. These can also reduce the level of soiling of the nappies themselves.

Certain routine observations are made when changing the person. His skin is checked for any signs of redness or rashes which may be the first indication of an impending pressure sore or other skin breakdown. The caregiver also observes whether the urine has an unusually strong smell which may indicate a urinary tract infection or that the person is dehydrated and that his urine is overconcentrated. If the caregiver suspects either of these causes the person has his temperature taken. An increase in temperature (pyrexia) may be another indication of systemic infection. The person's intake of fluids is also increased, and it would be wise to record exactly how much fluid the person was receiving daily. A clean specimen of urine would be obtained and sent to a laboratory for culture tests to identify positively whether or not an infection is present.

Faecal incontinence

The goals of management in urinary incontinence are also applicable to the person who is incontinent of faeces. There will be the same frequency of checking and even more scrupulous washing and drying during nappy changes.

Observations of the person's skin condition

are also made when changing. Any abnormalities of the faeces are noted, for instance, if they are unduly loose and foul smelling this may indicate a gastrointestinal infection. Stools which are very hard may again indicate dehydration. Other abnormalities can be detected by observation of faeces such as blood and intestinal parasites such as tapeworm.

Preventing complications

One of the most important aspects of the management of elimination is the prevention of complications arising from the handicapped person's disordered elimination patterns.

Many profoundly multiply handicapped people are prone to recurrent episodes of severe constipation. Several factors are responsible for this:

1. The level of immobility causes weakening of the abdominal and perineal muscles.
2. Gastric motility is reduced.
3. The person's diet may contain insufficient roughage and dietary fibre.
4. The person may be receiving insufficient fluids. If the person is kept in the lying position for long periods of time normal stimulation of the urge to defaecate does not take place.
5. There may also be specific neurological damage affecting the nerve supply to the gastrointestinal tract.

As severe constipation is a painful and distressing condition it is important that care staff are aware of the various measures which can be taken to minimise the possibility of its occurrence.

Exercise is an important part of the prevention of constipation. The provision of suitable exercise for the profoundly handicapped person is closely interrelated to programmes of physiotherapy and positioning for daily activities. Simple exercises can be performed by care staff such as floor mat exercises and music and movement sessions.

Dietary measures also play an important part

and the diet should contain a high percentage of fibre or roughage which can be found in foods such as wholemeal bread, green vegetables, fresh fruit, bran cereals and baked beans. The person also requires an adequate fluid intake.

Despite careful attention to exercise and diet some profoundly impaired people will require regular help from laxatives or enemata. Where this is the case there should be a clearly recognised policy for the administration of these medications. Oral laxatives are preferable to suppositories or enemata as they do not involve invasion of body privacy and are much less uncomfortable for the handicapped person. Where oral laxatives are found to be ineffective a laxative suppository or an evacuant enema may be prescribed. The method for administering these preparations is given in Box 9.2.

An important principle to remember before administering any laxative or evacuant enema is that the care staff must be sure that the stools which are to be passed will be soft and formed. If this precaution is not taken then the profoundly handicapped person may have to strain in severe tenesmic pain and distress trying to pass a large bulk of very hard stools. Anyone who has experienced such pain will vouch for its severity.

If the person has not had a bowel movement for several days then a rectal examination is carried out in order to ensure that the person's stools are sufficiently soft not to cause pain and discomfort when they are passed. Should it be discovered during this examination that the person's stools are unduly hard, then a stool softening preparation such as dioctyl medyl syrup or perhaps an olive oil enema is given prior to attempting evacuation of the faeces.

One of the most serious consequences of disordered bowel function is that the handicapped person may not have a bowel movement for such a long period that he develops faecal impaction where a large mass of hard faeces occludes the bowel and is very difficult to remove. Faecal impaction may make the person appear irritable and distressed. If the caregiver palpates the person's abdomen she may well be able to feel the mass within the bowel. This diagnosis can be confirmed if a rectal examination is done. If the mass is low down in the descending colon it will be easily felt.

Care staff should be alert to the possibility of faecal impaction in the handicapped person prone to constipation. This condition has often been misdiagnosed and the handicapped person has been sent to the local general hospital suffering from an 'acute abdomen' or 'query appendicitis'.

The signs of faecal impaction are sometimes deceptive in that small amounts of faeces often leak around the site of the impaction giving the false impression of regular or even loose bowel movements. If faecal impaction is suspected or discovered the person may have his level of fluid intake increased. Providing the site of the impaction is low down the caregiver can often remove it by very gently removing small pieces of the impacted mass at a time using a well lubricated glove. If the mass is higher up in the bowel then further medical advice should be sought.

A manual evacuation of faeces is a very unpleasant and distressing event for the handicapped person who may well not understand the necessity for it. The procedure is always carried out with the greatest care, reassuring and calming the person both during and after the event.

The other most common problem associated with disordered bowel function is diarrhoea. This is often caused by simple dietary indiscretion but occasionally it may have an infective cause as in gastroenteritis or dysentery. In a ward or unit for perhaps 20 or more people these and similar infectious disorders tend to spread at a rapid rate. Physical isolation of the infected person or persons and the instigation of a barrier nursing regime with scrupulous hygiene measures may prevent the spread of these and similar infections.

In a ward or unit where perhaps all of its residents are incontinent it is the responsibility of the care staff to ensure that the environment remains as pleasant and odour free as possible. Smells of urine and faeces which are present long after toileting procedures have been carried out make working and living conditions very unpleasant for all concerned.

Unpleasant odours will be reduced if the person is washed and changed immediately. Soiled or wet linen is put directly into the appropriate receptacles which should always be covered by a lid; if bags are used, they are tied at the neck. Receptacles are kept in one toilet area where the door can be closed. The ward or unit is kept well ventilated and windows are opened where weather and climate permit. Proprietary air fresheners are used by care staff in areas prone to unpleasant odours. Discussions with the supervisor of the cleaning staff could also be valuable and provide helpful suggestions for the cleanliness of wards and living areas.

Helping the person achieve beneficial postures, positions and movements

As the majority of profoundly multiply handicapped people suffer from physical handicap including almost total immobility, a large part of the daily care of such a person involves helping the person to adopt beneficial postures and positions related to the daily activities of living such as feeding, playing and sleeping. A programme aimed at good functional positioning actively attempts to prevent secondary physical deformities from developing in the handicapped person.

Due to the extent and severity of physical problems faced by most profoundly handicapped people it is important that the team involved in their care includes a qualified physiotherapist, who can organise programmes of movements, exercises, positions and strategies for prevention of deformities. It is surprising that many wards are often without this essential service. Oswin (1978) suggested that many physiotherapists felt that care staff were not in sympathy with their aims, and made little or no attempt to carry on programmes of positioning or movements when the physiotherapist was absent.

Nurse or care staff co-operation with

Box 9.2 Administration of an evacuant suppository/enema

Definition

This procedure involves introducing a solution or suppository into the lower bowel in order to ensure the later expulsion of the solution along with faeces and flatus.

Rationale for carrying out this procedure

To remove accumulated faeces from the lower bowel which the person is unable to void by himself.

Objectives

To ensure the effective expulsion of faeces from the lower bowel. To carry out the procedure as quickly and efficiently as possible, causing the minimum of discomfort and possible embarrassment to the person.

Equipment required

Evacuant suppository/Evacuant enema
Bowl of warm water
Lubricant, e.g. Vaseline or K Y Jelly
Dressing towel or paper roll
Disposable gloves
Disposal bag.

Technique

Prepare and assemble all equipment in advance. It will prolong an unpleasant procedure unnecessarily if things have to be fetched in mid-procedure.

Have the enema sitting in the bowl of warm water at approximately 38°C. This makes administration of the solution more comfortable for the person. The heat also serves to stimulate nerve endings within the intestinal mucosa.

It is best to have the person lying on his bed on his left side. This aids the flow of the solution into the descending colon. The dressing towel or paper should be placed under his buttocks to protect bedcovers. The tube of the enema is lubricated with the K Y Jelly. The tip of a suppository is dipped into the warm water. The person is then helped to raise his knees as far up as possible.

Gently separate the person's buttocks and insert the tube of the enema into the rectum for approximately 3 inches. If any obstruction is encountered **do not** force the tube.

The plastic bag is slowly rolled up from its base thus injecting the solution into the rectum.

With a suppository the caregiver wears a disposable glove with the index finger lubricated. The suppository is then gently inserted into the rectum and pushed up as far as the finger will reach.

Dispose of enema and gloves into disposal bag.

The person is then taken to a toilet and placed in a comfortable and dignified position for defaecation. However, in exceptional circumstances, for example the person suffers from very severe physical deformities, it may be impractical for him to sit on a toilet seat even with support. In these instances the person may be left in bed with the caregiver in attendance while the enema or suppository has its effect. Here, the bedcovers are protected by plastic drawsheets and the person is carefully covered and screened in order to ensure privacy.

Routine observations are made of the faeces and any abnormalities noted such as abnormally hard stools or the presence of mucus or blood.

After the procedure the person is left in a clean and fresh condition. The profoundly multiply handicapped person may find this a tiring procedure so a short rest or sleep afterwards may be beneficial.

As with all procedures the caregiver then evaluates the procedure to ascertain whether the objectives were achieved.

---

physiotherapists is so crucial that it is unlikely that an effective service involving management of the handicapped person's physical status can be achieved without it. It may help to promote this spirit of co-operation if the physiotherapist was to carry out programmes and demonstrate techniques in the ward or unit where care staff can become more involved, rather than in the physiotherapy department. Care staff might find it useful to ask the physiotherapist's advice on how good techniques of positioning, movement and handling could be integrated into the person's activities of daily living, in order that physiotherapy might not be seen as an isolated therapy session but as being relevant to the person's everyday life.

Systems of treatment of cerebral palsy and physical handicaps

Since the 1940s there have developed numerous schools of thought and philosophies of treatment regarding the management of cerebral palsy.

The most widely known of these philosophies which may be known to care staff are those of:

1. *Karl and Berta Bobath*. They suggest that the person's movement disorders are due to the persistence of infantile reflexes such as the asymmetric tonic neck reflex. Due to the continuing presence of these abnormal reflexes, normal reflex patterns which would help to co-ordinate and control normal move-

ments cannot develop. Treatment is therefore aimed at minimising these abnormal reflexes.

2. *Temple-Fay*. This approach was again neurological but differs from the Bobaths' approach in that, instead of attempting to eliminate abnormal reflexes, it seeks to use these in order to facilitate movement patterns.

3. *Doman-Delacato*. This controversial system of treatment was pioneered by adherents of Temple Fay. The 'Institute for the Achievement of Human Potential' in America has attracted large numbers of parents from all over the world who are taught 'patterning' movements which are to be performed with the child. This is a very intensive system of treatment which can require the assistance of five helpers at any one time.

4. *Peto*. A Hungarian Professor has developed an educational approach called 'Conductive Education' whereby the person is treated by one person — the conductor. This approach uses both neurological concepts and learning theories. The person is encouraged to carry out all activities by themselves with only advice and encouragement from the therapist.

Most workers would agree however that no one school of thought is an ideal method for the treatment of all physically handicapped people.

For this reason an eclectic approach is very popular among therapists working with profoundly multiply handicapped people. This style of therapy selects ideas from any of the different philosophies according to the needs of the individual handicapped person and the skills available to the therapist. The most notable proponent of the eclectic style is Sophie Levitt.

In recognition of the very important fact that each person's motor behaviour and physical handicap is unique it is not possible to produce a set of exercises or positions which tells us to do this with any spastic person or do that with any ataxic person, only some general guidelines and ideas will be given on management of the more common problems of daily living.

Aim

Our aim as care staff is to consider all of the handicapped person's needs as we plan and provide his care.

We have previously seen how an activity such as feeding is closely interrelated with other areas of care. A similar situation exists within activities such as positioning and exercises. For instance, in selecting a good side lying position for an immobile person we may be achieving the following aims:

1. Allowing any secretions to drain from the mouth on to a tissue.

2. Making bi-manual hand activity more achievable.

3. Providing an opportunity during positioning for communication and handling between the person and his caregiver.

4. If we choose a corrected side lying position using carefully placed foam shapes and pillows, we may also be helping to minimise or prevent the development of positional physical deformities.

Positioning

Sitting. The importance of being able to sit up is sometimes overlooked by care staff. The person who is left lying down for lengthy periods of time is deprived of much environmental stimulation. In addition he will be unable to learn to perform many activities due to lack of opportunity. When the person is helped to sit up with support he is able to look around and to take part in activities in a much more normal fashion such as feeding and playing.

Many profoundly handicapped people lack the trunk and head control to sit independently and require some means of support. This may be provided by means of a specially constructed wheelchair which is padded to provide additional support. If this means of support is used on its own, it could prove disadvantageous. The person may be confined to this special chair for all activities and for large parts of the day as the chair provides his sole source of postural support. Another problem is that often the person will have to be reclined far back in the chair if he is not to tip forwards. This can almost defeat the purpose of attempting to achieve an upright sitting position.

It is much more beneficial for the person to be fitted with a body brace made from Plastazote. This is a high density polythene foam which is moulded to the exact contours of the person's body and can be fitted with a head-piece to help support the person's head when sitting upright. These braces provide improved support for the spine thus helping to prevent deformities such as scoliosis (Fulford et al, 1982).

Care staff must ensure that people who have been supplied with such aids wear them as directed. Special care needs to be taken that the person does not develop any sores or skin abrasions as a new jacket may chafe the skin initially. These Plastazote jackets are washable and very easy to keep clean.

Non-ambulant residents who have a satisfactory level of postural control will have their own wheelchair. It is important that wheelchairs are not used simply as chairs or as means of transport but as aids to helping the person achieve an improved sitting balance. The wheelchair has footrests to prevent the person's feet from dangling or dragging along the floor. 'Wings' at the sides may offer some support and prevent the person from tipping sideways. Where the person tends to slide forward in the chair a groin strap may be used. It is very uncomfortable and detrimental for the handicapped person if he is allowed to sit slumped down in his chair with his bottom at the front of the seat and his back rounded (Fig. 9.11). The person will be more comfortable if he sits with his bottom well back in the chair and with his back straight (Fig. 9.12).

Chairs can be fitted with a table so that the person has the opportunity to handle toys and see objects within his reach. A table can also help prevent the person from slumping forwards.

The same principles of ensuring that the wheelchair is the correct size and type for the person and that the person is sitting in it

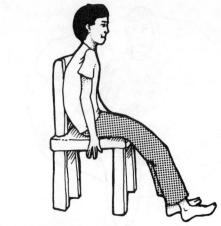

Fig. 9.11 Sitting slumped.

Fig. 9.12 Sitting properly.

comfortably and well supported apply to any ordinary chairs which the person may use.

There has been an increasing use of bean-bags or sag-bags in wards and units for handicapped people. These can be very comfortable to sit in if the person has few physical handicaps. However, bean-bags are unsuitable as chairs for immobile people. They offer no support for the person's spine and invariably the person slips into a curled up or lying position perhaps with his arms flexed inwards, his legs scissored, and his head tipped backwards (Fig. 9.13).

Standing. While a good sitting position is desirable it is even more important that the person's positions are changed frequently during the day. This is important for the

Fig. 9.13 Unsuitability of bean bags.

Fig. 9.14 Prone standing board in use.

neuromuscular system, the integrity of the skin and for experiencing new stimuli.

The severely physically handicapped person can be helped to experience the standing position for periods during the day by placing him on a prone standing board. These boards usually incline at an angle of approx 45°. The person is placed against the board and support straps are fixed to the legs and trunk. The board has a table at about shoulder height so that the person can engage in some activity with his hands (Fig. 9.14).

There are also special tables which have cut-out sections where the person can stand supported by straps and a backpiece. In this position he can enjoy play on the table top.

Lying. There are times during the day when the person may lie down for a nap or simply as another variety of position. However, lying the severely physically handicapped person on his back will encourage deformities such as scoliosis and 'windswept hips'; the person may also inhale secretions or vomit (Fig. 9.15).

When a side lying position is chosen, the person is laid on a floor mat with a pillow or sandbag at their back to prevent them from rolling over. A nappy or tissue is placed under the face to absorb any secretions which drain

from the mouth. Another pillow or wedge is placed between the hips to keep them in abduction (Figs 9.20 & 9.21). Both hands are brought forwards and some toys placed within the person's reach.

If a prone lying position is chosen, then the person lies over a foam wedge. This has the advantage over flat lying in that the person will find it much easier to use whatever head control he has, and also to reach out for toys or objects which are placed within his reach. This position is especially good as it encour-

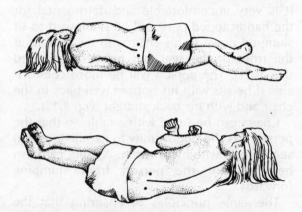

Fig. 9.15 Uncorrected side-lying positions encourage deformities.

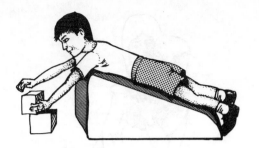

Fig. 9.16 Prone-lying over a foam wedge.

ages the adoption of a symmetrical body position (Fig. 9.16).

Hand function. Many profoundly multiply handicapped people have difficulty in using their hands perhaps due to asymmetrical tonic neck reflex or a very limited range of shoulder and arm movements. This means that he will not be able to bring his hands to the midline where he could look at them and play with them. This can also happen if the person is poorly positioned.

Even if a good range of shoulder and arm movements is present the cerebral palsied person often has no ability to grasp. The thumbs are flexed across the palm of the hand and the fingers clench tightly over it. This wrist is often also bent (Fig. 9.17). Care staff can help the person to become more aware of his hands during their daily activities with him.

Positioning again is very important in enabling the person to have his hands in front of him where he can more easily see and play with them. Unfortunately they are often allowed to dangle over the sides of his wheel-chair which can be dangerous.

Care staff can stimulate awareness of hands when carrying out activities such as bathing. Gently open the clenched hand by first straightening and turning out the arm. The hands can then be soaped and rubbed. Special

Fig. 9.17 Clenched thumb in palm.

'feelie mats' and surfaces of different textures offer a variety of tactile sensations. Some jam or syrup placed on a finger may encourage the person to bring a hand to his mouth. Noisy toys such as rattles tied to the hands may also stimulate hand movements.

Correcting asymmetries

One of the main aims of good positioning and handling of the handicapped person is to try to counteract asymmetries of the body and to train symmetrical postures and movements. This is very important as asymmetrical patterns can eventually lead to serious deformities.

Care staff should look out for the person who sits with his head turned to one particular side, or the person who uses the one arm and hand continually or the person who is able to 'bottom-shuffle' along the floor but always using the same side of the body. These patterns can be discouraged by stimulating the use of the other side of the body, e.g. by talking to the person from the other side or presenting material to the person's least used hand.

Handling

Care staff who are inexperienced in working with severely handicapped people often show a degree of reluctance and uncertainty when handling the handicapped person. This is very understandable, for a very frail multiply handi-capped child often looks as though he might 'break' were he to be lifted too roughly. However, this reluctance to handle can often lead to the person being restricted and deprived in his level of movement experiences and opportunities for learning. Also he will be deprived of much needed physical contact through touch and careful handling.

Careful handling by all care staff is important if the person is to have a wide range of move-ment experiences and helps to ensure his comfort during carrying and positioning; it can also help to prevent the development of secondary physical deformities. Specific hand-ling techniques may be decided upon after discussion with the physiotherapist; however some general guidelines will be given.

Handling should always be done gently and carefully. Tell the person what you are about to do. Never snatch or grab the person suddenly as unexpected movements can frighten the person and increase spasticity or trigger off abnormal reflex patterns. Help the person attain body symmetry when carrying out any handling. When helping the person to move from one position to another, perform the movement slowly in order that the person is given the chance to participate actively in it where possible. When lifting the person who has very little postural control of his head, trunk and limbs, do not pull him up by the hands leaving his head to hang backwards. Instead, raise him gently by holding each shoulder.

Avoid carrying the severely handicapped person as if he were a baby, with one arm under the shoulders and another behind the knees (Fig. 9.18). This encourages spinal curvatures, allows the person no chance to move actively, and greatly reduces the visual field. Another poor carrying position is where the caregiver holds the person around the waist. This is especially bad for the spastic person as he will tend to extend his hips and legs and will often scissor them.

It is better to carry the person astride your hip or abdomen with his legs well parted. This encourages outward movement of the hips

Fig. 9.19 Good carrying position.

and bending of the knees. While one hand supports the person's bottom the other can support his back which will be much straighter. The person's head is now at a better position for looking around and engaging in conversation (Fig. 9.19).

When handling the person always encourage any purposeful movements which the person initiates, for example helping to push an arm into a jumper sleeve.

Both the caregiver and the person must have confidence in the handling. If the person feels insecure this can cause him to go into abnormal reflex or spasm patterns.

For more detailed advice and illustrations showing how to handle the physically handicapped person correctly, readers are referred to Nancie Finnie's widely recommended book *Handling the Young Cerebral Palsied Child at Home*. Although primarily intended for parents who are caring for their handicapped child at home it contains much information and clear illustrations which would be invaluable for care staff working with the profoundly multiply handicapped person.

Physical deformities

There are many types of deformities which can develop in the person suffering from severe cerebral palsy, such as contractures, 'windswept hips' and spinal deformities (Scrutton, 1978). The severely physically handicapped

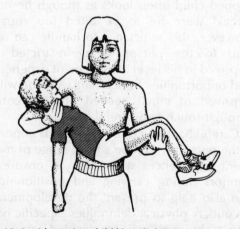

Fig. 9.18 Avoid carrying child like a baby.

person is very prone to the development of secondary physical deformities. As well as creating problems for the handicapped person, these deformities pose problems for care staff, e.g. trying to fit a nappy on to a person whose hips are so tightly drawn together and legs so scissored that they cannot be separated, or trying to put a pair of trousers on to the person whose legs are severely contracted in the bent position.

There are many factors which may contribute towards the development of physical deformities:

Immobility. This causes muscles to atrophy and shorten. Tendons and ligaments lose their elasticity and fixed contractures can result.

Muscle imbalance. If muscle tone is impaired as in hypotonicity where the muscle tone is reduced or in hypertonicity where the tone is greatly increased, bones can be pulled out of alignment by the abnormal pull of the surrounding muscles and deformities can result.

Asymmetry. Asymmetries can arise through muscle imbalance or as a result of the person maintaining a constant preferred position which almost always involves one side of the body only. If an asymmetry is allowed to persist it may lead to an incorrectable physical deformity.

Abnormal reflex patterns. Asymmetric tonic neck reflex or extensor reflex can interfere with development of normal postures and positions, thus creating deformities.

Growth factors. Deformities can often present during periods of growth spurt such as adolescence.

Position. The positions in which the person is placed throughout the day and night can also be a cause of serious deformities (Fulford & Brown, 1976).

Prevention of deformities. Frequent changes of position are planned throughout the day for the person. The person is encouraged to experience regular varied movements which follow as normal a pattern as possible. Both passive and, where possible, active movements have a part to play. Passive movements, however, are a poor substitute for active

movements initiated and performed by the person himself.

Passive movements are not entirely satisfactory as they have traditionally been interpreted by care staff as simply picking up limbs and putting them through a limited range of movements (Seivwright, 1982). This regime of passive movements however neglects important areas such as the hips and spine. Of far greater benefit to the person is a planned programme of functional movements and positions which can be used as part of all of the person's daily activities (Finnie, 1974; Levitt, 1983).

Attempting to force or stretch spastic muscles will only increase the level of spasticity. Instead the limb is moved very gently and smoothly. Massage of the muscles may also help to decrease the level of spasticity within the muscle. Music and movement classes can also be helpful in providing the handicapped person with a scheme of exercises and beneficial movements. To be effective these sessions should be held on a regular basis, and where possible with the guidance of the physiotherapist. The aim is that although the exercises may be entirely passive to begin with, the handicapped person will eventually develop a conditioned reflex whereby he will recognise a particular tune and move appropriately. As group exercises these sessions provide an invaluable communal activity, something that is often missing in the lives of severely physically handicapped people.

Individual exercise sessions also have a part to play as they can be adapted depending on the nature of the person's handicaps. The Doman-Delacato 'progressive patterning' exercises have evolved from the stages of movement development that non-handicapped children would go through. The movement patterns are divided into six stages ranging from prone lying with head and trunk rotation from side to side, through to a walking pattern. The most severely physically handicapped or immobile person may only be suited to the first three stages of prone lying with patterned movements being performed by the trunk, limbs and head.

This system of treatment is very labour intensive as it is recommended that these patterning sessions are carried out at least five
times per day for 5 minutes each time. The
exercises also require at least five helpers: one
to handle each arm and leg and one to handle
the person's head. Rotas involving over 20 volunteers have been used to maintain these intensive programmes.

The theory behind these treatments is that
'silent neurological pathways' can be opened
by the constant repetition of the movements
performed during the patterning. However the
treatment has been the subject of much controversy. Its critics claim that it raises parents'
hopes unduly that the treatment will 'cure'
their child's handicaps, and that research-
based evidence as to the validity of its claims
is either unacceptable or non-existent (Masland, 1966; Zigler & Seitz 1975). On the positive side the schemes of exercises do have
definite aims which allow care staff to work
with a programme which has identifiable treatments and a measurable sequence of pro-
gressions. The very intensive nature of the
patterning exercises may benefit the person in
that for periods of 5–15 minutes he will be receiving the individual attention and stimulus
of approximately five people. Viewed simply
as exercises, the patterning movements do
seem very suitable methods of correcting abnormal reflexes and carrying out an effective
range of passive movements on the trunk and
limbs. This should help greatly in the prevention of secondary physical deformities. For a
detailed account of how to perform these patterning exercises, see Levitt (1983) and Beasley
(1974).

Another method of providing individual exercises can be used if the residential facility
has a hydrotherapy pool. Pool activities can
provide many benefits for the profoundly multiply handicapped person:

To provide a change of environment.
To encourage relaxation.
To improve the circulation.
To encourage active movement.
To encourage self help.

To encourage play and recreational activities (Mason, 1975).

This is an area where care staff and physiotherapist can work very closely together.

Some general points regarding the management of the profoundly handicapped person
who has superimposed physical handicaps can
be made.

1. Techniques of moving, positioning and
handling are not the exclusive province
of the physiotherapist but should be part
of the skills of all caregivers involved with
the profoundly multiply handicapped.
2. It is impossible to divorce the techniques
and principles of good positioning and
handling from the person's activities of
daily living such as feeding, sleeping, sitting and moving. It is counterproductive
to divide the person into 'areas' for each
therapist such as mouth for the speech
therapist, limbs for the physiotherapist
etc. All disciplines must co-operate and
work effectively to provide total care for
the handicapped person.
3. Programmes of positioning and exercises
must be repeated regularly and frequently to be effective. Instant results are
neither looked for nor expected.
4. The needs of each physically handicapped person will be different due to
the wide variety of manifestations that
this handicap may take. The nature of
each individual person's handicaps has to
be considered and his care planned
accordingly.

Helping the person to rest and sleep

Many profoundly multiply handicapped people
display erratic or unusual sleep patterns. It is
thought that the ability to sleep deeply
develops along with maturation of the central
nervous system. An area deep within the brain
called the hypothalamus is thought to have a
prominent part to play in arousal and sleep.
There has been a tendency to underestimate

the importance of sound sleep and think of it as a very negative state where nothing is really happening. However, it is now widely recognised that a disturbed sleep pattern can seriously affect a person's emotional and physical wellbeing.

Ask a mother with a young bably who cries inconsolably night after night how she feels during the day as she tries to cope with all of her activities and relate to her family, having had little or no sleep. At the very extreme of this process of sleep disturbance it has been a common technique of physical and psychological torture to force a person to stand for many days and forcibly to prevent him from sleeping.

In addition to central nervous system damage there may be other factors which prevent the profoundly handicapped person from having a sound night's sleep. His level of activity during the day is an important consideration. If left to lie in bed or to sit in a wheelchair for an entire day, a person is unlikely to sleep well during the night. Here a pattern of sleep reversal may occur whereby the person may sleep during the day and be alert during the night. Sleep can also be disturbed by pain, discomfort, drug effects, hunger or thirst, or strong emotional and environmental factors.

There are several ways in which care staff can help promote a sound night's sleep. It should be beneficial if the person's day has been filled with interesting activities. Changes of position, play and games, exercises, music and movement, going for walks or playing outdoors can all be used to provide a variety of activities.

It is very difficult to fall asleep if you are hungry or thirsty. Unfortunately in many residential facilities the handicapped person may have his last meal of the day at around 4.00 pm. In this case a light supper including a warm milky drink should aid more restful sleep (Southwell et al, 1972). Being wet or soiled may cause discomfort and difficulty in getting to sleep, so night attire should be checked and changed if necessary.

There is often a quiet period in the evening just before bedtime when care staff can spend time in holding and settling the handicapped person. Care staff can hold or sit the person on their knee, talking to him and rocking him gently. This would also be a good time to tell bedtime stories or simply to talk to the person and try to evoke a response. Oswin (1978) found, through observation in several units for multiply handicapped children, that children were receiving an average of 5 minutes of mothering attention (cuddling, play and talking to) in a 10 hour period.

During the night, care staff have to perform certain tasks such as changing the person's position, washing and changing the person who is wet or soiled and perhaps administering medication. As far as possible such activities should be carried out concomitantly in order to minimise the disturbance to the handicapped person and those around him. Continued crying or restlessness can often be a sign of a physical illness or an acute painful episode such as headache, toothache or earache. Crying and restlessness may also accompany an epileptic seizure.

Night-time positioning is an integral part of the positioning programme which is aimed at reducing or preventing the development of secondary physical deformities. If the severely physically handicapped person were to be placed in bed in the supine position, he would tend to adopt a preferred position from which he could not move for the entire night.

This position of lying on his back is the worst possible position for the severely physically handicapped person as it leads to the development of positional deformities such as 'windswept hips', flexion contractures of the limbs and spinal deformities such as scoliosis (see Fig. 9.1). For the immobile person even side lying positions are of little help in preventing these deformities as they require to be supported and adapted.

The aim of these special positions is to help to counteract any incipient deformities by using padding in the form of pillows or preferably individually tailored and cut pieces of high density foam. The person's hips are kept well apart by placing a folded pillow between the thighs. This helps to prevent the legs from scissoring and developing contractures in the adducted position. A pillow, sandbag, pad or folded towel is placed at the person's back to prevent him from rolling over (Fig. 9.20).

Extra padding or foam blocks are often used with the side lying position to try to counteract any curvature of the spine. For instance if the person has a spinal curvature to his right side:

When lying on his right side a pad would be placed under his ribs (Fig. 9.20).

When lying on his left side a pad or block would be placed under his hips (Fig. 9.21).

If the person has been used to lying in a preferred position he may indicate discomfort and attempt to resist these new positions, but it is important that this programme of good positioning be continued throughout the night if the efforts of care staff during the day are not to be negated.

If for any reason, such as an acute chest infection, a side lying position is contra-indicated, the person is sat up in as symmetrical a position as possible. His head is supported and not allowed to extend backwards. Arms and hands are brought forward in the midline and hips and knees are bent in a sitting position. A sandbag at the person's bottom can prevent the person from slipping down the bed. This position helps to counteract abnormal reflex patterns such as extensor and

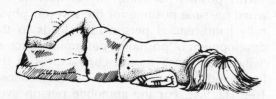

Fig. 9.20 Side-lying position — pillow between knees and pad under ribs to correct right scoliosis.

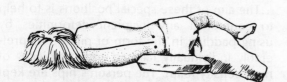

Fig. 9.21 Side-lying position — pillow between knees and pad under hips to correct left scoliosis.

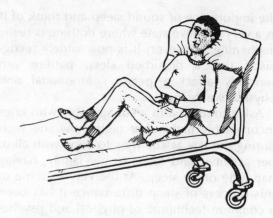

Fig. 9.22 Sitting up in bed with good support.

asymmetric tonic neck reflex. It is also a good position for allowing play and a good view of the person's surroundings (Fig. 9.22).

Drugs have a limited role in helping the multiply handicapped person achieve a good night's sleep. If a person does not fall into a deep sleep at 7.00 p.m. and awake again at 7.00 a.m. he does not have a 'sleep problem'. Hypnotic drugs are only requested when all other measures previously outlined have been conscientiously tried but have been insufficient on their own to help the person to sleep.

Among the most commonly used of these hypnotic drugs are nitrazepam (Mogadon) and chloral hydrate. If a person is prescribed these drugs, the caregiver must administer the exact dose. It should not be assumed that giving the person an increased dose, will help him to sleep more soundly.

Helping the person to select suitable clothing and helping with dressing

Institutional uniform. When we choose clothes to wear we do not think only of protecting ourselves from the weather, but of many aspects of clothing. We may wish to cover parts of our bodies to preserve our modesty or we may wish to show off parts of our bodies. We also reveal a great deal about our beliefs, attitudes and position in society by the way in which we dress. Sadly this same amount of thought is often not shown when clothing is selected for the profoundly handicapped person, especially in large institutional facilities.

The clothes which many people in residential care wear immediately proclaim to the world that they are 'patients from the hospital' or that they 'come from that home'. There are two extremes found here. One is where the person wears obviously institutional clothes which are invariably communal, ill-fitting and in some dull nondescript colour. At the other extreme we may find that staff have been given money to buy clothes for the person and have selected clothes that are totally inappropriate, e.g. a middle aged or elderly resident wearing orange jeans with a multicoloured shirt. The reasoning here seems to be that bright colours and big patterns equal non-institutional dress. In this area female residents seem to fare the worst. Dressing people in colours and styles which are incongruous with their ages and lifestyles results in their looking every bit as institutionalised as the grey shadowy figures who walk the corridors of some of our large institutions.

Care staff who appreciate the important role which clothing plays in the life of the handicapped person will realise that clothing and grooming can have a marked effect on the attitudes and behaviours of those who come into contact with the handicapped person. It is best if each person has his own personal clothing which he has helped to select wherever possible, and that each person's clothes are kept in his own wardrobe or locker. There are still institutions which preserve, at least unofficially, the practice of communal clothing although many have worked hard to end this anachronism.

Selection of clothes. There are special considerations which care staff make when selecting clothing for the profoundly multiply handicapped person. It is best if clothing is not bought as a mass purchase by the hospital or home but that it is individually purchased at 'High Street' stores. Wherever possible the handicapped person should be given the opportunity to participate in selecting his own clothing. This may not be possible for the most profoundly handicapped person, but even the very severely handicapped person may be able to indicate a preference for a particular colour or garment by a subtle gesture such as a nod or a smile.

If the handicapped person is not present when clothes are being bought for him it is important that care staff have an accurate list of his current measurements; guesses should never be made as the handicapped person may be small for his age and may have physical deformities.

The clothes chosen are usually loose fitting as tight clothing can cause skin irritation and discomfort. Tight clothing can also inhibit movement, make any physical deformities more obvious and can be very difficult for the person to put on and take off, especially if the person has only a limited range of movements. The profoundly handicapped person may require several changes of clothing in any one day, as a result of incontinence or feeding difficulties. People who wear support body braces also tend to perspire profusely.

For these reasons hard wearing and easily washable fibres are chosen such as cottons or polyester mixes. Garments which require hand washing or dry cleaning are best avoided unless efficient facilities exist for their cleaning. With the enormous range of choice of attractive, and relatively cheap, clothes available in shops and stores today there is no justification for the handicapped person being stigmatized as a result of his dress. For further specialist advice on the problem of clothing for the handicapped person, the Disabled Living Foundation at 346 Kensington High Street, London W14, provides a Clothing Advisory Service.

Dressing and undressing. The normal child will only begin to co-operate with dressing by putting out an arm or leg at around 1 year of age. He will be about 5 years old before he is dressing himself reasonably competently.

It is likely that most profoundly handicapped people will only be able to offer minimal assistance and will require to be dressed by their caregiver. It is important that all of the person's clothes are assembled and ready before beginning to help him to dress.

This saves the caregiver from making repeated trips to the wardrobe and disrupting the dressing exercise.

The person should not be 'bundled' into the clothes to get the job done quickly. Dressing affords the caregiver the chance to show the person a good position, to help make him more aware of his body, to perform a limited range of passive movements and to communicate with the person through talk and careful handling.

Depending on the nature of his physical handicaps the person is dressed in the sitting or lying position. It is a good idea to vary the position used for dressing in order to provide some variety of movement experience for the person. Lying on his back on every occasion is not beneficial. If the person has a more affected side this is dressed first. Try to straighten gently any stiffly flexed limbs and put the limb into the sleeve or trouser leg rather than pulling the clothes over the flexed limb and missing an opportunity to exercise it.

It is essential to talk to the person as you dress him. Explain what you are doing, name the different parts of his body as you dress them and talk about the colours of the clothes. Sighted people may enjoy being dressed sitting in front of a mirror where they can follow their movements as they get dressed. The caregiver observes closely for any sign of active co-operation from the person such as pushing an arm into a sleeve and encourages such developments.

People enjoy being told how nice they look or how pretty their clothes are. The severely handicapped person can often respond positively to such praise and encouragement. The less severely handicapped person may benefit from a more structured programme aimed at teaching dressing skills (see Ch. 8).

Helping the person with personal hygiene and skin care

Personal hygiene

The maintenance of a high level of personal hygiene is very important for the multiply handicapped person as any neglect can result in physical problems such as skin disorders and perhaps a reduced level of social interaction. Extra care is required if he is incontinent or prone to excessive perspiration due perhaps to his wearing special aids or appliances or to his sitting in a plastic or vinyl covered wheelchair for long periods.

The profoundly multiply handicapped person requires a daily bath or shower, preferably in the morning prior to the day's activities. A daily bath is not essential simply to ensure skin cleanliness and freshness, but it performs several other important funtions. Bathtime gives the caregiver the opportunity to examine the person's skin closely for any signs of redness or rashes which may indicate an incipient pressure sore. Any nappy rashes or other skin irritations can be noticed also.

Bathtimes also provide an ideal opportunity for play, fun and stimulation between the handicapped person and his caregiver. The method of bathing 20 to 30 people in the shortest possible time and with the minimal amount of play and interaction is more akin to a sheep dip and has no place in the care of the handicapped person.

When bathing the severely physically handicapped person it is important to wash carefully those 'awkward' areas such as skin folds, the inguinal areas and in between clenched hands. Any crusts which have formed in the nose or eyes should be removed by gently cleaning with a moistened cotton tipped bud.

Careful drying after the bath is important as areas which are left wet can cause chafing and soreness of the skin. Before dressing, talcum powder or deodorant is applied to the skin. Zinc and castor oil cream should be smoothed over the perineal region prior to putting on the person's nappy. However, avoid the excessive use of toiletries. It may be uncomfortable for the person if talc and cream are allowed to cake into lumps on his skin, thus negating their purpose.

Hair is shampooed frequently with a shampoo suited to the person's hair type. People with persistent dandruff will benefit from a special anti-dandruff shampoo. Hair should be dried in an attractive style with a hairdryer and not left to dry as a straggly mess.

Each person has a toilet bag containing his own toiletries. This practice is often started in residential facilities only rapidly to fall into disuse. It is an important part of individualising care and is a practice worth trying hard to maintain.

Skin care

The profoundly multiply handicapped person is in constant danger of developing sores or decubitus ulcers. Such sores can be difficult to heal, especially in the debilitated person. For this reason and also because of the pain and discomfort that they cause to the handicapped person, the prevention of pressure sores is a constant concern.

Factors which predispose the multiply handicapped person to developing pressure sores are:

1. immobility
2. thinness and debilitation
3. damage to the central nervous system, including sensory loss
4. having unusual bony prominences due to physical deformities
5. incontinence, with possible consequential skin breakdown
6. iatrogenic factors (factors resulting from medical/nursing care practices) such as the person being dragged up into a sitting position rather than being lifted, and the person being left in one position such as lying in bed or sitting in a wheelchair for several hours
7. vascular factors such as peripheral vascular disturbance resulting in poor circulation.

Prevention of pressure sores

This is not an isolated treatment which is carried out once or twice a day, but rather it is an awareness of the problem of pressure sores which guides the actions of the caregiver as she works with the handicapped person.

Basically, pressure sores are caused by unrelieved pressure. The multiply handicapped person therefore requires to be moved frequently throughout the day. Pressure sores can develop just as easily while the person is sitting in a wheelchair as they can if the person is lying in bed. These changes of position are viewed as part of the person's total care as this is also an integral part of maintaining good postures and positions and in the prevention of secondary physical deformities.

Regular and frequent checks are necessary to ensure that the incontinent person is not left in a wet or soiled condition, as this can lead to skin breakdown. Diet is important in the prevention of pressure sores. The aim is to help the person to achieve the best possible nutritional status for his height, build and physical condition. A diet high in calories and protein may be appropriate for the person who is susceptible to developing pressure sores.

The integrity of the person's skin is checked when undressing, changing and bathing, particularly for any areas of redness. There are several areas of the body where pressure sores are most likely to develop and these areas should be examined especially carefully:

sacrum
heels and ankles
hips
shoulders
occiput (back) of the head, especially in hydrocephalus
buttocks.

If an area of redness is noted it is vital that all pressure is kept off of this area.

The practice of vigorously rubbing a person's skin in order to stimulate the circulation has been shown by research to increase the likelihood of pressure sores developing (Dyson, 1978). This practice should be abandoned in favour of brief gentle rubbing when washing the skin. An overview of the pathogenesis, prophylaxis and treatment of pressure sores can be found in Torrance (1981).

Other skin problems

In common with most young people the handicapped person going through adolescence may suffer from acne. Skin cleanliness helps prevent pores being blocked and a proprietary deep cleansing lotion may be useful here after routine face washes. If the acne is very severe an antibiotic such as tetracycline may be prescribed. If the person tends to rub or scratch the affected areas his nails are kept clean and short in order to prevent further skin abrasion and infection.

People who have to wear any kind of orthopaedic brace or appliance may suffer from skin abrasions, redness or sores. This is especially common where the appliance is new, where perhaps it has not been put on properly or where the appliance has been outgrown by the person and is now too small, or where the person has to wear plaster of Paris casts following orthopaedic surgery.

Dental care and oral hygiene

Healthy teeth and gums are important in that they allow proper biting and chewing, help in proper speech development and give us an attractive appearance. In addition to the range of problems which can affect the non-handicapped person such as dental caries, gum disease and toothache, the profoundly multiply handicapped person may be faced with additional dental problems:

Malocclusion. This is commonly found in people with cerebral palsy. The teeth are irregularly arranged in the jaws which results in the accumulation of food debris with a consequent rise in the level of decay and gum disease. Malocclusion also adversely affects the person's appearance.

Bruxism. Bruxism or tooth grinding is more common in severely handicapped people and can result in increased and irregular wear on the teeth.

Poor oral clearance. Many profoundly handicapped people lack the ability to use their tongue and lips effectively. This can result in an excessive build up of plaque on the teeth with a resultant increase in decay and gum disease. Some profoundly handicapped people who also suffer from epilepsy may experience difficulty in clearing food from their teeth and gums due to hypertrophy or overgrowth of their gums caused by the anticonvulsant drug phenytoin (Epanutin).

Enamel deficiency. Malformations and deficiencies of tooth enamel are also more common among people with cerebral palsy (Rosenstein, 1978).

The mentally handicapped person living in a residential facility may suffer from dental and oral problems of an iatrogenic nature. Many wards and units relegate dental care to a low position of the list of priorities, and the standard of dental care is often poor as a result.

Other dental problems can be created for the handicapped person if he is receiving an especially high calorie diet. This diet tends to consist of sugary foods. Programmes involving the use of sweets to reward good behaviour can also unintentionally increase the chances of tooth decay occurring.

Should the non-communicative profoundly multiply handicapped person develop oral pain or toothache he may be unable to communicate this effectively to his caregivers, with resultant periods spent in pain and discomfort. If the profoundly handicapped person were to lose his teeth through decay it is almost certain that he would be unable to co-operate in the wearing of dentures. This would adversely affect his appearance and although the person himself may not express this, appearance can affect the amount and quality of the care that he receives (Berscheid & Walster, 1974).

Toothbrushing. There are many practical difficulties involved in efficiently cleaning the mouth of a severely handicapped person. He may dislike the procedure and offer resistance to it by constantly moving the head and biting on the toothbrush. Problems encountered during feeding such as a bite reflex or tendency to gag and choke can also make tooth cleaning difficult.

The object of toothbrushing is to remove plaque from the teeth, to remove food debris from spaces between the teeth and to massage gums (even those without teeth benefit from brushing). An additional aim is to leave the person's mouth feeling clean and fresh. In normal practice it is best to use a fluoride toothpaste or in special circumstances where the person may have a particular problem such as dental plaque or inflammation of the gums (gingivitis) a chlorhexidine gel may be used (Gibbons, 1983).

A good position for toothbrushing is standing behind the person while supporting his head and opening his mouth with the free hand. When using this method it is important to let the person know that you are going to clean his teeth, in order that he is not suddenly frightened. Another position, suitable for adults, is for the person to sit on the floor below the caregiver who can sit on a chair and hold the person's shoulders with his legs. This leaves both hands free for toothbrushing.

Each person should have his own toothbrush which is kept in his toilet bag or on a toothbrush rack. The latter method has the advantage of allowing the brushes to dry out between use. The wide range of toothbrushes available makes choosing the correct type difficult, however a small headed brush allows better access to corners of the mouth. A dentist or dental hygienist may help to select the proper toothbrushes for each handicapped person. It is best to replace toothbrushes approximately every 2 months.

Oral hygiene

Profoundly multiply handicapped people often breathe through their mouths. This can cause the mouth, tongue and lips to become dry and cracked. If left unattended this condition can lead to an increased risk of tooth decay and unpleasant halitosis. To prevent this the person is given regular small drinks to help to keep his mouth moist. The lips can be kept in good condition by smearing them regularly with petroleum jelly.

The person's mouth is cleaned occasionally with a solution of sodium bicarbonate in warm water using a foam tipped stick or preferably an index finger with some clean gauze swabs wrapped around it. This is effective but the taste may be unpleasant for some people. Chlorhexidine mouth washes have also been found to be effective in inhibiting the formation of plaque and gingivitis.

Dental hygienist

One of the most effective improvements in dental services for the mentally handicapped person has been the increasing use of the dental hygienist. The hygienist has an important role to play in the prevention of dental and oral problems through regular dental inspections and treatments. If the hygienist carries out her treatments in the ward or unit and not in the surgery, care staff can observe the techniques used by the hygienist.

Care staff often remark on how dramatic is the difference between their teeth cleaning techniques and those employed by the hygienist. The hygienist therefore has an important role to play in teaching good dental care practices not only to the person with the handicap but also to care staff. The handicapped person should receive a dental examination at approximately 6-monthly intervals.

Most of us are usually apprehensive at the thought of a visit to the dentist and the profoundly multiply handicapped person may also find this a frightening experience. For this reason alone the escorting of people to the dental surgery should not be relegated to the level of a 'deliver and dump in the waiting room' exercise.

An experienced caregiver who has a good rapport with the person accompanies him to the surgery. She will ensure that she has with her all of the information that the dentist may require such as records, the care plan and prescription sheets which lists any medication that the person is receiving. The caregiver stays with the person throughout the procedure to assist the dentist if required and also to comfort and reassure the person. If the person is to undergo general anaesthesia, then a trained nurse who is fully conversant with how to recover a person from an anaesthetic should accompany him.

Helping the person to avoid dangers in the environment

It is difficult to list every accident which can happen and prescribe preventive action for these. Many people however feel that the profoundly multiply handicapped person is very unlikely to have accidents due to the fact that he may lead a life of little mobility and therefore incur little risk, unlike the more lively and mobile handicapped person who will run around and explore while showing little regard for any dangers. This is unfortunately a belief which leads to complacency.

Constant vigilance is required from care staff if the person's environment is to be kept safe. Accidental burns can be caused by serving food which is far too hot. Filling baths with hot water before adding cold is also a potentially dangerous practice as the handicapped person may put a limb into the water before the cold water has been added. The common radiator can also cause severe burns if the person is left sitting too close and is unable to communicate his feelings of pain and discomfort to care staff.

Aids and appliances can often be involved in accidents. If people in wheelchairs are not given tables to place their hands and arms on, their arms can hang at the sides of the chair where fingers may be caught in the spokes. People should never be wheeled in a chair with their arms hanging over the sides. Painful injuries can easily result if the caregiver tries to push the person's chair through a narrow doorway.

There are potential dangers even in bed. If the person is a restless sleeper cot sides may be kept in position to prevent him from falling out of bed. Occasionally, padded cot sides may be necessary to protect the people who

repeatedly injure themselves against the cot sides or bed rails perhaps as the result of particularly severe seizures. This procedure is not routine for all handicapped people simply because they are in residential care or because they are severely handicapped as it cuts down the person's view of his surroundings causing an unnecessary degree of sensory deprivation.

Florence Nightingale said that a prime function of a hospital is that it should do the sick no harm. This is equally true for any place of residential care.

Helping the person with communication

Although communication is discussed more fully in Chapters 10 and 11 several aspects are closely related to physical care of the profoundly multiply handicapped. The handicapped person may have many problems which will make communication between him and his caregivers difficult such as the inability to speak or to indicate his needs by gestures; there may also be sensory problems such as deafness and/or blindness. When so much of the profoundly handicapped person's day may be involved in physical aspects of care, communication between the person and his caregiver should be an integral part of these care procedures.

When carrying out any care procedure with the handicapped person communication and rapport with the person is established by using every available channel of communication — verbal and non-verbal — play, touch and handling. It is often difficult for care staff to see the importance of talking to the handicapped person who seems not to understand or respond. This seeming lack of response often leads to the caregiver giving up her attempts at verbal communication. However, the development of responses and rapport takes some time and care staff should not become discouraged if immediate responses are not forthcoming. The caregiver may try to vary her voice to make it as understandable and as interesting as possible in order to evoke a response from the person. A funny voice or a whisper in the ear can sometimes produce a smile.

Non-verbal forms of communication such as the use of facial expression by the caregiver can give greater emphasis to what is being communicated. Touch is a very important system of non-verbal communication as the experiments of the psychologist Harlow (1971) showed. He discovered that baby monkeys when deprived of physical contact failed to develop normal patterns of interaction, became aggressive and anti-social and were unable to mate or to act as parents to young monkeys. Similar adverse effects have been described in human subjects (Pratt & Mason, 1981).

Feelings of affection, security and fun can all be conveyed by touch and handling. The way in which a person is lifted from his bed or carried to the bath can be done in such a way as to let the handicapped person experience warmth, security and enjoyment. Fun and enjoyment can also be conveyed by tickling and through games such as 'round and round the garden' and 'hickory dickory dock'. Seemingly unresponsive children will often smile and show pleasure during such simple physical contact exercises.

Pain and distress

One of the most vital areas of communication with the profoundly multiply handicapped person is that of detecting signs of pain, distress or discomfort which the person may be showing. It is a common fear of most parents whose child has to go into hospital that the staff will not know if he is upset or in any discomfort (Fraser & Ozols, 1980, 1981). Non-handicapped people can indicate pain or distress relatively easily. They can complain of pain and describe and locate it. They can use gestures to point to painful areas or to relieve the pain by, for example holding a sore head or stomach. They can also cry, groan and moan very expressively. There are however many profoundly multiply handicapped people who are unable to make known their pain and discomfort by any of these means.

The profoundly handicapped person is as likely to suffer from earache, toothache, headache, indigestion, constipation, cramp/muscle spasms or any other painful complaint. When he is trying to indicate pain and distress the signs may be very subtle and their detection calls for acute powers of observation on the part of the care staff:

Crying — this may not be loud overt crying and is often unaccompanied by tears.

Vocalisations — grunts, groans and moans.

Facial expressions — grimaces or 'pained looks'.

Nonverbal body communication — holding the jaw when there is toothache or drawing up the knees when there is abdominal pain.

Undirected agression — self injurious behaviour.

Movement disorders — any movement pattern which is abnormal for the person, e.g. restlesness, fidgeting and fussing behaviours or alternatively a reluctance to move.

Anorexia — loss of appetite is a common feature of pain and distress (Fraser & Ozols, 1980, 1981).

The signs and signals may be such a subtle part of the person's behaviour pattern that they may only be noticed by the observant caregiver who is experienced in working with the particular handicapped person. For this reason information regarding how the person indicates discomfort and/or pain is written in his care plan or casenotes. This information is important for any new care staff or therapist who may be working with the person.

The subject of pain and distress signs forms part of every admission interview with parents of profoundly handicapped people. Parents should be asked how their child shows pain and distress, and reassured that this information will be used by all those caring for the handicapped person in order to detect any pain or discomfort promptly.

Care staff should not underestimate the importance of this aspect of communication. If the person's caregiver is unaware of this area or has poor observational skills, then the profoundly handicapped person can be left to suffer pain and distress. This is incompatible with achieving the best quality of care for the handicapped person.

Helping the person with recreation and occupation

The provision of suitable recreational and play experiences forms an important part of giving physical care. When we think of how a parent carries out physical care activities with his/her child we see that these are often enriched by including recreational or play activities. Routine tasks such as dressing and bathing are often made into games. The caregiver should try to think of ways in which she can bring this extra dimension into her physical care of the multiply handicapped person (see Ch. 12).

Helping the person to learn

Many workers in the field now view mental handicap as primarily a learning disorder. It follows therefore that when providing physical care we try to increase the handicapped person's level of independence and knowledge as we do so. With the profoundly multiply handicapped person this may be very difficult indeed, yet improvements are possible although these may appear very slight. The person may learn to turn his head towards a stimulus when lying over a foam wedge or may try to push his arm into his sleeve when dressing or may smile and show pleasure when being handled in a particular way. These improvements may only come after many months of effort from care staff, yet they are improvements which indicate that the profoundly handicapped person has learned.

Physical care activities will take up a large part of the person's day and these activities are viewed as potential learning experiences. Otherwise physical care may become almost a passive routine whereby the caregiver performs care tasks on rather than with a person. How can these activities of physical care give the person a chance to learn?

The activities are used as opportunities to build a relationship and establish empathy with the handicapped person. This rapport cannot be established overnight. The handicapped person has to become accustomed to his caregivers, to trust their handling, to recognise their voices and to sense their affection. It is perhaps unreasonable to expect the profoundly multiply handicapped person to show signs of progress if these relationships have not been made.

New responses and behaviours will not be learned quickly by the profoundly handicapped person. Care staff frequently become disheartened when they have tried to evoke a smile or a response from a person for many months and have been met with a blank response. The caregiver should not give up trying.

If we wish the person to have the best possible chance of making a desired response we can try to be consistent in how we carry out the physical care. In presenting the same activity in the same way we give the person a chance to become familiar with the activity and possibly to anticipate a response or action. The handicapped person may become confused if his care is carried out by many people in many different ways. This confusion may arise as a result of the system of caregiving where care staff are allocated jobs instead of people to care for. Here the caregiver may find herself performing the same task on several people. This contrasts with a system of care where a caregiver is responsible for caring for all of the needs of a specified group of people. However, it is important that we do not confuse consistency in care with propagating and being unwilling to change out-dated and unsatisfactory institutional care practices.

REFERENCES

Balla D 1976 Relationship between institutional size and quality of care: A review of the literature. American Journal of Mental Deficiency 81: 117–125
Beasley N A 1974 A sensory motor training programme

in the special care unit. In: Better services — the realities. Association of Professions for the Mentally Handicapped Ist Annual Congress Report, London

Berscheid E, Walster E 1974 Physical attractiveness, Advances in experimental social psychology, vol 7. Academic Press, London

Chaney R H, Eyman R K, Miller C R 1979 Comparison of respiratory mortality in the profoundly mentally retarded and in the less retarded. Journal of Mental Deficiency Research 23: 1–7

Cleland C C 1979 The profoundly mentally retarded. Prentice Hall, New Jersey

Craft M (ed) 1979 Tredgold's mental retardation, 12th edn. Bailliere Tindall, London

Department of Health and Social Security 1971 Better services for the mentally handicapped. HMSO, London

Drillen C M 1958 Growth and development in a group of children of very low birthweight. Archives of Diseases of Childhood 33: 10–18

Dyson R 1978 Bed sores — the injuries hospital staff inflict on patients, Nursing Mirror 146: 30–32

Finnie N 1974 Handling the young cerebral palsied child at home. Heinemann Medical, London

Fraser W I, Ozols D 1980 Cries of pain and distress in the severely mentally handicapped. In: Mittler P (ed) Proceedings of the 5th Congress of the International Association for the Scientific Study of Mental Deficiency, Jerusalem

Fraser W I, Ozols D 1981 Detecting pain and distress in the profoundly retarded, In: Mittler P (ed) Frontiers of knowledge in mental retardation. Vol 1 — Social, educational and behavioural aspects. International Association for the Scientific Study of Mental Deficiency, Amsterdam

Fraser W I, Ozols D 1981 He sounds and looks sore — Professionals' evaluation of the profoundly handicapped person's pain and distress signals. In: Fraser W I, Grieve R (eds) Communicating with normal and retarded children. Wright, Bristol

Fulford G E, Brown J K 1976 Position as a cause of deformity in children with cerebral palsy. Developmental Medicine and Child Neurology 18: 305–314

Fulford G E, Cairns T P, Sloan Y 1982 Sitting problems of children with cerebral palsy. Developmental Medicine and Child Neurology 24: 48–53

Gibbons D E 1983 Mouth care procedures. Nursing Times 79: 30

Goffman D 1961 Asylums. Penguin, Harmondsworth

Harlow H F 1971 Learning to love. Albion, San Francisco

Henderson V 1969 Basic principles of nursing care. S Karger/International Council of Nurses, Basel

Holt K S 1970 The quality of survival for birth and life. Maternal and Child Care 6: 211–214

Innes G, Johnston A W, Millar W M 1978 Mental subnormality in North East Scotland: A multi-disciplinary study of total population. Scottish Health Service Studies No 38. HMSO, Edinburgh

Levitt S 1983 Treatment of cerebral palsy and motor delay, 2nd edn. Blackwell Scientific, London

Masland R L 1966 Unproven methods of treatment. Paediatrics 37: 713–714

Mason C 1975 Pool activities with the multiply handicapped child. Nursing Mirror 71:50–52

McFarlane J, Castledine G 1982 A guide to the practice of nursing using the nursing process. C V Mosby, London

Moores B, Grant G W B 1977 Optimists and pessimists: Attitudes of nursing staff towards the development potential of mentally handicapped patients in their charge. International Journal of Nursing Studies 14: 13–18

Moores B, Grant G W B 1977 Feelings of alienation among nursing staff in hospitals for the mentally handicapped. International Journal of Nursing Studies 14: 5–12

O'Reilly D E, Walentynowicz J E 1981 Etiological factors in cerebral plasy: An historical review. Developmental Medicine and Child Neurology 23:633–642

Oswin M 1978 Children living in long stay hospitals. Spastics International Medical Publications/Heinemann Medical Books, London

Oswin M 1978 Holes in the welfare net. Bedford Square Press, London

Paneth N, Kiely J L, Stein Z, Susser M 1981 Cerebral palsy and newborn care III: Estimated prevalence rates of cerebral palsy under differing rates of mortality and impairment of low-birthweight infants. Developmental Medicine and Child Neurology 23: 801–807

Penfold J 1976 The education of the child in special care: conference report. Petras Division, Newcastle upon Tyne Polytechnic, Newcastle upon Tyne

Pratt J W, Mason A 1981 The caring touch. HM+M Publishers, London

Richards N C G 1977 Treatment of choking. Nursing Times 73: 856–857

Robinson H B, Robinson N M 1965 The mentally retarded child. McGraw-Hill, New York

Roper N, Logan W W, Tierney A J 1980 The elements of nursing. Churchill Livingstone, Edinburgh

Rosenstein S N 1978 Dentistry in cerebral palsy and related handicapping conditions. Thomas, Springfield, Illinois

Scrutton D 1978 Developmental deformity and the profoundly retarded child In: Apley J (ed) Care of the handicapped child. Spastics International Medical Publications/Heinemann Medical Books, London

Seivwright J 1982 An unconventional approach to therapy. Remedial Therapist 4:21

Sontag E, Burke P, York R 1973 Consideration for serving the severely handicapped in the public school. Education and Training of the Mentally Retarded 8: 20–26

Southwell P R, Evans C, Hunt J N 1972 Effect of a hot milk drink on movements during sleep. British Medical Journal 2: 429–431

Stevens M 1976 The educational and social needs of children with severe handicaps. Edward Arnold, London

Swartz J D 1979 Foreword. In: Cleland C C (ed) The profoundly mentally handicapped. Prentice Hall, New Jersey

Torrance C 1981 The perennial pressure sore. Nursing Times Publications, London

Warburg M 1977 Blindness among 7600 mentally retarded children in Denmark. Proceedings of Study Group on Infants and Children with Visual Defects — April 1977, University of Nottingham

Wehman P, Bates P 1978 Education curriculum for

severely and profoundly handicapped persons: A Review. Rehabilitation Literature 39: 2–14

Wright E C, Abbas K A, Meredith C 1974 A study of interactions between nursing staff and profoundly mentally retarded children. Apex: Journal of the British Institute of Mental Handicap 20: 14–17 and 102–103

Zigler E, Seitz V 1975 On 'An experimental evaluation of sensory/motor patterning': A Critique. American Journal of Mental Deficiency 79: 483–492

FURTHER READING

Albin J B 1977 Some variables influencing the maintenance of acquired self-feeding behaviour in profoundly retarded children. Mental Retardation 15: 49–52

Azrin N, Armstrong P M 1973 The 'mini-meal' — a method for teaching eating skills to the profoundly retarded. Mental Retardatation 11: 9–13

Baker M, Jupp K, Myland E, Thurlow O 1981 A suggested curriculum for the profoundly handicapped child. Apex: Journal of the British Institute of Mental Handicap 8: 132

Ball T 1971 A guide for the instruction and training of the profoundly retarded multi-handicapped child. Santa Cruz County Board of Education, California

Ball T S, Hendricksen H, Clayton J 1974 A special feeding technique for chronic regurgitation. American Journal of Mental Deficiency 78: 486–493

Ball T, Serick, Payne L 1971 Long term retention of self help skill training in the profoundly retarded. American Journal of Mental Deficiency 76: 378–382

Banks S N, Mendleson M A 1974 A comprehensive program for multihandicapped mentally retarded children. Journal of Special Educators of the Mentally Retarded 11: 44–49

Barolatromana G, Davis R 1980 Neurophysiological mechanisms in abnormal reflex activities in cerebral palsy and spinal spasticity. Journal of Neurology, Neurosurgery and Psychiatry 43: 333–342

Bartholomew L 1980 Special care units: the shape of things to come? Apex: Journal of the British Institute of Mental Handicap 8: 48–50

Barton E S 1973 Operant conditioning of appropriate and inappropriate social speech in the profoundly retarded. Journal of Mental Deficiency Research 17: 183–191

Bellamy G T, Peterson L, Close D 1975 Habilitation of the severely and profoundly retarded: illustrations of competence. Education and Training of the Mentally Retarded 10: 174–186

Berkowitz S, Sherry P, Davis B 1971 Teaching self feeding skills to profound retardates using reinforcement and fading procedures. Behaviour Therapy 2: 62–67

Berkson G, Landesman-Dwyer S 1977 Behavioural research on severe and profound mental retardation. American Journal of Mental Deficiency 81: 428–454

Blackwell M W, Roy S A 1978 Surgical routines for profoundly retarded patients. American Journal of Nursing 78: 402–404

Bloxham E, Swallow J N 1975 The dental treatment of institutionalised mentally handicapped people: A two year report. British Dental Journal 139: 145–146

Bobath B, Bobath K 1975 Motor development in the different types of cerebral palsy. Heinemann Medical, London

Brewster L 1979 A survey of multiply handicapped blind children in the West Midlands Health Region. Apex: Journal of the British Institute of Mental Handicap 7: 78–79

Brown J E, Davis E, Flemming P L 1979 Nutritional assessment of children with handicapping conditions. Mental Reardatation 17: 129–132

Brown H S, Milner A, Penn R D 1979 Pathophysiological mechanisms in cerebral palsy. Journal of Neurology, Neurosurgery and Psychiatry 42: 606–618

Budd B, Evans J 1977 What is their future? An experimental project in conductive education with the multiply handicapped. Apex: Journal of the British Institute of Mental Handicap 4: 18–22

Burton T A, Hirshoren A 1979 The education of severely and profoundly retarded children: are we sacrificing the child to the concept? Exceptional Children 45: 598–602

Burton T A, Hirshoren A 1979 Some further thoughts and clarifications on the education of severely and profoundly retarded children. Exceptional Children 45: 618–625

Caunter M, Penrose J 1983 Solving feeding problems. Nursing Times 79 (51): 24–26

Caunter M 1983 Physiotherapy in mental handicap. Nursing Times 79 (49): 54–57

Christian W, Holloman S, Lanier C L 1973 An attendant operated feeding programme for severely and profoundly retarded females. Mental Retardation 11: 35–37

Clements J 1976 Training programmes for the multiply handicapped child. Apex: Journal of the British Institute of Mental Handicap 3: 14–17

Close D W 1977 Community living for severely and profoundly retarded adults: A group home study. Education and Training of the Mentally Retarded 12: 256–262

Council on Exceptional Children 1977 Hey don't forget about me: Education's investment in the severely profoundly and multiply handicapped. Council on Exceptional Children, Reston Virginia

Culley W J, Middleton T O 1969 Caloric requirements of mentally retarded children with and without motor dysfunction. Journal of Paediatrics 75: 380–384

Dawson M J 1980 Nursing care of the institutionalised profoundly retarded. New Zealand Nursing Forum 8: 8–10

De Vore S 1978 Individualised learning programme for the profoundly retarded. C C Thomas, Illinois

Douglas B L 1975 Dental care of the special patient in the hospital environment. International Dental Journal 25: 206–209

Eldridge H 1983 Double handicap: classification and causes. Nursing times 79 (48): 51–52

Endres J, Thamann A 1969 New perspectives in applied nutrition for mentally retarded children. Mental Retardatation 7: 44–47

Garn S M, Weir H K 1971 Assessing the nutritional status of the mentally retarded. American Journal of Clinical Nutrition 24: 853–854

Glover E, Mesibon G B 1978 An interest center sensory stimulation programme for severely and profoundly retarded children. Education and Training of the Mentally Retarded 13: 172–176

Goode D, Gaddy M 1976 Ascertaining choice with alingual deaf-blind and retarded clients. Mental Retardation 14: 10

Groves I L, Carroccio D F 1971, A self-feeding programme for the severely and profoundly retarded. Mental Retardation 9: 10–12

Grunewald K 1974 International trends in the care of the severely profoundly retarded and multiply handicapped. In: Meolascino F J, Pearson P H (eds) Beyond the limits, inovations in services for the severely and profoundly handicapped. Special Child Publications, Seattle, Washington

Hardman M L, Drew C H 1978 Life management practices with the profoundly retarded: Issues of euthenasia and withholding treatment. Mental Retardation 16: 390–396

Hengen M 1980 The role of the dental hygienist in the dental care of the cerebral palsy patient. Dental Hygiene 54: 472–473

Hereford S M, Cleland C C, Fellner M 1973 Territoriality and scent marking: A study of profoundly retarded enuretics and encopretics. American Journal of Mental Deficiency 77: 426–430

Hobson P A, Duncan P 1979 Sign learning and profoundly retarded people. Mental Retardatation 17: 33–37

Jones A M 1979 Overcoming the feeding problems of the mentally and physically handicapped. Journal of Human Nutrition 32: 359–367

Kanthor H, Pless B, Satterwhite B, Myers G 1974 Areas of responsibility in the health care of multiply handicapped children. Paediatrics 54: 779–785

Kass L 1979 Dental health program for the institutionally mentally retarded. Dental Hygiene 53: 76–78

Knott G P 1979 Attitudes and needs of parents of cerebral palsied children. Rehabilitation Literature 40: 190–195

Kucherawy D A, Kucherawy J M 1978 An electrical communication system for a nonverbal profoundly retarded spastic quadriplegic. Education and Training of the Mentally Retarded 13: 342–344

Lancioni G E 1980 Teaching independent toileting to profoundly retarded deaf-blind children. Behaviour Therapy 1: 234–244

Landesman-Dwyer S, Sackett C P 1978 Behavioural changes in nonambulatory profoundly mentally retarded individuals. Monograph of the American Association for Mental Deficiency 3: 55–144

Levine M, Elliot C B 1970 Toilet training for the profoundly retarded with limited staff. Mental Retardation 8: 48–50

Loynd J, Barclay AA 1970 A case study in developing ambulation in a profoundly retarded child. Behaviour Research and Therapy 8:270

Luckey R, Addison M 1974 The profoundly retarded: A new challenge for public education. Education and Training of the Mentally Retarded 9: 123–130

MacAndrew C, Edgerton R 1964 The everyday life of institutionalized idiots. Human Organisation 23: 312–318

MacAndrew C, Edgerton R 1964 IQ and the social

competence of the profoundly retarded. American Journal of Mental Deficiency 70: 612–621

McGavern M L, Cleland C C, Swartz J D 1974 Locating the profoundly retarded. Mental Retardation 12: 49–50

McGuire T 1979 The multi-handicapped blind in hospitals for the mentally handicapped. Regional Review 65: 4–7

Mason C 1975 The multiply handicapped child. British Journal of Occupational Therapy 38: 226–227

Michaelis G 1977 The physiotherapist working in special care units. Parents Voice 27: 8–10

Miller C J 1976 Children with feeding problems. Child: Care, Health and Development 2: 73–76

Miller M 1979 Oral hygiene management of the moderate to severely mentally retarded child. Dental Hygiene 53: 265–268

Miller S R, Miller T, Repp A 1978 Are profoundly and severely retarded people given access to the least restrictive environment? Mental Retardation 16: 123–126

Minge M, Ball T 1967 Teaching of self help skills to profoundly retarded patients. American Journal of Mental Deficiency 71: 864–868

Mori A A, Olive J E 1978 The blind and visually handicapped multiply retarded: suggestions for intervention in infancy. Journal of Visual Impairment and Blindness 72: 273–279

Morse J 1979 A programme for family management of the multiply handicapped child: Tempo as a clinical model. Rehabilitation Literature 40: 134–145

Murray R 1976 Providing medical care for the profoundly retarded requires initiative and innovation. Canadian Journal of Psychiatric Nursing 17:39

Myland E, Thurlow O 1981 A suggested curriculum for the profoundly handicapped child. II classroom organisation and routine. Apex: Journal of the British Institute of Mental Handicap 9: 87–88

Myland E, Thurlow O 1982 A suggested curriculum for the profoundly handicapped child. III integrating the special care class. Mental Handicap: Journal of the British Institute of Mental Handicap 10: 114–115

Naor E M, Balthazar E E 1975 Provision of a language index for severely and profoundly retarded individuals. American Journal of Mental Deficiency 79: 717–725

Norris D 1977 Severe handicap — some considerations. Parents Voice 27: 4–5

Norris D 1982 Profound mental handicap. Costello Educational, Kent

Norton Y 1975 Neurodevelopmental and sensory integration for the profoundly retarded multiply handicapped child. American Journal of Occupational Therapy 29: 93–100

Oswin M 1973 The empty hours. Pelican, Harmondsworth

Oswin M 1977 Physically handicapped children in long stay hospitals. Child: Care, Health and Development 3: 349–355

Oswin M 1977 These children are not vegetables. Parents Voice 27: 7–8

Penrose J 1983 Does he take sugar?: Communication with multiply handicapped people. Nursing times 79 (48): 52–54

Pilling D 1973 The handicapped child: Research review

Vol III. Longman/The National Childrens' Bureau, London

Pressland J L 1980 Educating 'special care'children: A review of the literature. Educational Research 23: 20–33

Rago W V 1977 Identifying profoundly mentally retarded subtypes as a means of institutional grouping. American Journal of Mental Deficiency 81: 470–473

Rago W V, Cleland C C 1978 Future directions in the education of the profoundly retarded. Education and Training of the Mentally Retarded 13: 184–186

Remington R E, Oxen T, Hogg J 1977 Auditory reinforcement in profoundly retarded multiply handicapped children. American Journal of Mental Deficiency 82: 299–304

Rogow S M 1978 Considerations in the assessment of blind children who function as severely or profoundly retarded. Child: Care, Health and Development 4: 327–335

Rogow S M 1981 Developing play skills and communicative competence in multiply handicapped young people. Journal of Visual Impairment and Blindness 75: 197–202

Ross T 1983 Are you sitting comfortably: Remodelled seating for profoundly handicapped people. Nursing Times 79 (51): 8–10

Scottish Home and Health Department 1980 Provision for profoundly mentally handicapped children three years on — A progress report by H M Inspectors of Schools. HMSO, Edinburgh

Scully C 1976 Something to bite on: Dental care for mentally handicapped children. National Society for Mentally Handicapped Children and Adults, London

Segal S S 1970 Assessment of the child with multiple handicaps: Symposium proceedings. National Fund for Research into Crippling Diseases, London

Simon G B 1981 The next step on the ladder: assessment and management of the multi-handicapped child. British Institute for Mental Handicap, Kidderminster

Smith M C 1970 Residential care of the severely and profoundly retarded child. Australian Journal of Mental Retardation 1: 30–33

Smith J M, Murphy J W 1978 Non-vocal communication with the multiply handicapped child. Apex: Journal of the British Institute of Mental Handicap 6: 16–17

Sontag E 1977 Educational programming for the severely and profoundly retarded. Council for Exceptional Children, Reston, Vancouver

Storm M, Willis J H 1978 Small group training as an alternative to individual programs for profoundly retarded persons. American Journal of Mental Deficiency 83: 283–288

Swartz J D, Cleland C C, Altman R 1971, Time Capsules for research in profound retardation. Mental Retardation 9: 29–30

Tesini D A 1981 An annotated review of the literature of dental caries and periodontal disease in mentally retarded individuals. Special Care Dentist 1: 75–87

Thompson G A 1979 Operant control of pathological tongue thrust in spastic cerebral palsy. Journal of Applied Behaviour Analysis 12: 325–333

Tizard J P M 1980 Cerebral palsies: Treatment and prevention. The Croonian Lecture 1978. Journal of the Royal College of Physicians of London 14: 72–80

Townsend P W, Flanagan J J 1976 Experimental preadmission program to encourage home care for severely and profoundly retarded children. American Journal of Mental Deficiency 80: 562–569

Usulan M M 1979 Orientation and mobility for severely and profoundly retarded blind persons. Journal of Visual Impairment and Blindness 73: 54–58

Van Etten G, Arkell C, Van Etten C 1980 The severely and profoundly handicapped. Mosby, St Louis

Walsh S, Holzberg R 1981 Understanding and educating the deaf-blind severely and profoundly handicapped: An international perspective. C C Thomas, Illinois

Wasch S W 1981 Hospitalisation of profoundly and severely mentally retarded children. Children's Health Care 9: 126–131

Webb R L 1969 Sensory motor training of the profoundly retarded. American Journal of Mental Deficiency 74: 283–295

Webb Y 1980 Feeding and nutrition problems of physically and mentally handicapped children in Britain. Journal of Human Nutrition 34: 281–286

Webb R C, Koller J R 1979 Effects of sensorimotor training on intellectual and adaptive skills of profoundly retarded adults. American Journal of Mental Deficiency 83: 490–496

Wehman P 1979 Curriculum design for the severely and profoundly handicapped. Human Sciences Press, New York

Weir K 1979 Psychological factors in feeding disorders occuring in mentally or multiply handicapped children. Child: Care, Health and Development 5: 285–294

Williams C 1978 An introduction to behavioural principles in teaching the profoundly handicapped. Child: Care, Health and Development 4: 21–28

Wood M 1982 Music for the profoundly handicapped. British Institute for Mental Handicap, Kidderminster

Wyatt W J 1978 Hearing test for a profoundly retarded human subject. Perceptual and Motor Skills 46: 91–94

Zysman S A 1980 Therapeutic feeding: A method of training the profoundly mentally retarded multiply handicapped. Dissertation Abstracts International 40 (12-N) Pt 1 5838–5839

Zigler E, Balla D 1977 Impact of institutional experience on the behaviour and development of retarded persons. American Journal of Mental Deficiency 82: 1–1

Bronwen Burford

10

Communication through movement

- *Communication does not depend on verbal skills and is a two-way process*
- *Cultural, social and environmental factors influence non-verbal expression and communication*
- *Movement can be functional, recreational, educational, artistic and therapeutic and the context in which the movement occurs gives it meaning and purpose*
- *Lack of interactional synchrony can cause difficulties in communicating and the formation of relationships*
- *Communicating effectively through movement requires that care staff monitor their own actions and are sensitive to the cues, reactions and mood of the mentally handicapped individual*

INTRODUCTION

In everyday life when communication is usually sufficiently successful to fulfil our needs and enable us to cope adequately with our lives, words such as 'interaction', 'expression', 'relationships' and 'interpersonal communication' are often seen as vague areas with no real meaning which can be scientifically investigated. They are just 'something' which 'happens' and we take for granted with little thought as to how we acquire them or the mechanisms involved when we utilise them. When these mechanisms break down or do not occur, perhaps in our attempted transactions with someone who is profoundly mentally handicapped, we begin to realise that these vague areas are of importance in everyday life and are more than just 'something' which 'happens'.

The ways in which a person communicates depend on his needs, intentions and abilities. The most useful and successful form of communication for people who are profoundly mentally handicapped is likely to be non-verbal, since they are unlikely to be able to communicate through speech and will have little, or even no, understanding of language. Additional physical handicaps may restrict a person's ability to use non-verbal means for communication and expression, but this ability can be utilised if it is adapted to fit the person rather than the person to fit into a method.

We are particularly concerned here with the social relationships between people during communication rather than the transmission of facts. Danziger (1976) gives a good description of this aspect of communication when he says that this involves 'influences on the target of communication.' This could describe the goal in developing ways of communicating with the profoundly handicapped person and others who are non-communicating, i.e. to influence the individual during our communication with him in such a way as to bring him out, little by little, to join the social world to the best of his ability, however limited, and perhaps help him to learn that his contribution can also influence us. He might learn that he can have some degree of control over his world.

When we begin studying non-verbal communication, its research and literature, we seem to enter a world which isolates and examines microscopic details and then attaches high significance to them. Yet these details *are* significant and play an important role in everyday communication.

ROLE OF NON-VERBAL COMMUNICATION

Body communication plays an important part in our lives from infancy. Its usefulness, perhaps more apparent during the pre-linguistic phase of development, does not diminish with the development of speech. The role of non-verbal communication is a multi-purpose one. Its roles and structures are the subject of much theory and research.

Let us take a brief look at these explanations of the role of non-verbal communication. For instance, Farb (1973) believes that speech determines the gestural system, as he calls it, and that the individual speech community determines exactly which movements will be used, just as the community determines the language that will be spoken. He says that when someone learns a language he also un-

consciously learns an accompanying gestural system.

Birdwhistell (1968) believes that there is a 'language' of movement which is comparable to spoken language. He sees communication as a multi-channel system with all channels being equally necessary to the whole. Though no single channel is in constant use, there are always one or more channels in operation (Birdwhistell, 1971). The fact that language is characteristic of humans does not lead to language being the central or the most important communication channel, Birdwhistell says. Interaction does not stop when the people involved stop talking.

Argyle (1972) believes that non-verbal communication appears to be part of an overall system with complex rules of structure and sequence. He says it must be accepted that most human social behaviour involves speech. Much speech is accompanied by non-verbal communication which may depend on structures similar to speech or even have been learnt as part of the skill of verbal communication.

Movement is a useful and powerful aid to language and the rhythm and intensity of speech can be matched by similar rhythm and intensity in movement. Our speech is accompanied by non-verbal signs and cues which can complement, enhance or contradict what we are saying. Sometimes we may consciously select certain non-verbal features carefully to emphasise what we wish to convey, e.g. facial expression to emphasise displeasure, or a certain stance of the body to convey an outward appearance which belies our inner state. However, for a large part of the time we can be unaware of our constant use of such features as gesture, eye contact and posture and indeed we may have movement habits of which we are completely unaware.

In our everyday lives we are constantly assessing the general attitudes or mood of the moment of other people through their non-verbal behaviour. Our interpretations are usually subjective and not necessarily accurate. However, accurate or not, we use our observations to adjust our attitudes and behaviour in a particular situation and to form judgements on people.

Channels and codes

Communication requires the use of channels through which messages can be sent and codes to carry the message. Two main channels are the verbal and non-verbal and these can be subdivided into a multiplicity of more channels, e.g. people can communicate non-verbally through gestures, touch, facial expression, or with their eyes. The meaning of the messages any one channel conveys can vary, depending on the context in which it occurs and on other messages being transmitted at the same time.

Limited range of channels

The profoundly mentally handicapped person often does not use a wide variety of channels for communication. Those he does use are likely to be non-verbal. Where physical handicap limits the use of non-verbal channels, we have to look at what means of communication, or channels, he has left. If someone is blind, has very little independent movement and does not use or understand language, then touch, tone of voice and vocalising will become important as a means of communicating *to* the person. Communication *from* him need not necessarily be through the same channels, e.g. he may use facial expression. Observation will show how the responses are expressed. Even if the response was more of an expression of pleasure than a deliberate attempt to communicate, it would still provide some indication that the approach was having an effect. Familiarity through regular contact with the person will show what means he uses to express himself and to communicate. Through time some two-way communication may develop.

Two-way communication with the profoundly handicapped person is difficult to instigate.

Even where he will readily respond in some way to communication attempts from others, initiation is often lacking and the interchange-ability and adaptation — features of two-way communication — are missing.

Picture a child mentally handicapped and unable to speak, who smiles at others, laughs appropriately, seeks and reaches out to others, looks at another, vocalises to another in a communicative way — he already possesses some interactive skills and will seek out and initiate contact. He is an *active* participant in interaction. Now picture a child who, also unable to speak, never smiles, does not laugh except inappropriately to himself for no apparent reason, who does not seek and reach out to others, does not look at another, does not vocalise or, if he does, appears not to direct it to any communicative purpose — he does not display interactive skills. He gives no feedback to those who attempt to communicate with him and so 'communication' with him is one-sided. He is not a participant in interaction and the task here is to find a starting point which will enable us to develop some way of communicating with him.

Picture a child between these two extremes, also unable to speak, who smiles when approached, laughs when amused by others, who does not reach out first to others but smiles and cuddles in when picked up, who looks at another and vocalises when played with — he already possesses some potential for developing interactive skills, but he is a *passive recipient* rather than an *active participant*. He is not good at making the first move and depends on others to approach him first. Some children who are seen as good communicators are, in fact, passive recipients. Their responses are pleasing and they can show obvious enjoyment when with others, but closer examination will show it to be very one-sided, highly dependent on the adult and limited in range.

The development of two-way communication enables the tiny, enclosed world of the profoundly handicapped person to be extended to include other people. The more active he can be in this communication the more opportunity he will have to expand his world.

Non-verbal features

There are many non-verbal features which could be illustrated and discussed. It is not the purpose here to survey and discuss the extensive literature available on non-verbal communication, but to draw attention to the multitude of channels available and the need to understand their use in successful interaction. Non-verbal features include posture, gesture, gaze, facial expression, touch, proximity, tone of voice, among others. These in turn can be subdivided, e.g. gesture could mean head nods, hand movements, arm movements. These in turn could be further divided into smaller parts. Birdwhistell (1971) has 57 different symbols for the face.

Areas of non-verbal communication which have been found to be particularly relevant and useful when working with the mentally handicapped person will now be considered in more detail, but their study here and the features outlined are not exhaustive.

Proxemics

The term proxemics was first used by Hall (1966) and is concerned with the space between and around people. First of all let us look at proximity, or interpersonal distance as it is also called and which is the term we shall use here.

Interpersonal distance. Interpersonal distance is the distance maintained by participants during interaction. This is not so much dictated by the physical space available but more by the social and emotional aspects of the encounter. If someone places himself closer than we feel the depth of our acquaintance allows, we adjust the distance until we feel more comfortable. With an intimate friend the same closeness would probably be acceptable. The less distance between the interactants, the greater the degree of intimacy in the relationship is likely to be. During everyday interaction we monitor and adjust the distance

between ourselves and those with whom we communicate. This distance is not a static measurement but a fluctuating one, determined by factors such as social relationships.

Interpersonal distance varies not only according to social factors, but is also different between cultures. An example is the difference found by Watson & Graves (1966) when comparing Arab and American male students during conversation. The Arabs preferred a greater degree of closeness than the Americans, with a more direct eye contact and a more direct orientation to others. Hall (1966) first described Arab–American differences from his observations, noting the discomfort Americans felt at the intensity of the encounter, while the Arab felt alienated by the lack of intensity from his American counterpart.

The mentally handicapped child does not always successfully manage the adjustment of interpersonal distance, to fit in with our cultural and social norms. Sometimes he seems to be totally unaware of this need for adjustment. He may approach everyone from complete stranger to close relative with extreme closeness and touching. Many people, when visiting a residential or educational centre for mentally handicapped people, will have encountered this type of greeting as if they were close, intimate and life-long friends. In this context its intention is understood. However, if a stranger were to approach us in the street in a similar manner we would have a less pleasant reaction, perhaps anger or a feeling of anxiety and fear. Similarly, if the mentally handicapped adult were to approach strangers in the street, particularly children, in this friendly, intimate manner, it could be unfortunately misinterpreted. Consideration should also be given to preparing the person to adapt to our non-verbal culture, alongside the other skills considered necessary for a more independent lifestyle.

There is the opposite situation, of course, where a child will maintain a large distance between himself and others. If someone attempts to decrease this distance he immediately adjusts it. If the physical confines of the room or space make this impossible he is likely to become anxious and upset. Such children are withdrawn and unwilling to communicate, but they are aware of others, unlike those who have not yet become aware of the separateness of self from others and the need to communicate.

The child who distances himself often seems to have a very sensitive 'monitoring' of the whereabouts of those around him and makes adjustments to changes in this to maintain the status quo, often without giving the appearance of noticing someone's approach.

Personal space. Interpersonal distance can be observed by both participants. There is also the personal space of the individual, which is the area surrounding a person's body exclusive to that person (Hall, 1966); it 'belongs' to him. Personal space is not observable and others can 'intrude' without realising it. Since it is not observable it is likely that it serves an *intra-personal* function (Strube & Werner, 1982).

This space does not remain fixed. It can vary in shape and size, remaining close to the person or extending beyond his reach. A perceived threat of someone approaching too closely may result in the space being expanded. It is a psychological part of the person and acts as a protective zone (Strube & Werner 1982). It is his psychological space.

Although we can map the pattern of where a person moves in the space around him, the boundaries of his psychological space are difficult to determine. Some mentally handicapped children seem to have no protective boundary. We can move right up to them and engage them in activity without any sign of upset, remaining much closer than we would usually do with others. Other children have a large personal space and can be seen to become anxious, upset and sometimes aggressive when this space is violated. Someone may simply have approached them in a normal, everyday manner. It can be puzzling in these situations to know what you have done wrong when the child reacts adversely.

Through observation and carefully trying various ways of approaching the child — from the side may be more tolerable than from in front — and noting how close it is possible to get before the child reacts, one can begin to guess the extent of the psychological space he needs. Through gentle and sensitive intervention he may be helped to decrease this space and thereby reduce the number of probable anxiety-provoking situations. If the child is standing, then walking up to him should be possible, but if he is sitting or on the floor, then getting down on the floor to his level may sometimes help.

Orientation. The orientation of interactants to each other is another factor which is of significance in social relationships. Orientation normally varies from head-on to side-by-side and varies with the nature and purpose of the interaction. People working in co-operation are more likely to be side-by-side whereas those in competition are more likely to be head-on (Argyle 1972).

Besides the varying nature of the interaction, culture also produces differences in orientation. The most common orientation in Britain is 90° (Argyle, 1972). Arabs prefer a direct head-on orientation (Watson & Graves, 1966).

Orientation can take on a useful role when working with the child who keeps apart from others. By varying the angles of approach and using some angles well outside the norm for everyday interaction, it is possible to build up tolerance and acceptance of another's presence.

Some children, though wishing to communicate, may have difficulty in working out the correct orientation for interaction. Recently, a teacher colleague described how a boy in her class, who had severe communication difficulties, was beginning to make attempts to communicate with others. He tried to engage another child in conversation but stood behind her to do this. The girl, who herself was not very skilled, looked around but remained standing in the same position. The boy seemed to realise something was wrong and moved to stand by her side. This time she noticed him and standing side-by-side he attempted to carry on a conversation which was limited not only by their general lack of skill, but also the awkward orientation.

Physical contact. Those cultures which use large interpersonal distances also seem to discourage the use of touch (Danziger, 1976). Jourard (1966) found large differences in the frequency of contact per hour of couples in cafes in cities of different countries. These countries were not all separated by long geographical distances. For example, Paris was compared to London and the frequency of contact was Paris: 110 per hour, London: 0. The other cities were San Juan (Puerto Rico) 180 and Gainsville (Florida) 2.

In parts of Africa and Asia two interactors may hold hands, have a hand on the other's knee or have legs intertwined. This bodily contact is normal in public in that part of the world, providing another channel for communication (Argyle, 1973).

Again, not only cultural factors affect the use of touch. Touch can play a part in communicating emotional warmth and closeness, but it can also convey status and power. Within cultures there are also individual differences. Some people touch more than others; some have a great dislike of being touched. When accidental touching occurs we apologise and move back or if it is unavoidable, as when sharing a seat on a crowded bus, we may tense the side in contact and adjust our position to make the contact as minimal as possible.

Some mentally handicapped children do not like being touched. The more severely handicapped they are, the more distressing it is likely to be for them since, by necessity, they will require much more handling and physical contact during their physical care. Sometimes observation will show that they can, in fact, tolerate touch if it is gentle and restrained, but what they are really protesting about is handling, when being dressed for example. Handling is quite a different experience from touching. The child who becomes upset at touch in general is more likely to display a more general aversion to involvement with other people.

Looking. Looking plays an important regulatory function during interaction which will be discussed later on in the chapter.

Besides mutual direct eye contact there is also looking at the other which is not reciprocated, and mutual gaze avoidance. As with other non-verbal features, emotional, social and cultural factors affect looking behaviour.

Attention has been drawn to 'looking' to make a point about encouraging eye contact in children. Some mentally handicapped children avoid eye contact, or even generally looking towards another, and others do not appear to be aware of the need or purpose of looking.

Lack of eye contact is one sign among others that a child is not able or does not want to enter a relationship or even acknowledge others. It is a small physical effort to move one's head and direct the eyes at another, but the emotional journey can be a long one. Children who find eye contact difficult may find it less difficult — never easy — to make contact with another through some other non-verbal channel first, e.g. hand, foot, and develop a relationship in this way. As trust develops, looking and direct eye contact may improve. It should be emphasised that the process is likely to be a long one and efforts to achieve this need to be both constant and consistent, slowly building on a non-verbal 'conversation' through hands or whatever means has been found to be best. The prime focus in this way of working is, of course, developing a relationship rather than aiming solely to increase the frequency of eye contact for some other purpose.

Gesture. The amount of gesture used by different cultures varies. An Italian will use far more gesture than a Scot. There can also be a variation in meaning, with the same non-verbal signal either having different meanings or having different signals for the same meaning. This could lead to possible misunderstanding and confusion if the two cultures meet.

LaBarre (1947) tells of such a misunderstanding, when he was working alongside an American Indian woman, Old Mary Buffalo of the Kiowa. He asked her where something was and although it was clear she had heard him she continued working, apparently ignoring his request. He repeated the request several times until, with them both now in a state of puzzlement and exasperation, she fetched it for him — from where it had been in plain sight. She had indeed replied to his initial request, repeatedly, but by pointing with her lips.

Shaking the head is a sign for 'no' in many different cultures, but Sicilians indicate it by laying back the head (Danziger, 1976). The head nod for 'yes' is said to be unknown among the Ainu of Northern Japan. They indicate 'yes' by gracefully bringing both hands up to the chest and waving them downwards, with the palms upward (LaBarre, 1947).

Some of the examples given to illustrate cultural differences in non-verbal communication may seem to be taken from, by now, dated sources. Nevertheless, even today with modern communication systems and travel enabling greater mixing with and awareness of other cultures, differences can still be seen. Recently a television travel documentary showed a group of Japanese tourists being welcomed aboard their cruise ship by the British captain who greeted them by shaking hands. The difficulty and awkwardness the tourists experienced with this form of greeting was obvious, yet in Britain a 'simple' handshake is not seen as a source of difficulty. It would be interesting to observe a group of British tourists coping with a typical Japanese greeting.

Of course gesture does not just consist of specific signs. When we gesture as we speak we are not simply signalling a series of specific meanings, and looking at them in isolation will not give us precise information as, say, a head nod might. Rather, they convey emotions and attitudes.

We do not have to be speaking when we gesture nor does the movement have to be expansive. For example, a previously outgoing person, after months of withdrawal and total lack of movement, apart from the functional to get from A to B, begins to respond to others with microscopic movements. These tiny movements are meaningful far in excess of the happy extrovert who flings his arms out in greeting to a friend.

Posture. Gesture may be distinguished from posture in a broad sense, by saying that it is a structured movement of part of the body whereas posture is a structured arrangement of the body in space (Firth, 1970).

Posture is affected by various factors, especially along the tense/relaxed dimension (Argyle, 1972) — emotional state, relationship to and feelings about others present, and culture. This is an important point in that posture is less well controlled than face or voice and there could be leakage (see later section) (Ekman, 1966). In a meeting the high status person is likely to have a more relaxed posture than the low status individual.

Some cultures have careful distinctions in posture on the basis of sex, others on age, and status (Hewes, 1955). These are seen as an integral part of the rules of etiquette and strictly enforced. In Britain we do not have such strict rules, but if we were visiting a culture which did we would have to beware of misunderstandings. In the Northern Solomons a woman who sits with legs stretched out is seen as giving an open invitation to sexual intercourse (Hewes, 1955).

Non-verbal leakage

Mention was made in the previous section of leakage. What we are really feeling can leak through the appearance or performance we may have set up to give an impression to the contrary.

Imagine you are at an important interview for a job which carries responsibility and requires leadership qualities. You wish to present yourself as knowledgeable, confident and well suited to the task, although at this moment you are extremely nervous, particularly as the other candidates seem confident and very able. During the interview you strive to hide your nervousness and verbally you succeed, managing to keep your voice steady and giving some good answers. However, your body tells another story — your posture is tense, you constantly rub your thumb against a finger and your smile is fixed.

Some people, aware of the possibility, will

be able to have more control over this leakage. It is probably easier to tell non-verbal lies with the face than it is with hands, legs and feet (Ekman & Friesen, 1969). Ekman & Friesen describe legs and feet as being the primary source of leakage and deception clues, whereas the face is likely to be the major non-verbal liar.

We are not always so consciously aware of non-verbal leakage and the conflicting messages we can send. A mother greets her child with open arms as he runs up to her and then hugs him, but her body remains rigid. Another mother greets her child in a similar way, but envelops him as she hugs him so that the mother and child are moulded. This child is likely to get more emotional warmth from his mother's greeting.

Awareness of this possibility of leakage can be useful. I worked with one young mentally handicapped woman whose whole body gave a strong message of total lack of interest in my presence. She sat immobile, huddled in with her head down low and impervious to any attempt to involve her in any communication. The message was loud, and clear, except for her eyes which almost swivelled out of their sockets in her efforts to track my movements about the room.

It is worthwhile remembering, though, that the observer can also be the observed. We should be aware of our own non-verbal behaviour and the possibility of giving adverse messages to those we are trying to help.

Regulatory function

The non-verbal components also have a regulatory function during conversation. They provide interactants with much of the feedback they need in order to maintain the fluency of the conversation. In the course of a conversation a person will at different times have the roles of speaker and listener. There needs to be some way of allocating these roles.

Kendon (1976) in his investigation of gaze-direction during long utterances — defined as lasting 5 seconds or more — found differences

between the same person when speaker and listener. A in the role of speaker tends to look away as he is about to speak. During the time he speaks he alternates between looking at and looking away from B his listener. B meanwhile has been looking at A for longer and more steadily. As A is about to finish speaking he looks up. Now B if he wishes can take his cue and begin speaking. A now becomes the listener and looks more steadily and for longer at B than he did while he was speaking to him. This regulation enables the conversation to run smoothly. To achieve a smoothness, each person involved must monitor the actions of the others in the conversation. This information helps each person to regulate his contribution and to maintain the interchangeability necessary for successful interation.

There is obviously more than gaze-direction involved. The other non-verbal features also have a role in directing and allocating listener and speaker roles and providing feedback to the speaker of the effects on the listener of what he is saying. If someone's reaction to an idea or suggestion you are outlining is very important, you will scrutinise that person's non-verbal behaviour as you put forward your proposals, trying to assess how they are being received.

MOVEMENT

It is difficult to interact with someone who does not look at you or turn his body even slightly towards you and who has a blank face. Such a person is unable to participate effectively in reciprocal communication. In attempts to encourage communication with the mentally handicapped person who has poor interactive skills, reference to and the use of non-verbal features is needed. However, emphasis is also needed on *how* the person moves as well as noting *which* part is moving. This should then be extended to note how the whole body moves, not just the part, e.g. hands, on which the main attention is focused. This is a more extensive view of moving than considering individual features.

Studies in non-verbal communication tend to be specialised concentrating, often at very great depth, on one or a few aspects, e.g. smiling, gaze-direction, as a glance through the literature on non-verbal communication will show. In the improvised type of movement we are now going to consider we do not study a small area of the body in isolation — attention has to be paid to the whole body, the movement of one part in relation to another and the manner in which the person moves, e.g. with force, gently, quickly. If I am working with someone who is only moving his fingers I concentrate on his fingers, but I am also aware of the rest of his body, which even in stillness is part of the interaction, and am ready to incorporate any further movement into the improvisation if it seems this would help. The person's movement should be observed through looking at the total movement of the body and how the person moves in the space around him, as well as touch, distance and other non-verbal features.

Movement is a complex subject for study. The vastness of its meaning and its wide variety of purposes can lead to many people using this one word but who are not in fact, talking about the same thing. Movement plays more than one role in our lives — it is found in many contexts and in widely varying forms. For example, it can be functional, recreational, educational, artistic and therapeutic. Each of these areas is concerned with different objectives, skills and benefits. At times one area may merge into another, at other times the context is so different that the only common factor is that some form of movement is involved.

If we could strip away the surroundings from someone who is moving, whether a crowded pavement, playing field, theatre, or social gathering and look at the movement alone with no clues from the surroundings as to its purpose — no street scene, no sports equipment, no stage, no fellow conversationalists — it would be very difficult to perceive the purpose and meaning of the movement observed. We would have no clues as to the size of the space, the relationship between the mover and the space and the objects in it and the degree of relationship, if any, between the mover and those around him. It is the context in which the movement takes place which gives it its meaning and defines its purpose.

We are concerned here with communication *with* and *through* movement and it is the social context which helps give the meaning to what is being expressed and communicated.

However, a person's movement is not only affected by the external environment. There are also intangible factors from within the person which can both prompt and influence the way in which he moves. Movement provides a link between inner self and the outside world. When we are working with people who have difficulty in communicating verbally, then working with them through the medium of movement can establish a link. This link can provide a channel for communication and expression of feelings, moods and needs and the means for forming relationships through which growth and development can occur. This non-verbal link is how we develop our early relationships as we shall see later in the chapter.

Having looked at the factors which give meaning to movement, we now have to look at the movement itself. In the type of work we are concerned with here, one has to develop powers of observation in order to break down the movement into smaller, more easily observable parts. Then we have to isolate the part(s) to begin working with — though never ignoring the rest — and build this up into movement which is based on co-operation and the involvement of all who are taking part.

Looking at an action will yield some information, but looking at *how* it is done will greatly increase this information. If we get into the habit of breaking down an observed action into smaller parts we usually find many difference between individuals doing the same action and these differences will often hold the key to successfully working with someone. For example, observing someone in a rocking action — is he rocking quickly or slowly;

forwards and backwards or side-to-side; how much does he use the space around him; is he tense or relaxed? Other questions might be — is there a rhythm; what is the rest of his body doing; are his arms involved in the action and how are they placed; how does he hold his head; where does he focus his attention; are there other stereotyped movements occurring as part of the whole rocking action? Sometimes when working with someone who spends a lot of time rocking which is presenting a barrier to contact, joining in with this initially often helps to break through this barrier. This in turn allows a more varied type of movement to be introduced which is more conducive to working together. It is important to remember to join in with *how* it is done, but there are pitfalls. It should not just be a mechanical imitation but an attempt to begin working with the person as he is now rather than imposing a pre-arranged set of ideas.

The patterns of our everyday movement reveal and are moulded by many different factors. Some patterns are transitory, affected by momentary moods and reactions, whereas others are a more permanent feature moulded by the type of person we have become. Some patterns can be controlled by the environment — it is unlikely that we would display the same movement behaviour in a relaxed and informal situation as we would at a crucial meeting at work. Some will be affected by our emotional state — the person who is depressed will not display the same movement as the same person in a happy, energetic state. This all emphasises the need for careful and consistent observation over a period, before any interpretation of value can be put on observation of movement. Observing movement and interpreting it should not be seen as the same thing. Objective observation of movement is possible, interpretation of what is observed is much more open to question and differing opinions and should be approached with caution. This is not to suggest that we should not interpret movement — we do this constantly — but we should always be aware of its subjective na-

ture, especially, when applying this in a 'clinical' or 'educational' setting.

As previously indicated, cultural influences play an important part in how we use and interpret movement. If someone visits a foreign culture, his communication non-verbally can be adversely affected. Similarly if, through profound mental handicap, a person has been impaired in his ability to be influenced by and adapt to the culture, communication difficulties can occur. Sometimes the manner in which some mentally handicapped people move, especially the more isolated and disturbed individuals, seems to be strange because it does not conform to our cultural and social ideas of what is 'normal' or 'correct' movement, e.g. someone may constantly move his arms and hands in a stereotyped pattern in front of his face. Although the actual ingredients of such movement are the same as the ingredients of our 'normal' movement, it is the way in which they are put together which makes them seem so different, e.g. the way the person uses the space around him and the timing of his movement. Added to that is the difficulty in perceiving its meaning or purpose. My thoughts when observing this sort of movement are that it seems to have high intra-individual value but little, if any, interpersonal purpose.

This sharing of ingredients means that movement can provide a common factor between those who do not and cannot communicate effectively and those who wish to find a link with them through which communication and expression can be developed.

COMMUNICATION AND EXPRESSION

At this point we should digress slightly and take a look at the words 'communication' and 'expression' a little more closely and the need we have for both.

Communication and expression are interrelated but they are not different words for the same meaning. The interrelationship is complex and the superficial examination here will only be sufficient to highlight the fact that there is a difference between the two.

If one person is transmitting factual information to another the communicative purpose is obvious and there is no emotional involvement. However, supposing A is extremely angry with B, he may not feel satisfied until B has 'received the message and understood'. On the other hand A may feel better at giving vent to his anger regardless of whether B or anyone else has understood or responded to this. We have a need to express inner experiences, but it is difficult to draw the line between the need for this to be understood and the need for expression, regardless of response (Parry, 1967). Not all non-verbal behaviour is deliberate communication.

This leads us to consider another factor affecting communication and expression. Frowning can convey disapproval, but if others do not understand what a frown means it is unable to convey this disapproval. Posture may indicate something about a person's emotional state, but if this cannot be interpreted correctly by others then nothing can be communicated through this posture (Danziger, 1976). Non-verbal behaviour has to be decoded before it can be understood. It does not have to be decoded into words — an appropriate response to the message is what is required (Danziger, 1976).

In this chapter the word 'communication' is used to mean that something, whether an emotional feeling or factual information, can be conveyed from one person to another. The word 'expression' when used indicates an expression of inner experiences, irrespective of whether it is understood by others. Expression, without communication, can be of value.

EARLY INTERACTIVE DEVELOPMENT

Communication through non-verbal channels plays an important role in helping the baby to join in social interaction with other people and it is through non-verbal channels that his first relationships are formed. The young baby is immature and lacking in skill in his interactions with others. He is dependent on adults to use their skill to compensate for this. Through his encounters with other people he begins to learn about the world around him. Other people are very important in providing experience for the young baby. Bullowa (1979) aptly describes this importance — 'At first an infant's world is almost exclusively a world of people and what they do with and to and for him.' There are parallels with the profoundly mentally handicapped child and his difficulties in joining the social world. This is not to advocate that he should simply be treated like a baby but that whatever his age, other people are extremely important and 'what they do with and to and for him'. The quote from Bullowa seems just as relevant in this context.

When working with profoundly mentally handicapped people, one is immediately aware of the extreme difficulty in communicating with them in any way and of the accompanying difficulty in forming relationships. The problems of communication are apparent to any person meeting this group for the first time. Living in a highly verbal world with little conscious attention being paid to the non-verbal aspects of communication, although they are always present, it is difficult to communicate and form relationships with people who are totally non-verbal and who do not pick up non-verbal cues from others. Thus, they are denied the opportunity to develop relationships, particularly special relationships deeper than the casual contact of everyday interactions.

During early interactions in the first 6 months of life the baby learns about cues and regulations in responding to, initiating and ending interactions with his caregiver and acquires the skills necessary in coping with social interaction (Stern, 1977). He develops conversational skills long before he speaks. There is strong evidence to suggest that the infant has an awareness of how other people communicate and that he is pre-programmed to react to social communication (Trevarthen et al, 1981) — that he is biologically tuned as Newsom (1979) describes it. At a very early age he is able to respond to and influence the communication of others (Trevarthen et al, 1981).

Language is now being related to pre-verbal communication patterns established between caregiver and baby in the early months of life rather than at the beginning of the second year (Schaffer, 1977). It is now believed that the development of verbal communication is related to the infant's ability to participate in these interactive sequences during the first year (Bruner, 1974). Language acquisition has been firmly placed within a social setting (Schaffer, 1977).

Adults adopt a conversational style with babies who are too young even to make a vocal response (Snow, 1977). The caregiver treats even the smallest behaviour as if it were meaningful (Snow, 1977). The adult provides the responses for the baby until gradually the baby is able to take more of an active part in the 'conversation'. For example, the baby sneezes or hiccups and the adult builds a conversation round this, playing both parts. Gradually an interactive structure begins to develop and this happens very early. The baby realises through these many conversations that others pay attention to his movements and vocalisations and that they produce certain effects. In time he begins to use these movements and vocalisations with purpose, anticipating that others will respond to him in certain specific ways (Schaffer, 1977). Even at the age of 2 months babies can stop and start activity, which is essential for two-way exchanges. (Trevarthen, 1979).

The ability to perceive and respond to the signals, cues and sequences of movement, which are part of social interaction, provides the child with some necessary pre-requisites for forming relationships. All our early relationships are formed non-verbally, the first being the important one between primary caregiver and the baby. As a child the profoundly mentally handicapped person is often denied the important early relationships through which he could learn and develop. He does not give out the crucial cues and responses necessary for successful two-way

interaction nor does he respond to them in others. Attempts to interact with him remain totally one-sided. Given no feedback the adult has great difficulty in establishing communication.

If a child does not interact with others these early relationships cannot be formed. If the child does not develop the ability to interpret meaning in other people's movement a most important mode of communication is unavailable to him and he is at a distinct disadvantage. This limited interactive experience further limits his experience of self and others.

Babies communicate effectively and in a varied expressive way through non-verbal channels before the onset of speech. Speech when it comes is an addition to the now familiar process of interaction. Without speech modern day living would be extremely difficult but, as we have seen, the non-verbal components of interaction do not disappear when talking begins. They continue to add to the meaning of what is being said and at times are more valuable than the spoken word. Many people with profound mental handicap will not develop speech, but will be able to take part in non-verbal 'conversations'. These conversations have to be built up slowly and consistently with an adult who has a perceptive, flexible and adaptable approach similar to the approach used by caregivers with their babies. In his interactions the mentally handicapped person will not necessarily achieve the skill, variety and effectiveness of the baby who follows the normal path of development, but it can still be sufficient to allow him to join us in the social world. No speech does not mean no communication.

INTERACTIONAL SYNCHRONY

In filmed sequences of interaction, adult to adult as well as adult to child, the co-ordination of people's movement often resembles a dance. This dance has been referred to as interactional synchrony. This refers to the synchronisation of the movements of interactants during conversation and of the individual with his own vocal patterns. Its inclusion here is considered necessary because knowledge of the existence of interactional synchrony and self synchrony is useful but it is a brief mention only. As with limited non-verbal and interactive skills its impairment can have an effect on the quality of our interactions.

When a person speaks his words are accompanied by body movements which are in precise synchrony with his speech, and people listening to someone speaking also move in synchrony with the pattern of the speaker's speech (Condon, 1979). Condon refers to the inferred inner processes the person uses to bring about synchronisation as 'responsive entrainment'.

Interactional synchrony can be observed even when individuals are not looking at each other but where the flow of speech can be heard (Danziger, 1976). Babies also move synchronously with adult speech and this has very early beginnings indeed. Condon & Sander (1974) found that 1-day-old infants synchronised their movements with tape recorded and live human speech, but not with recordings of isolated vowel sounds and regular tapping sounds. This synchrony was subsequently observed as early as 20 minutes after birth (Condon, 1979). Trevarthen (1979) says that it is possible that the newborn infant does become locked into adult speech, with the speech sounds acting as pacemakers for the infant's limb movements, but that much of the timing of these movements comes from the infant's own motor pacemakers. He views the infant as less passive in his entrainment doubting that such synchronisation plays a part in language development.

Raffler-Engel (1981) states that an adult or older child wishing to join a group conversation will establish interactional synchrony with the group members before beginning to speak, unless he wishes to take over leadership. In contrast a toddler will dyssynchronise to gain attention. Raffler-Engel (1981) suggests three distinct periods — the infant synchronises, the toddler dyssynchronises and the older child synchronises once again — but

says that the ages at which these changes occur have not yet been specified.

Bower (1977) describes the movement synchrony of babies as distinctively social behaviour. The synchrony of the day-old babies observed by Condon & Sanders was elicited only by human speech and not by other sounds. This synchrony, when it occurs between a mother and baby, is very important in conveying a feeling that the baby is responding (Bower, 1977) — that they are on the same wavelength. Where a baby does not display interactional synchrony, caregivers find it difficult to get on the same wavelength.

Cultural differences could affect synchrony. Although people from different cultures may be able to speak to each other in the same language their different body movements may hinder interactional synchrony and create communication difficulties. Communication can break down where, because of brain damage or mental disturbance of some kind, the individual is unable to synchronise his movements to his own vocal patterns and those of other people. Research findings have shown a wide range of children with learning difficulties to have a degree of difficulty in moving synchronously with human speech and sound (Condon, 1979). Condon also says that the greater the degree of autistic-like isolation of the individual the greater the degree of disturbed synchrony seems to be.

When synchrony is impaired for some reason, communication can become almost impossible with the resulting lack of formation of relationships. It is possible to overcome this sometimes by adapting to the movement of the person with difficulties. Lewis (1978) cites as an example a mother who was unable to form a bond with her baby who suffered from cerebral palsy and whose jerky movements made it difficult for her to synchronise with him. When shown how to move in the same way as her baby, copying his abrupt actions, it is reported that she was able to achieve the synchronisation needed to help form the bond.

Moving in a way which is adapted to suit impaired synchronisation is, of course, cutting across cultural and social norms. It can be embarrassing to adapt one's movement to movement outwith the 'norm' in front of others, particularly where done in a residential or institutional setting rather than the family home. The former is likely to provide a setting with several or more onlookers. This is not to provide an excuse for not doing so, but rather to give the reason why it can be so off-putting. Such adaptation, however discomfiting it may initially feel to the caregiver, can provide a useful means to creating a bond. The individual may not move in any synchronous fashion with himself and may not be aware of the movement of others or be able to adapt to them. By establishing synchrony with him by adapting to his manner of moving, i.e. on a very one-sided basis, we are able to convey a feeling of 'sharing' with the mentally handicapped person. It helps to alleviate some of the isolation of the individual who cannot adapt to or understand the world around him and the people in it. In time it might sometimes be possible to involve some adaptability from both participants.

The point that there is more than an exchange of verbal messages during interaction has already been stressed, as has the involvement of non-verbal features and how they are utilised. Now the synchrony of movement during interaction with its likeness to a dance has been added. People are daily engaged in countless interactions, often with no awareness of the complexities involved. However, lack of synchrony in interacting, although so often not consciously missed, can diminish interactive effectiveness.

COMMUNICATING THROUGH MOVEMENT — GENERAL POINTS

There are many factors to be taken into account when attempting to develop communication, interaction and relationships through movement with those who are profoundly mentally handicapped. One chapter in a book cannot cover all the possibilities, developments and pitfalls which might be encountered. Human communication in general and all its variables cannot be condensed in this way. This section is intended to provide some very general guidelines. Much depends on the quality of input and sensitive awareness of the caregiver.

We have to be continually aware of the effect our activities may have on participants. If they experience anxiety or discomfort they may withdraw or fail to respond. We have to be aware of the effect on someone when we approach him closely or engage him in activity which at first will have no meaning for him. We should also be aware of misinterpreting his perhaps unconventional attempts to communicate with us. Neither should we assume that any activity or general movement will feel to everyone else as it does to us. Amongst people at any level of intelligence, experience of the same movement can vary greatly. Some movement may be pleasant for one person, but perhaps feel uncomfortable to another, depending both on individual personality differences and current psychological state. If a group of people were asked to run across a large hall or open space and to take a leap into the air with body stretched out wide some might enjoy doing so while others might dislike the exposed feeling it gives. The person for whom it is a pleasant experience might find it less so if it were a day when he was beset by personal problems and disappointments — he just does not feel like taking a joyous leap into the air.

The pleasing or uncomfortable experience of a certain way of moving does not necessarily remain static. Moods can have an effect. We might find that a child who enjoyed rocking, bouncing and swinging the previous day does not feel like these activities the following day. He may be in a quieter mood seeking close physical contact and gentle rocking. Since we are trying to develop communication channels and some degree of relationship, particularly as caregivers, rather than teaching specific activities it does not matter that we have to change what we are doing. The movement is a means to an end and not the end itself. It should be adapted to meet the needs of the individual concerned.

Some children who enjoy activities such as swinging and rocking may, through time, develop non-verbal 'signs' which they use to 'ask' for the activity. For example, imagine a child who particularly enjoys being swung or perhaps rolled along the floor. If in the course of play and general interaction periods with adults, he is repeatedly swung or rolled along the floor he may begin to anticipate what comes next. As you bend to pick him up and swing him round, he may lift up his arms in readiness. As this becomes established the adult can begin waiting until the child lifts his arms before repeating the swing. In the beginning the activity has to be introduced by the adult during each encounter. Some children eventually begin to produce their home-made signs without this introduction each time. Some also begin to develop other signs for similar activities they especially enjoy.

The key word is enjoyment. As we have seen, not everyone enjoys close contact with others, being touched or lots of movement activity. Such children are unlikely to develop a home-made sign to initiate something they dislike. The child who thoroughly enjoys a rough and tumble play session or expresses pleasure at a few activities is more likely to develop some way of asking for these activities.

These signs or cues may be gestures which are idiosyncratic. The beginnings have to come from the child's actions rather than the adult deciding how it will be done. Different children may use different gestures to indicate the same activity. Although some children do signal clearly with intention from the beginning that they wish something to be repeated, it can have more vague beginnings. The gesture which eventually becomes a deliberate action with specific meaning is often initially a random movement which is not planned and carried out with specific intentions. The gesture becomes specific because the adult acts on it as if it had a certain meaning.

If working with a child in this way, then success will depend on how much the child enjoys the activities, and how well we observe his actions, and are able to pick up cues from him. In time the child may lose interest in a particular activity and will stop using the sign he has devised for it, but he will retain the lesson he has learned about communication. In general this can all be viewed in two ways:

1. The activity itself. B will lift his arms when he wants to be swung round. C will hold her hand out in a certain way when she wants you to rock her. E will lie on the floor and raise his arm when he wants you to roll him over.
2. The communication involved. B, C and E have all found a way of exerting some control over events in their world. They can initiate this activity. If several signs exist they can make a choice from several possibilities and make this choice known — they can direct a play session. It is often difficult to encourage a profoundly mentally handicapped child to initiate and this provides some means for doing so.

When children do develop their own ways of asking for something they enjoy it arises out of a personal desire. This method of asking is not derived from imitating the adult and it does not follow that the child will then be able to progress to copying and using signs with a specific unvarying meaning as in a system such as Makaton. The development of idiosyncratic gestures of his own may be the highest level he can achieve.

Activities should be done *with* the child rather than *to* him. They are carried out in partnership. By working *with* the child, the adult will gain a sense of the strength, speed and intensity of the action the child prefers. Two people working through the same series of activities with the same child can produce entirely different results. In one case the child may express his usual enjoyment, whereas in the other his enthusiasm may be subdued. This does not imply that the action should always be fast and furious. One activity at a time taken slowly and very gently may be the most suitable in some cases.

Appropriate stimulation. This leads on to a point which should be made about the amount of stimulation a child receives. Lack of stimulation is quite rightly often stated as one of the deficits in the care provided for mentally handicapped people. However, this is not a simple black and white issue of stimulation being good and lack of stimulation being bad. A more correct term might be lack of *appropriate* stimulation. A mentally handicapped person surrounded by noises, voices, activity, musical sounds and a variety of objects may be suffering from a lack of appropriate stimulation as much as the person who has no stimulation at all. While some people may thrive on being surrounded by a variety of stimuli, others cannot tolerate this. The flood of stimuli causes them to withdraw and shut it out. Some become distressed by too much going on around them. Presenting one thing at a time in a quiet atmosphere at a slow pace provides their appropriate stimulation.

The same applies to our manner. A loud voice and animated, exaggerated movement may be the correct approach in working with one person whereas with another we may need to speak softly, or even remain silent, and to keep our movement contained and to a minimum. Using the sound of our voice and speaking to the mentally handicapped person is very important, but there are times when it is best not to speak and we should be sensitive to this. In quiet moments during interaction the sound of a voice may be an intrusion, spoiling the atmosphere which has been built up through non-verbal channels. The decision about when to remain silent cannot be based on hard and fast rules. It depends very much on the sensitive judgement of the person making the decision.

Adaptable approach. We are concerned with sympathetic, sensitive intervention which is adaptable and which has an aim — to establish and/or maintain relationships. Adaptation is an important word to remember. We tend to lapse into movement which feels comfortable to us and forms part of our usual manner of moving. In day to day activities this need not necessarily be of any consequence — unless

faulty movement habits place undue stress on our bodies — but when we are using our movement to work with other people it does become very important. Rocking a child can be comforting and soothing but, as illustrated earlier, the rocking action is the end product of many different movement factors. If we are working with someone who prefers a slow rocking action and we fall into our preferred fast and vigorous rocking, then the experience can be unpleasant and discourage the wish to remain and co-operate with us. This is an example of obvious differences. The differences in timing and intensity of movement can vary more subtly, so it does necessitate a continual checking of our own movement to ensure we have not lapsed into our own comfortable patterns.

Another example might be where we have discovered after a long period of trial and error that someone enjoys having his hand tapped. It might be that when this is done he stops his stereotyped mannerisms, ceases grinding his teeth and turns his head towards us with a hand held up waiting for us to repeat the tapping. Then simply to tap his hand in any way might be successful, but it could also be that he likes having his hand tapped with a certain amount of force and a certain timing. Perhaps he likes the sensation of bursts of hand tapping with pauses in between, or he might like having the palm of his hand tapped but not the back. It was said at the beginning of the chapter that when we enter the world of non-verbal communication we enter a world of microscopic detail. This also applies to our use of non-verbal communication and movement in work with the profoundly mentally handicapped person which is aimed at developing communication and expression and forming relationships. Tiny details, often idiosyncratic, can mean the difference between success or failure. Looked at in isolation and out of context and then judged by the standards of the outside world, their relevance seems negligible. To say in passing that A likes having his hand tapped does not convey the full significance of the channels of communication this might open up, particularly to people who have little experience of working with the mentally handicapped population. In the extremely limited world of the profoundly mentally handicapped person these tiny details which would usually seem very trivial can assume much importance.

Those we are likely to work with in movement using this adaptable and flexible approach will vary tremendously, both in the manner in which they move and the amount of movement they use. For example, some seem to be always on the move, never being still for a moment. Others rarely move, even when they have the physical capacity to do so. These differences are found whether or not the person has additional physical handicaps. One person may move as much as the limits of his physical handicap allow, whereas another person similarly handicapped moves much less.

Sometimes when a person appears to be moving around continuously, observation will show the movement to be limited and repetitive. The manner of moving and the actions are always the same. Where the variation of expressive movement is limited, the aim of intervention is initially to work with the movement the person already displays and slowly channel this into a more varied type of movement. There will have to be many encounters before this can happen.

Of course not all participants co-operate and for a variety of reasons. We are particularly concerned here with people whose profound mental handicap has made it extremely difficult for them to develop any communication skills; who appear to be totally unaware of their surroundings; who, even when unhampered by physical handicap, lack the curiosity about and understanding of their surroundings to put their mobility to good use; who, if left on their own, would perhaps lie on the floor or roam about aimlessly. There are also those who deliberately block out their surroundings and withdraw from others, or whose difficult behaviour hampers attempts to establish contact with them. Whatever the problem, we have to work hard to find a starting point, experimenting

with different ways of moving with the person and of approaching him with regard to interpersonal distance and spatial orientation. Sometimes we have to react to any movement however slight and however random it may seem.

Often barriers in the form of stereotyped movement or the dislike of intrusion in the personal space, or both, may have to be faced. There are those who indulge in stereotyped activity throughout most of their waking day. For example, they may move their arms, hands and fingers in a repetitive pattern, focussing on this movement rather than looking at others or the activity around them. They will carry on with this movement regardless of surroundings — a crowded shop or empty room makes no difference to them. Another person might pace about in an unchanging floor pattern, with or without accompanying repetitive body movements. Stereotyped movement, whatever the actual actions involved, is often done to the virtual exclusion of everything else. This type of movement can stimulate, relieve boredom and provide a secure barrier. It very effectively blocks out the surroundings, making communication attempts difficult and sometimes impossible. Even where we can approach the person closely without adverse effect, his postural and movement barriers can shut us out.

We have to be careful not to impose too quickly and for too long. Let us take as an example an attempt to intervene in the repetitive patterns of someone who moves around with an unchanging floor pattern and constantly taps one hand with the other in front of her face. It might be too much to join in with the floor pattern, remain close and intervene directly with the hand movements by moving a hand in between her hands and face. Again the process of breaking down the movement we observe into smaller parts and deciding which to use is important. Perhaps we might find that the person can tolerate sharing the floor pattern if we keep at a distance. Through time we can aim to get closer then begin reaching out at times to touch the outside of her hand, then gradually work our hand into being involved in the hand movements. If the stereotyped actions serve as a barrier to contact with others it may be that initially these actions will increase in intensity in attempts to keep you out, but perserverance with sensitivity helps to overcome this. As with any type of work with profoundly mentally handicapped people the process is slow and painstaking and has to be constantly repeated and reinforced.

The many different problems that we might encounter and try to alleviate create many different ways of working through movement in this flexible and adaptable way. The nature of the problem can make the work look entirely different with different people. Work with a very agile, active and highly distractible child will not look the same as work with a child who prefers to remain huddled in a corner on his own. However, there is a general theme running through any approach which may be used. This is that the movement generated by the participant is reacted to and elaborated on like a very one-sided conversation, which eventually begins to have meaning for the participant, until a more deliberate movement interaction gradually develops. The opportunity is given time after time, usually over many months, for a conversation to develop, expand and become more recognisable not only to participant and caregiver, but also more obvious to other people who are then able to become involved. In this way the work begins to be generalised, moving out from a very specific but idiosyncratic meaning to a general ability to take part in a two-way exchange with others.

Two-way communication does not require equal amounts of input from each participant. When communicating with a profoundly mentally handicapped person, the caregiver may have a greater input both verbally and non-verbally, but the other person may be responding equally intensely within his own limitations. Neither is it necessary to exchange factual information. If one looks at mother-infant interaction sequences it is not possible to see an exchange of factual information, but one is in no doubt that the infant and his mother are communicating.

The caregiver should be aware of the timing of movement, the need for different amounts of input with each person and the way in which the person uses the space around him. It is important for the caregiver to be sensitive, to give the mentally handicapped person time to respond and, where possible, to direct exchanges in his own time and in his own way. In time he may become more able to adapt to others and share interactions on a more equal basis.

There will obviously be different degrees of success. For example, some may become able to respond to others when approached and remain in contact for brief periods or occasionally make the first approach. Others may form deeper relationships and, where this is the case, students and others who are likely to be in a particular hospital ward or residential establishment for a short time should take care when establishing and forming these relationships. When that person leaves, the mentally handicapped person loses someone to whom he has become deeply attached and possibly very dependent. He will not be able to understand why the person is no longer there and this can have an adverse effect. It is important for transitory staff to bear this in mind when attempting to establish and develop ways of communicating. This is not to say that in these circumstances communication should not be attempted but that it should be tempered accordingly.

Similarly, if a caregiver is successful in building up a relationship with someone who has previously been non-communicating and who relates to the caregiver and no one else, the responsibility is enormous. Where possible this should be shared, and can be done by teaching and involving other staff in the non-verbal 'language' and 'conversations' which have evolved. Others may not be able to become so adept or fluent in this 'language' but it does relieve the burden of being the sole communicator and could also be providing opportunities for new developments through contact with a variety of people.

The effect of mental handicap on a person's ability to interact with others creates many similar problems within this group of people, but the uniqueness of each individual means that a blueprint for successful interaction cannot be applied mechanically in an unvarying form to each person. This is no different from the development of interaction with non-handicapped babies. Stern (1977), in describing the process the mother goes through of learning to interact with her baby, says that it can be a lonely one, based as it is on continual improvisation in which the 'steps and notes' have never been written down. Although there are similarities between caregivers, each mother and baby will also show differences. Learning to interact is a creative and personal process for both mother and baby. However, these mothers do not have to work so hard to establish interactions — their babies come into the world primed to take part in interactions with others (Newson, 1979). The caregiver who wishes to interact with a profoundly mentally handicapped person often has to work hard to find a starting point. Without this it can be difficult to develop interaction. Whoever we are dealing with and whatever the problem, once we have found a starting point the way is open to establish and develop our dialogue — we have achieved communication through movement.

SUMMARY

People can communicate through non-verbal channels whether or not they are talking to each other and at times this can be more powerful than the spoken word. Mentally handicapped people, especially the more severely handicapped, may have a limited range of non-verbal channels through which they can communicate and express themselves, but with good observation and sensitive adaptability by the caregiver these can still be used effectively.

Some of the features of non-verbal communication which can be of particular relevance to profoundly mentally handicapped people and others who find it difficult to communicate are interpersonal distance, personal space, orientation, physical contact and looking towards and at others. These need to be considered when working towards communication with those people who distance themselves and protect themselves from other people.

Cultural, social and emotional factors all influence the way in which we communicate and express ourselves non-verbally and these have to be considered when we are working with others through these channels and when using observation to provide some information about a person. Gesture and posture, for example, can provide us with information about someone but the variety of factors which affect the gesture he makes or the posture he adopts should be taken into account.

From an examination of the detailed world of non-verbal communication we proceeded to look at human movement and its complex nature. The context in which the movement takes place gives it its meaning and defines its purpose. In using movement in the manner described here as a way of developing communication with someone whose skills are extremely limited we are concerned with communication with and through movement, set within a social context.

The external environment is not the only factor affecting movement. Intangible factors from within the person also have an effect and movement can provide a link between inner self and the outside world, and between one person and another. The ingredients of expressive movement are the same whether or not the movement looks strange or normally acceptable and this provides a common factor which can be used to form a link between people.

It is important to look at how a person is moving as well as the action itself. Observed actions can be broken down into smaller parts and in doing so we will usually discover many differences between individuals performing the same movement. It is these differences which often hold the key to success in working with someone. Care should be taken in the interpretation of someone's movement and this should not be confused with objective observation. The subjective nature of interpretation should always be acknowledged.

Communication and expression do not have exactly the same meaning. There is sometimes a need to express oneself whether or not it is understood with clarity by others, and sometimes a need to communicate something clearly. The mentally handicapped person should have an opportunity for both communication and expression, and where speech does not exist or is limited, then non-verbal channels can provide the means to do this.

The beginnings of communication are found very early in life. Through interactions with the primary caregiver and others around him the baby is able to join the social world and to form early relationships. He is practised in conversation before the onset of speech. Difficulties which arise when this process does not proceed smoothly demand hard work and sensitivity from the caregiver, with a need to find a starting point which will form the initial link.

Another feature present early in life and important to successful interaction is interactional synchrony, in which the movements of people talking to each other are co-ordinated and resemble a dance routine. The consequences of lack of interactional synchrony can result in difficulties in communicating and forming relationships.

The final section outlines general points which would need to be considered by caregivers when communicating through movement. No blueprint can be offered for human communication, only general guidelines and hints. All the hints are centred on the caregivers' ability to adapt to others, to monitor their own actions and their effect and to be sensitive to the cues, reactions and mood of the mentally handicapped person. Stimulation should be given careful thought and presented in a way which is appropriate to the needs of those for whom it is intended.

Adaptability is essential with the end product being more effective communication rather than the quality and complexity of the actual movement involved. Effective communication then opens up the way to form and consolidate relationships with the mentally handicapped person and to allow him to express something of himself which may be impossible through speech. Communication through movement can be a richly varied and expressive experience.

REFERENCES

Argyle M 1972 Non-verbal communication in human social interaction. In: Hinde R (ed) Non-verbal communication. Cambridge University Press, Cambridge

Argyle M 1973 Social interaction. Tavistock London

Birdwhistell R L 1968 Kinesics. In: Argyle M (ed) Social encounters. Penguin, Harmondsworth

Birdwhistell R L 1971 Kinesics and context. Essays on body-motion communication. Penguin, Harmondsworth

Bower T G R 1977 A Primer of Infant Development. Freeman, San Francisco

Bruner J 1974 From communication to language — A psychological perspective. In: Lee V (ed) Language development. The Open University, London

Bullowa M 1979 Prelinguistic communication: A field for scientific research. In: Bullowa M (ed) Before speech: The beginning of interpersonal communication Cambridge University Press, Cambridge

Condon W S 1979 Neonatal entrainment and enculturation. In: Bullowa M (ed) Before speech: The beginning of interpersonal communication. Cambridge University Press, Cambridge

Danziger K 1976 Interpersonal communication. Pergamon Press, Oxford

Ekman P, Friesen W V 1969 Non-verbal leakage and clues to deception. In: Argyle M (ed) Social encounters. Penguin, Harmondsworth

Farb P 1977 Word Play. Coronet, London

Firth R 1970 Postures and gestures of respect. In: Polhemus T (ed) Social aspects of the human body. Penguin, Harmondsworth

Hall E T 1966 The hidden dimension. Doubleday, New York

Hewes G 1955 World distribution of certain postural habits. In: Polhemus T (ed) Social aspects of the human body. Penguin, Harmondsworth

Jourard S M 1966 An exploratory study of body-accessibility. British Journal of Social and Clinical Psychology, 5: 221–231

Kendon A 1967 Some functions of gaze-direction in social interaction. In: Argyle M (ed) Social encounters. Penguin, Harmondsworth

LaBarre W 1947 The cultural basis of emotions and gestures. In: Polhemus T (ed) Social aspects of the human body. Penguin, Harmondsworth

Lewis D 1978 The secret language of your child. Pan Books, London

Parry J 1967 The psychology of human communication. University of London Press, London

von Raffler-Engel W 1981 Developmental kinesics: How children acquire communication and non-communication. Infant Mental Health Journal 2: 84–94

Schaffer R 1977 Mothering. Fontana/Open Books, Glasgow

Schaffer R 1977 Early interactive development. In: Oates J (ed) Early cognitive development. The Open University, London

Snow C 1977 The development of conversation between mothers and babies. In: Lee V (ed) Language development. The Open University, London

Stern Daniel 1977 The first relationship: Infant and mother. Fontana/Open Books, Glasgow

Strube M J, Werner C 1982 Interpersonal distance and personal space: A conceptual and methodological note. Journal of Nonverbal Behaviour 6: 163–170

Trevarthen C 1979 Communication and co-operation in early infancy: A description of primary intersubjectivity. In: Bullowa M (ed) Before speech: The beginning of interpersonal communication. Cambridge University Press, Cambridge

Trevarthen C, Murray L, Hubley P 1981 Psychology of infants. In: Davies J A, Dobbing J (ed) Scientific foundations of paediatrics. Heinemann Medical, London

Watson O M, Graves T D 1966 Quantitative research in proxemic behaviour. In: Argyle M (ed) Social encounters. Penguin, Harmondsworth

11

Verbal communication and non-speech systems of communication

- Understanding of language precedes expression
- Assessment of an individual's comprehension, listening skills and expressive abilities is essential to plan therapy
- Assessment must take account of a mentally handicapped person's level of ability, chronological age and interests
- Communication skills must be practised and used outside therapy periods
- Non-speech systems are useful where verbal skills are limited

Verbal communication
   Prevalence of problems
   Normal language development
   Assessment of abilities
   Evaluation
   How to help
   Criteria for intervention
   Priorities
Non-speech systems of communication
   Introduction
   Manual systems
   Written systems
   Rationale
Summary

The following chapter outlines normal language development, areas of communication break-down, and some techniques which can be used in assessing and remediating these areas with mentally handicapped people, in co-operation with the people in their environment. A list of priorities is proposed in terms of those most likely to benefit from intervention, and the criteria for intervention are discussed. The chapter ends with a description of non-speech systems of communication.

VERBAL COMMUNICATION

Prevalence of problems

A number of surveys of speech problems in mentally handicapped people have recently been completed. Leeming (1979) found that about two-thirds of school age children did not use grammatical sentences, and half of this number were 'at or below the level of initiating single words'. Under a quarter of the children could follow complex instructions, and a quarter failed even to respond to their names, or other sounds. Of the children who had some speech, a third were intelligible, and another third had some articulation problems. Whelan & Speake (1977) in a survey of adult training centres found that speech therapy input was high on the list of required professional input, and unpublished work (Stansfield, 1981) found that nearly three-quarters of adults in training centres had some difficulty with communication, and about a third of the clients had the potential to benefit from speech therapy. It can be inferred that hospital residents, with their more restricted environment, are even more likely to benefit from work to improve their communication. The Quirk report (DES, 1972) stated that a first priority in developing the speech therapy service should be the provision of services for the mentally handicapped, and especially working with other professionals such as nurses and teachers.

Interprofessional co-operation is of critical importance in all the work described below, and a basic knowledge of the normal development of speech and language helps nurses, teachers, and others to understand the reasons for the way work is carried out.

Normal language development

A great deal of study has been done on the early development of language, and there are conflicting theories ranging from the behaviourist view (Skinner, 1957) that all language is learned, and human babies only copy what is said around them, through to Chomsky (1957) who said that a child has an innate ability to create language.

Recent work has attempted to steer a path between these two extremes, suggesting that infants have innate abilities to learn language (Slobin, 1973; Lenneberg, 1967) but need to hear language before that ability can be used. It is also now widely accepted that other aspects of a child's development affect his ability to learn language, so in the first 6 months especially, gross and fine motor, visual perception and social development are also very important (Bruner, 1974).

Language begins to develop with the baby's first cry, and to some extent learning continues throughout life, although by adulthood it is mostly only new vocabulary that is being learned. The first 5 years are the most important, both for speed and complexity of learning. In the first months interaction between the parent or caregiver and child is essential in enabling a child to communicate in later life. A system of turn-taking can begin with the first feed session, with the pattern of baby sucking/parent speaking/baby sucking. Very often a parent attributes social responses to the baby, e.g.:

Mother Are you going to have some more? (Baby closes eyes.)
Mother Oh you've had enough. Let's get the wind up then. (Baby burps.)
Mother Oh you are clever!

Even when there is no response, the parent leaves time before beginning to speak again — part of the pattern of 'motherese' (Ferguson & Snow, 1978) — which enables babies to learn language. Most people speaking to babies change the way they speak: pitch is higher, there is a greater range of intonation and stress, a greater range from soft to loud, and speed is slower.

In addition, it is social custom for all visitors to make a baby centre of attention, thus adding to the child's awareness of communication. This can be an additional handicap to the older mentally handicapped child, who is just beginning language. He is too big and 'unbaby-like' to elicit attention and the 'motherese' speech which aids further language acquisition.

Normally, understanding precedes expression and this rule works from the earliest months.

From 0–4 months, infants are beginning to learn the intonation patterns of their own language; they jump when hearing a sudden noise, become quieter when they hear a familiar voice, and begin to appear to listen to a speaker. The only intentional communication before about 3 months, however, is eye contact. Of course, babies do cry, smile and gurgle, but these are comfort/discomfort signs and occur whether or not anyone is there to notice.

By 3 months there is occasional vocalising in response to sound stimulation or speech, and crying, cooing and gurgling does begin to have different meaning. As anyone who has had a child will know, a 3-month-old baby can howl in the middle of the night and stop the minute he is lifted, thus showing that he wanted attention, not feeding. Some consonant-like sounds begin to be heard by about 3–3½ months. Up to this age the sounds produced are thought to be innate (even deaf babies begin making noises), but the infant very soon begins to use the sounds heard around him.

Between 3 and 6 months a baby begins to recognise familiar sounds — musical toys, cup and spoon, and familiar voices — and will turn towards things he enjoys: he is able to recognise different voice tones.

By 6 months, tongue control is increasing; babble chains of 'mamama', 'bababa', 'gagaga' are heard and this is a continuous process involving learning from the environment (Weir, 1966). The baby occasionally experiments with consonant sounds not heard in his language, but is generally becoming closer and closer to his own language, so that by 9 months there may be long intonated babble chains that sound like his own language. These babble chains are often interpreted as 'words' too soon, so that 'dadada' may be understood by the parents to mean 'daddy' and greeted with delight! This, of course, brings us back to interaction. The child whose 'dadada' is responded to by: 'Where's daddy, yes, daddy's coming — oh, here is daddy,' will learn to use 'dadada' as a word referring to daddy much sooner than if the parent says, 'Yes, that's right,' or says nothing.

Between 6 and 9 months the child is beginning to recognise words like 'no', 'daddy' etc. and between 9 and 12 months begins to respond meaningfully to a few words.

A breakthrough in cognitive development occurs at about 8 months when the child begins to realise that an object that is out of sight still exists, and can be found. This is known as object permanence (see Ch. 5). From this stage on, thought and language become progressively more closely related (Bruner, 1974).

At 12 months a child can understand single words and very simple commands. To begin with, words are understood specific to context. 'Chair' may mean one particular chair. 'Where's daddy?' may gain a response at home, but not in a neighbour's house. First words appear between 12 and 18 months (Gilham 1979), and between 18 and 24 months at least a few two-word sentences will be heard.

By 2 years a child understands short sentences, often repeats words an adult says (echolalia) and uses between 50 and 150 words with meaning. Two-word 'sentences' are heard increasingly in the next few months, usually starting with noun-verb combinations, 'daddy — gone', 'him got', and by 2½ years three-word sentences are also heard, e.g. 'him hit James'. Vocabulary also increases rapidly over the 2–3 year period, but because it may be inadequate for a child's needs, he may occasionally hesitate or repeat sounds when he is unable to find the right word, e.g. 'Mumumum there's a a a thing in the s,s,sky' when the 'thing' is not a bird or plane, words the child knows, but helicopter which he does not. This is 'normal' non-fluency and can continue until about 4 years.

From 3–5 years the sounds produced in speech become more similar to the adult norm, although some substitutions continue to be made. Sentence length and construction increase in complexity and grammatical structures are used correctly more often, although irregularities are occasionally regularised (e.g. sheep — sheeps; run — runned) until the child is about 4½ years old. By 5 years of age almost all the normal development of language has taken place. Such subtleties as self-regulation of behaviour, using inner language and discourse on abstract ideas obviously continue to develop for several years. Vocabulary also continues to increase and change up to the mid or late teens before becoming specialised as a person enters work and becomes involved in individual social activities.

A 5-year-old, however, should have adequate language skills in terms of sounds, sentence structure and comprehension and expression of meaning, to communicate with most people in his environment.

Assessment of abilities

A mentally handicapped person's communicative abilities must be assessed in the field of his everyday life. A variety of methods can be used to assess hearing, physical ability to produce speech, voice, fluency, phonology and language but very few tests are specifically designed for mentally handicapped people and difficulties can be experienced in finding materials suitable for the level of ability, chronological age and interests of the person concerned.

Many people have stereotypes of the way they expect, e.g. someone with Down's syndrome to speak (Gibson, 1978) but while the disorders to which he may have a predisposition should be kept in mind (Ingram, 1976), communication should be investigated without prejudice.

Hearing

Anyone with difficulty in hearing speech will experience some problems in learning to produce it accurately, therefore a record of the person's hearing acuity is important. Recent research (Nolan et al 1980) has found that almost 50% of mentally handicapped adults in an adult training centre they surveyed had some degree of hearing loss.

Initial tests of hearing can be done by nurses or other professionals involved with the mentally handicapped person as follows:

Stand 1.2 m behind client and have another person standing in front.
Clap hands.
Rattle keys.
Jingle coins in your hand.
Shake high-pitched rattle.
Bang drum.

Ask the person in front to note any reaction, e.g. movement, change of expression.

Stand behind the client and ask him to perform tasks of which he is capable — 'stand up', 'sit down' etc., getting progressively quieter as you give the commands.

If there is a lack of response, or a hearing loss is suspected for any reason, a medical officer should be asked to arrange a hearing test (audiological assessment). This is important to rule out hearing loss as a contributing factor to a mentally handicapped person's problems, or to identify the degree of hearing loss.

Oral examination

Considerable control of movements of the tongue, lips and soft palate and adequate structure of the mouth (hard palate and teeth in particular) are necessary for normal speech (Fig. 11.1). The oral examination is to check that there are no physical problems which would interfere with the development of speech (Crickmay, 1975).

Hard palate. This should be intact and gently arched. A client with a cleft palate may tend to have nasal escape of air even after a cleft has been repaired. In Down's syndrome clients the hard palate is frequently vaulted — high arched and narrow — and this can distort the resonance patterns of the voice.

Teeth. Ideally, the teeth should be even and straight and any dentures should be adequately fitted. Dental caries (bad teeth) resulting from infrequent brushing or weak enamel can cause halitosis — itself a barrier to communication.

Case examples

Angus, aged 18 years and profoundly handicapped, was overweight and physically

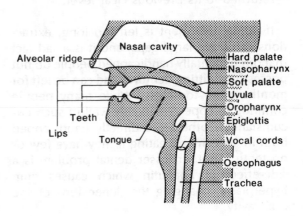

Fig. 11.1 Organs of articulation.

unattractive. He refused to allow a tooth-brush inside his mouth and as a result his breath became more and more unpleasant and fewer and fewer people would go close enough to him to communicate effectively. Eventually, he had some dental treatment under anaesthetic and five very decayed teeth were removed. After this, with a lot of help and encouragement from the ward staff, and with a very soft toothbrush at first, he began to tolerate tooth-brushing and the halitosis was reduced. This had the added benefit of staff being prepared to get physically close to him again and therefore increasing his opportunities for communication.

Brian, aged 32, years was referred by the Adult Training Centre (ATC) he attended because his speech had suddenly deteriorated over a period of 6 weeks. He spoke with his mouth almost closed and was extremely difficult to understand. When askesd to open his mouth for an oral examination he was unwilling but was persuaded and as soon as he opened his mouth wide his upper dentures fell out completely! The ATC staff then recalled that he had been absent for a few days about 6 weeks previously and, on contacting his parents, discovered that it was because of extraction of all his teeth and the fitting of dentures. Brain returned to the dentist for a refit and once he had well-fitting dentures his speech returned to its previous clear level.

If dental treatment is left too long, extractions can leave large gaps, and it is a sad fact that often mentally handicapped people do not possess well-fitting dentures and can be left for months quite toothless. While many people continue to cope remarkably well in such circumstances, others are directly handicapped both in speech and eating if they have few or no teeth. Another lesser dental problem is a side-effect of Epanutin which causes gum hyperplasia, changing the dimensions of the oral cavity.

The alignment of upper and lower teeth is worth noting. A tongue thrust can push the upper teeth out of line and a protruding lower jaw can cause problems in producing some consonants, for example f, m, b.

Soft palate. The soft palate should rise to form a closure with the pharyngeal wall (see Fig. 11.1) during most of speech. This is difficult to assess as saying 'ah' produces tension and can force the soft palate up even if it does not normally move adequately. If the soft palate does not rise or does not touch the pharyngeal wall the usual result is some hyper-nasality or nasal escape of air during speech.

Lips. Lip closure is necessary for several consonants, and fine movements are required for sh, s, oo, ee, amongst other sounds. It also means that drooling is less likely to be a problem.

Tongue. Fine tongue movements, particularly of the tongue tip, are required to produce speech and therefore the ability to move the tongue rapidly and accurately and to point the tongue tip is important. If there are problems with the physical structure of the mouth, dental or ENT opinions should be sought through the medical officer as appropriate.

Investigation of difficulties in tongue movement ought also to be requested from the medical officer and an opinion given on whether difficulties are a result of dysarthria or dyspraxia.

Voice

The degree of loudness, nasality, pitch and usage of air during speech are important in voice production, and in addition there may be particular problems such as hoarseness. In isolation any one abnormality would be unlikely to interfere with communication, but a combination of difficulties, e.g. a loud, hypernasal, hoarse, low-pitched voice may be enough in itself to reduce intelligibility.

Before any work is begun on a voice disorder of a child or adult, an ENT investigation should be sought to rule out any physical problems (Greene, 1980).

Fluency

Speech therapists tend to use two terms, stammer and stutter, interchangeably to indicate a degree of non-fluency. This can range between mild repetitions of a sound, syllable, word or phrase: 'm-m-m-my book', hesitations: '......... my book', prolongations: 'mmmmmmy book', intrusive sounds: 'er — my book' and blocks, where intense muscular effort is used before a sound explodes into being. Any of these can be associated with an avoidance of eye-to-eye contact and facial or body movements. Other non-fluent behaviours include disorders of speed (excessively slow, fast or accelerating speech) and of stress (for instance where every syllable is of equal length, 'the te-le-phone is ring-ing').

Theories about the causes of non-fluency seem to be almost as numerous as non-fluent speakers (Andrews et al 1983) and no research findings are currently available on the efficacy of treating mentally handicapped stammerers.

Phonology

The phonemes (consonants and vowels) of a particular language need to be produced accurately at the beginning, middle and end of words and in blends of sounds for intelligibility to be maintained, e.g.

```
p
pig   happy      cap
Spy              clasp
```

Some tests (Ingram et al, 1971) assess a person's developmental level of articulation but it is often more useful to map the production of consonants in speech to give an idea of any underlying problems.

Disorders of phonology and articulation can be due to a hearing loss or physical problems (dysarthria, dyspraxia) (see above). A listening problem, reduced auditory memory, perception or sequencing skills can also be a cause (Johnson, 1979).

Language

This is by far the most important aspect of a speech therapist's work with mentally handicapped people. Investigation of how much is understood (comprehension), both of single words and longer utterances, and of *listening* skills (auditory attention, memory, and discrimination) is the first area of assessment, followed by the person's expressive ability — how he expresses meaning, and uses sentences and vocabulary. A list of commonly used tests is shown on pages 246–7 along with their advantages and disadvantages for use with a mentally handicapped person.

Checklists are becoming more popular as a way of including the primary caregivers — parents, nurses — in the assessment of a mentally handicapped person's abilities. Of particular value are those by Kellett (1976) specifically on language development, Cunningham & Sloper (1978) based on normal infant development tests for 0–2 year olds and the Portage Guide to Early Education which covers general pre-school development from 0–6 year olds. All these checklists are of value in asking the people who know the mentally handicapped person best, to assess his level of functioning.

Patchy development of language skills is common in mentally handicapped people, but some aspects seem more prone to breakdown than others. It is frequently found that comprehension and expression of single word vocabulary are well ahead of comprehension or expression of longer utterances (Renfrew, 1972) possibly due to limited auditory attention skills.

In adults, experiences and preferences will determine the vocabulary so that developmentally advanced concepts may be known, while much simpler ones are not. Comprehension and expression of grammatical structures can also be well behind that of meaning (Fig. 11.2) e.g.

Therapist What is the man doing?
Child (describing the picture) Brush leaves.

Fig. 11.2 Stimulus picture. (Reproduced by courtesy of LDA, Park Works, Wisbech.)

The information is present but except for correct word ordering, grammar is not (a complete answer would be: He is sweeping up the leaves).

Careful observation must also be used to assess the mentally handicapped person's functional communication (communicative competence). Parents, care staff and teachers are consulted to see if they agree with the speech therapist's assessment of the problems, as obviously the people living with a patient have a much clearer picture of the mentally handicapped person's use of communication.

Evaluation

After assessment of the different areas of communication skills an evaluation of results needs to be made. Additional handicaps such as hearing, vision, gross or fine motor deficits may reduce scores and here again the opinions of caregivers are of immeasurable value.

Case examples

Dianne, aged 8 years, a new girl in the school, scored very badly on several language tests and her teacher was quite surprised by this, as in class she appeared one of the more able children. There were no records on the school notes of any particular problems. but consultation with the parents revealed that she had a progressive deterioration of vision and that the only area where she could see clearly was the very centre of normal visual range. She had managed to hide the problem quite well in school until entirely new material was presented to her. A teacher of the visually handicapped was approached for advice on handling the problem.

Evelyn, aged 17 years, had recently started at a new Adult Training Centre. Her understanding was very good on testing but she seemed unable to name even the most common objects. No physical problems were found and so she was observed in a group of other clients and it became apparent that she was not unable to speak, but merely unwilling with strange adults she had never met before. Over a period of 2 months she began first to use a few single word answers and eventually sentences which were at the same level as her comprehension skills.

How to help

Hearing

Someone with a suspected hearing loss can be helped by everyone in his environment:

Make sure the speaker's face is in direct light. Have the mentally handicapped person facing the speaker.
Make sure that he watches the speaker's face.
Use a slightly raised voice.
Speak slowly and clearly.
If necessary, repeat the words.

Tongue and lip movement

There are numerous exercises for helping to improve tongue, lip and soft palate movement (Crickmay, 1975), some of which are shown below. These can be used with guidance from a speech therapist and should never be continued if the mentally handicapped person shows obvious distress.

Use a mirror and ask the mentally handi-capped person to imitate you as well as possible.
Push the tongue out and in, slowly then quickly.
Move the tongue from side to side.
Push the tongue up to reach the nose.
Push the tongue down to reach the chin.
Move the tongue outside, round the lips, first clockwise then anticlockwise.
Move the tongue round between the lips and the teeth.
Pull faces in front of the mirror.
Ask him/her to put his tongue on the part of the lip (upper or lower) that you just touched.
Try to hide the lips completely.
Purse the lips.
Grimace to pull the lips back towards the ears.
Try combinations of any two movements.

The following activities may appeal to children and the developmentally young:

Put a small amount of any of the following on the mentally handicapped person's lip (any position) and see if he can lick it off.

Chocolate ⎫
Blackcurrant ⎪ Squeezy food
Strawberry ⎬ flavourings
Raspberry ⎭
Honey
Jam
Vermicelli
Malt spreads
Diluted vanilla ⎫ Essence
Diluted almond ⎭

Do the same and ask him to use the lips *only* to remove the substance.

Put spots of the same substances immedi-ately beyond the boundary of the lips. Ask him to lick them off.
Put a spatula, lolly stick or similar just between the patient's lips — encourage him to maintain lip closure while you 'try' to pull out the stick. Don't let him hang on by the teeth.
Always end with an activity that the mentally handicapped person can achieve with ease to complete the session successfully.

Voice

With voice disorders, intervention must be considered very carefully. If direct work is to take place, the mentally handicapped person must realise that the voice is a problem and co-operation is required to change it. Direct speech therapy can involve relaxation exer-cises, breathing exercises and self-monitoring by a variety of specific exercises including tape-recording and self-perception depending upon the type of disorder. Indirect work can be as basic as giving a good normal pattern for imitation. A person speaking excessively loudly can be spoken to in a quiet voice thus encouraging a reduction in volume; one with excessive nasality can be encouraged to open his mouth wider to balance oral and nasal resonance and a male with an excessively high voice could be designated a male member of staff with whom to spend more time so that the normal male vocal range is heard frequently. A voice disorder in a mentally handicapped child or adult would very rarely be treated directly, unless it is a major cause of unintelligibility and the only barrier to effec-tive communication.

Fluency

The basic clinical criteria for treatment of a mentally handicapped stammerer is the same as that for 'normal' non-fluent speakers — that if they are not aware of the non-fluency as a problem, then regardless of how severe it may seem to others, it is only treated indirectly

(Gregory, 1979). Insight into the fact that there is a problem and a willingness to co-operate to change the speech pattern must be present before direct therapy is undertaken. Assuming that intervention is considered appropriate by the speech therapist there are many methods available to increase fluency and reduce associated problems, e.g. of anticipation and expectation of difficulties, avoidance of people, situations, words and sounds by a progressive desensitisation programme. This involves building up fluency skills and confidence in a series of situations in which it is progressively more difficult for the stammerer to remain fluent, making sure of consistent success at each level, before moving on. Indirect methods mainly directed at primary caregivers include the following advice on how to react to a stammer — do's and don'ts to avoid increasing the non-fluency:

Do speak simply and clearly yourself.
Do give the stammerer time to speak.
Do let him finish what he has to say without interruption.

Don't say 'Stop and start again'.
Don't pretend you've not heard him speak.
Don't draw attention to the way he speaks by telling him to 'think first' or 'speak more slowly'.

In mentally handicapped people non-fluency can be due to a limited vocabulary and this, of course, can to some extent be rectified indirectly by work on language skills (see below).

Phonology

Vowel patterns, and some consonants obviously vary in different parts of Britain and intelligibility within a person's own community is the aim when work on production of sounds is commenced, not the production of 'Queen's English'.

Once the sound system has been analysed and causes of problems identified auditory discrimination work is usually the first part of rectifying a problem. As there are so many causes of articulation difficulty, this is another area where specific speech therapy advice is needed before trying to help the mentally handicapped person. Telling him to 'say s', for example, is almost guaranteed to fail.

Direct intervention for a sound production disorder is unlikely to be successful if the mentally handicapped person has a mental age of less than $3\frac{1}{2}$–4 years overall and language intervention work will usually be of greater benefit (Berry, 1969). Speech therapists rarely work on sound production with normal children below this age for the same reasons as noted in the discussion of voice and fluency — that insight and co-operation are essential to effect change. Listening games can be introduced which help to increase the person's perception skills (McCartney & Byers Brown, 1980). Exercises such as the following can be used:

Ask the client to copy a rhythmic pattern of clapping hands or tapping on a table, short short: long short. Begin with two sounds and work up to five or six.

Ask the client to identify common noises, e.g. running water, spoon banging cup, saucepan lid. Show objects and make the sound. Hide objects behind screen, make one of the sounds. Remove screen. Identification of the sound heard is by pointing or naming the correct source.

Ask for identification of musical instruments. For example cymbals, drum, bell. Gradually instruments which sound similar can be introduced, e.g. large and small triangle, similar bells, melodica and mouth organ.

Ask for identification of the location of a sound made behind, above etc.
With eyes open.
Blindfold.

Use pictures of animals and either make the animal sound or use a tape-recording. Ask for identification of the animal which produced that sound.

After listening work is successful, specific techniques are introduced to elicit a particular sound, e.g. /f/ can be demonstrated using a mirror; /k/ from coughing. The sequence of production is then as follows:

Production of the sound in isolation, imitating someone else.

Production of the sound in nonsense syllables, e.g. 'b' — 'bee',, 'eeb', 'eebee'.

Production of the sound in a word, in imitation (using a small selection of familiar, useful words).

Production of the words learned.

Naming a picture.

Completing a sentence.

In phrases.

In sentences — structured conversation.

Production of the sound generalised to other words.

This technique works well with children but with adults the pattern tends to break down after stage 4 so that generalisation is not a feasible goal for adults (McCartney & Byers Brown, 1980). Ultimately, with any mentally handicapped person, it may be necessary to accept less than perfect speech, so long as therapy has reached the mentally handicapped person's maximum potential, thus: 'thi i a fa ka' or 'dith ith a pat tat' when the correct words would be 'This is a fat cat' (Fig. 11.3), may be the best which can be expected.

Fig. 11.3 Naming a picture. (Reproduced by courtesy of LDA, Park Works, Wisbech.)

Further emphasis on sound production can lead to much more severe communication problems, such as a refusal to speak at all, violence or total withdrawal.

Case example
Conn, aged 35 years, had a fairly severe sound production problem and although he could correct himself in single words he was quite unable to do so when he was talking spontaneously. A well-meaning aunt who had visited one speech therapy session decided to correct Conn every time he said a sound wrong, despite advice to the contrary. She came back some days later, very upset because Conn had first refused to look at her and finally rushed out of the house and slammed the door in her face. She never stopped trying to correct him. Speech therapy had to avoid direct articulation work and go on to more general listening skills for some months before Conn would try his single words again.

Language

Almost without exception, language intervention work is based on normal development, regardless of intrusive problems such as excessive activity or socially unacceptable behaviour. There are many programmes available to encourage and increase communication, including general developmental stimulation (Bluma et al, 1976; Cunningham & Sloper, 1978; Curtis & Hill, 1978); language, comprehension and expression stimulation (Peabody Language Kits; Jeffree, 1976; GOAL), and those specifically for comprehension (Learning to Listen) or expression (Gillham, 1980, 1983).

Most of the kits and books were originally designed with children in mind, as until recently the communication problems of mentally handicapped adults have received little attention (Whelan & Speake, 1974; Leudar et al, 1981), but with imagination childish materials can be substituted by ones designed to appeal to adults when this is necessary. Although the individuality of a person is obviously of primary importance, common language disorders of mentally handicapped people can be grouped to some extent.

Language problems

Group One. Verbal comprehension, expression and non-verbal skills all at the same level.

In children, work on attempting to increase language skills should be closely associated with cognitive, fine and gross motor, self-help and socialisation skills. A system such as Portage (see above) can be used to monitor and encourage progress and obviously primary carers have the most time and knowledge to plan goals.

In adults, if language skills are at the same developmental level as all the other skills then intervention would not be relevant. If, however, the communication skills are much lower than, e.g. self-help or socialisation abilities as is common, then an attempt would be made to increase communication competence. With children and adults, this is usually done through play materials (Jeffree & McConkey, 1974) and using carefully graded commands and commentary on the activities as they go along in addition to encouraging any expressive language and expanding upon it.

Case example
Fraser, aged 4 years, was understanding simple sentences but using only about three words, 'dad, no, more.'
Therapist I've got a toy bus. I'm going to push the bus to you.
(Fraser picks it up.)
Therapist Push the bus to me.
(Fraser pushes bus.)
Therapist I've got the bus. I'll push the bus fast.
Fraser Bus.
Therapist Yes bus. I pushed the bus.

Group Two. Verbal comprehension and expression below non-verbal abilities.

This is often the case with deaf people or where there is a specific language disorder,

and mental handicap does not exclude these problems. Many mentally handicapped people, however, have such a problem with no demonstrable cause. Such people are able to communicate by understanding and using such things as facial expression, gesture, proximity and touch and these methods in addition to speech can be used to encourage an increase *in verbal* communication. If this does not improve, however, it is still possible to use a standard gestural system to help everyone in the person's environment to use the same non-verbal language (see below). Signing can be introduced as a first attempt to increase communication as it frequently has the effect of reducing frustration and subsequently encouraging the emergence of verbal expression (Moores, 1980).

Case example
Gareth, aged 53 years, had been a hospital resident since he was 7 years old, but was only referred for speech therapy when the department expanded. On testing, his understanding was at about a 3 year level, but he used only single words. Attempts to increase the number of words were initially unsuccessful and so Makaton was introduced (a language programme to teach signing), as he already had quite a number of gestures understood by those around him. Over a year of intensive work, with cooperation from everyone he knew, Gareth learned 25 Makaton signs and began to put them together into two and three-word phrases. In addition be began to *say* two and three-word phrases firstly using the same words as the signs but gradually adding new ones. Although his expressive skills never reached his level of understanding, he did maintain the use of two and three-word phrases after therapy was discontinued.

Group Three. Verbal comprehension better than expressive abilities.

This group includes physically handicapped people where muscle co-ordination or muscle tone (as in spastics) severely reduces the ability to use facial expression or gesture as well as speech. It may also include some autistics, emotionally disturbed and depressed patients.

Verbal expression is increased by encouraging any utterance and rewarding it, then only accepting sounds progressively closer to the required utterance (word or phrase), e.g.

Attempts
a
oo
poo
boo
book

Another 'ploy' is to give the person a forced choice, 'Shall we look at the book or look in the box?', making sure that one or other is a desired object in the first place. With physically handicapped people specific exercises to improve tongue, lip and soft palate control can also be used (see p. 231).

If expressive language or gesture is physically or emotionally impossible, however, a picture, photo or Blissymbolics communication board may be introduced. Commercially produced boards are available or one can be designed for an individual by those who know his basic needs. Blissymbolics is a system of written symbols which is easier to learn than reading. The mentally handicapped person may point to the picture or symbol representing his requirements. (See pp. 242–3 for an outline of these systems.)

Case example

Harriet, aged 21 years, had been admitted to hospital because of her severe physical handicap but was also considered severely mentally handicapped. She was unable to communicate except by eye contact, but was referred for speech therapy at the request of a student nurse who was writing a case study. It quickly became obvious that Harriet could identify pictures by correctly looking at the one named and a tentative attempt was made to introduce Blissymbolics. Within 6 months Harriet had progressed to a board with 400 symbols on it and, despite her physical handicap, for the first time in her life was able to express herself. She

continued to live in the hospital but began attending a day centre for physically handicapped people, where she was able to use the Blissymbols to good effect.

Group Four. Verbal expression better than verbal comprehension.

Known as Cocktail Party syndrome, this occurs in some autistics, many hydrocephalics and often in children who are mentally handicapped but come from highly articulate or highly intelligent families where talking well is at a premium. On analysis sentence structure is occasionally at a lower level than expected and it can be the sheer volume of talking which gives the impression of advanced expression. Where the structure is advanced, content is usually lacking, irrelevant or delayed echoing of someone else's utterance (Tew, 1979).

Case example

Ian, aged 29 years, a new arrival in the hospital, was referred when the speech therapists were taping a number of people to demonstrate 'good speech patterns'. He had lived in the south of England, had an immaculate Oxford English accent and at first appeared to be anything but mentally handicapped. Over a short period of time, however, it became apparent that Ian had major problems.

Therapist I'd like to tape your voice if that's all right.

Ian My mother and father said they would take me to the zoo on Saturday if it doesn't rain.

Therapist Do you like the zoo?

Ian When I lived in London we always used to have cake for tea at grandma's.

Therapist Oh, that's nice — can you see a picture of a cake here?

Ian But grandma doesn't live in London now, so we have eskimos for tea instead.

Therapist Ian show me the cake.

(Ian picks up picture of a spoon.)

Therapist (picks up correct picture) Here is the cake.

The procedure with such people is to ignore all expressive language which is not directly relevant to the immediate situation and concentrate on comprehension, repeating commands until they are obeyed (or at least an attempt is made), then repeating again and peforming the action for the mentally handicapped person if he really does not understand.

Criteria for intervention

Two considerations should be made before work on communication skills is commenced.

— It must be possible to motivate the person to communicate.
— There must be a situation to encourage communication when the person is not receiving speech therapy.

There is no point in taking someone for speech therapy unless there is a need for and encouragement of the skills they learn in daily life.

Case examples
John, aged 35 years, was able to produce grammatical sentences in response to questions but as a rule he reduced utterances to the minimum: 'Out — Saturday — home — dad — pub' meant 'I'm going home for the weekend and dad will go to the pub with me.' Obviously, however, he managed to express his meaning so that almost everyone in his immediate surroundings understood him — and there was no motivation for him to increase his grammatical ability.

Kate, aged 12 years, and profoundly handicapped, spent 5 minutes with a new nurse gesturing and saying 't-t-t'. 20 minutes later she was found to be wet. As a result, she was reprimanded because she *could* toilet herself, but the gesture she had used was the Makaton sign for toilet. It was not Kate's fault she was wet, neither was it the new nurse's as he had not been informed of the system of signs and sounds used — but communication had obviously broken down, leading to an uncomfortable, unhappy, frustrated child and an annoyed and frustrated nurse. The remedy was to improve communication between the various staff involved with the child.

Lewis, aged 50 years, was withdrawn and spoke rarely although he understood simple commands on the ward and responded appropriately to situations. After a period of speech therapy he began to speak more and to seek out members of staff to demonstrate his new skills. There were 40 other men on the ward and an average of three staff at any one time so he was actively discouraged from making approaches as he reduced the time available for all the other important aspects of nursing duties. The result was a return to the withdrawn Lewis and consequently a less 'troublesome' patient. The remedy was to work with Lewis in a group, so that he began to talk to other residents, not just staff. Intensive work on the ward proved that long-term communicative residents could actually reduce an excessive workload by increased responsibility for their own actions.

The criteria for formal intervention to improve a mentally handicapped person's communication skills are a potential for improvement and development of these skills and, with some patients, the maintenance of skills which may otherwise deteriorate through, for instance, lack of practice.

Priorities

The prorities for work on communication fall, to some extent, into age bands although it cannot be stressed too much that each person should be regarded as an individual and all aspects of a problem be thoroughly investigated before work is begun or decided against. The groups are:

Pre-school children regardless of apparent level of ability
School leavers
16–25 year olds

Younger school age children
Older adults/less able adults.

Pre-school children

The first group, pre-schoolers, is of fairly obvious importance, as this is the period of fastest development (Mittler, 1976). There is a case for a 'developmental therapist' for young mentally handicapped children, with one person involved in all aspects of development, rather than the family having a long stream of clinic appointments and professionals visiting them at home. The developmental therapist could be *any* professional trained in normal development. A research project in Exeter (Carlyle, 1980) used occupational, speech and physiotherapists, nurses, a teacher and an experienced parent in the role. A major strength of each of these people was that they knew what they did not know and if a specific problem arose they called in the relevant specialist immediately.

Older school age children

Traditionally, the younger school children have been receiving therapy and, because of lack of time, the older ones have not been fitted in unless their communication problems were very severe. Clinical experience suggests that work with particularly the more able older children can be much more effective than when they were younger, and Leeming (1979) noted a spontaneous increase in abilities between 12 and 14 years. Specific problems with language, phonology, fluency and, very rarely, voice (loudness, nasality etc.) can be tackled using the child's awareness and insight to achieve results. In addition, social skill development and such things as interview techniques can be practised in co-operation with the primary carers, teaching staff and, occasionally, potential employers.

Young adults

It has been noted in clinical observation (HARC, 1981) that there seems to be a spurt of development from about 16 to the early 20s in many mentally handicapped people. Whether this is an increase in the ability to learn, application of knowledge previously acquired or other reasons is unclear. It will be interesting to note if there is any change when children leaving school have received a full-time education instead of the 'training' to which they were entitled before 1974 in Scotland and 1971 in England and Wales. Previously, mentally handicapped children attended junior training (occupation) centres, under social work department control. The instructors were not required to be qualified, and although many had an interest in helping the children develop, the emphasis was often very heavily on physical care. Since the change in the law, qualified teachers have been employed to work with all children of school age, early diagnosis and assessment is much more closely related to educational input (Leeming, 1979), and physical, social, emotional and cognitive development are now seen as being equally important in the children's education.

Much of the need for young adults is similar to that of school leavers, especially as again, specific speech therapy usually stopped early in their school career. Many gaps in knowledge appear on testing individual young adults and language work has been shown to be effective, especially where adult training centre staff, parents or other primary carers carry through the programme.

A speech therapist can assess, design programmes and then act in an advisory capacity with general language work, in addition to taking individual sessions to work with specific problems.

Younger school age children

This has traditionally been the commonest target group for intervention in the past. One of the main reasons for putting the group so low on the list is that in schools, teachers themselves are becoming more and more aware of, and able to apply language development techniques to work on general language skills and they are also incorporating the work into all the school activities from toileting to pre-reading and reading skills.

The days of a child being hauled out of a classroom for half an hour's 'speech' a week are, thankfully, diminishing and there is much more co-operation between therapists, school staff and the child's home.

A therapist may see children individually, but also work alongside teachers in the classroom on language development. Parents can now be invited to school on an 'open house' basis, but home visits can be made (with the parents' permission), so that both parents can be seen and any work be discussed in more detail. Most school children also have a small notebook which contains ideas for practice work from the school and comments on the usefulness and success of this work from the parents.

In this way, communication between all those involved with the child can be kept at a high level, and behaviours which occur in only one situation can be noted.

Case example

Marie, aged 6 years, had started school late because of recurrent bouts of illness. At school, she used only a very few single words and work began on trying to encourage two-word phrases. Then the parents reported that she used short sentences when speaking to them and suggested the work was too easy for her. Over a period of a year, the parents visited school about once a week, and Marie's teachers and other people who worked with her visited home during the holidays. Marie always spoke freely to her parents, and eventually began to use the short sentences in school.

Older and less able adults

With older and less able adults a thorough assessment of the potential for change has to be made and this can take weeks or even months. Some older adults, particularly in hospital, may well have been admitted with no formal assessment of their abilities and there

are still, rarely, people referred who appear severely mentally handicapped but who are predominantly hearing or physically handicapped (see Harriet above) and who, when introduced to a non-verbal communication system, show that they are able to communicate. Intervention at a very basic level, for example introducing new people and experiences, can have quite dramatic results, even with older people, in particular with 'institutionalised' residents.

Case example

Michael, aged 56 years, who had been hospitalised since he was 8 years old, was referred because he never talked. Investigation showed that he had a very limited environment and nothing new ever happened for him to talk about. Direct speech therapy was never introduced but a volunteer was found who took him out and spent a lot of time with him and eventually Michael began to return to the ward telling people where he had been and what he had done. He had always had the ability to talk but previously his routine was so predictable that he felt no need to do so.

There are, of course, people for whom intervention has little or no value as ways have not yet been found to help. Unfortunately, these are often most obviously handicapped in communication, profoundly handicapped adults who have not yet appeared to benefit from previous intensive input. It must, however, be stressed that many profoundly handicapped adults have had no input, intensive or otherwise, and they must be given the opportunity to benefit from some stimulation. Mentally handicapped voice and fluency disordered people are another group of people for whom intervention is of dubious value, although this ia a matter of some controversy at present (McCartney, pers. comm.).

With mildly mentally handicapped it can be possible to effect change but the prerequisite is that the patient must understand that there is a problem, and that he needs to work hard if it is to improve. Without insight, therapy can be at best ineffective and at worst can make a problem worse (see above).

NON-SPEECH SYSTEMS OF COMMUNICATION

Introduction

Formal systems of communication using non-verbal channels have existed for many years, but it is only recently that they have been accepted as valid methods of enabling those mentally handicapped people who have inadequate or non-existent verbal skills to increase their ability to communicate (Kiernan, 1977). Non-speech systems can be divided into two main groups; a manual (signing) system is used as a means of comprehension and expression, while a written system is primarily useful as a means of expression by the mentally handicapped person. It must be noted that verbal comprehension and expression is the major aim, as this is the least conspicuous and most socially acceptable method of communication. However, use of a non-speech system can have the advantage of reducing frustration level in a person whose verbal skills are limited, and frequently this can also lead to increased verbal abilities. Below is an outline of the systems most commonly used in Britain.

Manual systems

Amer-ind is a signal system based on American Indian hand talk (Skelly, 1979). It is a system of mimed gestures which are generally easy to interpret, even by untrained observers. There is only a small number of signs to learn, which can then be joined together as necessary to demonstrate longer ideas. As the system operates at a very basic level, however, it cannot be used to introduce abstract ideas, and it has no grammatical rules. It is most useful for people requiring a simple gesture system for indicating basic needs.

The Makaton vocabulary is a language programme designed specifically to teach signing to deaf, mentally handicapped adults (Walker, 1973). The signs are derived from British Sign Language (BSL-the national sign language evolved and used by the British deaf community), but they are organised into the word order and grammatical structures of spoken English. Grammatical spoken English should always accompany Makaton signing when used by a non-mentally handicapped person. There are some minor problems with this system. Signs do not correspond directly with either BSL or spoken English, and to be used to its best advantage, everyone in the

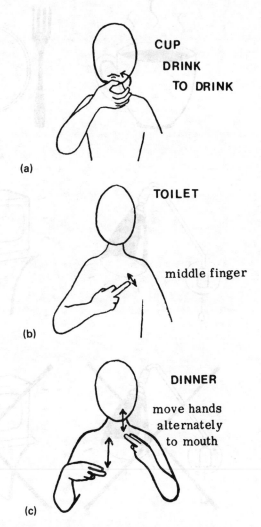

(a) CUP / DRINK / TO DRINK

(b) TOILET — middle finger

(c) DINNER — move hands alternately to mouth

Fig. 11.4 Makaton signs. (Reproduced from the Line Drawing Illustrations, 3rd edn, August 1980, for the Revised Makaton Vocabulary, with the permission of Mrs M. Walker, Project Co-ordinator, Makaton Vocabulary Development Project.)

Fig. 11.5 Picture communication board. (Reproduced by courtesy of the College of Speech Therapists.)

environment needs to know the system (see case example, Kate, p. 00). These disadvantages are however counteracted by the many advantages of the system. The vocabulary is presented in nine stages of progressively more advanced words and concepts, following the normal developmental pattern of English. In the first four stages, many of the signs are mimes (Fig. 11.4) and therefore easy to understand. The organisation of workshops for parents and professionals to learn the system is extremely efficient, and possibly because of this, Makaton is the signing system most widely used with mentally handicapped people in Britain (Stansfield, 1982).

Paget Gorman Sign system (*PGSS*) was originally designed for deaf people who tended to reject it in favour of their 'native' British sign language. It is an artificial language with a one-to-one relationship between English meaning, grammar and vocabulary, and that in sign (Paget et al, 1968). The signs have a logical progression. Basic concept signs have elements added as required, so that all the signs about a particular concept (e.g. animal) have the same basic hand shape. As with Makaton, the system is taught following normal development of English but, with the total number of signs available (over 3000), it would be almost impossible for any truly mentally handicapped person to learn the full form, especially as many of the signs are very similar and most are not mime, but abstract. The system is not widely used with mentally handicapped people.

A disadvantage amongst the signing systems is that they are mutually incompatible, and an aim for the future may be to find one system to be used throughout Britain, just as there is one major spoken language.

Written systems

Picture boards and photo communication boards are often used as a means of encouraging expression (Fig. 11.5). Some are produced commercially, but they can be designed to suit an individual person's needs. Their advantages are that the pictures are easy

to recognise and indicated by the board's owner, and can motivate further attempts to communicate. They are, however, only a very concrete form of expression, and communication using them can only be at a very basic level.

Blissymbolics was originally designed to overcome language barriers between readers of different linguistic backgrounds (Bliss, 1966) but it has become widely used as a method of communication for physically handicapped people. The symbols are abstract, but the system is logical, with symbols built up from a few basic elements (Fig. 11.6). In addition, on the communication boards the symbols all have the written word underneath, reducing the difficulty level for the recipient (Fig. 11.7). A trial introduction of this system can show if a severely physically handicapped person is capable of abstract thought. A cognitive ability of about 3 years, and intact visual perception channels are necessary for the system to be used successfully which limits its usefulness with mentally handicapped people, but as a means of enabling communication by a person whose primary handicap is physical, Blissymbolics can be invaluable.

Non-verbal systems of communication can be used as a single approach, but occasionally two systems can be combined, so that for example a person comprehends Makaton, and expresses himself using a Bliss board.

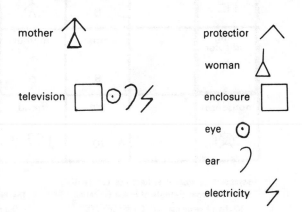

Fig. 11.6 Logical build-up of Blissymbols. (Reproduced by courtesy of Blissymbolics Communication Institute.)

My Name is:

no	thanks	one	question	I, me	past action indicator	(to) walk, go	to, towards
—!!	♡⚓	1	[?]	$\perp_1$	△	>l	
goodbye	sorry	two	what	you	action indicator	(to) come	and, also
o←→	♡↓)	2	?	$\perp_2$	∧	→l	+
not		three	where	he, him	future action ind	(to) make	good
—l		3	?	λ3	'	△	♡+!
opposite meaning		four	boy	she, her	(to) do, act	(to) know	bad
↓		4	♀	λ3	∧	⌒	♡—!
plural indicator		five	girl	it	(to) be	(to) think	more
. ×		5	♀	l	Φ	⌒	×
combine indicator		six	man	animal	(to) have	(to) put	on
⊕		6	⋀	⋔	±	×	×
similar sound		seven	woman	bird	(to) be able, can	(to) sleep	in, inside
ll=2		7	Y	Y	∨	⊡	□
similar		eight	father	flower	(to) want	(to) wash, bathe	out, outside
ll=		8	⋏	♀	♡)	⌒	□
thing indicator		nine	mother	toy	(to) like	(to) cry	up
□		9	⋏	□∧♡↑	♡+!	⚬↓	↑
nonsense!		ten	friend	name	(to) give	(to) help	down
⊗!		10	⊥♡+!	⊘	⚓	∧	↓

Blissymbolics Communication Resource Centre (U.K.)
South Glamorgan Institute of Higher Education
Western Avenue, Llandaff, Cardiff, CF5 2YB

Materials from:-
The Blissymbol Programme, Heathfield School
Oldbury Way, Fareham, Hants, PO14 3BN

Core Vocabulary
(October 1979)

A

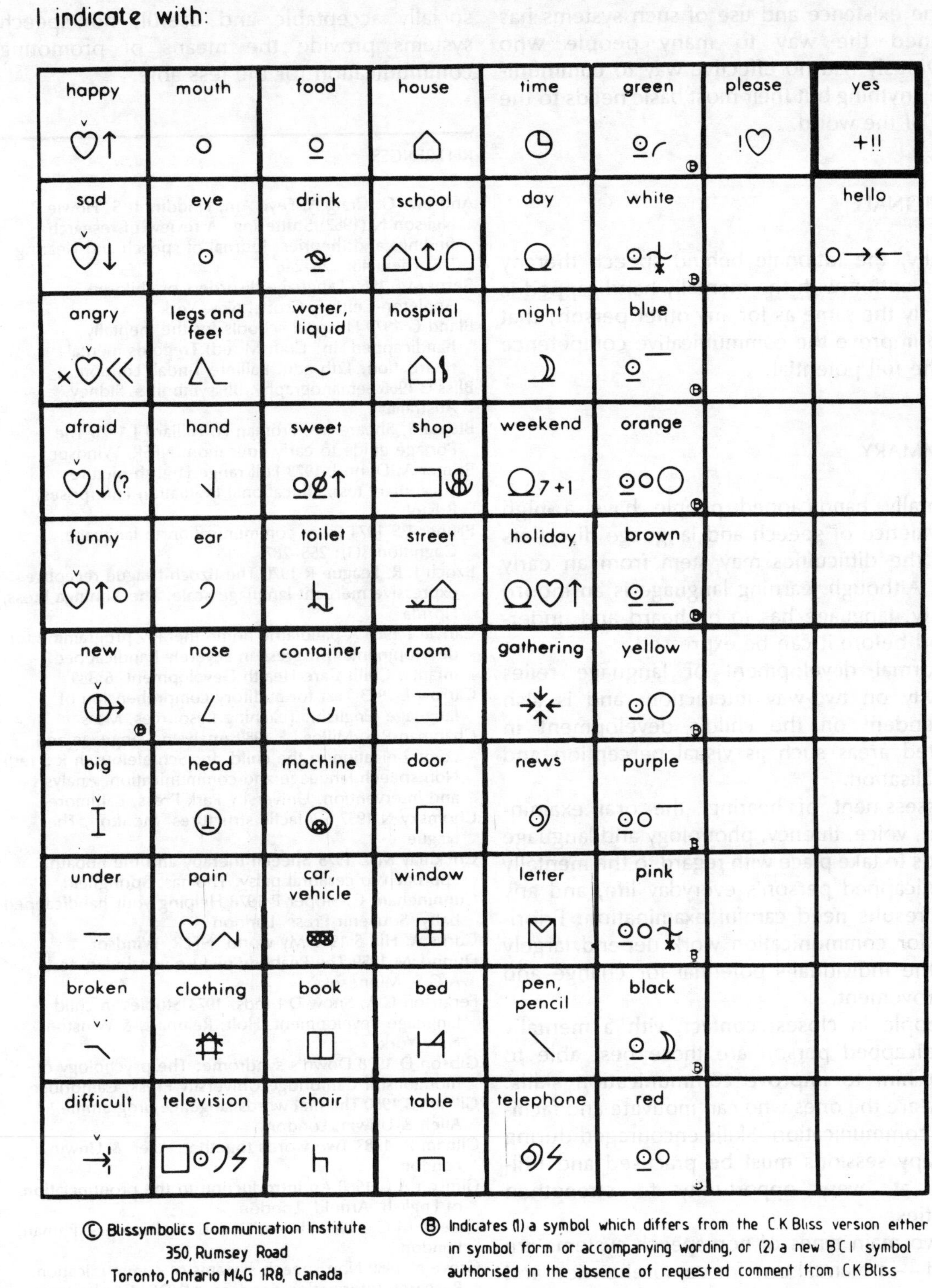

I indicate with:

happy	mouth	food	house	time	green	please	yes
sad	eye	drink	school	day	white		hello
angry	legs and feet	water, liquid	hospital	night	blue		
afraid	hand	sweet	shop	weekend	orange		
funny	ear	toilet	street	holiday	brown		
new	nose	container	room	gathering	yellow		
big	head	machine	door	news	purple		
under	pain	car, vehicle	window	letter	pink		
broken	clothing	book	bed	pen, pencil	black		
difficult	television	chair	table	telephone	red		

© Blissymbolics Communication Institute
350, Rumsey Road
Toronto, Ontario M4G 1R8, Canada

Ⓑ Indicates (1) a symbol which differs from the C K Bliss version either in symbol form or accompanying wording, or (2) a new BCI symbol authorised in the absence of requested comment from C K Bliss

B

Fig. 11.7 Blissymbolics core vocabulary. (Reproduced by courtesy of Blissymbolics Communication Institute.)

The existence and use of such systems has opened the way to many people who previously had no effective way to communicate anything but their most basic needs to the rest of the world.

RATIONALE

Finally, the rationale behind speech therapy intervention with the mentally handicapped is exactly the same as for any other person; that is to improve the communicative competence to the full potential.

SUMMARY

Mentally handicapped people have a high prevalence of speech and language disorders and the difficulties may stem from an early age. Although learning language is an inborn ability, language has to be heard and understood before it can be expressed.

Normal development of language relies heavily on two-way interaction, and is also dependent on the child's development in related areas such as visual perception and socialisation.

Assessment of hearing, the oral examination, voice, fluency, phonology and language needs to take place with regard to the mentally handicapped person's everyday life, and any test results need careful examination. Priorities for communication work depend largely on the individual's potential for change and improvement.

People in closest contact with a mentally handicapped person are those best able to help him to improve communication skills. They are the ones who can motivate and facilitate communication. Skills encouraged during therapy sessions must be practised and utilised at every opportunity to strengthen abilities.

Two main types of non-speech systems are used — a manual one for comprehension and expression and a written one mainly for expression. Although verbal skills are the most socially acceptable and useful, non-speech systems provide the means of promoting communication for the less able.

REFERENCES

Andrews G, Craig A, Feye Am, Hoddinott S, Howie P Neilson N (1982) Stuttering: A review of research findings and theories, Journal of speech and Hearing Disorders 48: 226–246

Berry M F 1969 Language disorders of children. Appleton-Century-Crofts, New York

Bland G 1979 Hospital schools for the mentally handicapped. In: Craft M (ed) Tregolds mental retardation, 12th edn. Balliere Tindall London

Bliss C 1966 Semanography. Blissymbolics, Sidney, Australia

Bluma S, Shearer M, Froman A, Hilliard J 1976 The Portage guide to early education. NFER, Windsor

Brimer A, Dunn L 1973 Full range English picture vocabulary test, Educational Evaluation Enterprises, Bristol

Bruner J S 1974 From communication to language. Cognition 3(3): 255–287

Bzoch K R, League R 1970 The Bzoch-League receptive expressive mergent language scale. The Anninga Press, Florida

Carlyle J 1980 A paediatric home therapy programme for developmental progress in severely handicapped infants. Child Care Health Development. 6:339

Carrow E 1973 Test for auditory comprehension of language (English). Teaching Resources, Mass

Chapman R S, Miller J F 1980 Analysing language and communication in the child. In: Schiefelbusch R S (ed) Non speech language and communication. Analysis and intervention. University Park Press, Baltimore

Chomsky N 1957 Syntactic structures. Moulton, The Hague

Crickmay M C 1975 Speech therapy and the Bobath approach to cerebral palsy. Thomas, Springfield

Cunningham C, Sloper P 1978 Helping your handicapped baby. Souvenir Press, London

Curtis A, Hill S 1978 My world. NFER, Windsor

Dunn L M 1959 The Peabody picture vocabulary test. A G S, Minnesota

Ferguson C A, Snow D I (eds) 1973 Studies in child language development. Holt, Reinhart, & Winston, New York

Gibson D 1978 Down's syndrome: The psychology of mongolism. Cambridge University Press, Cambridge

Gilham B 1980 The first words language programme. Allen & Unwin, London

Gilham B, 1983 Two words together. Allen & Unwin, London

Gimson A C 1980 An introduction to the pronunciation of English. Arnold, London

Greene M C L 1980 The voice and its disorders. Pitman, London

Grove N 1980 Non speech systems of communication. Research Information Services. MVDP, Camberley

Hester Adrian Research Centre 1981 Current research. University of Manchester, Manchester

Ingram D 1976 Phonological disability in children. Edward Arnold, London

Ingram T T S, Anthony A, Bogle B, McIsaac M W 1971

Ingram T T S, McIsaac M W Anthony A, Bogle B, 1971 The Edinburgh articulation test, Churchill Livingstone, Edinburgh

Jeffree D, McConkey R 1978 Extending language through play. Special Education Forward Trends 1(3): 13–16

Jeffree D, McConkey R 1978 Let me speak. Souvenir Press, London

Johnson J P 1979 Nature and treatment of articulation disorder. Thomas, Springfield

Keane V E 1972 The incidence of speech and language problems in the mentally retarded. Mental retardation 10(2): 3–5

Kellet B 1976 An initial survey of the language of ESN(S) children in Manchester. The results of a teacher's workshop. In: Berry P (ed) Language and communication in the mentally handicapped. Edward Arnold, London

Kiernan C 1977 Alternatives to speech. A review of research on manual and other forms of communication with the mentally handicapped and other non-communicating Population. British Journal of Mental Subnormality 23: 6–28

Laver J 1980 The phonetic description of voice quality. Cambridge University Press, Cambridge

Leeming K, Swann W, Coupe J, Mittler P 1979 Teaching language and communication to the mentally handicapped. Evans Methuen Educational, London

Lenneberg E 1967 The biological foundations of language. Wiley, New York

Leudar I, Fraser W I, Jeeves M A 1981 Social familiarity and communication in Down's syndrome. Journal of Mental Deficiency Research 25:133

McCartney E, Byers Brown B 1980 A speech teaching scheme for use by ATC instructors. British Jovrnal of Disorders of Communication 15(2):103

Moores D F 1980 Alternative communication modes. In: Schiefelbusch R S (ed)Non speech language and communication. Analysis and intervention. University Park Press, Baltimore

Nolan M, McCartney E, McArthur E, Rowseen V J 1980 A study of the hearing and receptive vocabulary of the trainees in an adult training centre. Journal of mental deficiency Research 24(4): 271

Paget R, Gorman P, Paget G 1968 A systematic sign language. RNID, London

Renfrew C 1972a Action picture test. Renfrew, Oxford

Renfrew C 1972b Word finding vocabulary scale. Renfrew, Oxford

Reynell J K 1977 Reynell developmental language scales (revised). NFER, Windsor

Skelly M 1979 Amer-Ind gestural code based on universal American Indian hand talk. Elsevier, New York

Skinner B 1957 Verbal behaviour. Appleton Century Crofts, New York

Stansfield J 1981 Speech therapy survey of ATCs in Lothian region. (unpub discussion paper)

Stansfield J. 1982 Current trends in speech therapy with mentally handicapped people: Bulletin of the College of Speech Therapists, London

Slobin D 1973 Cognitive prerequisites for the development of grammar. In: Ferguson C A, Snow D I (eds) Studies in child language development. Holt, Reinhart & Winston, New York

Swann W, Mittler P 1976 A survey of language abilities of ESN(S) children. Special Education Forward Trends 3(1):24

Tew B 1979 The cocktail party syndrome in children with hydrocephalus and spina bifida. British Journal of Disorders of Communication 14(2):87

Walker M. 1973 An experimental evaluation of the success of a system of communication for deaf mentally handicapped Adults. Unpublished thesis, University of London

Walker M 1980 Line drawing illustration for the Makaton vocabulary. MVDP Camberley

Weir R 1966 Some questions on the child's learning of phonology. In: Smith I. Miller G A (eds) The genesis of language. MIT, Cambridge Mass

Wetherby B, Striefield S 1978 Application of a miniature linguistic system on matrix training procedures. In: Schiefelbusch RL (edd) Language intervention strategies. University Park Press, Baltimore

Whelan E, Speake B 1977 Adult training centres in England and Wales. Report of the first national survey. NATMH Manchester University

Whelan E, Speake B 1978 Learning to cope. Souvenir Press, London

Whurr R 1974 An aphasia screening teet. University of Reading, Reading

RECOMMENDED READING

Berry P 1976 Language and communication in the mentally handicapped. Arnold, London

Mackay G, Dunn W 1981 Early communication skills. Faculty of Education, Glasgow University Glasgow

APPENDIX

Test	Age range	Advantages	Disadvantages	Comments
Aphasia Screening Test (Whurr)	Adult (Aphasic)	1. Acceptable to more able adults. 2. Materials are not childish. 3. Limited sections can be used without disturbing the overall result. 4. Gives a useful insight into visual as well as verbal comprehension.	1. Very repetitive. 2. Each individual section is limited in context. 3. Rote speech, reading and writing sections are inappropriate for many mentally handicapped people.	Designed for adult stroke patients. Investigates visual and auditory comprehension, and expression. Very useful. British (1974).
Bzoch-League Receptive-Expressive Emergent Language Scale	0 — 36 mths	1. Begins at birth. 2. Requires no active co-operation. 3. Can be filled in by the primary carer.	1. Based on normal development; therefore statements such as 'learns more new words every week' appear. 2. Some of the behaviours expected of a given age level are rather optimistic. 3. Only three behaviours for comprehension, and for expression are given at each age level.	An observational checklist of comprehension and expressive skills. American (1970). Broadly useful.
Carrow Test Of Auditory Comprehension of Language (English)	3–7 yrs	1. Pictures are the medium, therefore acceptable to mature individuals. 2. The person only needs to point to the relevant picture. 3. Gives a basic 'age level' upon which to base work. 4. Language becomes abstract and sophisticated at the top of the scale. 5. Errors can be broken down into different grammatical functions.	1. Requires the ability to recognize pictures. 2. There is a 1 in 3 chance of being correct. 3. Some of the pictures, and many instructions are rather American for British people. 4. There is no ceiling therefore the whole test must be administered. 5. Test takes about 20 mins to administer; can become boring.	A picture pointing test, with a choice of 3 pictures for each test item. American (1973).
English Picture Vocabulary Test.	3–18 yrs	1. There is a wide age range. 2. Pointing to the relevant picture is all that is required. 3. There is a ceiling to the number of errors a person is allowed to make. 4. Quick to administer.	1. Requires the ability to recognize pictures. 2. There is a 1 in 4 chance of being correct. 3. Some of the stimulus vocabulary is dated.	A picture pointing test of comprehension of single words, with a choice of 4 pictures for each test item. British (1973) but based on the Peabody Picture Test (American) (1959).

Test	Age Range	Advantages	Disadvantages	Comments
			4. The test claims to give a 'mental age', but in fact only gives a 'vocabulary comprehension age'.	
LARSP (Language Aquisition, Remediation and Screening Procedure)	9 months–4½ yrs	1. Records spontaneous speech and therefore avoids the artificial language of some standardized tests. 2. All the person's utterances are analysed. 3. The profile emphasizes abilities, not disabilities.	1. There can be difficulties in taping a long example of spontaneous speech. 2. Transcription and analysis is time consuming.	A tape recording of speech is transcribed, and analysed in terms of sentence, phrase and word structure, thus giving a basis for a remedial therapy programme. Useful for therapy planning in complicated cases, otherwise too time-consuming. British (1976).
Renfrew Action Picture Test	3–7½ yrs	1. Very quick to administer. 2. Cues are allowed, to encourage a reticent person. 3. Discrepancies between the expression of meaning and grammar are shown up. 4. It gives a good initial idea of the person's expressive language.	1. The expected replies are 'normal' for middle-class southern English speakers. No account is taken of regional, social variations in scoring.	A series of specific questions designed to elicit particular information and grammatical structures. Very useful. British (1972).
Renfrew Word-Finding Test	3–8½ yrs	1. Mentally handicapped people seem to enjoy naming pictures. 2. It demonstrates any word-finding problems. 3. There is a ceiling to the number of errors a person is allowed to make. 4. It can be compared with the lower end of the EPVT.	1. The pictures are not always easily recognized, even when the word is known. 2. The vocabulary is weighted towards the middle class (e.g. there is a large number of different animals to name).	A picture naming test of expressive single word vocabulary. British (1972).
Reynell Developmental Language Scales	1–7 yrs	1. Quick to administer. 2. The comprehension section requires minimal cooperation (usually pointing). 3. A basic 'language age' is given.	1. The toys are too small. 2. Some of the pictures are of middle-class situations and dated at the upper levels of the test.	A test of language comprehension and expression using pictures and and toys. A useful test on which to base other assessments. British (1977).

GLOSSARY

Amer-ind	Basic gesture system.
Articulators	Tongue, lips, soft palate.
Auditory discrimination (Perception)	The ability to listen to and recognise differences between sounds (e.g. bell and drums; 't' and 'k' etc.).
Auditory sequencing	The ability to recognise and reproduce sounds (noises, words, nonsense syllables etc.) in a particular order.
Drooling	Dribbling.
Dysarthria	Reduction in muscle movement (e.g. of tongue and lips) due to poor nerve control.
Dyspraxia	Reduction in voluntary movements (e.g. of tongue and lips) resulting in many different articulation problems.
Echolalia	When the client echoes (parrots) back part of what you said to him/her.
Falsetto	Excessively high voice (e.g. man trying to sound like a woman).
Flaccid	Floppy. Poor muscle tone.
Halitosis	Bad breath.
Hypernasal	Too much sound vibrating in the nose (e.g. cleft palate).
Hypertonic	Very tight muscles — usually limited in speed and movement.
Hyponasal	Too little sound vibrating in the nose (e.g. if someone has too large adenoids).
Hypotonic	Reduced muscle tone.
Incisors/ Incisors	Front four teeth top and bottom.
Ingressive air stream	Breathing in (speaking on ingressive airstream — talking as taking air in.
Initial sound	First sound in a word.
Interdental	With the tongue between the teeth.
Jargon	Meaningless chatter — sounds like speech, but is frequently just random combinations of sounds.
Makaton	Language programme to teach signing.
Malocclusion	Unevenly matched teeth, often with a wide gap between to top and bottom teeth.
Medial Sound	Middle sound in a word (usually referring to consonants).
Open syllable pattern	The final consonant is missed off (e.g. cat becomes ca).
Overbite	Top teeth well in front of bottom teeth at rest.
Perseverate	Continuing to give the same response long after it is appropriate — e.g. always pointing to the first picture on a page, even if the correct one is the second or third.

12

Play

Philip Darbyshire

- *Play helps self-expression, acquisition of essential skills, social interaction and understanding of the world*
- *Care staff may need to initiate play for the mentally handicapped*
- *Care staff should not be discouraged by lack of immediate response*
- *Play should not become a dull, routine chore*
- *Physical contact should be used whenever possible with the severely handicapped*

INTRODUCTION

Play is a vital part of every child's development. It is one of the principal ways by which he learns to express himself, to master skills, to understand his world and to relate to other people. Many adults often think of children as 'just playing', and of play as a purposeless activity which occupies children and keeps them out from under their feet when they are busy, or at best an amusing way for children to pass the time. Play however is of far greater importance than this.

NATURE OF PLAY

Play is a very difficult concept to clarify and throughout the literature on play there is no universally accepted definition or classification system.

> Play is that self-initiated activity and experience which is as essential as life itself to the child, for it is the very stuff of his life; it is predominantly the way by which he discovers the world and by which he becomes an integrated person. (Isaacs, 1951)

> The child gains experience in play. Play is a big part of his life. External as well as internal experiences can be rich for the adult, but for the child the riches are to be found chiefly in play and fantasy. Just as the personality of adults develops through their experiences in living, so those of children develop through their own play and through the play inventions of other children and

of adults. By enriching themselves children gradually enlarge their capacity to see the richness of the externally real world. Play is the continuous evidence of creativity which means aliveness.

Play provides an organisation for the initiation of emotional relationships and so enables social contacts to develop (Winnicott, 1974).

In addition to attempting to define play it is also informative to consider those characteristics which distinguish play from other activities of childhood.

Garvey (1977) lists five main characteristics of play:

1. 'Play is pleasurable and enjoyable'

This is an obvious feature of a child's play. Morris (1977) describes several 'play signals' such as smiling, laughing and play screaming which indicates that 'this is not serious, I am only playing.' However, the child may still be enjoying his play even if it is not accompanied by such overt signs.

2. 'Play has no extrinsic goals'

Play is activity for its own sake and, although this is not to deny its great value to the developing child, the child has no aims or goals in mind when playing, he simply enjoys the act.

3. 'Play is spontaneous and voluntary'

A child does not normally have to be persuaded to play and even in the absence of toys babies will play with their fingers and toes and older children will invent imaginary toys and situations.

4. 'Play involves some active engagement on the part of the player'

Play is very much an active process; children *do* things when playing: The child who is sitting reading a comic or watching television or sitting around looking bored cannot be said to be playing.

5. 'Play has certain systematic relationships to what is not play'

Play involves various behaviours and activities which at first may seem to serve no social or biological function, but these play activities are vital to the child's future motor, social, cognitive, perceptual and language development.

Indeed if play were only an interesting way in which children amuse themselves then it would not have received the vast amount of investigation and analysis from developmentalists and behavioural scientists that it has merited.

THEORIES OF PLAY

Around the late 19th and early 20th century several psychologists from many differing schools of thought had brought various insights into understanding the nature of play.

Surplus energy theory

This was one of the earliest attempts to explain the nature of play. The English psychologist and philosopher Herbert Spencer described play as being a result of the build up and subsequent expenditure of surplus nervous energy. Although this was an attractive theory at the time, modern developments in knowledge of nervous system physiology have outdated this theory.

Recapitulation theory

This theory was proposed by an American psychologist, G. S. Hall. He saw play in evolutionary terms, whereby children are an integral part of the evolutionary process from animals through to man and this process is reflected in their play, i.e. their love of water, climbing and swinging from trees and 'camping' in the garden. Although few researchers now accept this theory it did cause many more people to observe closely the behaviour and play activities of children.

Practice of skills theory

This theory, favoured by a Swiss philosopher, Karl Groos, was developed from a close study of the behaviour of animals. In accordance with Darwin's theories of natural selection, he argued that animals perform actions to enable their species to adapt and survive. He believed that through play children learned actions and skills which would be essential for their development into adulthood.

More modern psychologists have also studied play and children's behaviour from different standpoints.

Sigmund Freud

Freud was mainly concerned with the imaginative and fantasy aspect of the child's play and its relationship to emotional development. He saw play as the projection of the child's desires and wishes and as a means to master situations and resolve inner tensions. Freud believed that all behaviours have a cause, including the various types of children's play, and his work in this area gave rise to the use of play in psychotherapy treatments for disturbed children — often referred to as play therapy.

Jean Piaget

Piaget has been a major influence in the field of developmental psychology, and was mostly concerned with the cognitive and intellectual development of the child, and it is mainly as a vital factor in this development that he discussed play.

Piaget describes the intellectual development of the child as following four main stages (see Ch. 7):

Sensory-motor stage	birth–2 yrs
Pre-operational stage	2–7 yrs
Concrete operational stage	7–11 yrs
Formal operational stage	11 yrs onwards

Complementary to these he describes the development of the child's play as also following a definite sequence of stages comprising both social and symbolic elements:

Social element

Solitary play	birth–2 yrs
Parallel play	2–3 yrs
Associative play	3–7 yrs
Co-operative play	7 yrs onwards

Symbolic element

Sensory-motor play	birth–15 mths
Object play	15 mths–2 yrs
Symbolic/Representational play	2–8 yrs

Millar (1968) states that:

'Piaget's theory gives play a clear biological function as active repetition and experiment which "mentally digests" novel situations and experiences. It affords a coherent description of the development of successive activities from pushing hanging rattles to acting out stories and playing rugby or chess.' (p. 56)

DEVELOPMENT OF PLAY

In discussing the development of play it is useful to study the theories of Piaget as these provide a framework for explaining the different types of play exhibited by the developing child. However, when using the previously mentioned system of classifying the development of play it is very important to realise that these categories are not mutually exclusive and that certain types of play activity may fall into more than one category. Also the age ranges given are approximate. Each child is an individual and his play develops at his own rate.

Solitary play

This type of play is characteristic of the first 2 years of life. The child will sit with a selection of toys and will play happily with them but for fairly short periods of time. He will enjoy exploring and manipulating toys, mostly with his hands and mouth.

The child at this stage likes to have a parent near to hand and will enjoy limited periods of play with them but is relatively unconcerned with other people. Provided that the child's basic physiological and comfort needs have been met he will instigate and perform his play predominantly by himself.

Parallel play

During this stage the child will play beside other children. They may show each other their drawings or toys and sit at the same table but there is little reference to or co-operation with the other children.

Associative play

It is at this stage that the child may initiate activities with other children and groups of children. Initially it may appear that the children are playing at the same game but in fact each child is concerned only with his own part in it.

Co-operative play

Millar (1968) quotes Piaget as saying 'that really co-operative play develops only after the age of 7 or 8' (p. 178) although examples of attempts at co-operative play can be seen at an earlier age.

During this stage of play children will initiate group play with others and will co-operate in keeping the game going. This is the stage of playing at houses, tea-parties and 'mothers and fathers'.

Competitive play such as cowboys and Indians and sports games, and play with rules such as group play activities where certain rules have to be followed if the child is to be allowed to participate, are later features of this stage of play.

Sensory-motor play

This type of play is evident during the first 18 months. Millar (1968) states that:

The co-ordination of perceiving and moving, and progressive refinements in adapting to the way in which the world is arranged is one of the main developments of the first 18 months of life. (p. 111)

The development of the child's play in this period is thus closely related to his development in other areas such as locomotor, cognitive and perceptual skills.

The very young baby will enjoy kicking his legs, reaching, and exploring various parts of his body. As his motor development progresses through the stages of sitting, crawling, standing and walking, these activities will be incorporated into his play.

His manipulative skills also develop rapidly during this period. The infant will first grasp hold of a parent's finger and will soon be handling objects such as large beads and rattles. The child's desire to explore his surroundings is intense, everything is reached for, and all objects grasped.

His play at this stage is characterised by much repetition of an activity, e.g. shaking a rattle, dropping a toy out of his pram for mum to recover, and laughing at every 'peek-a-boo' game.

As his manipulative skills develop so do his perceptual abilities and during this period he is learning of the relationship between himself and objects by activities such as reaching for and dropping toys, catching a ball and building blocks.

Object play

The child's play progresses from sensory motor play where toys are explored and played with, with no real regard for their function, to the stage of object play where the child will begin to use the toy or object for its intended purpose, i.e. he may push his car along the floor or pretend to drink from a toy cup.

Object play usually begins at around 15–18 months and the child's play with objects and toys becomes more skilful as his range of experiences increases and his imagination develops.

The child learns that spoons can be put in the mouth but toy cars cannot, that a bat and ball are compatible as a plaything, that behaviours can be transferred to objects, i.e., the 'a spoonful for me, a spoonful for dolly,' feeding game and that she can create imaginary objects in play such as a bottle to feed dolly with.

Of object play Garvey (1977) has said:

> More and more meaningful associations accrue to objects, and play with objects is combined with other aspects of play . . . All through these changes however objects continue to arouse curiosity and the desire to learn. They provide enjoyment in mastering their use or in understanding the properties of things and they also continue to facilitate social contacts and to assist in the expression of ideas and feelings.

Symbolic/representational play

This stage of play occurs between the ages of approximately 2–8 years and it is significant that during this period the child's development in speech and language is at its most marked. The child can now communicate by meaningful gestures and words.

Pretend and imitative play are very noticeable during this stage. The child will invent imaginary toys and people: the settee will become a boat, and a blanket draped across two chairs will become a house. The child will also imitate people and scenes familiar to him.

Of symbolic play Millar (1968) states:

> Piaget's notion of symbolic play as 'assimilation' of events in symbolic form probably sums up best, at present, the exploring manipulating, repeating, varying, confirming and classifying of impressions, events and feelings which can be observed in children's make believe play. If so, make believe play belongs with all those processes and structures which underlie the coding, storing, checking and recoding of information, and which appear to keep the human brain pretty busy. (p. 156)

PLAY NEEDS OF THE MENTALLY HANDICAPPED

Play should be an essential part of every child's development and this is no less true for the mentally handicapped, whose play needs are essentially the same as for any other child. However, the nature and extent of the child's handicap(s) can accentuate, prolong and intensify these needs. Difficulties experienced by the mentally handicapped person in learning how to play can be considerable.

The non-handicapped child develops play skills through a highly active process of constantly exploring, touching, seeing and hearing his environment and the people in it. It is through this active process that the child makes sense of his perceptual world. This level of activity and inquisitiveness is frequently absent in the mentally handicapped child. Many parents of mentally handicapped children describe the child's infancy as being characterised by inactivity and lack of response: 'He was a good baby.' 'He never cried.' 'She slept most of the day'. 'He was so easy to care for.' 'She was never a demanding baby.' are all frequently heard comments.

Yet this lack of activity and curiosity, far from indicating that the baby is 'good', is a sign that exceptional effort should be made by the baby's parents or carers to involve the child in activity and provide suitable stimulus to help the baby progress in development.

These characteristics of the play of many mentally handicapped children — lack of imagination and lack of desire to discover — are often exacerbated by some of the additional handicaps from which the child may suffer. The more common of these additional handicaps are cerebral palsy and associated physical handicaps, sensory handicaps such as varying degrees of blindness and deafness, and communication problems such as lack of speech and language development.

The mentally handicapped child can therefore be said to play less than the nonhandicapped child. His play may be very unimaginative and repetitive and he may show little desire to explore and discover new forms of play. His level of concentration may also be poor and he may quickly lose interest in a toy or activity.

These are formidable problems for the child and his family to overcome but for the mentally handicapped child in institutional care the problems involved in meeting his play needs are far greater.

Play and institutional care

The results of poor institutional care, whether it be in a children's home or children's ward of a mental handicap hospital are so damaging to the child that it is essential for all staff involved in child care to be aware of the causes and effects of institutionalisation' and how this condition is directly linked with poor 'mothering' (by this is meant personal, affectionate care given by either a man or woman) and lack of action geared towards meeting a child's play needs.

The character of the institution is an important factor in influencing the child's play and some researchers argue convincingly that institutional life actually retards a child's play.

Bowlby (1976) found that children living in institutional care played less, and that their play was more stereotyped, unimaginative and immature than non-institutionalised children and stated that:

> The child is not encouraged to individual activity because it is a nuisance; it is easier if he stays put and does what he is told. Even if he strives to change his environment he fails. Toys are lacking; sometimes the children sit inert or rock themselves for hours together. Above all, the brief intimate games which mother and baby invent to amuse themselves as an accompaniment to getting up and washing, dressing, feeding, bathing and returning to sleep — they are all missing.

The reasons why institutional models of care seem to have a retarding influence on the child's play are numerous and complex but such features as absence of 'mothering', the system of management of the institution, care staff work procedures and the actual physical environment have all been implicated.

Since the work of Bowlby and others over 30 years ago it would be reasonable to expect that some of the worst features of institutional care such as poor 'mothering' and inadequate opportunities for play activities would have been eradicated or at least, substantially improved upon. More recent research however has found that the same poor standards of institutional care and lack of both facilities for play, and an appreciation of the vital importance of play for the developing child are still widespread.

Either the lessons have not been learned or more probably the resources in terms of finance, staff, and staff training have not been made available to effect the necessary improvements. It is doubly shameful however that some of the worst features of poor institutional care are to be found in institutions which claim to provide care for mentally handicapped children.

The most important and influential research into the lives of mentally and physically handicapped children has been done by Maureen Oswin and three of her books, *The Empty Hours, Holes in the Welfare Net, and Children Living in Long Stay Hospitals* are essential reading for all those concerned with the care of mentally handicapped children.

In *The Empty Hours* written in the late 1960s she identified other characteristics of the play of institutionalised children: the suddenness and brevity of their play, the requests for adults to perform the play activities for them, the attempts of the children to gain physical closeness to an adult during play, the holding of toys and objects rather than playing with them, and the lack of play initiative. She also wrote that:

> The staff did not participate in the children's play, and ward duties such as bed straightening or repetitive dusting came before the play demands of the children; children would sometimes be calling out for paper and pencils, and for books and cuddles, but the nurses were too busy completing their set rota of duties and so they did not respond to the children.

Some 10 years later in 1978 she could again write:

> The dearth of personal attention and the hours of loneliness appeared to be the cause of some children developing odd habits of occupying themselves. 14-year-old Sally (11 years in hospital) had a habit of chewing the straps of her wheelchair. One June afternoon she spent from noon until 4

pm and from 5.30 until 8.20 pm sitting in her wheelchair and chewing the end of the strap that secured her. Nobody spoke to her or touched her during that time.

Oswin was by no means alone in her observations. The National Development Group for the Mentally Handicapped was set up in 1975 to advise on the development and implementation of better services for mentally handicapped people and their families.

In its first report (1978) it stated that:

> We have encountered a variety of views on the provision of play and leisure equipment and on occasions a lack of understanding or appreciation of their value in development, where they are still considered of secondary importance to medical and nursing needs. We still encounter the view that 'toys will only be broken' which although true of all children, is used here as a reason for not providing them. In many hospitals: toys, stimulating mobiles and pictures are available, but often they are locked away in cupboards out of reach of the children for most of the day or so placed that the children cannot see them.

The National Development Group also stated in a later report (1978),

> The Development Team reports have noted many examples of practices which should not be found in any service (including):
>   children left for long periods lying on the floor, unable to contact anyone or anything.
>   lack of attention to play needs, absence of toys or other play materials.
>   toys hanging from the ceiling.
>   lack of play space for children both inside and outside the living units.

From all of these and similar observations of the damaging effect of neglecting the mentally handicapped child's needs for play activities and stimulation it must be obvious that meeting the play and 'mothering' needs of the mentally handicapped child is every bit as important as caring for his other basic needs such as food, comfort and cleanliness.

PLANNING FOR PLAY

When planning how best to meet the play needs of the mentally handicapped child certain points must be considered. Although play should be incorporated into the activities of daily living such as dressing, washing and feeding, there should be certain times of the day allocated for more formal play sessions.

It is rarely beneficial for the mentally handicapped child to be surrounded by 'educational toys' and a 'stimulating environment' if no member of the care staff will actively engage with him in play activities. Play skills do not develop by some sort of diffusion from the 'stimulating environment' to the child. They must be actively encouraged.

It is important that the child is assessed with a view to planning and providing the most suitable play activities for him as an individual. However, as assessment has become rather a fashionable term, the situation must be avoided where assessment is carried out for its own sake. Assessment must form a basis for action.

Several methods of assessment already incorporate the use of play (Newson & Newson, 1979) and the assessment of play skills such as the Observational Play Repertoires (Mogford, 1979) which are 'an attempt to construct a guide to the observation of the play of handicapped children with a range of four selected toys. The purpose is to offer a structure for the clinician who is trying to acquire experience in this skilled task, and to provide a method of pin-pointing a child's achievements and difficulties in play.'

SELECTING SUITABLE TOYS AND PLAYTHINGS

It is beyond the scope of this chapter to list and describe all of the toys and playthings that may be suitable for use with the mentally handicapped (see Further Reading, p. 262 for more detailed sources). However, certain principles are important when trying to choose toys and playthings which will be beneficial in play activities with the mentally handicapped.

The Toy Libraries Association in 'Play, Toys and Toy Libraries in Mental Handicap Hospitals' lists various points to consider when choosing toys and playthings for a mentally handicapped person:

a. *Attraction*. Is the toy or subject of the toy attractive to the person playing with it?

b. *Type of toy*. Is the size, shape, weight and strength suitable for the use you are going to put it to or can the player manage it physically?

c. *Coping*. Can the player cope with the toy and get rewarding results from it?

d. *Development*. The toy or play activity should allow the development of skills or ideas but not necessarily in conventional terms, that is, the play may not take the form we would expect.

e. *Imagination*. Does the toy allow for imaginative play?

f. *Success*. Does the toy allow a high rate of success to be achieved by the player? Success builds confidence and the desire to try something a bit harder the next time.

g. *Response*. Does the toy give a very large response for a small amount of effort?

h. *Concentration*. Do not use toys or play games which involve long periods of concentration if the mentally handicapped person's concentration span is short.

i. *Visibility*. Make sure that the toy you use does not conflict with or gets lost in the background (i.e., table top, floor covering), especially with partially sighted people.

j. *Suitability*. Older people may be humiliated by being expected to use 'baby toys' so consider this when choosing an activity.

Head & Mogford (1979) list four criteria for use when choosing a toy:

1. Does this toy or game, given careful demonstration and introduction to the child, catch her interest, tempt her to explore, or involve her in any way?

2. If the toy or activity does this, can I, or the child, develop this first response in one or more ways?

3. Does the toy, or can I, provide clear messages of success and achievement?

4. Does the toy allow the child to reach towards higher levels of achievement when she is ready? Does it present a challenge, and not simply a rehearsal of what she can already do?

Toys however, no matter how carefully they are selected do not cause play to occur and if simply surrounded by toys and left to his own devices the mentally handicapped person is highly unlikely to develop play skills or to improve those that he has. The toy chosen should serve as a tool through which the child and carer can interact more productively.

Toy safety

The question of toy safety is of vital importance to all children but is especially relevant to the mentally handicapped who may have little idea of what constitutes a 'dangerous' toy. For this reason the onus for protecting the child from any danger or injury during play rests with his care staff.

Fortunately governments, manufacturers and parents have become much more aware of the problems of toy safety and stringent safeguards and controls exist to govern the materials used in the construction of toys — The Toy Safety Regulations. These regulations have been very successful and accidents to children as a direct result of toys are very infrequent.

Vigilance is always necessary however and care staff should consider before giving a child a toy:

Can the child break it easily?
Are the surfaces smooth and free from cracks, sharp edges, etc?
Is it hygienic and can it be kept clean?
Is it safe for the child to chew or suck?
Does it have any small or loose parts which could be swallowed?
Is it suited to his age and abilities?

Staff should also ensure that toys are properly stored and cared for and that any broken or incomplete toys are removed from the children.

TECHNIQUES OF PLAY

Before commencing a play session it is important that the child be in the best possible frame of mind so that he may enjoy and benefit from the session. The child should not be hungry, soiled, wet, tired or in an uncomfortable position.

As previously mentioned many mentally handicapped people will not initiate play by themselves. Toys therefore, have to be demonstrated to them repeatedly. This is a difficult task for many care staff as they may feel that they are 'getting no response' or 'feel stupid' playing with someone who 'can't play,' but perseverance is essential at this stage.

Results are rarely dramatic and immediate when working with the mentally handicapped and it is important that the initial response to a play activity is not taken as being indicative of the person's potential for improvement. The mentally handicapped person may react to a new play activity by becoming anxious and upset or by trying to avoid it. It is therefore important that new activities are introduced gradually and repeatedly.

Certain methods of teaching skills developed from behaviour modification techniques can be used to build up the play skills of the mentally handicapped person. These include:

Be specific. Set definite aims and objectives. Phrases such as 'helping the child reach his maximum potential' and 'stimulate the child' are really meaningless whereas 'I want the child to reach for a rattle'or 'build a tower of four bricks' are observable improvements in the child's level of functioning.

Break complex tasks into simple components. This often makes it much easier for the child to succeed in the task.

Record your observations. It is easy for information on how the child's play has progressed to be 'lost' in verbal communication between the many care staff involved. Records can also show slow improvements which may otherwise go unnoticed and lead to the discouraging assumption that no improvement has been made.

Show the child exactly what you want him to do. It is not enough to simply say to the child what you wish him to do. You must also demonstrate the action to him and may have to do this many times.

Give the child a good chance to succeed and reward him when he gets it right. The task should be made simple enough for the child to achieve and much praise and attention should be given when the child succeeds.

Although these techniques have been found to be useful in teaching a variety of skills including play skills to the mentally handicapped, a flexible approach should be employed by care staff.

As previously stated, play should be spontaneous, voluntary and above all **fun**.

Staff should be flexible and patient with the child during play and refrain from imposing too strict a control over the play activity; let the child learn from his experiences and mistakes and allow him to use his own initiative. Otherwise, the whole essence of play may be lost and the play session may become another dull routine chore for both the child and the care staff.

TYPES OF PLAY ACTIVITY

The various types of play which can help the mentally handicapped person can be listed under the following broad and often interrelated headings:

Exploratory play
Energetic play
Manipulative play
Social play
Imaginative/symbolic play
Hobbies/leisure activities.

Exploratory play

In order to explore his immediate environment the child must be encouraged to use all of his senses of touch, smell, taste, hearing and sight as best he can. Toys which are intended to stimulate the child into using these senses should be brightly coloured, easy to grasp, and make a noise such as a rattle or musical toy.

Mobiles, cradle-play and 'pop-up' toys can encourage the child to reach out and handle them.

Toys which produce a surprise such as 'jack in the box' provide a fun reward for the child's explorations.

A 'rummage box' full of articles of different shapes and textures can also be used to encourage exploration and object recognition, for instance, finding the soft toy, or the ball.

Activity boards are excellent toys for encouraging exploratory play. These can be bought commercially or are easily made by threading rings, bobbins and large beads on to a board. Large activity boards can be made to take up a whole area of wall and can incorporate doorbells, mirrors, handles, sliding bolts, telephone dials and almost anything else which would encourage the child to handle and explore it.

Energetic play

The mentally handicapped person can enjoy energetic and rough and tumble play as much as the non-handicapped person and consideration should be given to this area of play to ensure that the person is not being overprotected.

Active physical play such as running, jumping, skipping and climbing is very valuable in improving locomotor and co-ordination skills. They can also be used as group activities in helping to promote better social interaction.

A soft play area is an excellent resource to have available for energetic play. This is usually a room or part of a room, which is covered in thick foam padding. Here the child can be as active and adventurous as he wishes but will not be hurt if he falls. This is particularly good fun for those people who are unsteady in walking or are prone to epileptic seizures.

An adventure playground is also a great asset in providing for energetic play. Chutes, swings and climbing frames are among the most useful items here. However, it is important that, when using equipment in an adventure playground, the person is supervised as accidents to children in playgrounds are fairly common.

Manipulative play

The development of manipulative skills is closely related to other factors such as perceptual abilities and the degree of hand-eye co-ordination.

Initially, toys should be light, easy to grasp, and interest the child by their colour, texture and sound. Suitable toys here would include rattles, teething rings and cradle toys. More advanced toys may be introduced later such as building blocks, threading beads, 'Lego' type construction sets and abacus type toys.

Manipulative play can also be incorporated into the child's activities of daily living such as brushing teeth, combing hair, drinking from a cup and fastening buttons.

Social play

Learning to play happily with other children is one of the major developmental tasks facing the mentally handicapped child. The child who shuns the company of others, refuses to participate in group activities and loses his temper when his every wish is not granted is likely to be viewed increasingly as being a major 'behaviour problem'.

Social play can be introduced into most play sessions and suitable activities include assembling a train set or house of bricks, any card games such as 'snap', board games such as 'ludo', and group games such as 'cowboys and indians' can all be used to encourage co-operation, sharing and turn-taking.

Imaginative/symbolic play

We have already noted that this type of play is often lacking among the mentally handicapped, so help is needed to facilitate it.

Toys such as 'Wendy houses', 'play people', dolls' houses and adult clothes for 'dressing up' are ideal items although these will be too advanced for many mentally handicapped people. However, simpler items such as paper and paint, sand pits and water play areas can be of equal value to the more severely handicapped child.

Ordinary objects should be used to try to encourage 'pretend' play, where an object represents another object, or try to get the child to imagine objects and situations where they can be used. This type of play is particularly useful in helping with language development. If the child has no speech start by trying to get him to make sounds during play such as making the sound of a car while playing with one.

If some speech is present simple games such as nursery rhymes and 'round and round the garden' are useful. Here the child can fill in a missing word such as 'one step, two steps, tickle him under . . . there' where the child can soon learn the anticipated word easily and have fun while learning to speak.

Hobbies/leisure activities

Throughout this section we have discussed play as relating predominantly to children and particularly mentally handicapped children.

This, however, is not to say that the mentally handicapped adolescent and adult have no need for recreation and leisure activities. It is a mistake to assume that because a mentally handicapped person has reached a certain age that he suddenly no longer requires 'play' activities. Wherever possible the activities and playthings selected by and for adults should reflect their age group. There is something very sad about seeing a middle-aged or elderly mentally handicapped lady wandering around clutching an old doll or soft toy.

There are numerous recreational and leisure pursuits in which the mentally handicapped person can participate such as art and craft work, musical activities and recreation and sports activities — see Further Reading for more detailed suggestions.

PLAY FOR CHILDREN WITH SPECIAL HANDICAPS

There is no clear definition of the profoundly and multiply handicapped child but such children may suffer from several additional handicaps such as immobility due to severe cerebral palsy and sensory defects, usually varying degrees of blindness and/or deafness. With this type of child it is especially important to look beyond his obvious handicaps and to try to understand the practical implications of them in terms of his play needs and how best to meet them.

This child's physical handicaps and resulting relative immobility have very damaging effects on his opportunities for play. The child is completely reliant on others to provide play activities for him. He is often unable to take part actively by shaking a rattle or reaching for a toy. This immobility also seriously restricts his opportunities for interaction with other people.

In view of the extent of the child's physical handicaps it is probable that he will be receiving physiotherapy treatment. Play can be made a valuable part of this treatment. (Finnie, 1974)

Normally a child may be content to lie on his back or in a sandbag and play with toys, but this is one of the worst possible positions for immobile children. These children must be placed in a variety of beneficial positions throughout the day which will increase their prospects of initiating more normal movements and allow them to see their surroundings from more than one viewpoint. Frequent changes of position are also vitally important to prevent such physical problems as pressure sores and positional deformities such as 'windswept' hips and scissoring of legs (Darbyshire 1980a, b).

Foam wedge shapes are useful for these children; the child can be laid prone over the wedge with head and arms over the edge. Toys should be placed just within the child's reach. This position encourages better head control and makes it easier for the child to reach for toys.

If the child has to spend long periods in a wheelchair musical toys, mobiles, etc can be attached to it. A wooden frame can also be set up around the chair with toys dangling from it within the child's reach.

Although the child may be very severely physically handicapped and may seem very frail he can still enjoy certain 'rough and tumble' play activities such as being swung in a blanket. It is best if these activities are done in a soft play area or on foam floor mats.

Certain new developments in toy manufacture may be very useful for this group of children. These are the new range of electronic toys. Some of these toys can be operated by the slightest pressure on a pressure plate which can be placed in front of the child. This is obviously very useful for immobile and paralysed children who may have an extremely limited range of purposeful movements. The pressure plate can be made to operate almost anything from flashing lights to cassettes of taped music.

In view of the severity of these children's mental and physical handicaps a major source of play and stimulation for them must be their care staff. Every opportunity should be taken when working with the child to provide enjoyable physical contact. Some ways of doing this are by:

Cuddling. This is important for everyone including the profoundly handicapped child, as it gives a feeling of security and warmth and the chance to speak softly to the child, while rocking him. Cuddling should not be restricted to the times when the child is crying and upset.

Touch/Tickling. With children who may also have sensory handicaps such as deafness or blindness, the sensation of touch assumes even greater importance. Simple touch games such as 'round and round the garden' can often elicit a response from the child, but much trial and error is usually required to discover what the child enjoys. Tactile senses can also be stimulated through activities involving sand, water and multi-textured toys such as 'feelie' boards.

Voice. Although not a method of physical contact it is very important to speak constantly to the child as you work with him. It is not always easy to chat away interestingly to a child who seems never to respond to you but

it is very bad care practice not to try. The child may have no understanding of language so try to vary your voice tone to make yourself sound as interesting as possible.

The great advantage of this type of physical contact/social play is that it can be practised whenever the care staff are working with the child during activities of daily living such as bathing, feeding and dressing. No extra staff or special equipment are required, only thoughtful care staff.

LEARNING ABOUT PLAY

In order to learn about play and how to provide satisfying play activities for the mentally handicapped there is no real substitute for practice. Actually playing with the mentally handicapped is the best way to develop play skills. There are a great many useful books on the subject of play in general and play for the mentally handicapped which will provide new ideas and possibilities for trying out.

Many organisations concerned with the mentally handicapped take great interest in play, and provide a very valuable service in publishing literature on play, advice on toys and playthings, and organising seminars and courses on play and related topics.

The Toy Libraries Association

This organisation was formed in 1967 by the mother of two handicapped children. It has now expanded into a national organisation which will provide information on many aspects of play and suitable toys for handicapped children. They will advise and assist anyone who wishes to establish a Toy Library in their hospital or area. As well as organising regular conferences, seminars and courses on how to organise toy libraries, and the provision of play for the handicapped, they publish many relevant booklets and literature on play activities for the mentally and physically handicapped.

The Spastics Society

This society is also active in providing information on play for handicapped children especially the physically handicapped.

Castle Priory College is under the auspices of the Spastics Society and organises numerous short courses on various aspects of care of the handicapped. Of particular interest would be the course entitled 'Play activities for Young Children with Handicaps'.

The Joint Board of Clinical Nursing Studies developed a course in Child Development (No. 965) and a follow-on course to this on Play (No. 969) for qualified nurses. However, these courses are dependent on centres providing them and on there being sufficient applicants. For further details contact The English National Board.

Playbus schemes are operated by many local authority social services departments and their staff can offer much information, advice and practical experiences. A special playbus staffed by two qualified play leaders was being organised by the Save the Children Fund to tour various mental handicap hospitals offering advice and information to hospital staff on play and playthings for the mentally handicapped in hospital.

For further information on these organisations and the courses which they provide please write to them at the address given under 'Useful Addresses'.

SUMMARY

Play is an essential part of every child's development. It is one of the main ways in which he learns to understand his world and the people in it and to master essential skills. Play has been studied extensively by behavioural scientists and they have brought valuable insights into a child's play. The development of play is often discussed using the framework which compliments Jean Piaget's stages of the child's cognitive development. This framework comprises both social and symbolic elements and the play follows the sequence of solitary, parallel, associative and co-operative, and sensory motor, object and symbolic play.

Play is equally important for the mentally handicapped and their play needs are largely the same as those of the non-handicapped people but the play of the mentally handicapped child tends to be characterised by certain difficulties such as lack of imagination, activity and concentration. Also a dependence on adults to play for the child is common.

Play should be used throughout the day by care staff to complement the child's activities of daily living, but more structured play sessions should also be organised. The mentally handicapped child may be very poor at initiative play and for this reason it is important that care staff actively engage the child in play. Being surrounded by toys and 'stimulating' sights and sounds does not cause the child to play.

Careful thought should be given to selecting suitable toys and play activities for each individual child. Consider his stage of development, abilities, the nature and severity of his handicap(s) and of equal importance: does the toy provide enjoyment and fun for the child?

Before starting a play session care staff should ensure that the child is not hungry, uncomfortable, wet or tired. Try not to feel self conscious or worry about 'looking silly' when playing. Try not to become discouraged if the child fails to play or respond immediately. This is to be expected and does not mean that the child will never learn.

The various types of play — exploratory, energetic, manipulative, social, symbolic and hobbies/leisure activities — are all important for various mentally handicapped people. There is immense scope for a variety of play and recreational activities within these categories — play should not be allowed to become a dull routine chore as this destroys its very essence.

Although we have concerned ourselves mostly with the mentally handicapped child, many of the principles and ideas relate also to the mentally handicapped adolescent and adult for whom recreation and leisure activities are also a basic human need and must be provided for.

Play is characterised by activity on the part of the player but some mentally handicapped people are unable to use activity in play, especially the profoundly multiply handicapped for whom very severe mental handicap is exacerbated by physical and sensory handicaps. Their needs however are no less than for the less severely handicapped. Due to the degree of immobility and inactivity the care staff must make a special effort to play with the child. The severely physically handicapped child needs to be placed in various beneficial positions during the day and the imaginative placing of toys and mobiles can make sitting in a wheelchair or lying prone over a foam wedge more interesting for the child. Physical contact is also an extremely important channel of communication which should be used whenever possible with this group of children.

This chapter is a brief overview of play and its importance both in child development and for care staff working with mentally handicapped people. For those staff who wish to learn more about this subject, there is a great deal of literature on play and all its related aspects which they should read. There are also several organisations actively concerned with play and the provision of play activities for the handicapped. They would be willing to provide and help, advice and information.

REFERENCES

Bowlby J, Fry M 1976 Child care and the growth of love. Pelican, London, p 64

Darbyshire P 1980a Nursing care study: A severely mentally and physically handicapped child. Nursing Times 76(2): 64–68

Darbyshire P 1980b Play and profoundly handicapped children. Nursing Times 76(35): 1538–1543

Department of Health and Social Security 1978a National Development Group for the Mentally Handicapped First Report 1976–77. HMSO, London, p 48

Department of Health and Social Security 1978b National Development Group for the Mentally Handicapped. Helping Mentally Handicapped People in Hospital. HMSO, London, p 13–14

Finnie N 1974 Handling the young cerebral palsied child at home. Heinemann, London

Garvey C 1977 Play. Fontana/Open Books, London, p 10–11

Head J, Mogford K 1979 Using toys and playthings. In: Newson J, Newson E (eds) Toys and playthings. Penguin, Harmondsworth, p 197

Isaacs S 1951 Social development in young children. (Students' abridged edn) Routledge and Kegan Paul, London, p 210–213

Millar S 1968 The psychology of play. Penguin, Harmondsworth

Mogford K 1979 The observational play repertoires. In: Newson J, Newson E (eds) Toys and playthings. Penguin, Harmondsworth, p 172–189

Morris D 1977 Manwatching. Cape and Elsevier International Projects, London, p 267–271

Newson J, Newson E (eds) 1979 Toys and playthings. Penguin, Harmondsworth, p 159–171

Oswin M 1971 The empty hours. Allen Lane/Penguin, London

Oswin M 1978 Children living in long stay hospitals. Spastics International Medical Publications/Heinemann Medical, London, p 101–102

Toy Libraries Association 1980 Report of the Working Party of the Toy Libraries Association 1979–1980. Play, toys and toy libraries in mental handicap hospitals. Toy Libraries Association, p 19–20

Winnicott D W 1970 The child, the family and the outside world. Penguin, Harmondsworth, p 144–145

FURTHER READING

Axline V M 1947 Play therapy. Haughton Miffin, New York

Axline V M 1978 Dibs: In search of self. Penguin, Harmondsworth

Bruner J, Jolly A, Sylva K (eds) 1976 Play: Its role in development and evolution. Penguin, Harmondsworth

Jeffree D, McConkey R, Hewson S 1976 Let me play. Human Horizon Series, Souvenir Press, London

Leland H, Smith D E 1965 Play therapy with mentally subnormal children. Grune and Stratton, New York

Lindquist I 1977 Therapy through play. Arlington Books, London

Matterson E 1970 Play with a purpose for under sevens. Penguin, Harmondsworth

Piaget J 1972 Play, dreams and imitation in childhood. Routledge and Kegan Paul, London

Roberts V 1971 Playing, learning and living. A and C Black, London

Sheridan M D 1977 Spontaneous play in early childhood. National Foundation for Educational Research Publication, London

Tizard B, Harvey D (eds) 1976 The biology of play. Heinemann, London

Weller B 1980 Helping sick children play. Bailliere Tindall, London

Winnicott D W 1974 Playing and reality, Penguin, Harmondsworth

PLAY ACTIVITIES

Lear R 1980 Play helps: Toys and activities for handicapped children. Heinemann, London

Toy Libraries Association Publications (see below for address):

The Good Toy Guide.
Choosing Toys and Activities for Handicapped
Children.
For Busy Hands.
Hear and Say.
Play for Mentally Handicapped Adults.
Design and Make Magnetic Board Toys.
Encouraging Language Development.
I can use my hands.
Mucky Play.

USEFUL ADDRESSES

The Toy Libraries Association
Seabrook House
Wyllyotts Manor
Barkes Lane
Potters Bar
Herts ENS 2HL

Handicapped Adventure Playground Association
Fulham Palace
Bishops Avenue
London SW6 6EA

Disabled Living Foundation
346 Kensington High Street
London W14 8NS

*National Society for Mentally Handicapped Children and
Adults (MENCAP)*
117–123 Golden Lane
London EC1Y ORT

Spastics Society
12 Park Crescent
London W1N 4EQ

(Information & Equipment)
16 Fitzroy Square
London W1P 5HQ

Pre-School Playgroups Association
Aveline Street
London SE11

Down's Babies Association
Queenbourne Community Centre
Ridgacre Road
Quinton
Birmingham

National Association for Hospital Play Staff
Mrs S. Burt
22 Kings Road
Tonbridge
Kent

*National Association for the Welfare of Children in
Hospital* (NAWCH)
Exton House
7 Exton Street
London SE1

British Toy Manufacturers Association
80 Camberwell Road
London SE5 OEG

Castle Priory College
Thames Street
Wallingford
Oxon Ox10 OHE

Save the Children Fund
157 Clapham Road
London SW9

MANUFACTURERS AND SUPPLIERS OF TOYS ESPECIALLY SUITABLE FOR HANDICAPPED CHILDREN

Educational Supplies Association
Pinnacles
PO Box 22
Harlow
Essex CM19 5AY

Community Playthings
Carvell
Robertsbridge
Sussex
TN32 5DR

James Galt & Co.
PO Box 2
Cheadle
Cheshire

Fisher Price Toys Ltd
Scottish Life House
29 St Katherine Street
Northampton

Hestair Kiddicraft Ltd
Godstone Road
Kenley
Surrey

Hamley Brothers Ltd
200 Regent Street
London W1

Huntercraft Silverbands Ltd
4 The Castle House
Long Street
Sterbourne
Dorset

Kidstuff Education Division
WCB Containers Ltd
Oldham Street
Denton
Manchester M34 3RS

*Pethna Toy System (Electronic Toys for the Profoundly
Handicapped)*
Bryn Roberts
26 Sandway Road
Wrexham
Clwyd
North Wales

Many of these manufacturers will supply product
information and catalogues on request.

13

The family

Gail Ketley-King

- *A grief response may be the parents' reaction to news of a child's mental handicap*
- *Family care can create practical, financial, emotional and social problems*
- *Practical counselling about physical care of the child is essential as is emotional counselling to help the parents cope*
- *The family situation should remain as normal as possible with the needs of the whole family catered for*
- *Comprehensive information about local and national specialist services and helping agencies should be made available to families*

HISTORICAL BACKGROUND

Attitudes to the care of the mentally handicapped have changed dramatically this century. Until the mid-1950s the usual policy was one of segregation from the rest of society, but with the Report of the Royal Commission on the Law relating to Mental Illness and Mental Deficiency (1954–57) policy altered. The report suggested a shift of emphasis from hospital to community care. Residential and hospital care were felt to be appropriate only where home care placed an undue burden upon the family, or where there were special circumstances. The Mental Health Act (1959) and the Scottish equivalent Mental Health Act (1960) which evolved from the findings of the Commission, embody these principles.

This policy reorientation was subsequently reinforced in two further official documents: 'Health and Welfare: The Development of Community Care' (1963) and the White Paper 'Better Services for the Mentally Handicapped' (1971). The latter emphasized that 'mentally handicapped children and adults should not be segregated unnecessarily from other people of similar age, nor from the general life of the local community . . . . Each handicapped person should live with his own family as long as this does not impose an undue burden on them or him, and he and his family should receive full advice and support . . . . When a handicapped person has to leave his family home, temporarily or permanently, the substitute home should be as homelike as possible.'

To this end there followed a 20-year drive to reduce the numbers of mentally handicapped children and adults resident in hospitals. The Education Act (1970) further signalled the move away from segregation towards an acceptance that the problems of the mentally handicapped are essentially social and educational rather than medical. It is now accepted (Court, 1976; Jay, 1979) that hospitals are inappropriate places for children to develop, and that the mentally handicapped person has as much right as his normal counterpart to the social and medical resources which exist in the community.

The attitude change was partly the result of Bowlby's work (1951), and was encouraged by several further studies in the 1960s and '70s. There is much evidence that severely mentally handicapped children develop faster if brought up at home rather than in an institution, and that an appropriately stimulating environment is an important factor in encouraging their abilities (Tizard, 1960; Lyle, 1960; Centerwall & Centerwall, 1960; Stedman & Eichorn, 1964; Shipe & Shotwell, 1965; Bayley et al, 1966; Carr, 1970). Aspects of hospital care which were thought to be antitherapeutic were the homogeneity of child grouping and the emphasis on institution rather than child oriented regimes. What is more, both the development of speech and language and the child's behaviour were found to improve when children were moved from large institutions to smaller units.

Further studies (Leck et al, 1967; Kushlik, 1970; King et al, 1971; Bone et al, 1972; Jones, 1975) show that the medical needs of the mentally handicapped are no greater than those of the population as a whole, and that they can survive in the community with varying degrees of support. The indications are that not only is community care more desirable for the individual but that it is considerably cheaper than hospital care.

The change in emphasis resulted in great reductions in the numbers of mentally handi-

capped people resident in hospitals. 'Mental Handicap: progress, problems and priorities' (1980) shows that in the 1950s 84 000 mentally handicapped adults and children lived in hospitals compared with 49 200 adults and 7100 children in 1969. These figures had dropped to 44 100 and 3900 respectively by 1980. It is now estimated that 90% of severely handicapped children and 40% of severely handicapped adults live at home with their parents. In Leicestershire (Kerry, 1980) half the mentally handicapped population lives at home, and 6% live with parents who are over the age of 60 years. 8% of those providing care are unmarried, divorced, separated or widowed and are, therefore, single-handed. Bacquer (1977) reported that three-fifths of mentally handicapped people live at home and, like Kerry, found that many of the parents were over the age of 80. Many of the mentally handicapped in this study were also multiply-handicapped.

As more children remain at home and more adults are discharged from hospital, the real meaning of community care is becoming apparent to more and more parents who shoulder the burden. In an ideal world these parents would be supported by family, friends and neighbours as well as by statutory social, education and health care services. Suitable accommodation, appropriate social, medical and recreational facilities and access, where needed, to short-term care facilities, would be available. In practice, a parent looking after a mentally handicapped offspring may receive pitifully little support. Some battle on until they are of an age when they are physically incapable of coping further, and even then hospital residential care may be unacceptable to them. Whilst the Attendance and Mobility Allowances and the provision of education for all children have alleviated some of the problems these parents face, enormous gaps remain in services, and those which are available may be unused because of the parents' ignorance of them.

If community care is to mean care in the community, by the community, and not merely family care, then families of the mentally handicapped need support and resources throughout the child's life, not just at times of crisis. For our therapeutic interventions to be maximally effective we must understand the common themes of a family's reaction to the discovery that one of its members is mentally handicapped. We must appreciate the problems which they meet, and we must anticipate, and so prevent, the adverse effects upon the family which may result from caring for a mentally handicapped member. This chapter aims to describe these responses, to outline the difficulties, and to indicate the ways in which professionals, and particularly the social worker and community mental handicap nurse may help the family cope with them.

FINDING OUT

In the author's experience most parents make a reasonable adjustment to the news that a child is mentally handicapped, but sometimes there is more suffering than there need be. Over and above their personal distress, they run the risk that their relationship with the child or with the existing family members will be seriously distorted. However, with timely advice about resources and, more particularly, through the provision of adequate counselling, coupled when necessary with occasional short-stay residential care, parents may be helped to enjoy their child and to maintain a normal family life.

The emotional response

The news that a child is mentally handicapped comes as a sudden blow to the parents whose response to it resembles that of a grief reaction. Before the child can be accepted as handicapped they must mourn the loss of their normal child (Solnit & Stack, 1961). This is true not only for parents whose child's handicap is diagnosed at birth but also, perhaps even more so, for the parents of a child whose disorder becomes apparent later. In the latter case there is already an established relationship with the child, so that whilst the grief may be more intense there is possibly less chance of subsequent rejection. Occasionally parents report that the final confirmation of the diagnosis comes as a great relief, presumably from the anxiety created by a long period of uncertainty.

Several models have been suggested (Solnit & Stack, 1961; Cohen, 1962) to aid our understanding of the bereavement process. Drotar et al (1975) describe five stages in the parental response:

1. Shock
2. Denial
3. Sadness and anger
4. Adaptation
5. Reorganisation.

A variety of mental and physical symptoms which have been described in bereavement proper (Murray Parkes, 1965) also occur in parents' grief for their handicapped child. These are a normal part of the grief response, and include insomnia, weight loss, restlessness, irritability and outbursts of anger.

The first response is one of emotional shock, which is accompanied by a sense of numbness. One mother, Chris ('Tears and Joy', 1981) recalls her experience: 'Our daughter was $2\frac{1}{2}$ years old before we realised, because she looked perfectly normal. She was a very good baby; I didn't have a lot of problems except, looking back on it, she was uninterested in things. . . When we were actually told in words that she was mentally handicapped it came as a terrific shock. I found it hard to accept because she looked so normal . . . Initially my husband took it very badly . . . he was totally embarrassed about it. He got up off his chair . . . and he just ran out . . . I just sat there. I didn't feel like crying, I didn't feel like doing anything. I just felt stunned. But it hit me later that day . . . Next morning he said "Well, we've got to accept it, we've got to get on with it and do the best we can for her." . . . . It was hard, and it took us months to adjust.' Another parent (McCormack, 1978) remembers: 'I refused to see James for 10 days. I wanted him put away so that I could forget he ever existed. I didn't believe it was possible to love a child like that. I think I was in a state of shock. It seemed like a nightmare . . . Once I had James in my arms I accepted him, it was as simple as that. I wasn't happy, not for a long time, but I accepted.'

Depression of mood is, perhaps, an inevitable component of grieving. This sadness is accompanied by social withdrawal and feelings of personal inadequacy. These are normal, albeit extremely painful and disabling, responses. Olshansky (1962) goes so far as to suggest that parents of retarded children experience chronic sorrow, to a greater or lesser extent, throughout their lives. A parent of a Down's syndrome boy (Hannam, 1975) remembers his response following his son's birth: 'The feeling of guilt was, at first almost unbearable. I felt an almost Old Testament sense of having somehow done wrong and that this was a punishment . . . . Having a mentally handicapped child made me feel that I had failed. . . I was ready to reject him, and even prepared to consider killing him. I believe that these feelings of ambivalence are entirely natural, but they are nevertheless frightening, and it is perhaps better to express them then have them increasing the mounting feeling of guilt and inadequacy.' It helps if parents are encouraged to express these normal feelings, and skilled counselling, offered at the appropriate time, may facilitate grieving and promote a better long-term adjustment. Unresolved grief is detrimental not only to the parent but to the whole family, and ways in which they can be helped with their grieving will be mentioned later.

Grieving involves a working through of feelings of disbelief, rejection, envy, personal inadequacy, personal failure, loss of self-respect and loss of self-esteem. Former hopes and expectations must be replaced by a new reality. Ambitions and aspirations for the child must be abandoned and substituted by more realistic goals. It is a turbulent period, not only for the parents but also for the professionals who are involved. The parent may harbour unpleasant, disturbing and unwelcome thoughts and feelings. It is better that they

should be aired than concealed. One of McCormack's (1978) mothers is clearly grieving when she talks of the envy she feels towards the parents of normal children: 'I would be inside, mopping up the sick, because that's what always happened when I was trying to feed him, and I could look out of the window and see the woman next door in the garden, playing with her lovely little toddler. I used to cry and cry.' Such feelings may be reactivated by important reminders such as pregnancy in a friend, the birth of a new baby, or the first day when a normal child sets off to school. The delay in the developmental milestones of handicapped children means that the normal joys experienced by parents are so much harder to share with others.

Grieving takes time and will depend on the strengths and weaknesses of both the parents and the services. Generally, 6–12 months is considered to be a usual period for adjustment to a severe emotional trauma like bereavement but, in the case of mental handicap, the trauma is prolonged indefinitely, as the child serves as a constant reminder of what has been lost. The component stages are neither separate entities, nor do they occur sequentially, but tend to overlap and recur with varying frequency and duration. Only the initial stage of emotional shock seems to be limited in duration. For the remainder, time must be allowed for the expression of feelings, the assimilation of information and subsequent formulation of questions, since if they remain unanswered, uncertainty, frustration and anxiety will delay the onset of resolution. How successful is the process of working through the grief will largely determine how well the parents, and hence the rest of the family function in the future.

COPING

However well-informed or supported parents may be, it is inevitable that they will experience great anxiety. Understandably, they discover their own ways of minimizing their pain, ways which are analogous with the defence mechanisms described by dynamic psychotherapists. Some are helpful, but others — particularly when they are exaggerated — merely solve one problem at the expense of another.

Humour

In the play 'A Day in the Life of Joe Egg' (Nichols, 1967), Brian and Sheila use humour to alleviate some of their distress. As another character in the play remarks, 'the sick joke kills the pain but leaves the situation as it was.' One of the author's clients, whenever she talked about the difficulties her severely mentally and physically handicapped child encountered, referred to this as a '3-year handicap race'.

Rationalisation

All parents try to make what sense they can of the handicap and its implications. Most are desperate to find some explanation for the child's condition, and if a medical explanation is not sufficient parents may adopt a misguided reasoning of their own. Some may believe that the handicap has been caused by an unusual event, illness or mishap. Others may regard it as a punishment from God, the result of an extra-marital relationship, or a just reward for a contemplated abortion.

Avoidance

Many parents are extremely sensitive, if not even ashamed, about their child's handicap. Two of McCormack's (1978) mothers say: 'I'm ashamed of myself but when I take her out in the pushchair I wrap her up well so that people won't see there is anything wrong', and 'I used to keep my daughter shut in the garden playing alone, while all the normal kids played in the road, till one of the neighbours told me I was a fool.' Because of their discomfort, parents may retreat from neighbours, friends, local welfare clinics and mother and baby groups in order to avoid awkward moments and embarrassing glances. An obvious physical defect in the child, or overt behavioural problem, will exacerbate this difficulty. Severe restrictions upon the social lives of both the child and the family may result.

As a result of avoidance, the parents' social anxiety is never given the opportunity to habituate, so that, as the family becomes increasingly isolated, alternatives become more and more difficult. Even within a family the subject may be avoided. Unknowingly, fathers may increase their own avoidance by working away or working longer hours, so that the mother and child become even further isolated within the family. The marital relationship and, of course, the sexual relationship, are frequent casualties. Mere fear of a further pregnancy can lead to avoidance of sexual contact, which in turn may develop into a complicated psychosexual problem which will require great skill if it is to be overcome. Sexual avoidance is reinforced by allowing the child to share the same bedroom or, quite often, the same bed as the parents.

Anger

The expression of anger brings relief of tension and frustration to many parents. Others find this extremely difficult and become embroiled in a destructive circle of resentment, guilt and over-protection. A certain amount of anger towards the hospital, its personnel and its services may be a normal component of grieving. However, persistent overt anger can distort the family's attitudes, and hence its functioning. Other parents may deny their anger and become caught up in an effort to 'make up' to the child for the condition which causes such guilt. They develop a habit of overprotection, perhaps involving social workers, health visitors and others who provide material support, and this sows the seed of later management problems and family restrictions. Yet other parents direct their anger at one another, or towards a normal sibling, who now becomes the scapegoat for the family's inability to express its anger about the handicap. In this way normal family activities become increasingly restricted so as to accommodate the handicapped child, and the circle of resentment, guilt and over-protection is completed.

Denial

Possibly because the full extent and implications of the handicap are too painful for a parent to bear, it is not unusual for the severity of the handicap to be minimised or even denied entirely. Whilst denial may be a normal part of parental adjustment, it can also form a life-long attitude characterised by a belief that the child will 'catch up' or 'grow out of it', or that a cure may be found. A child's normal appearance, parental and family doubts about the validity of the diagnosis and a readiness to seek second and third opinions may reinforce the parents' view that the handicap is minimal. A recurrent failure to keep appointments, or a persistent tendency to be late for them, may be indications that parents do not appreciate the severity of the condition, and therefore the importance of subsequent assessment, treatment and after-care.

Many observers feel that a degree of denial is essential to reduce the severity of the chronic sorrow which parents experience. At certain stages denial may well be adaptive in as much that it allows the parents sufficient time to come to terms with reality.

THE PARENTAL RESPONSE: HOW IT CAN VARY

No two parents respond in quite the same way to the news that their child is handicapped. Several factors, some specific and others not so, modify this response:

1. The attitudes held by the parents towards mental handicap and its implications.
2. The age of the parents.
3. Previous experience of childbirth, miscarriages, stillbirth or delays in conception.
4. The child's position in the family: more may be invested in a first born child.
5. The attitudes of other key people, particularly the maternal grandmother. Gath (1978) suggests that in the extended family the key figure is the maternal grandmother, and that a close relationship between her and the mother is a helpful factor in terms of outcome.
6. Social class: professional parents may find the acceptance of the handicap more difficult.
7. Religious beliefs and support.
8. The family's lifestyle, career considerations and social mobility may be important.
9. The marriage: a disharmonious marriage, or the absence of a partner, makes smooth adjustment more difficult.
10. The nature and degree of the handicap which, again, may be most important to parents who value intellectual performance. Eaton & Weil (1955) give an account of the Hutterite community, a communal religious sect in the mid-west of the United States of America. Here, there is no emphasis on competition and achievement, and mental handicap is not regarded as a tragedy in the way it is in the rest of western culture.
11. Bonding: because of its own medical needs, the handicapped child may be separated from the mother at birth, thereby increasing the risks known to be associated with a failure of bond formation (Klaus & Kennell, 1970; Bowlby 1969, 1973, 1980).
12. The child's appearance: physical deformity may result in the uncommon response of immediate and permanent rejection.
13. The final factor which may influence parental response concerns the way in which parents learn of the handicap. As this is an area in which there is much room for useful improvement, it will be considered at length.

In the past and, one hopes, to a lesser extent now, considerable unnecessary suffering has been caused by inept handling of the initial interviews. Although telling people that their child is mentally handicapped can be a very difficult and emotionally demanding task, there is no evidence to suggest that the parents come to resent the informant as long as it is done with care and skill (Gayton & Walker, 1974: Cunningham & Sloper, 1977). However, parents do express dissatisfaction with the way they are told (Berg et al, 1969; Carr, 1970; Stone, 1973; Gayton & Walker, 1974; Cunningham & Sloper, 1977), and greater care and effort must be exercised here.

Before 1964 the only available guidelines were based upon the experiences of paediatricians. Some (Franklin, 1958) were in favour of allowing the parent to form a relationship with the child before being told of the handicap, whilst others (Parmelee, 1956) recommended informing the parents as soon as possible. Since then, several studies — all of them involving cases of Down's syndrome — suggest that parents prefer to be told the diagnosis as early as possible (Drillien & Wilkinson, 1964; Carr, 1970), and that they wish to be told the truth without the false reassurances which so often ease the task for the informant (Tizard & Grad, 1961).

It has been suggested that parents would not wish to hear the truth, and would be dissatisfied no matter how the news is delivered. However, it may be that some professionals do not realise that a parent's apparent failure to appreciate what has been said may be less of an indication of anger, resistance and denial than of the depth of their emotional shock.

Hannam (1975) quotes one mother: 'I felt unreal, that this could be me, that if I switched off and went back to sleep I would wake up and find I had dreamed it. I even did not want to see my husband in a way, because that would have meant facing reality', and another: 'Both my husband and I were in such an emotional state that it is quite possible that we may have been told (that their child had Down's syndrome) and just not heard it.'

The informant should always pay due regard to his own ability, or lack of it, to communicate clearly. Whilst it is easy and convenient to blame subsequent difficulties upon the parents' response rather than upon personal ineptitude, in the end the fault may often lie with the professional. Unlike the parent, who has never encountered the problem before, the professional should be fully prepared and should have a sound knowledge of the present state of research and resources. With this knowledge, and with the necessary skills, he should offer clear, factual information in an appropriately sympathetic way. Few, if any of us, are lucky enough to be born with these skills, but like other interviewing skills they can be acquired through interviewing and counselling skills training.

Several authors (Schumacher, 1945; Yates & Lederer, 1961; Richards, 1964; Wolfenberger, 1967; Pinkerton, 1970) stress the need for repeated interviews to help the parents to assimilate the information, to express their feelings, and to make what best adjustment is possible in the immediate situation. To achieve this the informant must explain the meaning of medical terminology, and fully examine the parents' understanding of the information they have been given and its implications. It is a time when the parents are being presented with complex, emotionally charged information and so it is not surprising that much time and repetition is needed to avoid parents being misinformed.

Always the parents should be informed together. Sadly, mothers have too often been given the news of their child's handicap at a routine out-patient clinic, only to be faced with the task of returning home, ill-prepared, to discuss uncertain details and anxieties with the father. To avoid these unfortunate situations Cunningham (1979) offers the following guidelines:

1. Most parents prefer to be told of the diagnosis as soon as possible.
2. Most parents feel that the child should be present at the time or that they should have immediate access to him.

3. Most parents appreciate being informed together. For a single parent, the presence of a close friend or relative is helpful.
4. The medical details should be given privately, as parents often resent the presence of other professionals at this stage.
5. Sufficient time should be allowed for information to be imparted, questions to be asked, and emotions to be expressed. Particularly important at this stage is specific information about the handicap, how it was caused, the likely outcome, and what the parents can do to help in the immediate future.
6. Where appropriate, written information should be offered.

Support for these guidelines comes from Gilmore & Oates (1977), Gath (1978), Lucas & Lucas (1980), and Tarran (1981), and they confirm the recommendations already made by Carr & Oppe (1971) and Spain & Wigley (1975).

FURTHER PROBLEMS: HOW THEY AFFECT THE FAMILY

Early problems

Looking after a mentally handicapped child poses practical, financial, emotional and social problems, particularly where the child has multiple handicaps. Any one, or any combination of them, may adversely affect the well-being of the family.

Housing

Initially many houses are quite unsuitable for caring for a mentally handicapped child, and the cost of adapting the property may be equally prohibitive. Bathrooms and bedrooms are normally on the first floor, and parents may experience great difficulty in getting a disabled child up and down the awkward, narrow staircase of the average house. Whilst a stair lift may be an answer, lack of funds or, where the accommodation is rented, lack of permission, render this solution impossible.

Butler et al (1978) felt that just over half of the families in their study were living in unsuitable accommodation. Of these 72% needed additional safety measures like escape-proof fencing, gates and locks. 39% of those living in unsuitable accommodation had already made alterations or had moved to more suitable property. However, only one in four had received any financial help, more than half of those who had applied for local authority financial aid having been turned down.

Financial problems

As well as the costs of providing suitable accommodation there are additional costs which arise directly from the child's condition or behaviour. Vomiting, dribbling and incontinence increase the costs of clothing and washing. Wear and tear to clothes, bed linen, carpets and furnishings may be excessive through constant cleaning, unorthodox use, or simple destructiveness. Loss of time from work, particularly where the father's employer is unsympathetic, reduces family income unless valuable annual leave is used in order that hospital appointments can be kept. Transport costs, particularly when special transport is needed, are frequently prohibitive. Additional heating, the inevitable loss of a potential income from the principal caregiver, plus the fact that not all parents of mentally handicapped children receive an Attendance Allowance further compromise a limited family income. Ultimately there is a considerable lowering of the standard of living.

Attendance

The need for constant supervision is the commonest day-to-day management problem which parents report, and it makes household tasks and the care of other children all the more difficult. Wilkin (1979) quotes one mother as saying: 'I can't get anything done because he's always running around. If he sits down, you've got to sit down with him. It's the constant attention that gets you down.' As well as disrupting normal household tasks the handicapped child often creates more work in terms of feeding, cleaning and, where there is incontinence, nappy changing. Many children continue to need night-time attendance, and even if the child sleeps well, evening time is taken up with household chores which otherwise might have been completed during the day. Inevitably, social life becomes severely restricted. Butler et al (1978) found mild restrictions in 32% and severe restrictions in 52%. Some mothers (Wilkin, 1979) accept this more easily than others who feel a greater need for more leisure time or for paid employment.

Recent studies (Hewett et al, 1970; Bayley, 1973; Carr, 1976; Butler et al, 1978; Wilkin, 1979) emphasize the daunting day-to-day practical problems for families with a handicapped child. Wilkin (1979) describes another mother as saying: 'I have to clean his room every day with Dettol. . . I have to bath him three times a day and do the washing every day.' 40% of Butler et al's (1978) sample of handicapped children were incontinent, one-third needed attention at least once a night, one-third could not be safely left unattended, and 40% of these mothers found it was a problem to take the child out either because of the physical difficulty of boarding buses or because of difficult behaviour which, alone, was the major problem for 24% of families. Still, the need for constant supervision, reported by 55%, came first in the list of most troublesome problems, with lack of personal hygiene (21%) coming a close third behind behavioural disorders. Butler et al also found that 40% of mothers received no help in caring for the child, and 82% had little or no help with housework. Whilst school time afforded some relief, most help was still offered by the father, whose time, by virtue of his having to work, was severely restricted during the day, when his assistance might have been most useful. Bayley (1973) and Carr (1976) found 'frequent' or 'considerable' help from friends, family and neighbours, but Wilkin (1979), who specifically examined the nature of the help offered, concluded that although friends and family assist with occasional babysitting and shopping, the very heavy burden of care continues to be borne, with very little support, by the mother.

Holidays

Holidays present difficulties over and above those encountered in day to day care. Holidays away from home present problems all of their own. Reluctance to travel far lest medical problems such as recurrent epileptic seizures should arise and unsympathetic attitudes from some holiday proprietors, restrict the family's choice so much that, especially when the adequacy of facilities is uncertain, many parents find a holiday away too burdensome to consider. If short-term care can be arranged for the child at least the parents may get away, but for a variety of reasons even this may not be acceptable for some.

Short-term care

Despite the need for respite from the constant care of their handicapped child, many parents are unable to come to terms with the idea of short-term care. Some feel guilty because they believe they are failing in their duty to the child. These parents need careful counselling to enable them to make proper use of care facilities. Even with a planned period in care they will be unable to enjoy the rest unless they are well prepared. They must feel that the child will be happy, well cared for, and that he will also enjoy his break from them. He will have the opportunity for new social encounters and friendships, and at the same time learn to cope with separations from the parents: separations which, in some cases, are destined to become permanent if long-term care is eventually required.

Education

Parents sometimes find themselves in the cross-fire of the continuing argument which rages between advocates of special education and of normal provision. Some readily accept a designated placement, but others attempt to secure what they feel is a more appropriate placement. Whilst schools and parents usually co-exist peacefully, the parent who presses for alternative provision runs the added risk of being unfairly labelled as hostile, guilt-ridden, or worse. Whilst there are educational psychologists who can offer advice about education, very often nurses and social workers, by virtue of their availability, are the first to hear of the parents' worries and complaints.

The effect on the family

Families with mentally handicapped children experience greater stress than others. Frequently, though not invariably, the mother is the principal caregiver and, with apologies to some fathers, it will be assumed here that this is usually the case.

The mother

Bradshaw & Lawton (1978) found that neither material circumstances nor the specific form of handicap accounted for much of the variations in maternal stress. However, their study, as well as that of Butler et al (1978) and Burden (1980) showed that greater stress is experienced with more severe handicaps. Lack of relief from continual supervision accounts for the depression reported by 61% of mothers (Hewett et al, 1970), and high rates of physical and mental ill-health are found in family members, particularly in mothers (Tizard & Grad, 1961; Carnegie Trust, 1964). Wing (1975) found that with severe handicaps 40% of mothers reported current psychiatric symptoms, and 17% had received treatment in the previous year. Wilkin (1979) supports this with the finding that 40% of mothers had physical complaints and 72% had mental health problems. Of these, depression, edginess, tiredness, exhaustion and 'bad nerves' were the main symptoms. 60% of these mothers did not go out to work, 40% were unable to get out in the evenings, and 90% had no personal free time at weekends. As a result of these sorts of restriction many mothers feel imprisoned at home and would welcome the chance of some personal 'space' away from the responsibilities of the home. Burden (1980) suggests that it is naive to think of a handicapped child causing mental ill-health in the mothers. He finds it more helpful to view the birth of a handicapped child as a 'critical life experience' for the mother, the effects of which interact with the effects of other critical experiences and the mother's own personality to produce a likelihood of depresssion or mental breakdown. Due to these variations there can be no one set of solutions.

The father

Less stress seems to be experienced by fathers than by mothers. Gath (1978) found that at 33% the percentage of mothers of Down's syndrome children who were depressed was double that of her control group, but between fathers there was no such difference in reported psychiatric symptoms. Only 18% of Wilkin's (1979) group of fathers experienced significant mental health problems. On the other hand Cummings (1976) feels that fathers do experience psychological stress, but suggests it is due to the negative effect of 'fathering a limited child relative to the traditional child-rearing roles and responsibilities of fathers.'

The marriage

Inevitably the marriage is a frequent casualty. The arrival of a mentally handicapped child may be a decisive factor in the break-up of an already shaky marriage (Gath, 1977) and, at the very least, may contribute to existing marital problems (Lonsdale, 1978). A parent explains ('Tears and Joy', 1971):

> It's a strain on your marriage initially. I felt guilty. I felt it was may fault that I had a child like that. My husband rejected the child completely, then he rejected me as well. There was a battle, but I didn't realise it was going on because I was so involved in my own grief and trying to accept that I had a mentally handicapped child.

Psychosexual problems are not unusual, resulting from the child's spending the night with his parents, from the unexpressed fear of a further pregnancy or from loss of libido due to exhaustion or depression. Divorce is common, occurring, according to a recent survey by the Welsh National School of Medicine, cited by McCormack, ten times more frequently than the national average. Similar figures were reported by Tew et al (1977), who found a divorce rate of nine times the national average in parents of spina bifida children. Earlier studies (Tizard & Grad, 1961; Carnegie Trust, 1964; Hewett et al, 1970) found lower divorce rates but, as Tew et al (1977) suggest, this may be due to differing methodologies rather than a specific influence of spina bifida per se.

The siblings

Parents often worry that a handicapped child will have a harmful effect on his siblings, perhaps due to a lowering of standards, imitation of unwanted or bizarre behaviour, reluctance to bring friends to the home and a fear of the unwelcome comments and questions of others.

There are several rather contradictory studies on the subject, of which few actually interviewed the siblings. However, it does seem that the apportioning of time rather than the actual presence of a handicapped child is an important factor. If the family's attention is directed exclusively towards the handicapped child then emotional and behavioural problems may be expected in brothers and sisters. Burdensome chores, restricted family life, sharing a bedroom, interrupted nights, inability to do homework, and lack of attention lead to jealousy and resentment felt, but rarely clearly expressed, towards the handicapped child. Not always do these problems remain within the family, for occasionally a normal sibling will present problems elsewhere, for example at school. This may be an important clue to stress within the family. Despite this, it is often the parents' own attitudes and adjustment which govern the non-handicapped child's response, and it has to be noted that some children seem to benefit from their handicapped siblings in terms of their own increased sensitivity to the needs of others.

The extended family

This subject has been less researched. Grandparents seem to react rather as the parents do, perhaps because they share common attitudes. Some may be towers of strength and yet others may be consumed with grief, robbed of the special delight a grandparent takes in a new child. Not uncommonly the grandparents experience precisely the same grief-related problems as have been described in the parents. Here, particularly skilful interventions may be needed to avoid dividing the parents' loyalties and to ensure that damaging compromises do not develop.

Further pregnancies

For completed families the question of further pregnancies is simple. Not so for parents who had planned further children, and for them this decision is fraught with anguish. There may be the real possibility of the handicap being repeated, or the worry of having insufficient time to devote to a new baby (Holt, 1958). Modern genetic counselling, which should be freely available to parents, may help them to settle one of these issues. However, for parents who do decide to embark on a further pregnancy, the practical problems of rest during the pregnancy, the confinement and the perinatal period must be anticipated, particularly where friends and relations are unable to provide sufficient support themselves.

Later problems

Adolescence

For the parents of non-handicapped teenagers adolescence is often a stormy time, but where the youngster is mentally handicapped there may be additional difficulties. Public ignorance of mental handicap can become more apparent at this age, when the handicapped youngster may be ostracized, bullied or victimised. Many people are less tolerant of moody, rebellious behaviour in handicapped teenagers than in normal individuals. To these worries are added fresh reminders for parents about their child's limited career and marriage prospects, and many parents face the fact that there will be no further generation in the family line.

Sexual awareness, which has received more attention with the advent of community care, group homes and desegregated hospitals, is now more widely accepted, and it is recognised that, like their contemporaries, mentally handicapped youngsters also have sexual drives. Greater anxieties may be posed for the parents of the mentally handicapped who, therefore, require advice about the sex education of their child and about practical issues like the need for contraception. Menstruation in girls, spontaneous erections in boys, and concern in both sexes about masturbation may be a great worry for the parents of a mentally handicapped adolescent. An accepting and non-judgmental attitude can be encouraged, but always there will be parents who find the subject so embarrassing that they stringently avoid it, hoping, presumably, that it will go away.

Employment and leisure

At 16 years of age the young mentally handicapped person ceases to be the responsibility of the local education authority, and his care is passed to the social services department. A lucky few gain places in Adult Training Centres but, for most, leaving school means a future of uncertainty and limited opportunity. Some may be accommodated in sheltered employment, but for many the prospect of work is remote, and their unfortunate families are left with the job of finding some leisure activity with which their chronically unemployed offspring call fill his time.

The future

A statement from the Hartcliffe Friends of the Handicapped ('Tears and Joy', 1981) summar-

ises the thoughts of many parents when they consider what the future holds for their children:

> We all find it difficult talking about the future. We want more information about what's going to happen to our children when we've gone, but when we ask people in authority they say 'Don't worry about it.' It's quite enough getting through our daily or weekly problems without having to think about the future, but it's always there. If that was solved, it would make day to day problems much easier.

The outlook is so bleak that many avoid the issue and it is, perhaps, one of the problems which is most difficult to overcome. As there is no simple solution, parents often battle on until they reach the inevitable point beyond which they cannot cope. In Leicestershire (Kerry, 1980) there are surprisingly high numbers of aged parents who are caring for mentally handicapped adults. Despite their devotion, the need for residential accommodation increases as the mentally handicapped grow and their parents become older. Problems of incontinence, feeding and carrying may be worse than they were in childhood, even though the handicapped teenager and adult may be easier to occupy with television, music and the like. In many cases, the abilities and disabilities of the handicapped individual, coupled with the extent to which the parental home can be modified, will be the deciding factors in whether residential care is eventually needed. Finally, whilst most parents welcome their new-found freedom once their mentally handicapped offspring has left home, there are some, who, because of insufficient preparation and inadequate support develop feelings of guilt or ambivalence about giving up their responsibility.

ASSISTANCE: HOW THE SOCIAL WORKER OR HEALTH CARE PROFESSIONAL CAN HELP

Can I see another's woe
And not be in sorrow too?
Can I see another's grief
And not seek for kind relief?

from 'On Another's Sorrow' by William Blake.

Faced with the multitude of emotional and practical problems which have been described, it is surprising that so many families manage as well as they do. Some families do, however, experience greater difficulties than others, and so services must be flexible. While some parents prefer to 'go it alone', others wish to be involved with every helping agency available. Some accept suggestions and others reject them. Some prefer a doctor-client relationship, whilst others like regular or intermittent support from paramedical and social workers. A further group thrives on the support of other parents either in a group or workshop. Only the parents can decide whatever best suits them. As much as is possible, the professional must respect this prerogative, but at the same time make available the whole range of appropriate services. According to Collins (1976), the father of a mentally handicapped daughter, these services should include:

1. A fully comprehensive assessment.
2. A practical programme to promote maximum development.
3. A picture of the scope of local services.
4. Resource services for implementation of programmes.
5. Deeper understanding of specific problems.
6. Contact with others in similar situations.
7. Information on future continuing services.

Social work skills

Although the term social worker is used in this section, often the community mental handicap nurse carries out a similar function but is unlikely to be involved in intensive case work. Providing information about the availability of resources is frequently one of the tasks of the social worker, whose job it often is to support the family throughout the child's life. Whatever role the social worker assumes, certain basic skills are essential. This list, which is by no means exhaustive, includes some of the qualities which the author considers important in a social worker's effectiveness with the

families of mentally handicapped children. Many of these qualities have been more widely accepted as those of the effective psychotherapist.

1. Warmth (Carkuff & Truax, 1967).
2. Empathy (Carkuff & Truax, 1967).
3. Ability to promote emotional expression.
4. Ability to cope with emotional expression.
5. Non-judgmental acceptance of clients.
6. Realism.
7. Ability to realise and highlight the positive rather than the negative aspects of a child's development.
8. Ability to liaise with and organise other resource agents.
9. Ability to persist with therapeutic interventions until they have been given a fair trial, particularly when improvement is slow and discouraging.
10. Ability to 'stay' with clients at difficult times.
11. Ability to encourage clients at these times, or at times when difficult therapeutic interventions are attempted.
12. Listening skills.
13. Ability to accept personal failure and therapeutic impotence.
14. Ability to maintain professional standards, for example, when unpleasant statutory duties are necessary.
15. Ability to interact with children.
16. Enthusiasm
17. Self-understanding.
18. Honesty with the clients.

Information

Parents repeatedly request more information about their child and about available services. However, Jacobs (1977) finds that not only are parents dissatisfied with the information they are given about the child's condition but they are poorly informed about specialist services, and have surprisingly little contact with helping agencies. Hence many parents are unaware of resources which might relieve their difficulties. A well-informed social worker should be able to act as a source of the information which a parent requires.

Under the following headings are lists of various agencies and possible assistance which may be of help to parents in dealing with specific problems (see Ch. 5 for more details).

1. Financial assistance

Attendance Allowance, Mobility Allowance, Invalid Care Allowance, Family Fund, local authority rent and rate rebates, road tax exemption, various charities.

2. Health care

Physiotherapy, occupational therapy, speech therapy, genetic counselling, family planning, the provision of enuresis alarms, wheelchairs, buggies, disposable nappies and laundry facilities.

3. Social and educational services

Creches, toy libraries, play groups, summer play schemes, Gateway clubs and home helps.

4. Residential and relief services

Long- and short-term care facilities, local baby-sitting groups, foster parent schemes, hospital care, hostel and group home accommodation, and various private sector schemes such as the Camphill Village Trust, Care Villages, Home Farm Trust, Rudolph Steiner Homes, etc.

5. Transport services

The Orange Badge Scheme, volunteer driver schemes and assistance from the DHSS or hospital.

6. Housing services

Home alterations, stair lifts, ramps, downstairs showers, etc.

7. Organisation of services

How departments operate and where they are: for example Area Health Authority, Education Department, Social Services Department.

8. Local and national voluntary organisations and charities

The National Society for Mentally Handicapped Children and Adults, the Voluntary Council for Handicapped Children, the Spastics Society, local self-help groups, parent groups and parent workshops.

9. Literature

For example: 'Help Starts Here', published by the Voluntary Council for Handicapped Children, selected texts and books written by parents of handicapped children.

10. Medico-technical information

Explanations of jargon and procedures.

A booklet which contains all the relevant information about agencies and entitlements is ideal, so that parents can refer to this without having to wait for the next meeting with their social worker. As much information is offered to the parents in the early stages, such booklets provide for that which is forgotten. 'Who Can Help', published by the London Borough of Wandsworth, and 'Coping with Mental Handicap in West Sussex', which followed Jacob's (1977) survey and recommendations, are two such booklets which are already available.

Practical counselling

Parents need a variety of practical advice about the physical care of their child. In particular they are concerned with feeding, dressing, prevention of physical deformities, skin care and dental care. Expert help can be offered by physiotherapists, speech therapists, health visitors and occupational therapists. Educational and clinical psychologists may assist with enuresis, soiling, pica, self care and conduct disorders and with sufficient skill and experience the social worker or community nurse may also be able to design and implement operant programmes for some problems like sleeping difficulties, behavioural problems and problems with toilet training. Of course the co-operation of the parent is essential, particularly as marital breakdown is known to occur less frequently where early intervention has emphasised practical involvement (Gath, 1978).

Early involvement may help to alleviate some of the guilt and frustration which can result from the parents' sense of helplessness and impotence, particularly if they are rewarded by obvious progress. The child, too, benefits from the closer relationship, and if the parents' involvement is correctly managed then they come to attribute success to their own, rather than to the professionals', abilities. Mittler (1979) believes that it is important to have a definitive plan for collaboration between parents and professionals. In such a partnership 'Professionals must find a balance between helping parents to learn professional skills while at the same time retaining their own sense of identity as parents.' Parent guides and parent workshops are specifically designed to involve parents actively in their child's management.

Parent guides

The Portage Guide has the advantage of being available in the home, and so offers the chance of early and sustained support. It employs precision teaching methods to achieve developmentally appropriate goals for the individual child. The therapist, whether a nurse, social worker or psychologist, demonstrates the programme and supplies a written description to which parents can refer later. Progress is carefully monitored and recorded to provide a clear indication of improvement. These programmes encourage the early stimulation of the child in his own home, and fosters a sense of coping and competence in the parents. Since the training sessions take only twenty minutes a day, the programme

does not interfere with the mother's domestic routine, and it means that fathers can be involved too. Revill & Blunden (1977) have confirmed that using the Portage Guide considerable developmental gains can be achieved.

Parent workshops, self help groups, parents' groups

A parent workshop is a series of meetings at which a group of parents discuss with professionals their problems and difficulties of caring for a handicapped child. According to Attwood (1978), a workshop 'enables parents and professionals to discuss the stages of child development, the types of developmental problems that occur with handicapped children, programmes to facilitate the attainment of the next stage of development, the management of behavioural problems, information on services available and the opportunity to discuss their feelings regarding their handicapped child.'

One advantage of a workshop is that it reduces parents' feelings of isolation. Fathers can usually attend with their wives, as the meetings are normally held in the evenings. This may provide the first opportunity for the parents to share their feelings and to learn together about their child and his problems. Through a workshop, parents come to understand what they can reasonably expect of their child and to set realistic goals. Furthermore, since the child's attitude towards himself and his handicap are determined by his parents' reaction to him and his disability (Heilman, 1950), the more positive the parents are, the better adjusted the child will be.

The relaxed atmosphere of the workshop encourages friendship and valuable social interaction between parents. Vicarious learning, particularly from observing other parents who have managed to solve the problem they have met, can often fill gaps where services fall short. One such workshop, which was run for ten weeks by the author, has resulted in a continuing self-help group which publishes a monthly newsletter, has monthly meetings, social evenings and family days, and provides babysitting and library services. The group has brought pressure to bear for the organisation of additional workshops, and is in the process of producing a local information and resources booklet as well as organising a befriending service for parents of children with recently diagnosed handicaps.

For some parents, the single most helpful intervention is their introduction to other parents via, for example, the National Society for Mentally Handicapped Children and Adults (MENCAP) or a Down's syndrome group. In some experimental schemes, such as the Pilot Parents' Scheme in Omaha, Eastern Nebraska, U.S.A., new parents are matched, as soon as possible, with experienced 'pilot' parents. This is especially helpful for parents who are not yet ready to make use of a group.

Many parents may wish to be involved with pressure groups so as to set about establishing better facilities. A group of parents in the London Borough of Islington have, through their concerted demand for local residential care, succeeded in establishing Field End House, a local hostel where care is shared between parents and residential staff.

Emotional counselling

In the author's experience, the task of emotionally supporting the parents of mentally handicapped children often falls to the social worker. Often this involvement will be right from the moment the parents are told of their child's handicap. Sometimes the referral will be later, should a paediatrician consider that the parents are experiencing difficulties in adjusting or coping.

An immediate requirement is comfort in order to help the parents with the painful appreciation of the news that they have been given. A skilled social worker will encourage the parents to express their grief, and will attempt, rather than discourage, a display of their distress. Before trying to establish facts and attempting to help the parents to work out realistic hopes for the child's future, they must have room to grieve the child they had hoped

for. Sometimes it will be necessary to encourage any anger, hostility or guilt which the parents feel, and at the same time to re-assure them that even though such emotions are disturbing they are, nevertheless, quite normal. Where the parents' grieving seems to be complicated, either in severity or duration, and there are clear avoidances of, for example, reminders of the child that has been lost, then guided mourning (Mawson et al, 1981) may be useful. This would involve gradual exposure to anxiety-evoking reminders such as photographs of the child, or some of the possessions and clothes he had at a time when he was considered to be normal. Occasionally encouraging the parents to record their feelings, particularly in the form of a letter written to the child that might have been, will help to neutralize emotionally laden ideas and so encourage resolution of the grief. In the end, no matter how much careful counselling is offered, there will be emotional upheavals. These should be anticipated so that reassurance can be given that, at these times, and at all others, support and back-up services will continue to be available.

The early years

Sometimes parents of mentally handicapped children become so involved in their care that the needs of other family members may be neglected. In order to avoid the difficulties which may ensue, the social worker should try to help, rather than tell, the parents to treat the handicapped child in a way which is more compatible with the needs of the whole family. This can be achieved in several ways:

1. By encouraging the parents to resume their personal social life as soon as possible. Parents often get out of the habit of going out together, and may neglect each other and some friends. A reliable babysitter, plus sound advice about problems, will pave the way for parents to feel free to enjoy their time together.

2. By encouraging the family to go out together and to enjoy normal family activities

like walking, swimming and going to the cinema.

3. By encouraging the whole family to mix with friends and neighbours, and to accept offers of help with supervising the child.

4. By encouraging and helping the parents to expect the most normal behaviour possible from their child. Parents must take a sensible, firm and consistent approach to the child's behaviour. They should be discouraged from making allowances solely because of the handicap. The social worker, the clinical psychologist, and the community nurse, should be able to offer advice about behavioural methods and programmes which will reinforce normal behaviour in the child.

5. By anticipating awkward situations which might arise with other people as a result of the handicap and, though role rehearsal, preparing the parents to cope with them.

6. By anticipating problems which brothers and sisters will encounter so that they may be avoided; for example, by providing a safe place for toys and books and somewhere for entertaining friends, or by setting aside for the normal child his own special time with his parents.

7. By airing the attitudes of the extended family, particularly the grandparents. They too may need help with grief which they may hide by avoiding the child and his family. Too easily this may be misconstrued, and much may be achieved by involving the grandparents within the family as early as possible.

8. By introducing the notion of short-term care so as to make available the opportunity for the family to have time to itself without the pressures of the child's care. Of course, parents of normal children benefit from time to themselves, and normally relatives and friends can provide the necessary supervision but for parents of a mentally handicapped child the issue is more complex. Firstly they are often more reluctant to leave the child, as they feel they cannot justify the need for a break, and secondly a handicapped child often requires special kinds of care and supervision which a friend or relative might be unable to

offer over a long period. Some challenging of the parents' assumptions about the morality of leaving the child and having time away from him may be needed before they will be able to accept short-term care, which can provide an answer that relatives and friends cannot.

9. By offering advice about any specific marital and sexual problems which may arise.

10. By providing access to information and advice about the implications of hereditary conditions, and those which are likely to deteriorate.

Childhood and adolescence

As the child grows and develops further problems arise, particularly in adolescence. Educational problems require active liaison with teachers and educational psychologists, and parents may need help with developing their child's leisure interests. After puberty, with the development of fertility and sexual awareness, the parents will require contraceptive advice and suitable literature about how to cope with the sexuality of a mentally handicapped child.

Once the child has left school the Careers Officers and the Disablement Resettlement Officer may advise about employment, training centres and sheltered workshops, or MENCAP may be able to link a young person with a supporter at work through its Pathway Scheme. Eventually the parents will have to make provision so that their handicapped offspring is able to live independently of them. Financial and residential provision will probably be the most pressing needs. Finally throughout the contact the social worker has with the mentally handicapped individual and his family, there will be additional unpredicted difficulties like death, divorce, illness and redundancy. At such times of crisis it will be necessary to intensify the emotional and practical support which otherwise is being provided continually, in order to assist the handicapped child and his family to make the best possible adjustment.

SUMMARY

Radical policy changes with respect to the care of the mentally handicapped have resulted in a shift from institution-based care to community care. This has placed a much greater burden upon the families who must care for their handicapped offspring.

In order to accommodate the fact that their child is handicapped, parents need to mourn for the child they had anticipated but have lost. For many the pain of having a handicapped child is life-long, and parents exhibit a variety of ways of coping with this.

Families with mentally handicapped children meet a number of subsequent difficulties, some emotional, some educational, and some material. These may, in time, exert a great strain upon the family structure, and can result in serious and, at times, irrevocable changes in family relationships.

The appropriate remedial help is not always available. As well as necessary medical and paramedical care much can be achieved by the interventions of a well trained social worker. Highly developed interactive skills are essential, and these must be coupled with an extensive knowledge of local services and an ability to use them.

Statutory and voluntary services can be supplemented by a variety of self-help methods which can be developed, with suitable guidance, by the parents themselves.

Acknowledgement

The author wishes to thank the British Association for Counselling for their kind permission to reproduce material which has already been published in 'Counselling' No 39, January 1982.

CASE STUDIES

Stephanie Price

Stephanie Price was 2½ years old when she was referred to the Paediatric Assessment Centre because of delayed speech and language development. Her parents felt there were no other problems and that, in time, her speech would improve naturally. In fact, at the end of the week's assessment, Stephanie was found to be severely mentally handicapped. No obvious cause was given, but it was suggested that the parents be referred for genetic counselling.

The revelation to the parents was devastating. They were so shocked that they sat in silence, unable to speak. Then they questioned the paediatrician about the certainty of his findings, and finally left the interview in a state of uncertainty and bewilderment. It was not clear that they had learned much from the interview.

After 3 days they were seen at home by the social worker. The weekend had been tearful and sleepless and they could scarcely believe what, to them, seemed to be a dream. They repeated mutual reassurances about Stephanie's normality, and the grandparents, whom they had telephoned, reinforced their incredulity by suggesting that the paediatrician 'did not know what he was talking about.' Their disbelief was accompanied by paradoxical requests for information about the handicap. As much as possible, the social worker answered these, and for the remainder it was suggested that the parents make notes in preparation for the next clinic appointment.

In subsequent interviews it was clear that they had experienced difficulty not only with medical jargon but with the implications of some of the paediatrician's statements like 'she will not develop at the same rate as her peers . . . she will develop at approximately half the normal rate . . . she will be slow.' They were desperate for reasons. Was it due to drugs taken in pregnancy or to toxaemia? Should Mrs Price have rested more? Was it due to 'his' side of the family — to his cousin with epilepsy? They scoured medical books loaned by friends or borrowed from the local library. Throughout their searching their doubts about the accuracy of the investigations continued, and still they wondered if a mistake had occurred.

Over the weeks the disbelief faded, and Mrs Price was able to admit that she had already wondered about Stephanie's slow development but had put it down to the fact that her own side of the family had always been dull at school, and slow to learn. However, because he adored her so much she had avoided discussing this with Stephanie's father, hoping to be able to 'bring her up to scratch' without causing him any worry about her disabilities. Having had no previous experience of children, and because he spent so much time away from home, Mr Price had remained quite ignorant of the problem until she attended for assessment.

They had hoped to embark on further pregnancies, but now they feared that they might not cope with another child and that the handicap might be repeated. A delay in referral for genetic counselling was the stimulus for Mr Price's anger. He directed this at the paediatrician and at the educational psychologist who had carried out the psychological assessment, questioning her credentials and her suitability for the task. This difficult period was punctuated by feelings of guilt so powerful that Mrs Price eventually became convinced that she was entirely to blame. Through the barrage of ill-feeling and self-blame the task of providing emotional support fell to the social worker.

Their physical health suffered. Mr Price lost his appetite and spent 2 weeks away from work. Mrs Price had recurrent digestive complaints, and both complained of insomnia and agitation. Their social life was wrecked. They avoided friends, and Mr Price ceased to talk, as he once had, about his daughter. He avoided all mention of his own family, and Mrs Price isolated herself at home, avoiding the shops for fear of awkward questions from other mothers.

Genetic counselling settled the matter of aetiology. The problem was the result of a 'one in a million' chance of these parents coming together. There was a one in four chance of further children being affected. Immediately Mrs Price's guilt lifted and her husband's anger dissolved. They became interested in finding ways of caring for Stephanie, and Mrs Price was once more able to take a loving interest in her husband. They decided to delay the decision about a further pregnancy until Stephanie reaches the age of 5 years.

At last they were able to make use of practical help. They asked to be put in touch with other parents, and they joined a self-help group. Mrs Price attended the Red Cross Toy Library and a peripatetic teacher for preschool children offered advice about suitable play material.

After 6 months their sorrow remained apparent, but they were calmer and had found the support of other parents immensely helpful. Strangely, the experience had brought them closer to one another, and they felt a mutual commitment to look after and support their daughter. To avoid their becoming exclusively involved in her care, the social worker's final intervention was to point out the responsibility towards one another and to suggest that their own social life should be developed. In this way the Price's were helped towards a more balanced attitude to their daughter's handicap and towards a rewarding marriage, as well as a satisfactory family life.

Gemma Knight

The second case study describes a girl who had spastic quadriplegia. Despite a chronological age of 14 months, Gemma Knight was at a developmental equivalent of only 3 months and was considered to be severely mentally and physically handicapped. Mrs Knight, her mother, had recognised the stiffness of her legs but thought that the problem was merely physical, and that Gemma was slow because she had been 'spoiled', but that she would eventually 'catch up'. By the age of 5 years would join her brothers at school and ultimately would follow in the family's footsteps by going to university.

Gemma had been born of a pregnancy which followed a difficult period in Mrs Knight's marriage, a pregnancy which she thought would alleviate the marital disharmony. It did not, and her husband left. He disclaimed any responsibility for the pregnancy and Gemma was born during the emotional upheaval of a divorce. Gemma was a source of great joy and comfort for Mrs Knight. She responded by trying to 'make up' for the loss of her father and, by her own admission, spoiled her by over-indulgence. Mrs Knight could not come to terms with the cerebral palsy and severe mental handicap, and told no one — not even close friends or relatives. Instead she maintained a pretence in which no one else knew of the periodic visits to hospital and, of course, no one ever dared to mention Gemma's obvious handicaps. Mrs Knight felt that she had failed, through her broken marriage as a woman, and through the birth of an abnormal child as a mother. Amidst these problems it was much too painful for her to talk of Gemma's condition.

Several therapeutic interventions were offered. Regular physiotherapy was coupled with close social work support and close liaison between the two services meant that questions raised with the physiotherapist in the morning session could be processed by the social worker later in the day. The social worker's first tasks were to determine:

1. how much Mrs Knight had been told about Gemma's condition,
2. her understanding of this,
3. her appreciation of its implications in terms of Gemma's abilities and disabilities.

This involved a discussion of normal developmental mile-stones, which was made easier by the fact that Mrs Knight already had two non handicapped children, as well as tactful exposure of her worst fears and her hopes and expectations for Gemma.

In fact, she had appreciated little of what she had been told at the previous clinic appointment, and she was quite certain that nothing had been said at the time of the birth, even though she was troubled at the time by the turmoil of the divorce. She remembered feeling the need to maintain her composure at the postnatal clinic appointment, and to appear sensible and intelligent. The paediatri-

cian appealed to her intelligence by assuming that she understood the terms 'spastic', 'quadriplegia' and 'educationally subnormal'. Occasional phrases like 'brain damage', 'retarded' and 'treat as normal' stood out in her memory, and she left the interview bewildered, too ashamed to reveal her ignorance to the paediatrician. Gemma's prematurity had further confused the significance of her delayed milestones, but behind the confusion lay Mrs Knight's unremitting fear that her daughter might be a 'total vegetable' who would be incapable of an independent or useful life. After all, no one had told her what to expect, and so she anticipated the worst for the much longed for little girl, who she had hoped would achieve academically, and who later would become a career woman.

Over the course of several interviews, and with the help of a paediatrician who was a skilled counsellor, Gemma's problems and their implications were discussed along with a full explanation of the terminology which Mrs Knight had been given. The future implications in terms of education, physical health, independent living and social development were explained as far as was possible, and Mrs Knight was put in touch with parents of handicapped children so that she might gain firsthand experience from those who had encountered these problems already. Practical help was provided through instruction in physiotherapy exercises, referral to the Red Cross Toy Library, and an introduction to a workshop for parents of mentally and physically handicapped children.

Because she feared that friends and relatives might respond with exaggerated pity or rejection, difficult and embarrassing encounters were role-played with the social worker to prepare her for the day she told them about Gemma. This she did, and 18 months after the first referral to the social worker she had regained her confidence, so that she was able to befriend other parents of newly diagnosed mentally handicapped children and had become a group leader in the parents' workshops. She had discussed Gemma's difficulties with her own family and friends, and was surprised by their sympathy and understanding. Furthermore, difficulties with her husband no longer caused the anguish they previously had, and she found she was able to take these in her stride.

Barry Ronson

The third case study concerns Mr and Mrs Ronson, whose only child, Barry, had been normal until he was 6 years old, when he was diagnosed as having a brain tumour. Major surgery followed, but there was considerable brain damage. From being a healthy, bright boy Barry became mentally handicapped with a hemiplegia, impaired vision and dysarthria. He could no longer attend his usual school and a place was provided for him at a school for the educationally subnormal.

Due to her inability to discuss it, and her avoidance of talking about its implications, it was clear that Mrs Ronson had not yet come to terms with Barry's handicaps. Nor had she grieved for him, since she avoided photographs taken of him before he became ill, and clothes which he used to wear. She could not talk of how he used to be, and yet had the constant reminder and unrelenting stress of his frequent admissions to hospital as well as his markedly altered and difficult behaviour. Moreover, she denied that Barry's change had created any problems, and she blamed her general practitioner and the hospital for his condition.

Her own health was affected by tiredness, loss of energy and a variety of fleeting, rather non-specific symptoms, which were thought to be psychosomatic. The marriage offered little support because her husband, who was clearly experiencing the same distress as she, was in no position to cope with her sorrow as well as his own. They lost contact with friends and family, and Mrs Ronson became isolated from her principal source of support, her own mother. Being an only child, and hence very special to his mother, Barry became overprotected. He was not allowed to play with other children or to engage in any hazardous activi-

ties. He received constant supervision even when this was unnecessary.

A period of 3 months after the initial involvement of the social worker, a crisis developed. Barry's condition deteriorated, which necessitated a hospital admission, possibly for further surgery. Mrs Ronson became extremely tearful and anxious. She cried bitterly, experienced severe panic attacks, and felt that she could cope no longer. Her husband was bewildered and quite unable to contribute anything constructive. Through intensive contact over the subsequent 3 days the parents were encouraged to grieve for their son by talking about how life had been. Their mourning was guided with the use of photographs of Barry, his clothing, and his possessions. Their unfulfilled expectations were aired, and they were encouraged to relinquish these in favour of more realistic aims. They were also encouraged to express their anger, resentment and hostility towards friends, family and health workers, including the social worker. Their mutual sense of inadequacy, personal failure and guilt were examined and tested, so that, where appropriate, some attempt could be made to restructure the irrational views which they had of themselves.

As the crisis passed the couple were able to receive Barry home again, but their anger towards the social worker intensified. They suggested that because therapy was so painful the contact should end. However, with tactful persistence and gradual, repeated exposure to those aspects which distressed them most, dramatic changes occurred. They requested literature about Barry's handicaps, and allowed Barry to play outside with local boys. Contact with the extended family was re-established, and maternal grandmother babysat once a week whilst the parents went out together, alone. Finally, Mrs Ronson took a part-time job.

Recently the couple have talked about becoming foster parents, and have expressed a desire to 'befriend' other parents who, like them, have recently learned of their child's handicap. Lately they have planned a holiday with old friends, whilst Barry is to have his own holiday with his grandmother.

John Robinson

The Robinson family is the subject of the fourth case study. Mrs Robinson was referred to the social worker for advice about family holidays and finance, because her husband had recently been made redundant from his work. She and her husband were 33 years old and had four children: Linda, the eldest, was 15 years old. David was 12, John 11, and Sally 6 years old. John had been severely mentally handicapped since birth, was doubly incontinent, non-ambulant and without speech.

The simple problem with which they presented seemed to be a request for help with much wider difficulties. The family was in a crisis and on the verge of breaking up. The parents argued incessantly. Linda demanded money to buy clothes with which to impress the local youths and regularly stayed out late at night in defiance of her parents' orders. David was truanting from school and had recently been caught in the act of 'shoplifting'. Sally was becoming 'cheeky' and disobedient.

Although they had not had a holiday for 12 years, Mrs Robinson's suspicion that her husband would object to a holiday with the rest of the family proved correct. The background to this emerged in subsequent interviews. Mr Robinson admitted that he had never 'got over' the initial shock of John's handicap. He had felt ashamed, and so would never agree to go on holiday with John. He refused to allow John to be taken to the local shops by his brothers or sisters, or to sit in the front garden for fear of attracting critical attention. His very manhood had been slighted, and had been only partially restored by Sally's birth. Mrs Robinson had been equally devastated but was the one who had to cope and keep the family together. Hard and tiring as it was, she refused to admit that John was any trouble to her at all. Linda, however, found his bruxism irritating, and was tired of babysitting. Even this anger was muted, and she was able to express little more than sorrow for the boy. David, who shared a bedroom with John, complained only that he was occasionally woken by him at night. Otherwise he loved him very much. Sally knew him as a brother, and her thoughts went no further than this.

Mrs Robinson had recently started work as a barmaid in a public house, ostensibly because of the need for the money, but she enjoyed meeting people, and dressing up and going out. She found her time away from home relaxing and yet still made no connection with John and the obvious problems he created for her. Mr Robinson would go to play darts in another public house, Linda preferred to meet with the local boys, and David stayed out of the house as much as possible. Eventually David 'got into trouble' with the police for stealing, and with the education authority for truancy.

Surprisingly, they had had no contact for 10 years with any agency which might have been of help with the management of John's handicaps. To the social worker there were eight obvious problems:

1. The parents no longer communicated with one another.
2. The whole family was locked into a bland denial that John presented any problems at all.
3. Mr Robinson had never accepted John as he was.
4. David was truanting and rapidly becoming delinquent.
5. Normal family life had ceased.
6. They were beset by financial difficulties.
7. There were obvious practical problems in caring for John.
8. Mother's health was poor.

The parents agreed to some interventions. The social worker liaised with the social services department's occupational therapist to provide a stair lift and bathing aids, whilst the Family Fund supplied a washing machine and tumble drier. Arrangements were made with the Electricity and Gas Boards, and a grant from a voluntary organisation helped alleviate some of their financial difficulties. A series of family interviews permitted family members to express their grievances and a tentative agreement was given to John's spending a weekend in short-term care. Finally some help was offered with David's problems which involved meetings with the school, the education welfare officer, the social services department, the educational psychologist and the leader of David's intermediate treatment group.

These interventions were partially successful. The practical arrangements were satisfactory. The marriage improved as Mrs Robinson gave up her job and Mr Robinson made more effort with practical tasks in the home. This meant that they then had more time to spend together and could go out together as a couple. Linda was more relaxed at home and became less demanding. She contracted to help more at home in return for the privilege of staying out late at night and of entertaining her boyfriend at home. However, David's position in the family turned out to be irretrievable. He continued to offend and appeared in court on two further occasions. Fortunately he had a strong relationship with the Intermediate Treatment worker who was able to support the recommendation that David be given a place in a children's home. His parents, particularly his father, who by now had disowned him, gladly accepted the recommendation. Despite much persuasion, which even involved John's spending an experimental night in care, Mrs Robinson could not come to terms with the idea of short-term care, and cancelled this arrangement at the last moment.

The social worker felt that the family's attitudes and behaviour had become so entrenched over the previous 11 years that it was unable to undergo any fundamental changes. Relationships in the family had become distorted by the myth that John was no trouble at all and by an unwritten rule that no-one should criticize him. Throughout John's life one sacrifice after another had accommodated him, culminating in the final sacrifice: the scapegoating and rejection of the son who rebelled.

Social work support will not stop here. More effort will be made to help the parents gain a more realistic perspective of the difficulties which John presents. At the same time it will be necessary to help them to plan for the future, and existing interventions with their marital problems will continue. Above all, care will be taken to ensure that Linda and Sally do not suffer the same rejection which has already ousted David from the family.

REFERENCES

Attwood A J 1978 The Croydon workshop for parents of pre-school mentally handicapped children. Child: Care, Health and Development 4: 79–91

Bacquer S A 1977 The inhibited pursuit of better life for the mentally retarded in the community. Research Exchange and Practice in Mental Retardation 3(2): 96–108

Bayley M 1973 Mental handicap and community care. Routledge and Kegan Paul, London

Bayley N, Rhodes L, Gooch B 1966 A comparison of the development of institutionalised and home-reared mongoloids. California Health Research Digest 4(3): 104–05

Berg J M, Gilderdale S, Way J 1969 On telling parents of a diagnosis of mongolism. British Journal of Psychiatry 115: 1195–1196

Better Services for the Mentally Handicapped 1971 Cmnd 4683. HMSO, London

Blake W On another's sorrow. In: Keynes G (ed) 1976 Completed writings. Oxford University Press, London

Bone M, Spain B, Martin F M 1972 Plans and provisions for the mentally handicapped. Allen and Unwin, London

Bowlby J 1951 Maternal care and mental health. World Health Organisation Monograph Series No 2, Geneva

Bowlby J 1969 Attachment and loss: I Attachment. Hogarth Press, London

Bowlby J 1973 Attachment and loss: II Separation, anxiety and anger. Hogarth Press, London

Bowlby J 1980 Attachment and loss: III Loss, sadness and depression. Basic Books, New York

Bradshaw J, Lawton D 1978 Tracing the causes of stress in families with handicapped children. British Journal of Social Work 8(2): 181–191

Burden R L 1980 Measuring the effects of stress on the mothers of handicapped infants: Must depression always follow? Child: Care, Health and Development 6: 111–125

Butler N, Gill R, Pomeroy D M, Fewtrell J 1978 Handicapped children — their homes and life styles. University of Bristol Publications, Bristol.

Carkuff R R, Truax C B 1967 Towards effective counselling and psychotherapy. Aldine Publishing, Chicago

Carnegie Trust 1964 Handicapped children and their families. Carnegie Trust, Dunfermline.

Carr E F, Oppe T E 1971 The birth of an abnormal child: telling the parents. Lancet II: 1075–1077

Carr, J 1970 Mongolism: telling the parents. Developmental Medicine and Child Neurology 12: 213–221

Carr J 1976 Effect on the family of a child with Down's syndrome. Physiotherapy 62: 20–24

Centerwall S A, Centerwall W H 1960 A study of children with mongolism reared in the home compared to those reared away from home. Pediatrics 25: 678–85

Cohen P 1962 The impact of the handicapped child on the family. Social Casework 43: 137–142

Collins M, Collins D 1976 Kith and kids: self-help for families of the handicapped. Souvenir Press, London

Court S D M 1976 'Fit for the Future'. Report of the Committee on child health services. Cmnd 6684. HMSO, London

Cummings S T 1976 The impact of the child's deficiency on the father: a study of mentally retarded and of chronically ill children. American Journal of Orthopsychiatry 46: 246–255

Cunningham C Parent Counselling. In: Craft M (ed) 1979 Tredgold's mental retardation, 12th edn. Bailliere Tindall, London

Cunningham C, Sloper P 1977 Parents of Down's syndrome babies: their early needs. Child: Care, Health and Development 3: 325–47

Drillien C H, Wilkinson E M 1964 Mongolism: when should parents be told? British Medical Journal 2: 1306–1307

Drotar D, Baskiewitz A, Irvin N, Kennel J, Klaus M 1975 The adaptation of parents to the birth of an infant with a congenital malformation: a hypothetical model. Pediatrics 56(5): 710–717

Eaton J W, Weil R J 1955 Culture and mental disorders: a comparative study of the Hutterites and other populations. Illinois Free Press, Glencoe

Franklin A W 1958 Care of the mongol baby: the first phase. Lancet I: 256–258

Gath A 1977 The impact of an abnormal child upon the parents. British Journal of Psychiatry 130: 405–410

Gath A 1978 Down's syndrome and the family — the early years. Academic Press, London

Gayton W F, Walker L 1974 Down's syndrome: Informing the parents. American Journal of Diseases in Children 127: 510–512

Gilmore D W, Oates R K 1977 Counselling about Down's syndrome: the parents' viewpoint. The Medical Journal of Australia 2: 600–603

Hannam C 1975 Parents and mentally handicapped children. Penguin, Harmondsworth

Health and Welfare: the development of community care 1963. Ministry of Health. Cmnd 1973. HMSO, London

Heilman A 1950 Parents' adjustment to the dull handicapped child. American Journal of Mental Deficiency 54: 556–562

Hewett S, Newsom J, Newsom E 1970 The family and the handicapped child. Allen and Unwin, London

Holt K S 1958 The influence of a retarded child upon family limitation. Pediatrics 22: 744–755

Jacobs J 1977. Symposium on professional relationships in the field of mental handicap: Improving communications between health service professionals and parents of handicapped children, a case study. British Journal of Mental Subnormality 23: 54–60

Jay P 1979 Report of the Committee of Inquiry into Mental Handicap Nursing and Care. Cmnd 7468. HMSO, London

Jones K 1975 Opening the door: A study of new policies for the mentally handicapped. Routledge and Kegan Paul, London

Kerry M 1980 Mentally handicapped people in Leicestershire. Leicestershire Area Health Authority (T), Leicestershire Social Services Department

King R D, Raynes N V, Tizard J 1971 Patterns of residential care. Routledge and Kegan Paul, London

Klaus M H, Kennell J H 1970. Mothers separated from their newborn infant. Pediatric Clinics of North America 17(4): 1015–1037

Kushlik A 1970 Residential care for the mentally subnormal. Royal Society Health Journal 90(5): 255–261

Leck I, Gordon W L, McKeowan 1967. Medical and social needs of patients in hospitals for the mentally subnormal. British Journal of Preventive and Social Medicine 21: 115–121

Lonsdale G 1978 Family life with a handicapped child: the parents speak. Child: Care, Health and Development 4: 99–120

Lucas P J, Lucas A M 1980 Down's syndrome: telling the parents. British Journal of Mental Subnormality 26: 21–31

Lyle J G 1960 The effect of an institution environment upon the verbal development of imbecile children III: the Brooklands residential family unit. Journal of Mental Deficiency and Research 4: 14–23

Mawson D, Marks I M, Ramm L, Stern R S 1981 Guided mourning for morbid grief: A controlled study. British Journal of Psychiatry 138: 185–193

McCormack M 1978 A mentally handicapped child in the family: a guide for parents. Constable, London

Mental Handicap. Progress, problems and priorities 1980: A review of mental handicap services in England since the 1971 White Paper 'Better services for the mentally handicapped'. DHSS, London

Mittler P 1979 Patterns of partnership between parents and professionals. Parents Voice June: 10–12

Murray-Parkes C 1965 Bereavement and mental illness Parts I and II. British Journal of Medical Psychology 38(1): 1–26

Nichols P 1967 A day in the life of Joe Egg. Faber, London

Olshansky S 1962 Chronic sorrow: A response to having a mentally defective child. Social Casework 43: 190–193

Parmelee A H 1956 Management of the mongol in childhood. International Rehabilitation Medicine 169: 358–361

Pinkerton P 1970 Parental acceptance of the handicapped child. Developmental Medicine and Child Neurology 12: 207–212

Report of the Royal Commission on the Law relating to Mental Illness and Mental Deficiency 1954–57. Cmnd 169. HMSO, London

Revill S, Blunden R 1977. Home training of pre-school children with developmental delay. Report on the development and evaluation of the Portage Service in South Glamorgan. Mental Handicap in Wales Applied Research Unit, Ely Hospital, Cardiff

Richards B W 1964 Mental subnormality in the general hospital. Journal of Mental Subnormality 10: 19–2

Schumacher H C 1945 Contribution of the child

guidance clinic to the problem of mental deficiency. American Journal of Mental Deficiency 50: 277–283

Shipe D, Shotwell A 1965 Effect of out of home care on mongoloid children: a continuous study. American Journal of Mental Deficiency 69: 649–652

Solnit A J, Stack M H 1961 Mourning and the birth of a defective child. Psychoanalytic Study of the Child 16: 523–537

Spain B, Wigley J 1975 (eds) Right from the start: A service for families with a young handicapped child. National Society for Mentally Handicapped Children, London

Stedman D J, Eichorn D H 1964 A comparison of the growth and development of institutionalised and home reared mongoloids during infancy and early childhood. American Journal of Mental Deficiency 69: 381–401

Stone H 1973 The birth of a child with Down's syndrome. Scottish Medical Journal 18: 182–187

Tarran E C 1981 Parents' views of medical and social work services for families with young cerebral-palsied children. Developmental Medicine and Child Neurology 23: 173–182

'Tears and Joy' 1981 Bristol Broadsides (Co-op) Ltd, Bristol

Tew B J, Lawrence K M, Payne H, Rawnsley K 1977. Marital stability following the birth of a child with Spina Bifida. British Journal of Psychiatry 131: 79–82

Tizard J 1960 The residential care of mentally handicapped children. In: Richards B W (ed) Proceedings of the London Conference of the Association for the Scientific Study of Mental Deficiency. May and Baker, Dagenham

Tizard, J, Grad J C 1961 The mentally handicapped and their families. Maudsley Monograph No 7, Oxford University Press, London

Welsh National School of Medicine. See McCormack M 1978

Wilkin D 1979 Caring for the mentally handicapped child. Croom Helm, London

Wing L. See Spain B, Wigley G (eds) 1975

Wolfenberger W 1967 Counselling parents of the retarded. In: Baumeister A (ed) Mental retardation. University of London Press, London

Yates M L, Lederer R 1961 Small, short-term group meetings with parents of children with mongolism. American Journal of Mental Deficiency 65: 467–72

14

Management of care

- Aim of care is to allow the individual to develop to his maximum level of independent functioning
- Care must be individually planned, consistent and continuous
- Care should be based on careful assessment and plans regularly evaluated
- Care is most effectively planned by a multi-disciplinary team
- All staff should be actively involved in setting team goals

INTRODUCTION

Society, which once condoned and even encouraged an institutional, custodial approach to care, has become more conscious of its duty to treat people with mental handicap the same as any other group. The view that people with mental handicap were a burden or even a danger to society is being replaced gradually by a growing acceptance that they are people in their own right, and given support and opportunities are able to enjoy a full and more meaningful life.

This growing concern for those with mental handicap and their right to be seen as people rather than patients has had some effect on the everyday care are provided in institutions looking after the mentally handicapped. Care is no longer being seen as an essentially passive exercise which provides for basic physical needs, such as food and warmth, in as efficient a manner as possible; rather now it is seen as creating a stimulating yet stable environment which affords mentally handicapped individuals the opportunity to develop to their fullest potential. This care may range from acquiring bladder control to learning how to prepare and cook a simple meal, and it involves providing a quality of life which does not fall below what is considered acceptable for the rest of society.

PURPOSE OF CARE

The ultimate aim of all care must be to allow an individual to develop to his maximum level of independent functioning. For development to take place, people, no matter how handicapped, must be given the opportunity to experience the usual physical and emotional contacts. They must be given responsibility for not only tending to their physical needs but for all their actions and activities. The individual must be allowed to make decisions about matters that concern him, but he must also learn to live with the consequences of his decision making, particularly if it was the wrong one:

> The right to freedom of choice for the retarded individual involves the right to fail.
>
> Blackwell, 1979

WHO PROVIDES THE CARE?

The needs of any individual or group cannot be met by any one person. Thus care of the mentally handicapped person cannot be considered the sole province of any one particular discipline. The needs of individuals demand that the provision of care requires the skills and expertise of a variety of specialists — a multi-disciplinary team. Using their combined efforts, the aim of the team is to teach the mentally handicapped person, no matter how handicapped, to live as independently as possible. The success, or otherwise, of the team is dependent upon the effectiveness of the care staff.

As a result of their 24 hr a day contact, care staff are best placed to identify the problems and difficulties that a person has in actually living from day to day. If therapists are to gain an accurate picture of an individual, they are dependent on the care staff supplying them with detailed and accurate information about the person. In turn, care staff are responsible for ensuring that therapy initiated by a specialist takes place wherever possible as part of the daily routine.

In hospitals for the mentally handicapped

the ward charge nurse is at the crossover point between therapists, who have specialised roles in relation to an individual, and the direct care staff whose comprehensive role is to teach the mentally handicapped person how to live and cope with living. He is best placed to balance the clinical and personal considerations in programming and also interpret and present the views of the different groups to each other. This unique position makes the charge nurse the most appropriate person to co-ordinate the activities of the team.

The idea of working as a member of a team, let alone co-ordinating it, is often a source of great consternation among nursing or care staff. So often one hears the comment that the team is ignorant of the person's real needs and merely interferes with the work of the direct care staff. The answer to this problem lies in the hands of the care staff themselves. If they wish care programmes to reflect what they see as a person's needs then they must be fully involved in the creation of those programmes.

HOW CARE IS PROVIDED

Any unit for mentally handicapped people will contain individuals with a variety of abilities and handicaps. The team running the unit is constantly faced with the problem of reconciling the needs of the individual with the demands of the group. To achieve an equitable solution the needs of every member of the group must be discovered so that any routine is developed around the individual and not a blanket treatment irrespective of differences.

For individual programme planning to be most effective it must be organised in a systematic and standardised way for everyone in the unit. This will ensure that all residents are given equal consideration and also help to reduce the tendency of a minority to dominate the attention of staff to the detriment of the majority. Of course certain individuals will always require more resources than others to meet their needs. However an organised system of determining needs, planning care and assessing its progress will help to ensure that, nearly always, insufficient resources are most effectively deployed. Programming encourages interaction to take place within normal activities and means that residents do not have to display inappropriate behaviour before staff will relate to them.

This approach does not mean that the unit becomes a highly structured, formal living environment. Rather, it allows the unit staff to assess accurately what their residents' needs are and the most appropriate way of meeting them. This will be as intensive or as low key as the unit staff themselves think necessary to meet the residents' needs adequately. It will certainly bring organisation and structure to the work of the staff, but not to the life of the resident, and in doing so allow a more effective distribution of their efforts.

A process which allows for future evaluation of planned nursing intervention is essential if care staff aim to monitor an individual's progress and utilise fully the contribution of a multidisciplinary team. In the past evaluation was either carried out as a particular problem arose and dealt with on a day-to-day basis, information being passed on verbally, or continuing needs were considered generally not individually. If needs are not met, problems will occur. The problem/progress orientated record system and the concept of the nursing process are effective methods of meeting needs as they provide a framework for individual care.

MANAGEMENT OF CARE

The management of care for people with mental handicap living in residential care has changed over the years, and is now becoming more structured. Until recently the major approach to care has been by means of the traditional case conference but this has come in for criticism:

1. Information concerning the client is often held by the respective disciplines involved in his care and is not always available to other disciplines involved in the care structure.

2. Clients' problems are not always defined at the case conference, e.g. due to the complexity and range of problems that some clients present. There is a tendency also for the obvious problems to be dealt with first.

3. When the problems are recognised, the treatment approach to care is often stated in general terms, and not in 'specific' treatment terms.

4. The clients' problems and treatment plans are not systematically and routinely assessed usually because of the time interval between each client being discussed. In some instances it can be months before a review of the client's case comes before the case conference.

The implication for the client is that difficulties in treatment and new problems emerging are not recognised quickly enough, this in turn sometimes compounds the problem and makes it worse.

5. Treatments are not routinely programmed — the problems of an urgent nature are given attention whereas the problems of lesser urgency are not always programmed. At the case conference usually a limited number of cases can be dealt with, i.e. one or two cases each week. The time factor in discussing each case can vary from weeks to months.

6. Important aspects of treatment within some programmes are not specified in enough detail. Without specific instructions or a step by step approach to the treatment of the client, staff can develop different approaches to the treatment. This inconsistency in turn confuses the client and retards his progress.

7. The recording of the client's progress and events often lag behind the events, so that treatment becomes out of step. Each discipline involved in treatment reviews treatment at a different time resulting in an individual's progress being assessed on a piecemeal basis during a period of several months.

As a result of these shortcomings of the traditional case conference approach, it became more and more obvious to the nursing staff who deal with the day-to-day management care of the client that a more structured, positive approach to the overall care for mentally handicapped residents was urgently required.

PROBLEM-ORIENTATED RECORD SYSTEM

One system of management care that was examined as a possible alternative approach was designed by Weed (1970). A problem-oriented record system, it is concerned with care from the medical viewpoint.

The basic components of Weed's system are:

1. Information base.
2. Problem list.
3. Treatment plan.
4. Progress record.

As a medical model, a major disadvantage of this system is that decisions on treatment are made by doctors despite the fact that the people who are closest to the care of the client are nurses, and their view of management care of the client may not be considered in the doctor's decision about the management of care. However, this drawback can be overcome by allowing all disciplines to take an active role in the planning and management of the client.

PROBLEM/PROGRESS ORIENTED RECORD SYSTEM

This system, an adaptation of Weed's approach, was designed principally by the nursing team, with the senior members of the nursing team contributing to the main structure, and other disciplines giving advice and support to the development. The nurse was strongly represented mainly because of the expertise the nurse has in recognising the problems of the client, and in developing the management of care.

As the system was designed to meet the individual requirements of the mentally handicapped person, its main advantage is that it can be adjusted and expanded to meet the changing needs of the handicapped person. In contrast to the conventional record system it outlines a whole multitude of reports and outdated material relating to the individual in a chronological way.

The conventional system makes it difficult to evaluate and assess current position of care without a painstaking search through the file. Furthermore you find that detailed progress of the individual is likely to be held by a number of other disciplines, e.g. social workers, speech therapists, psychologists so that there is a considerable degree of duplication. The advantage of this system is that it gives an instant profile of the individual that is available to all staff. The record system is held together in a clip folder, which makes it easy to add or delete sections as required and kept in a central file.

General structure of the system

The system is sub-divided into separate sections which are clearly named:

1. Information (general details).
2. Photograph of client.
3. Information and assessment data base contents.
4. Client's problem list defined.
5. Treatment programmes indicated for specific problems.
6. Progress records.
7. Summary records of progress.
8. Recreation/Occupation record.
9. Behavioural modification.
10. Drug application.
11. Community nursing/Social work record.

1. Information (general details) (Fig. 14.1)

General details of the client are recorded on admission, e.g. address, next of kin, date of birth, religion, family doctor, diagnosis, legal status, discharge date.

2. Photograph of client

A photograph of the client is included to aid easy recognition of the client by new staff and

GENERAL DETAILS

Name   *John Brown*

Address   *9 Oakpark Road*

Next of kin   *Parents (Same address)*

Date of birth   *10 March*

Admission date   *10 October*

Clinical diagnosis   *Moderate mental retardation Hyperactivity*

Family doctor   *Dr Smith, Health Centre*

Legal status   *Informal*

Religion   *Church of Scotland*

Discharge

Fig. 14.1 General details.

helps promote the idea of dealing with a person rather than a case.

3. Information and assessment data (Fig. 14.2)

The information contained within this section gives details of referral reasons, case history and updated assessments from the other disciplines directly involved in the patient's care, e.g. neurology, speech therapy, physiotherapy, psychology, social work, nursing.

The assessment reports outline when the person's situation was examined and details of problems and skills that the individual has; conclusions and recommendations are also included in these reports.

Date	Name: *John Brown*
	Preparation for town (1) Requires assistance in dressing ( ) (2) Minimum assistance required (√) (3) No assistance required ( )
	General behaviour Transport: *Bus* Response: *Poor* Remarks: *Appeared restless and agitated while travelling on buses.* Crowds: Response: *Fairly Good* Remarks: *Walks fairly well in large crowds, has a tendency to be familiar with strangers e.g. going up and talking to strangers.* Shops: Response: Remarks: *Similar forms of behaviour seen as expressed while travelling on buses e.g. restless behaviour, he wanders around the shops with no purpose in mind.*
	Recognition of common signs and items Remarks: *Difficult to assess owing to his poor communication skills.*
	Kerb drill/Green man crossings Response: Remarks: *Appears to have little or no knowledge of kerb drill.*

Fig. 14.2A–C Socialisation training programme assessment.

4. Client's problem list defined (Fig. 14.5)

The problems that the individual has should be itemised in order of priority. The list should also include the date the problem was recognised and the date when it is resolved. The problems are expressed in detail, e.g.

Violent behaviour
a. *To objects* — at times he will throw various objects which come to hand in order to get his own way.
b. *To parents and staff* — When confronted with controls and restrictions he will demonstrate violent behaviour towards

Date		
	Use of public toilets Remarks: *Uses the public toilets with some assistance being required.*	Response: *Fairly Good*
	Use of public transport Remarks: *Has very little knowledge of the general use of public transport.*	Response: *Poor*
	General hygiene skills (1) General Washing: *Requires prompting and assistance.* (2) Oral Hygiene: *As above.* (3) Bathing: *Enjoys his bath, requires general supervision.*	
	Domestic activity within house *Fails to achieve even the simplest form of domestic activity.*	
	Table etiquette *Reasonable level expressed, will use his fingers to eat if not supervised.*	
	Language development/Expression *Expressive language poor, has great difficulty in communicating his daily needs.*	

Fig. 14.2B

parents and staff alike, including kicking and striking out with his fists.

Urinary incontinence
Several times during the day, he will wet himself. This usually occurs shortly after mealtimes. There is no record of urinary incontinence at night.

Table etiquette
When left unobserved, he will eat with his fingers and steal food from other children. Note that he is able to eat with a knife and fork in a correct manner.

Kerb drill
He has little or no knowledge of how to

Date	**General interaction with adults/children** *Relates well to adults, does however find some difficulties in relating to his own age group due to his overactivity.*
	Social interests/Hobbies *Somewhat limited for a child of his ability.* *Spends most of his time viewing television.*
	Dressing/Undressing skills *No problems. Can dress himself fairly well.*
	Enuresis: day/night *No problems.*
	Assessment carried out by (1) *C/N R. Adams* (2) *S/N J. Jones* (3) *H/A K. Smith*
	Recommendations *(1) General control of his overactive behaviour.* *(2) Refer to speech therapist for programme development.* *(3) Instruct and develop his social skills in a broad area.* *(4) Expand his social development in all areas possible.*

Fig. 14.2C

cross the road, has a tendency to run out on to the road when in town or streets.

5. Treatment programmes indicated for specific problems (Fig. 14.6)

The treatment programme prescribed will give detailed specific approaches to the problem areas identified.

Each of the other disciplines is involved in the care management according to their specialist area.

Programme example
Violence to objects
When this form of behaviour occurs, he should be instructed to clean up any mess without any assistance from the staff. Give 'specific' instructions in simple verbal commands repeating them to him several times until he understands what is being required of him.

Care staff give explicit instructions, and do not engage in any other form of conversation unless it is relevant to the treatment programme. It is the responsibility of the

charge nurse to check intermittently to see that the instructions are being carried out.

The progress of the programme is accurately recorded so that evaluation of the treatment can be carried out. This treatment data will help in adjusting or modifying the programme according to the previous progress.

This form of approach to the care of the mentally handicapped person gives continuity and consistency to the management care.

Programme implementation commences when the nursing staff and other disciplines have agreed the planned course of action and are committed to carrying it out.

The planning for the treatment programme is discussed and designed at the case review meeting at which all other disciplines are represented.

6. Progress records (Fig. 14.7)

Progress reports are received from all disciplines who are engaged in the treatment programme of the client. They are written in a form so that reference is made to the

Name *John Brown*	Ward _____
Date	*Referral letter from family doctor* *John is a young adolescent boy who demonstrates a degree of behavioural and communication problems.* *His mother is becoming considerably harassed and finding his problems difficult to cope with at home. His sleep patterns are also giving rise for concern. He usually sleeps for about 3–4 hours each night.* *I would be grateful if you would assess the child to see if he would be suitable for inpatient care in one of your units.*

Fig. 14.3 Referral letter

Name	*John Brown*		Ward
Date	*Multi-disciplinary meeting*		
	After discussing the case in general, it was agreed to admit this child for a period of assessment/training as soon as possible.		
	Areas where priority attention should be given:		
	(1) Overactive behaviour.		
	(2) Language communication skills.		
	(3) Sleep patterns.		

Fig. 14.4 Report from multi-disciplinary meeting

previous progress report, and will refer to specific areas in the treatment plan.

The frequency of the reports can vary, depending on the treatment programme itself. The progress report can be daily, weekly or monthly. The reports are received by the nurse in charge, and filed into the respective section.

7. Summary records of progress (Fig. 14.8)

With progress reports being submitted by various other disciplines, a synopsis of all the progress reports is made by the charge nurse. The overall summary report can be presented at the multidisciplinary group meeting, which will take place each month. This should allow for every client's case to be reviewed and discussed on a regular basis.

8. Recreation/Occupation

A general record is made of the recreational developments of each client, as this can often be used as a way of measuring development of the individual. This will assist the staff in participating, and becoming actively involved in developing the most suitable form of recreation for the client. It is especially valuable to the student learner on placement, which usually lasts for 13 weeks.

9. Behaviour modification

Behaviour modification is now an accepted part of the treatment programme for many mentally handicapped people. Records of behavioural programmes are kept separate from the treatment records because of the complex nature of some of them.

The behavioural data may include:

a. Case history of behaviours, and referral source.
b. Psychological and nursing assessments of behavioural problems.
c. A specific list of behavioural problems.
d. Specific details of programme planning to modify the behaviour problems, including time sampling, and baseline records etc.
e. The programme may also include a home-based programme which will give

Name	*John Brown*	Ward

Date	Problem list
	(1) Overactive Behaviour
	John demonstrates a fairly high degree of restless behaviour. He cannot sit for any lengthy period of time; most of his time is spent in walking about in an aimless fashion. Therefore this form of behaviour brings him into conflict with his peer group which he disrupts by his actions.
	(2) Communication Skills
	His expressive language skills are poor; most of his speech is unintelligible. *This in turn leads to frustration and agitation on his part.*
	(3) Sleep Rhythm Patterns
	Most nights John settles fairly quickly on going to bed. He does however usually only sleep for a period of 4 hours, then he is up and in an active state.

Fig. 14.5 Problems defined.

overall details of the family description of the programme, and a record of previous professional help, if any.

The behavioural assessment at home will help evaluate self-care and domestic reactions:

Eating
Dressing
Toileting habits and problems
General hygiene skills in detail
Sleeping patterns
Domestic help at home
Development of language and communication skills between parents and siblings
Play — what level of play the child has reached with his family and other children, and within the neighbourhood.

Independent Function Skills
Physical disabilities — visual, hearing, motor — what they are, and in order of priority.
Aggression — detailed description of aggression made to staff or others and of events leading up to the aggression.
Disruptive behaviour, a detailed account of incidents and circumstances surrounding them.
Educational Developments.

Parent/relative/client interaction can sometimes be of prime importance when assessing and evaluating the overall problem.

Name   John Brown_____   Ward_____

Date	Treatment plans
	Overactive Behaviour
	Owing to the degree of restless overactive behaviour that John presents, it was decided at the multi-disciplinary group to try and stabilise his behaviour by the use of a controlled drug Ritalin (5 mg) administered twice daily and increasing the dosage where necessary.
	Communication Skills
	It was expressed by the speech therapist that John would probably benefit from the use of Makaton sign language. It was decided to start him off using the basic signs from stage I, and selecting the ones he would find easy to communicate with. The words selected were: toilet, sit, come, good morning, please and thank-you. Once these words were being successfully used the range would be increased to cover more of the aspects of his daily living.
	Sleep Rhythm patterns
	In order to establish a more acceptable sleep rhythm pattern, he should first of all have a set time for going to his bed each night. A small dose of triclofos (10 ml) should be given 1 hour before going to bed.

Fig. 14.6 Treatment programme.

10. Drug management & Epilepsy Frequency record (Fig. 14.9)

Where drugs are being used, a record of the prescribed drug is recorded along with any changes to the drug required, e.g. drug, dose, date, commencement date, discontinued date, comments.

Prominence should be given to any known allergies and record of any side-effects observed is noted.

11. Community/Social work report

With the extension of community care, nursing personnel are becoming increasingly involved in visiting and supporting the mentally handicapped person and his family.

The expertise and information the nurse can bring are often invaluable, e.g. the nurse may be the link between home and the hospital and other specialised services. Information

Name	*John Brown*	Ward

Date	Progress Reports
	(1) Overactive Behaviour *A noticeable decrease in the level of his overactive forms of behaviour since commencing Ritalin 3 weeks ago.* *He is now concentrating more on relevant subjects. His mother has also commented on the reduction of his overactivity and finds it a welcome change.* *(2) Since his overactivity levels have been reduced he is now concentrating more on the instructions from the speech therapist and nursing staff. He has picked up all of the signs that were given to him and he is using them approximately. With this level of progress it has been recommended to increase his vocabulary range further with the use of Makaton.* *(3) Sleep Rhythm Pattern* *John has responded well to the small dose of triclofos. He is now sleeping right through the night on the dose prescribed.*

Fig. 14.7 Progress reports

about the existence of local self-help groups can be given so that families can share experiences and reduce the feelings of isolation and frustration that may have evolved.

After a nurse has made a home visit, a generalised report is written and any specific aspects of the visit noted and highlighted for the attention of other disciplines, e.g. social worker.

THE NURSING PROCESS

'The nursing process is an orderly systematic manner of determining the client's problems, making plans to solve them, initiating the plan or assigning others to implement it and evaluating the extent to which the plan was effective in resolving the problems identified.' (Yura & Walsh, 1973). The process is broken down into five stages:

1. Assessment
2. Problem identification
3. Planning
4. Implementation
5. Evaluation.

Assessment

Assessment is the corner stone of the process. If the initial assessment is inaccurate or inad-

Name _John Brown_	Ward _____	
Date		Signature
	1st Report to Multi-Disciplinary Team	

1st Report to Multi-Disciplinary Team

John has settled into the environment and is responding well to the treatment plan. With the general reduction of his hyper-activeness he has now responded well in his major problem areas.
His interaction with his peer group is now more positive and he is now accepted.

His communication is improving and this in turn is opening up new dimensions to him, especially in the social areas.
His parents are pleased with the initial response to the treatment plan.

In view of these developments it was agreed to continue with the treatment plan and to review his progress in 4 weeks.

Fig. 14.8 Progress report for multidisciplinary meeting.

equate, then all subsequent phases of the process are rendered ineffective. When assessing residents it is vital that performance is recorded in an objective, standard way so that: (1) everyone involved understands what is going on and can use the same language (2) when evaluation takes place it becomes a simple matter of reassessment using the same method (3) evaluation is then a matter of comparing performance before and after the programme and not staff trying to think whether any change has taken place or not.

There are several assessment scales, charts and schedules available, which have been specifically designed for use with the mentally handicapped. These will provide a great deal of the information required to identify needs. However, it should always be remembered that assessment is not the sole province of prepackaged rating procedures. The staff in situ are best placed to determine the most

appropriate assessment method for the members of their own particular group. If possible the resident, his family, or friends who are involved with him outside the unit should be consulted so that a more balanced and accurate assessment may be made and a link established between staff and families. This link is vital if meaningful planning is to take place.

Problem identification

Problem identification is translating the information which the assessment has provided into written form so that problems identified can be placed in order of priority. This enables staff to determine which problem to tackle first, and those that can be left to a later date, given the normal situation of limited resources. It also helps to establish a sense of proportion when considering which are the most debilitating problems.

Name *John Brown*				Ward _____
Drug	Dose	Date started	Date stopped	Comments
Ritalin	*5 mg*			*Given in order to try to reduce his overactive behaviour*
triclofos	*10 ml*			*Given to establish a more regular sleep rhythm pattern.*

Fig. 14.9 Drug record sheet.

Priority or a hierarchy may be established by classifying problems as follows:

a. Major problems — those which cause great distress to the resident or others and which significantly affect his lifestyle.
b. Intermediate problems — those which do not cause distress but do affect the lifestyle and independence of the resident e.g., a resident unable to feed himself.
c. Minor problems (idiosyncratic traits) — those which do not affect lifestyle, e.g. nose picking.
d. Potential problems — those which staff perceive may occur in the future.

The resident's, and his family's, own idea of what are problems must always be considered.

Planning

Whenever possible when planning intervention the resident and his family should be involved. This not only helps in co-operation with the intervention but also the fixing of realistic goals. Totally independent functioning is not always an achievable objective. However, families rarely desire such a high level of ability if they are willing to care for their relative and it may only require one particular problem to be overcome before a family resumes providing care. Also for a programme to succeed fully there must be a consistent approach from everyone involved with the resident. If programmes are only applied by unit staff, then there is a real danger that any change achieved will be confined to the unit.

The following rules should always be observed:

a. State clearly and precisely the method to be used, how often it will take place, and the person to be involved in the implementation.
b. Set a specific target date for evaluating the effectiveness of the intervention.
c. Use small steps to change the behaviour.

Implementation

Successful implementation is dependent on (i) clear delegation of who will be involved in the activity — staff nurse/nursing assistant or another discipline if appropriate; (ii) staff involved in implementation must believe in what they are doing. Merely going through the motions as instructed will effectively destroy any programme no matter how well thought out.

There is no ready-made solution to this problem, but as all members of the team are vital to the effective implementation of any new programme, they should all be involved, and encouraged, and allowed to contribute to the construction of it. Time spent in this way at the outset of a new programme should be seen as an integral part of all programme design, and not just a public relations exercise. The significance of each individual's contribution will vary greatly depending upon training, if any, or experience or personal outlook. However, if everyone feels involved and is allowed to comment on the new ideas, then they are more likely to feel commitment to the final scheme. And if they have their questions answered or perhaps even their fears allayed before a programme gets off the ground, it stands a much better chance of being successfully implemented.

Evaluation

Evaluation is the assessment of the effectiveness of planned intervention. On the date set at the planning stage a meeting should be held:

(a) to discuss the effectiveness of the intervention and if the goal has been achieved
(b) if the goal has not been achieved an analysis of the process must be carried out to identify where it failed:
 (i) was the goal feasible?
 (ii) was sufficient time allowed?
 (iii) was the method of teaching change correct?
 (iv) have any other problems arisen or been identified, e.g. has it caused distress?
(c) new goals should be set or the time limit on the present ones extended
(d) staff performance should be evaluated — even if the programme has been successful and the goal achieved
(e) the results of the evaluation should be recorded;
(f) the process continued.

This process allows a methodical, flexible approach to the planning and delivery of care which is relevant to the individual needs and problems of the resident. It is a diagnostic and management tool which promotes problem solving, critical thinking, planned intervention, goal setting, and evaluation.

EFFECTIVE CARE

The stability of any group is affected by its morale. Residents' morale is directly linked to that of the unit staff. In a unit where morale is good the care given is more effective and the staff able to cope with periods of higher stress. The leader of the direct care team, the charge nurse or officer in charge, is the most decisive influence on the morale of his staff. It is his role to establish and maintain good morale in his unit. He achieves this by treating the residents as individuals, providing his staff with a sense of purpose, effective communication and effective leadership.

By regarding the residents as individuals the team leader immediately sets the example for his staff to follow as he functions as a model for them, observation and imitation being the principal methods by which they learn. Individual programme planning enables the team leader to organise his team more effectively while clearly defining the goals and policies of the unit and establishing what is expected of individual team members.

Having a sense of purpose leads to job satisfaction and this causes morale to increase. A sense of purpose is gained if the team leader delegates responsibility for care. Being held responsible helps build self confidence by indicating that staff are thought capable and reliable, and this in turn encourages the formation of strong working relationships based on trust and respect.

Good communication between staff, residents and their families, and other disciplines is vital if morale and thus standards of care are to be kept high. Confusion leads to misunderstanding and conflict which will destroy any care plan. Each team member must be aware of the team's objectives and the value of her particular role and contribution to the overall plan. How successfully this is achieved will depend largely on how effectively the leader communicates with his team.

Communication

A daily report is the major means by which information is disseminated and collected. It should take place as early in the workshift as possible, and should bring staff up to date with the current state of affairs in the unit and inform them of alterations to care plans. At this time, duties for the day should be allocated, forthcoming events publicised and unit policies reiterated and reinforced when necessary. However, as communication is a two-way process, this is the best opportunity for the direct care team to discuss and evaluate not only how effective individual care plans are proving, but also all aspects of the unit. Junior and untrained staff in particular must feel able to use this meeting to air their views. The team leader should encourage them to do so and in turn use this time to teach and explain to them the reasoning behind care plans and unit policies.

Regular unit meetings provide the oppor-

tunit for all involved with care to discuss problems and progress. It is important that these meetings are held frequently on a regular basis and not just when a crisis occurs so that issues are raised as a matter of routine. Planning and decision-making can then take place under a minimum of pressure. The unit charge nurse or officer in charge must use these meetings to confirm his position as co-ordinator of the multidisciplinary team by organising the agenda, chairing the meeting, ensuring that matters discussed and decisions reached are recorded and followed up.

Leadership

A good team leader makes himself available to his staff to discuss everything and anything about care. He is constantly appraising his staff's performance and giving encouragement and praise, criticism and advice, guidance and counselling where necessary. Keeping staff informed about their performance will encourage a sense of progress and sense of achievement which will keep morale high. Staff assessments provide the opportunity to take stock and set goals for staff, but this should also be a continual process and not just happen at the time of the assessment. The importance of staff compiling and maintaining a written record of their work has already been highlighted.

The effective leader defines the aims and objectives of his team, then plans and organises how these might be achieved. He sets the standard of performance required and supervises the individual members while encouraging the team and maintaining morale. A democratic style will get the best from the members of the team as they feel they are making a valuable contribution to achieving high standards of care. There will always be great variation in personality, capabilities and skills, but the good leader communicates with his staff and listens to their replies. He consults them and values their contribution. He delegates responsibility and gives support and encouragement. He is consistent in his approach and response to people. He teaches his staff and encourages them to learn new skills. He does not belittle them or take them for granted and is sensitive to their needs and counsels them on their personal and professional development. Discipline is not weakened but strengthened by this, as staff have respect for his judgement as well as his position and value his guidance.

Styles of leadership which are ineffective

The autocratic leader rules by fear. He issues decrees and does not consult his staff. He refuses to recognise the contribution of other staff and will not delegate responsibility. Staff make decisions for his benefit and not the residents' benefit. They gain little job satisfaction as they are made to feel unimportant and have no sense of responsibility. As a result, staff morale and resident care are poor.

The laissez faire leader abdicates all responsibility for his team. Staff have to muddle on as communication is poor and they are left to get on with their job without guidance and support. Standards are not set and consequently are very low. Responsibility is left to others and accountability denied. This leads to insecurity amongst staff and residents as both groups are aware of a lack of concern for them which saps morale.

BURN-OUT

A constant problem to be overcome amongst care staff is that of burn-out. This condition is generally characterised in previously caring, conscientious staff by a lack of concern for residents, apathy and a negative attitude to the development of themselves and residents. Staff begin their career with a fund of enthusiasm and a desire to help others and change things for the better. However after experiencing some failures and discovering that their efforts are not always appreciated by the residents they may start to question their own performance, feeling frustrated and impotent. Unless they receive guidance and support they will either resign or retreat behind a defence of increasing cynicism and apathy, rigidly adhering to their job description and doing only the bare minimum to satisfy their superior. Other staff may achieve their personal goals and having done so lose direction and interest. They begin to stagnate and become increasingly frustrated by their lack of enthusiasm. This leads on through increasing apathy and cynicism to the burnt out state.

Burn-out can occur at any stage in a career to any grade of staff. To help prevent it occuring at an early stage realism must be encouraged without stifling enthuisasm. When stagnation occurs in a more experienced person, changing the way they do their job is more important than changing the job as burn-out can often be taken to another post. A stable work environment with good interstaff communication and clear goals will provide staff with a sense of purpose and the opportunity to contribute to decision-making. Recognition of successes no matter how small increases satisfaction and enables staff to use their sense of achievement to expand and adapt their role. The team which recognises the importance of individual members and does not try to stifle their anger and frustration but encourages them to express their feelings and tries to channel these into improving care and their contribution to it, is the most effective way of counteracting burn-out. It will not always prevent the process occurring but will help people recover from it.

SUMMARY

Care is no longer restricted to providing for basic physical needs but is geared to the individual and his requirement for developing to his fullest potential. A multidisciplinary team approach is necessary to provide the variety of skills and expertise essential for responding to all the individual's needs.

Management of care has become more structured with the focus being switched from the traditional case conference to an individual problem-orientated record system. Individual problems are identified, treatment programmes agreed and progress continually and closely monitored.

The nursing process involves five stages: assessment, problem identification, planning, implementation and evaluation with the initial assessment being the most crucial stage.

Realistic goals must be set and the individual and his family should be involved in planning the intervention. The nursing process allows a flexible approach to the planning and delivery of care directly related to individual needs.

Purposeful team leadership is vital to the maintenance of effective care, and ensuring good communication between all members of the team is important for achieving positive results. Regular meetings should be held to discuss plans and policies as a matter of course and not when a crisis makes a meeting necessary.

Staff should be made aware of the problem of burn-out which usually manifests itself as a state of physical and emotional exhaustion with a total loss of purpose and enthusiasm. Positive management which ensures job satisfaction for individual members of staff may help prevent burn-out.

REFERENCES

Blackwell M 1979 Care of the mentally retarded. Little, Brown, Boston

Matthews A 1982 In charge of the ward. Blackwell Scientific, Oxford.

Moore J 1983 Burn Out — A new name for an old problem. Midwife Health Visitor and Community Nurse. 19(9): 348–352

Weed L L (ed) 1970 Medical records, medical education and patient care. Year Book Publishers, Chicago

Yura H, Walsh M B 1973 The nursing process: assessing, planning, implementing, evaluating. Appleton-Century Crofts Educational, Meredith Corp., New York

15

Isobel Hessler

Some ethical and legal issues

- *Professional carers are required to follow their given code of ethics to ensure right care is given*
- *No one set of rules covers all moral issues and there is no absolute right and wrong*
- *Primary relationships should be established with each mentally handicapped individual*
- *Rules, regulations and professional codes may be powerless against human weakness and dictates of conscience*
- *Laws can provide guidance in certain areas of care but cannot change society's attitudes*

INTRODUCTION

Care of mentally handicapped people and help for their families is seen in Britain as a team approach involving many professionals. Among these there may be doctors, psychologists, social workers, nurses and therapists. As a professional a person is required to behave in a certain way as outlined in the profession's code of ethics. A code of ethics of a professional group especially in the caring professions provides the people being cared for with reassurance that their interests come first, and that the highest possible standards of care will be given.

Training for, and obtaining professional qualifications, does not however automatically mean that the highest standards of care are given. Many factors influence the kind of care given such as:

— the carer's knowledge and understanding of mental handicap
— philosophies of care
— establishments where care is given
— interdisciplinary relationships
— power structures
— status
— staffing levels
— personal vs professional moral codes.

In some instances poor care, neglect and even ill-treatment of mentally handicapped people can and does occur.

This chapter is about care of mentally handicapped people in hospitals. It is about the moral problems which staff may have to solve in their day-to-day work especially where there are instances of poor care, neglect or ill-treatment. The chapter concentrates on care within a hospital setting because some of the most vulnerable people who are mentally handicapped are accommodated in hospital and therefore moral problems may be more pertinent. Most inquiries into cases of ill-treatment or neglect have occurred in hospitals. Although the emphasis is on hospital care, the contents will have relevance for all staff working with mentally handicapped people.

Morals and ethics can be difficult ideas to understand; therefore some examination of the theory of these is included. We look first at moral problems experienced by student nurses working in a large psychiatric hospital. It is hoped that by examining these problems, moral pressures on staff may be identified. We then look at the idea of mental handicap and at some day-to-day problems in care. Finally we look at codes of ethics, philosophies for care, guidelines for care and at a theoretical framework of morals, ethics and law.

COMPLAINTS MADE BY STUDENT NURSES IN A PSYCHIATRIC HOSPITAL

The following is a summarised extract of complaints from student nurses regarding care of patients taken from the 1972 Report of the Inquiry in Whittingham Hospital:

— patients were put to bed too early in the evening;
— 14 students alleged instances of cruelty had arisen but refused to substantiate incidents due to fear of discrimination;
— some patients who are incontinent are bathed with long mops;
— patients struck with key strap (some knotted) with or without cause;
— indigent moneys of patients spent on patients' behalf but goods do not reach patients;
— agitated patients tied by bed sheets on some geriatric wards;

— patients in bed being tormented and/or abused for the amusement of staff!

An extraordinary meeting was called to consider patient care in relation to Press statements on malpractices in patient care arising from the publication of 'Sans Everything'. It was moved that any resolution put forward should not use names of hospital personnel for fear that statements made might lead to prejudice and discrimination.

Why did student nurses make the complaints?

In student nurse training only a short period of time is spent in any one area of experience. It is common knowledge that a person perceives most keenly in the first 4–6 weeks in any new situation. After this time certain factors which would be questioned and measured against currently-held values may be no longer questioned but accepted as the status quo. Student nurses are also new into the professional area of care and may not know the professional values. They may therefore measure care against the personal system they have developed from childhood. Add to this the theoretical input of ideals of care and it may be seen how questioning and measuring of care occurs.

In common language this means that young people come into nursing with their own ideas of right or wrong. They see situations which require new understanding. Being newcomers to the profession they may not have the background knowledge to make professional judgements regarding whether a situation is right or wrong. The only thing they can measure the situation against is their own personal values or a different set of professional values if from another discipline. The main point being made here is that they actively question the kind of care given.

Example 1
A student nurse commences work in a hospital for mentally handicapped people. In her unit there are two male residents, aged 25 years old and 30 years old, who eliminate into bed pans sited on the floor at

night. The student questions this practice but accepts an explanation that this is the normal way for these particular residents. Though she considers this strange there are other facets of caring for mentally handicapped which are also strange.

A new senior registered nurse for the mentally handicapped joins the staff and is shocked and annoyed at this pattern of elimination for two physically grown men. She points out that this is wrong since it takes away from the dignity of the residents, and is among other things a danger to health since infection could occur.

Example 2
A student nurse is seconded to a psychiatric hospital for her period of psychiatric experience. She sees a depressed patient who is untidy, unhygienic and generally unkempt. The student considers this is wrong and she thinks that the staff should insist on the patient conforming to a higher standard of hygiene and grooming.

The ward sister explains that acceptance of this patient as she is now is of more therapeutic value to her self image and that insistence on someone else's standard at this point might be detrimental. This patient should be encouraged to improve her own appearance herself in her own time.

In both these instances questioning occurs. In the first example a lack of knowledge of mentally handicapped people is allowed to cloud judgement of a wrong action. In the second a lack of knowledge of psychiatric practice causes questioning regarding what is seen as wrong action.

Why were the students afraid to substantiate incidents?

The answer here might include the possible risk to themselves which could exist, risk of being shunned by other staff, risk of having to produce evidence in front of an examining committee, being feared by other staff. They might feel concern about any punishment which could occur to staff members accused — in other words they have more loyalty to the staff member than to the patient.

How do you feel when you suspect certain actions are wrong and feel you must do something about them? Who do you turn to?

How were the complaints made

Complaints were channelled through the Student Nurses' Association. Individual students are low in the power hierarchy and are vulnerable should they attempt to challenge accepted practices of those in power. As we see, however, from the complaints made, where practice offended the students' conscience and caused conflict then action was taken. In this instance the students grouped together and by remaining anonymous made complaints through a recognised channel.

Other actions which an individual or group could have taken include challenging the person who carried out the immoral act, reporting the act to senior staff in the unit, ignoring the act and thereby ignoring his conscience and somehow rationalising the malpractice. Alternatively the individual could resign or decide it was none of his business since he would be leaving the unit soon.

What is meant by malpractice or immoral acts? What made the students decide that practices they saw were wrong? The answers to these questions are important since it is necessary to recognise what is right or wrong action in caring for mentally handicapped people.

Before we go on to examine the content of one of the specific complaints in the Whittingham Inquiry we can look briefly at the ideas of morals and ethics in an attempt to clarify the issues.

DEFINITIONS OF MORALS AND ETHICS

The Oxford Dictionary gives one definition of morals as the distinction between right and wrong, and of ethics as moral principles, rules of conduct. Ethics are therefore the rules which can be used as a measure to decide what is right or wrong. What do these mean in practice, since there is no absolute right or wrong (though possibly many people will argue this point) and no one set of rules covers all actions in all situations?

Moral acts are social in nature, i.e. they involve people and the ways in which they behave toward each other. They involve the person who acts and others. Social acts in this context range from polite and courteous behaviours to moral behaviours.

Wright (1971) defines moral behaviour as consisting of all the various things people do in connection with moral rules. He identifies moral rules as those concerned with keeping promises, honesty, respect for the rights of individuals, sympathy for those in need, and of maintaining trust, mutual help and justice in human relationships. Wright's book deals in depth with these concepts and the reader wishing to study the subject of morals and ethics is recommended to such writers. As this chapter deals mainly with right or wrong action of care for mentally handicapped people, the ideas of morals and ethics here are the writer's interpretations and as such may be challenged.

Some human actions are very obviously wrong and society spells out the rules for these as the laws of the country. Breaking these rules is an illegal act and the courts of the country punish the offender. Other rules are embodied in the codes of ethics and breaking these rules is an immoral act and a person's conscience and/or a professional body inflict the punishment. Breaking rules which form the norms of a social group could be viewed as non-conforming and in this instance the group punishes.

People are required to conform to all of these areas of rules and it may be that at some point in time conflict occurs as to which set of rules takes precedence. Consider a group of adolescent boys where the norm is to demonstrate loyalty to each other by guarding territory and fighting anyone who invades it, though the law of the country states that fighting in public places is a breach of the peace. Which rules will take precedence?

Consider the group of people you feel closest to in your work situation caring for mentally handicapped people in hospital. Your work colleague acts in a way you consider wrong in his/her care of the mentally handicapped person. Where do your loyalties lie? Which rules do you follow — those of your group, or the hospital regulations or rules which state that such actions are wrong? Codes of ethics may depend on those who formulate them fully understanding the complexities and boundaries of the moral climate. Moral boundaries can change as new values emerge, e.g. in Victorian society it was considered immoral for people to expose their bodies on public beaches or swim unless they wore clothing which almost completely covered them. Compare that with modern British society where even nudist bathing beaches are allowed. There may however be moral principles which remain valid over time.

In order to judge whether an action is right or wrong a person requires to know which set of rules apply and whether they are relevant at this time and in the context of the situation.

In looking at the content of the complaints made by the student nurses one could readily state that certain of the complaints were obviously wrong actions and reasons could be given why. Other complaints however may be less easily seen as wrong and the underlying rules may be difficult to identify.

> In formulating a moral policy a person or group examines ethical principles, weighs available facts and then makes a decision about what should be done in any given situation. The process is basically the same for any human ethical decision no matter how far reaching the consequences.
> **In other words in deciding what is right or wrong the rules are examined, the facts of the situation are noted and a decision is made as to what to do.**
> Fromer 1981

What were the complaints about?

With this brief background of morals and ethics what can we discover about the content of the complaints made by the students? We can examine one of the complaints which is not so clearly wrong, where knowledge of underlying philosophies and rules for care of mentally handicapped people is necessary in order to judge.

Patients were put to bed too early in the evening. Let us examine this further. What do we mean by describing someone as a patient? In the situation outlined in the complaints patients were adult mentally ill and mentally handicapped people living in a large psychiatric hospital. Calling a person a patient labels him, and causes other people to see that person in a particular way. Labelling mentally handicapped people as patients can restrict the view of others to a purely medical idea of them. This label may also give directions for care and the rights of each party regarding the care, e.g. patients are often cared for in hospitals, and hospitals are institutions, places where public services are carried out. As such, establishment of a routine to ensure efficient service is given is important. Hospitals, however, may be designed to give a service to people who would possibly stay for a limited period of time to have treatment and then leave the institution. The mentally handicapped people in the psychiatric hospital mentioned were possibly long stay residents to whom the hospital was in reality their home.

It could be suggested that hospital care for mentally handicapped people is wrong unless they have a specific medical problem amenable to treatment or therapy and that no one person or institution can meet all of a person's needs. A hospital designed, however, to treat and return to home an ill person is not usually designed to provide for all the comforts of home. Home being the place where a person has the people and things around him which are most familiar and which make him feel safe and secure.

Mentally handicapped people can be patients, i.e. they can become physically or mentally ill. Mental handicap in itself is not an illness and enlightened thinking in this area now refers to people with mental handicap as either residents in long stay care, or to handi-

capped or disabled people, or intellectually handicapped. But the reality of the situation is that for some time to come a proportion of the numbers of mentally handicapped people in British Society will require to be cared for in residential establishments, and in hospitals. This means that staff will be faced with problems similar to the moral issues which gave rise to the complaints put forward in the Whittingham inquiry.

Unenlightened staff still viewing the mentally handicapped person as a patient would perhaps see nothing wrong in deciding what bedtime fitted best for the smooth running of the hospital ward.

What values did the student nurses hold in order to consider that the bedtime was too early? Perhaps they used the normalization philosophy of care which gives priority to the sameness of mentally handicapped people to the rest of society. Let us imagine that the people concerned with going to bed are: (a) a 60-year-old gentleman, (b) a 3-year-old child, (c) a 20-year-old woman, all physically well.

What would be a reasonable bedtime for each of them? Frequently elderly people may have 'naps' during the day and may not retire until late, possibly 10 p.m. or 11 p.m. Elderly people may require less sleep than in their younger days. A 3-year-old child requires at least 12 hours sleep so would probably need to be put to bed between 6 p.m. and 8 p.m. A 20-year-old woman would probably need 8–10 hours sleep but might be flexible in how she catches up — sleeping longer or going to bed earlier after a very late night. An estimation on what time is a suitable bedtime may therefore be related to each person's physical need for sleep and rest.

Where a person is a patient who is physically or mentally ill then his sleep requirements may be greater than usual. The values the students may have held regarding the normalisation philosophy could be that it is an adult's right to choose what is a reasonable bedtime for himself. They may have thought that bedtime on a ward should not be decided for administrative convenience or to suit ward staff's personal preference but rather decided on by the needs or desires of the mentally handicapped people concerned. What factors then govern the time for bed where there are perhaps 25 mentally handicapped people with serious disabilities being cared for by a small number of staff in a large ward in a hospital?

What are the moral questions that should be asked in this situation? What should staff do if they find themselves in conflict over such a situation? What other parallels to the bedtime situation are there in caring for large groups of mentally handicapped people in similar situations?

Perhaps you have mentioned toileting of all the group at the same time or everyone every time having the same set mealtimes. What may be happening, when this occurs, is block treatment of the group. This can give rise to staff ceasing to see people as persons within the group but rather as objects who require to be washed, fed and watered. Unless the moral dangers inherent in this situation are recognised and dealt with then instances of obvious immoral acts such as patients being struck can occur.

MORAL PRESSURES

When an obvious immoral act does occur then the moral pressures to take some action can cause great conflict. Some action to resolve the conflict does happen as outlined earlier. To speak out against dangerous situations which can give rise to immoral acts or against obvious immoral acts requires moral courage. Beardshaw (1981) gives a checklist of points to use in helping to know how to go about making complaints. In her conclusion however, she sees: 'making complaints as a negative approach to problems of mental hospitals and considers that an understanding of basic human frailty could be the foundation where open, constructive questioning and criticism would make formal complaining unnecessary. If this were combined with an approach to care centred on enhancing patients' individuality and preserving their rights, it would be

hard for malpractice to escalate into the patterns that recur in the long lists of inquiry reports.'

Summary

Mental handicap care is a team affair where professionals in the team are required to follow their professional code of ethics, in order to ensure that right care is given.

Codes of ethics are identified as rules which, if followed, give reassurance that right care is being given. Moral acts are concerned with keeping promises, respect for the rights of individuals, and sympathy for those in need.

When a person feels that aspects of care are wrong he feels impelled to take some action and it is here that moral pressure is greatest. However no one set of rules covers all moral issues and there is no absolute right or wrong, though this-is certainly debatable. Knowledge and understanding of the situation, rules used in the situation, facts of the situation all require examination in order to judge right from wrong in moral issues.

In order therefore to guide practice a clear idea of mental handicap and problems in care is necessary as is a clear philosophy of care and clear rules to follow, and an accepted system whereby staff who are under pressure can find help.

The next part of this chapter looks at the idea of mental handicap, at common problems staff may have which give rise to moral pressure, at the codes of ethics which govern the profession of nursing, and at rights of mentally handicapped people.

MENTAL HANDICAP — WHAT DOES IT MEAN?

What mental handicap means will depend on who you are. To a nurse, for example, it might mean she has a place of work to go to where mentally handicapped people are cared for in hospital. To the parent of a mentally handicapped person it can mean conflict of loyalties, joy in caring, worry, any one of a variety of emotions and thoughts. To a mentally handicapped person it can mean having to be what other people with the intelligence and the power want him to be, or where intelligence and power are allied to understanding and empathy it can mean being himself.

How can we understand the self of another person so that in our relationships we can make real contact and avoid the depersonalisation which can give rise to immoral acts? In society generally people are recognised by the characteristics of the roles they play, e.g. the postman delivers letters and is recognised by the uniform he wears. Through experience one knows how to relate to him and what to expect.

Knowledge at least, if not understanding, of most of the roles in life is obtained by either being at one time in that role, e.g. a child, a male or female, of British nationality, an adolescent, adult, or recognising characteristics of the role as normal. Normal here means that most people know what to expect from someone in that role. A person having mental handicap may not fit into any recognised picture of what is expected in any one role, except perhaps the stigmatising role — he's daft.

A baby is born and after 6 weeks the infant is beginning to focus with his eyes and to respond to tone of voice by becoming quiet, following with his eyes, and recognizing the touch and smell of his most constant carer. The infant born mentally handicapped might not show any usual observable response and the carer would not get the feedback expected. This can result in confusion for the carer who does not know what the right action to take would be in order to relate to this vulnerable little one.

If you saw an adult woman, about 30 years old, dressed in smart casual clothes you would probably not give her a second look. But if she suddenly began to jump up and down and to pace the room, or attempt to discover what was in your pockets or bag you carried — behaviour more characteristic of a 3-year-old child than a 30-year-old woman — how would you respond?

Would you be responding to the physical, chronologically aged woman or to the aspects of behaviour which are more characteristic of the child, or to both? Your knowledge and/or experience of 3-year-old children and adult women in normal society can give the rules for relating to either one of these persons within the mentally handicapped adult. The problem arises in combining ways of relating to both aspects of the person in a way which is considered moral by the wider society.

PROBLEMS IN DAY-TO-DAY CARE

Mentally handicapped children in long stay care in hospital

How much emotional involvement can a student nurse or staff member have with any particular child? This is a moral problem recognised by senior care staff in health and social services to the extent that for most children alternative forms of care such as fostering or shared care takes the place of hospital admission for long-term care. There are a number of children who are still in hospital so the moral problem is still one which needs looking at.

Children need love, security, stimulation, in order to develop. Interpretation of these is not so easy.

Love. The word love has many connotations. Here it is meant to convey such caring for the good of the child that one's own desires and wants take second place.

Example

A new young nurse commences work in a children's unit in a hospital for care of mentally handicapped children. She is particularly drawn to one small child and becomes so fond of him she asks to take the child home to her family for visits. If this child already has a close primary group such as his own or substitute parents, then those in charge who have the child's interests at heart will ask a few questions, and perhaps permit the visits.

Questions asked may concern how much

future contact the nurse intends to have with this particular child. What will happen when the nurse moves to another unit, has examinations to take, goes off on holiday, decides to leave nursing or get married? Who is going to be the one to gain the most out of the relationship? Will there be a possibility of emotional harm to the child? These questions would be in addition to those which would check out the factors related to physical comfort and safety of the child.

The main question to ask oneself is 'Why do I want to do this?'

Security. What spells security for a person? It could be a familiar routine or knowing what is going to happen. Having someone with you whom you trust in situations which are unfamiliar or frightening. Knowing what is going to happen is dependent on either it being explained to you in a language you understand or experiencing something and remembering it and recognising it again when it recurs. Mentally handicapped people may have difficulty in laying down information so that later it can be recalled. The more seriously mentally handicapped the person is, the greater is this a problem. Security therefore for the mentally handicapped child can be provided by an established routine which incorporates some rituals which the child finds meaningful.

Security is having people around you whom you trust and who understand the special ways of ensuring your comfort and safety. In hospital, who are the people closest to the mentally handicapped person? How secure can a child be if every few months, or even weeks, he receives intimate bodily care from a different person who after a few more weeks disappears? Possibly the only way to overcome this problem in a hospital is to ensure the child has a close primary group that remains consistent and identifies with him. The new nurse coming into this area of care can certainly contribute but she must be sensitive to the primary relationships of the child. This can especially apply where a child's parents are involved.

Security for a mentally handicapped person/child/adult can often occur through primary relationships with voluntary people who have no formal legal ties. These people can often give of themselves, of their time and other resources. When the death of the mentally handicapped person occurs these people may not always be considered in the grieving process or in the plans for burial. Happily in other instances these ties are recognised by care staff and these 'substitute' families are given the recognition they deserve, and the support they may need in their loss.

Stimulation. Moving from one stage of development to another is a gradual process. A new stage can suddenly appear when the person has built on his skills and a new large skill appears in his repertoire. Stimulation is necessary at every stage of the developmental process. A stimulus is defined in the Oxford English Dictionary as 'a thing that arouses to activity or energy' and '(physiological) thing that evokes functional reaction in tissues'. Human beings are stimulated through their senses such as the special senses of touch, vision, hearing, smelling, tasting, but also through a variety of other sensory messages which come from inside the body as, e.g. sense of hunger, thirst, and position in space.

The mentally handicapped person may have sensory organ impairment in addition to a deficit in nerve cells or damage to sensory nerve cells which means that only limited sensory information is being received and even that in no constant pattern. The new nurse to a children's unit should be morally aware of the part she is required to play in carrying out care. She should follow closely the instructions for methods of communicating with the child, for the kinds of play and activities designed to meet the special stimulatory needs of this child. The nurse's patience may be tried as often an activity, to be meaningful for the child, has to be repeated again and again.

To select an activity for the child simply to reduce the nurse's own boredom, or because knowledge of the child or activities is faulty, instead of as a stimulus which is meaningful for the child may be seen as immoral, though there may not be any set rules which convey this.

Primary relationships for mentally handicapped adults of low ability

Mentally handicapped people have difficulty in learning and adapting to the social environment. The level of functioning will depend on the degree of mental and physical impairment. An adult with profound mental handicap (low ability) may function at the mental age of an infant. This does not mean that this person is the same as an infant since the fact of living to an adult chronological age gives experiences which do bring about learning and adaptation. A person of low ability intellectually will require care and supervision all his life.

Infant development is dependent on bonding with a significant carer who stimulates and interprets the infant's world for him and in so doing also gains satisfactions. In hospital the adult with profound mental handicap may have been cared for by a succession of carers throughout his life. The query therefore is to what extent bonding with any one person could develop, and whether it is in fact necessary.

It is socially acceptable practice with a young infant to lift, hug, touch and play with him, activities which can mean close bodily contact. To act in such a way with an adult is not acceptable. However the infant within the adult mentally handicapped person may require just this kind of bodily contact to aid development.

How, within a moral framework, can this be provided? Indeed, to ignore such a need may be seen as immoral. Happily there are developments in care where by the use of specific therapies, e.g. drama, music, and movement, these needs can be met in a socially acceptable manner. This leads on to a further' problem in care for people of low and moderate ability who because of economic constraints are required to have as their family

a group of other mentally handicapped people in a hospital situation.

Neglect of residents who provide little positive feedback for the carer

By neglect is meant the lack of emotional involvement at a one-to-one level with a person who gives little or no response to attempts to communicate with him or who responds in a way which is not the acceptable norm. Examples may be of an adult, profoundly handicapped and perhaps blind, who either does not respond to attempts to gain contact with him or who responds by crying, or a mentally handicapped child who spits in one's face when attempts are made to communicate, or a child who shrinks away at any attempt to gain contact with him. It is perhaps understandable in these circumstances that staff unless directed to spend extra time with these people would choose instead to concentrate their efforts on mentally handicapped people whom they felt they could benefit and who might provide positive responses. In consequence those who may require more time than others of individual contact may instead get less.

Restraint — physical or medical

A child who requires close supervision and care to ensure he does not injure himself has safeguards in legal regulations which his parents or carers are required by law to follow, e.g. using a fixed fireguard in front of an open fire, or no child being left in the care of a minor, i.e. someone under the age of 16 years. Parents and other carers of young children also use various aids such as stair guards, restrainer harnesses for prams and push chairs and cots with adjustable sides.

Mentally handicapped adults of low ability also require close supervision and care to ensure they do not injure themselves. Providing safeguards as one does for a child is not simple, and moral problems of restraint can arise. The real problem may not lie in the fact of restraint but in the reasons why the restraint is necessary. If because of poor interpretation of need, or poor staffing levels an individual adult is restrained by being tied into bed with sheets, then perhaps the action could be viewed as immoral. Is this act always immoral? Would the time of day or night give any indication as to the morality? Would the prescription in the nursing care plan signed by a doctor that restraint at certain times is allowed and the method of restraint outlined make a difference to the morality? Would there be any difference in applying such restraint if the mentally handicapped person was of high ability? How moral is an act of holding down a disturbed or apparently disturbed person and injecting him with a tranquillising drug?

You can perhaps examine these factors by looking at who the restraint is for, why the restraint is required, what signifies the restraint, what is the result of the restraint for all concerned, and what rules are being followed.

Violence against the mentally handicapped person/violence against staff

The Oxford English Dictionary definition of violence is 'unlawful exercise of physical force, intimidation by exhibition of this'. Violent acts may be actual — striking, pushing, pinching, scratching — or acts of threatening violence. Mentally handicapped people in hospitals may be at risk not only from staff members but also from other residents in their group.

It is difficult to envisage circumstances where a caring person entering a profession, or someone who chooses to care for mentally handicapped people resorts to physical violence or tolerates intimidation of a mentally handicapped person. The complaints made in the Whittingham Inquiry do show however that such observations are reported and may occur. Employees in hospital have a duty under Section 7 of the Health and Safety at Work Act (1974) to take reasonable care for the health and safety of themselves and others who may be affected by acts or omissions at work.

With regard to violence to staff this puts responsibility on staff to be aware of the possible situations where violence could occur and to ensure they are cognizant with the professional way of dealing with this. The main method would of course be to aim to prevent violent behaviour. This means that members of staff noting any changes in a person's behaviour which could lead to episodes of violence have a duty to report these as they have a duty to report when the staffing situation is at dangerous levels either in number or in supervision of non-registered staff. Senior staff have a duty to ensure that untrained members of staff are taught how to relate in a constructive way with those mentally handicapped people who may become aggressive or violent.

Nurses may feel proud if they have worked short staffed and have managed to get through the routine work of care. If, however, the mentally handicapped person being cared for has only had his physical needs met and has been left feeling frustrated or insecure, then episodes of violent behaviour could occur. The work on the unit at a certain level might have been done but perhaps at the price of injury to the mentally handicapped person or to a staff member. Senior staff on a unit have a moral responsibility to ensure adequate staffing levels and to ensure all staff on their unit are aware of their responsibility in preventing violence and aggression. Two different examples follow of potentially violent situations.

Example 1
A middle-aged woman of moderate ability is in a general hospital. It is 1 a.m. and she is being assisted to the toilet as part of her care. She becomes aggressive and threatens the nurse accompanying her. This nurse calls her senior colleague and both approach the woman quietly and gently, and ask what is wrong. The senior nurse stands quietly and listens to what the woman is trying to say. She asks if they have come to take her away as during the day she had been threatened that she would be sent to

another hospital. The two staff comfort her and reassure her that she is not going to another hospital. They help her to the toilet, return her to bed, give her a cup of tea and she settles back to sleep. The staff make a verbal and written report in the morning and the senior nurse investigates the incident the woman referred to.

Example 2
In contrast a mentally handicapped man, while being helped to the toilet at 1 a.m., becomes aggressive and difficult. The senior nurse is called and he attempts to encourage the man to come out of the bathroom and return to bed, but the man begins to shout, threaten and becomes very upset. The senior nurse leaves him asking the other member of staff to remain observing, but at a distance while he telephones and makes arrangements for three other members of staff to come to help administer a prescribed drug. He does this taking care to preserve the man's dignity. The man is returned to bed and carefully observed for the rest of the night. In the morning the senior nurse makes a verbal and written report.

When a person is upset enough to pose a threat to himself or to others it is important that the people who make an attempt to calm him are those he trusts and has constructive relationships with.

Summary

Strategies can be developed for dealing with day-to-day problems in care. While mentally handicapped people require long-term care in a hospital, then the hospital will find ways of handling the problems which arise. Constraints which can lead to ethical problems can also act as a stimulus for innovative ways of caring. The strategy for preventing the development of malpractice may lie in ensuring all staff are aware of and committed to a humane philosophy of care where every individual person, handicapped or staff, is seen as someone with a need to belong, to have some status and to be important to someone.

It is essential to maintain a mentally handicapped person's individuality, and this can be achieved by providing for the establishment of a primary relationship for each mentally handicapped person. Current trends in Britain lean towards this idea which is a feature of care in America, i.e. advocacy. The more handicapped a person is the more vulnerable he might be and therefore would require a strong representative to monitor his care to ensure it is of the highest standard possible. Staff attitudes are therefore of prime importance.

PERSONHOOD

What signifies whether someone is seen as a person and not an object? Fromer (1981) writes about life as being a purely biological function and asks about factors which make human life different and what constitutes a person. She refers to criteria of personhood from Fletcher (1972) some of which will be discussed below.

Criteria of personhood (according to Fletcher, 1972)

Positive criteria

1. Minimal intelligence. An individual whose score on a Stanford Binet Intelligence test falls below 20 cannot be considered a person. Fletcher thought that a score between 20 and 40 put one in a category of questionable personhood. Many people disagree with the severity of Fletcher's criterion of intelligence, pointing to the thousands of profoundly mentally retarded individuals who would thus be denied personhood.
2. Self-awareness.
3. Self-control. An individual must not be totally subject to the will of others (except by force) but must have conscious control of his own actions and exhibit means-end behaviour. The temporary loss of control because of

illness or accident does not, of course, jeopardise one's personhood; the condition must be permanent.

4. A sense of time.
5. A sense of futurity.
6. A sense of the past.
7. The ability to relate to others. Fletcher makes no judgements about the quality of one's relationships — only that they should exist. To be a person, one needs to be aware of the personhood of others and to relate to others on a human level.
8. Concern for others. This does not necessarily mean altruistic or charitable concern but refers more to concern for the personhood or humanity of others.
9. Communication.
10. Control of existence.
11. Curiosity.
12. Change and changeability.
13. Balance of rationality and feeling.
14. Idiosyncrasy. To be a person is to be recognisable as a distinict individual, to have an identity, to be different from all other human beings.
15. Neocortical function. This is the criterion on which all the others are based.

Negative criteria

1. A person is not non — or — artificial.
2. A person is not essentially parental.
3. A person is not essentially sexual.
4. A person has no natural rights. Fletcher believes that the notion of human nature has given rise to the idea that people have natural rights to which they are automatically entitled as if these rights were absolute and eternal. Rights are granted by social systems and are not a requirement of personhood.
5. A person is not necessarily a worshipper.

Looking at Fletcher's criteria it might be seen how a mentally handicapped person who does not provide the expected responses which indicate personhood could be viewed as an object and treated as such. One does not need to use Fletcher's criteria alone; other factors

in society — the family situation a child is born into, the culture, the class — can indicate whether people view someone as a person and to what degree. If one accepts that a particular level of functioning is not indicative of personhood and that a mentally handicapped person falls into this category, how can we ensure that a high standard of care is given? How can we ensure that lack of personhood or depersonalisation does not lead to the mentally handicapped person being abused.

A child until he forges his own identity will be identified by the family he belongs to. Should the family be considered by society as an important one, then the child might be accorded the status and with that the respect and privilege which accompanies it. The respect and privilege are accorded to the child not because of himself but as a mark of respect to the family. If for some reason the family rejects the child it may be that society will also reject him. In these circumstances, therefore, if an individual is rejected because he does not meet the criteria of personhood or is depersonalised, he will require a strong person well respected, and/or a strong group to ensure he is afforded his rights and to ensure he suffers no abuse.

FRAILTY OF STAFF

The norms of a society mean that within a social group certain rules apply. These may be explicit, i.e. 'spelled' out, or informal, someone only knowing he exists when he has broken them. Informal rules are learned over time through contact with the group, learned by trial and error, the group rewarding acceptable behaviour and punishing that which is undesirable.

A person new to the group measures the norms against the system he already follows. If the new norms do not cause conflict then the person may feel comfortable and fit into the group. If a person breaks the norms of the group often enough the group may reject him. This might only serve as punishment if the person wishes to be a member of the group. Wider society also has norms or standards of behaviour which are desirable for the population as a whole or certain groups within the population. We have identified these as being incorporated in the laws of the country and in codes of ethics. Laws of a country are usually fairly easily identified. Rules in a code of ethics may be clear but problems can arise where different codes of ethics abound or conflict.

Human weakness or frailty can be the cause of a staff member caring for mentally handicapped people being unaware of the ethical code which governs care (though it is the responsibility of a professional person to know and follow the professional code of ethics). It can happen that the code is known but is so separate from everyday care that it has little significance for staff. Where violations of the ethical code occur as, for example, neglect and abuse of a mentally handicapped person, a staff member aware of this may not take any steps to prevent or report this, either because of lack of status and power in the group or because of lack of knowledge of where to go. The staff member may decide to obey the ethical code in his own area of work in a conscientious way but be unwilling to take any responsibility for his colleagues' actions. Where care of mentally handicapped people is in large institutions cut off from the rest of society, and especially where there is little or no knowledge of advances in care, then it might happen that small groups within the hospital will set their own norms. Isolation, lack of stimulation, lack of individual development programmes for all staff can lead to staff slipping into standards of care which are not desirable. It is the norms within the small groups that staff follow as their mode of conduct.

Student nurses and other staff who are passengers through these groups may not become committed to these norms. In some cases they will tolerate feeling uncomfortable if they see actions which conflict with their own code of conduct, because the time spent in the area may be limited. Unless their own personal code is seriously challenged they may take no action other than discussing problems with their peer group or close friends. This can defuse any feeling of tension or conflict, so instances of poor care may not be reported or dealt with. Students may also be able to distance themselves from any immoral situations as they do not carry the ultimate responsibility or accountability for care.

This responsibility is carried further up the hierarchy to the staff nurse or ward sister/charge nurse, who may not see instances of ill treatment or neglect. It may be that unenlightened staff who have been in a position of trust over a long period of time with autonomy of action, but little supervision or reinforcement for innovative examples of improved care, may become self interested and low in morale. They may become so entrenched that they feel inviolate and do not know when their own moral code is becoming eroded. Should however ill treatment or neglect of a mentally handicapped person 'come to light', then not having taken any action when it has been seen even though one was not responsible, renders a person as guilty as the person responsible for the ill-treatment or neglect. How can human weaknesses be overcome? Possibly by appealing to a person's conscience? It might be of value at this point to look at examples of how conscience develops.

Personal values and development of conscience

In a report carried out into children and their primary schools it was stated that moral development was closely associated with social and emotional development:

The child forms his sense of personal worth and his moral sense from early experience of acceptance, approval and disapproval; out of an externally imposed rule of what is permitted, arises a sense of what ought to be done and an internal system of control — a conscience. The very young child, limited in understanding, acts according to strict rules, even though he often breaks them. What is right and wrong relates closely to what his parents say and to the situations arising in the home. Later as the child develops intellectually and lives with others, his sense of right and wrong derives from a wider circle and becomes more qualified; the rules of the game are arrived at by consensus and are therefore modifiable by common agreement. (HMSO, 1967)

Wright (1978) describes the work of Kohlberg, an American psychologist, who developed a theory of how moral values develop. In his studies, Kohlberg set up situations which required children of varying ages to think through moral dilemmas, e.g. is a man whose wife is dying of cancer and who has failed to obtain an essential drug by legal means entitled to resort to stealing? In other words in any situation what should prevail: the rule of law or the needs of an individual?

An interpretation of Kohlberg's stages is of three levels, with each level having two stages. The first stage is carrying out an act to avoid punishment. The second is carrying out an act to obtain a reward. Stage three is where the act is carried out in order to please others within the family or social group. In the fourth stage action is done in obedience to the law. Stage five is where an action is carried out because of agreement in the society of individual rights involved even though the action may be contrary to the law. In stage six an action is carried out because of ethical principles — rules based on fundamental truths of justice and rights of human beings.

All movement through these stages is forward in sequence and does not skip steps. Children may move through these stages at varying speeds. An individual may stop at any given stage. Kohlberg's stages are interesting when we look at the human weaknesses of people and at where courage may be required to examine one's own moral position in relation to the care provided for mentally handicapped people.

Summary

It is impossible to ensure that a human being is viewed as a person and not an object. Human weakness can all too easily lead to situations of neglect or ill treatment of mentally handicapped people; isolation, lack of stimulation and lack of development of staff can result in lowered morale and the erosion of moral codes. Despite the existence of rules and regulations conscience may be the overriding factor guiding a person's actions.

ETHICAL PRINCIPLES IN PRACTICE

Ethical codes

The Ten Commandments found in the Bible are an example of the Jewish code of ethics which act as a basis for the rules which some Christian people accept as the guidelines for the way in which they conduct their lives. It could be argued that these rules were made for a different society and as such do not cover sufficiently the needs of current Christian societies because the moral boundaries have changed, e.g. 'Thou shall not commit adultery.' This is debatable.

Wright & Taylor (1970) give one reason for the formulation of a code of ethics as:

The survival of many species depends upon the development among their members of a cooperative and altruistic form of behaviour. This basic interdependence of members of a species leads to evolution of forms of social control. The human species is unique in that the main mechanism of social regulation is a system of conceptually formulated rules, conventions and values.

In other words a group, in this case mankind, continues in existence if they have, as a basis for their behaviour, regard for others and cooperation with others. In order to ensure this the group forms rules and holds certain values which other members of the group are expected to uphold. Ethical codes may give the guidance for the formulation of these rules. Ethical codes may however vary from society to society. In caring for mentally handicapped people it might be of value when faced with ethical problems to be able to identify where the values underlying the care or lack of care spring from. To help in this, some examples of sources of ethical codes are given.

Types and sources of ethical codes

Religious. We have already identified the Jewish code of the Ten Commandments. Others include the Islamic code found in the Holy Law from the Koran, and the Judaic code found in the Talmud.

Philosophical. Philosophy can be viewed as a love of wisdom, knowledge, especially that which deals with ultimate reality, or with the more general causes and principles of things (The Concise Oxford Dictionary, 1952).

As an abstract idea this might be difficult to understand. In a more simple way this might be seen as knowing the truth of something, e.g. to be wise is to know that from experience something is so, but not only to know that it is so but also to understand what makes it so. An adult playing with an infant may hide sweets under a series of cups and play a game. The infant may recognise that the sweets disappear and then reappear. To be wise to what is happening the infant would require to know that the sweets were under the cup and how they were put there, i.e. the truth of the situation.

Philosophies for care

The following are three examples of philosophies taken from Fromer (1981). They are the author's interpretations for the benefit of this chapter.

Socrates believed that 'the head should rule the heart' in determining ethical decisions. In a situation where ethical decisions need to be made then a decision must be based on what is right not on what the general consensus says is right. The decision must not be based

on what the consequences of the decision will be. The problem here of course is to identify just what action is right, especially in the complexities of care for mentally handicapped people.

Plato believed in justice and the principle of never harming anyone. He believed in knowledge as a virtue and ignorance as a vice and that knowledge underlies all virtues and just actions.

Kant believed that a person should be an end in himself and not used as a means to an end.

The idea of believing in a given philosophy provides guidelines for the kind of care to be given, just as in performing a task a person may have a clear aim in view which sets the goals to reach for. People may however have different philosophies in which they believe and aim for quite different things. Even within the caring professions there may be different professional philosophies even though the factors which identify a group as a profession are the same. An example of this might be seen in the different philosophies of medical versus nursing care, medicine being seen as more a treatment and cure philosophy, while nursing could be viewed as a care philosophy.

In religious and philosophical sources of ethical codes an individual may have a choice. In a profession however the person entering is required to become committed to the professional code which guides the care.

View of a profession

Dunkerley (1975) states that it is necessary for a professional group to develop a code of ethics to guide the conduct of the members of the group and to provide them with approval from society to pursue their profession Lord Cohen in a lecture on medical ethics said:

The essence of a profession is that though men enter it for the sake of their livelihood,

the measure of their success is the service they perform and not the gains they amass.
Phoon Wai On (1971)

In nursing, as one of the caring professions, the most commonly used philosophy of care is Virginia Henderson's:

> The unique function of the nurse is to assist the individual sick or well in the performance of those activities contributing to health or its recovery (or to a peaceful death) that he would perform unaided if he had the necessary strength, will or knowledge. And to do this in such a way as to help him gain independence as rapidly as possible.

This philosophy incorporates a wide view of the nurse in that it deals with assisting individuals in activities which contribute to health. Since health covers the whole person physically, intellectually, emotionally and socially, and as mentally handicapped people have a problem in learning and adapting to the social situation, then in the view of this philosophy nurses have a significant role to play in the care for mentally handicapped people.

Nurses, as a professional group, subscribe to a Code of Professional Conduct as outlined in the United Kingdom Central Council for Nursing, Midwifery and Health Visiting Code based on ethical concepts. A philosophy of care sets the aims. The codes of ethics give the rules to follow. In caring for mentally handicapped people the aim often given is of aiding the development of the handicapped person to the maximum of their potential. We said at the start of this chapter that care for mentally handicapped people in Britain was seen as a team approach. We have also identified ethical codes, philosophies of care and what makes a profession. All of these may be relevant in some aspect of care and may point staff in a general direction for overall care but these do not spell out the specific factors needed to ensure care really meets the needs of the handicapped person. To find this kind of information one can turn to the

Declaration of the United Nations Organization to the General Assembly:

The rights of the handicapped

1. The term handicapped designates each person is unable to procure for himself all or part of the necessities of an individual or social life because of deficiency, congenital or otherwise, in his mental or physical capacities.

2. The handicapped has an essential right to respect for his human dignity whatever may be the origin, the nature, and the gravity of his troubles and deficiencies; the handicapped has the same basic rights as his fellow citizens of the same age which implies in the first place the enjoyment of a decent life as normal and fulfilled as possible.

3. The handicapped has the right to medical, psychological and functional treatments, including artificial limbs and appliances, to medical and social rehabilitation, to education, to professional training and rehabilitation, to aids, counsel and services for placings and other services which could ensure the maximum use of his capacities and aptitudes, and would hasten the process of his social integration or reintegration.

4. The handicapped has the right to social and economic security and a decent standard of living. He has the right, according to his possibilities, to obtain and keep an employment or to carry on useful, productive and remunerative occupation and to join a trade union.

5. The handicapped has the right to have his particular needs taken into account at every stage of social and economic planning.

6. The handicapped has the right to live with his family or in a substantive home, and to take part in all social, creative or recreative activities. No handicapped should be submitted, in the way of residence, to distinctive treatment which is not required by his condition or by the relief which might be procured for him. If it is necessary for him to stay in a special establishment, the surroundings and lifestyle should be as much as possible those

of the normal life of people of his age group.

7. The handicapped must be protected against all exploitation, all regimentation, or discriminatory, abusive or degrading treatments.

8. Organisations for the handicapped could be usefully consulted on all questions concerning the rights of the handicapped.

9. The handicapped, his family and his community should be fully informed by all appropriate means, of the common rights contained in this declaration.

These rights are for handicapped people generally and not specifically the mentally handicapped person. There may be difficulty in interpreting point 6 in that the handicapped person's lifestyle should be as much as possible those of the lifestyle of people his own age group. In mental handicap it might be difficult to determine just what age group's lifestyle is applicable.

Rights of a person also imply an obligation on another person. So, if as in point 6 the handicapped person has the right to live with his family, then the family is obliged to have him live with them though this point does also say a substantive home. If every person is entitled to the same rights, whose rights take precedence? This situation can arise in a hospital ward where there are possibly a large number of mentally handicapped people living together, all of whom have the same rights to care. One of the problems that can arise for staff is how they can apportion their time to ensure that everyone gets the amount of care and attention which is their right.

Where moral rights are concerned each person must depend on others in his society granting him the right. Governments can legislate for people's rights by passing Acts of Parliament, however governments can also take away these rights. To ensure the more vulnerable members of a society get their rights, other stronger members will require to be unselfish and caring though they would need to ensure a balance of rights is maintained. To illustrate this we can look at the right of a mentally handicapped person of moderate ability to get married and to have children. We could say that certainly the handicapped person has the right to marry. Certainly he has the right to have a child. Society also has the right to say that those people who produce children have a responsibility to ensure they can provide for and look after their child. The child has a right to expect that he is cared for and helped to develop. If the mentally handicapped person or people require support and care from society for their own functioning how right would it be for them to have a child for whom they are unable to provide care. Whose rights take precedence?

Summary

Society requires some set rules to ensure its continued functioning. In caring for mentally handicapped people it might be useful to identify the underlying values for care, especially when faced with ethical problems in care. The United Nations' list of rights of the handicapped may prove helpful. Two other examples of citizens' rights can also be seen as applicable in current British society and as a humane philosophy to follow in considering the rights of handicapped people:

We hold these truths to be self evident that all men are created equal, that they are endowed by their Creator with certain unalienable rights, that among these are life, liberty and the pursuit of happiness. That to secure rights, governments are instituted among men, deriving their just powers from the consent of the governed. That when any government becomes destructive of these ends it is the right of the people to abolish it, and to institute new government, laying its foundation on such principles and organising its powers in such a form as to them shall seem most likely to effect their safety and happiness.

American Declaration of Independence
Thomas Jefferson 1776

The French in 1789 in 'The Rights of Man and Citizen' declared:

> The end of all political associations is the preservation of the natural and imprescriptible rights of man; and these rights are liberty, property, security, and resistance to oppression.
>
> Wright, 1977

Wright goes on to say that it is from bases such as the above that today's rights come, and that the history of democracy is an extension of the lists of individual citizens' rights, and of their conversion from moral claims to laws which can be enforced by the state. It is to these legal rights that attention is now turned.

LEGAL ASPECTS

Although legal rights stem from moral claims not all Acts of Parliament have their basis in moral claims. Some Acts may aim to do what is right for most people but some people's rights may take precedence. This can perhaps be seen in controversies which surround such issues as abortion and euthanasia. It is not the intention of this chapter to examine these issues though certainly the Abortion Act 1967 has relevance for mental handicap. Nowadays tests such as amniocentesis in early pregnancy can detect abnormalities in the fetus. The mother is entitled, as a right, to have the pregnancy terminated where the tests have shown that the child will be seriously handicapped.

Pressure groups can bring weight to bear on central government to amend such laws, each pressure group working from their own moral standpoint. Issues such as these involve people's basic philosophies and in a free society each person has entitlement to his own views and the right to make these known. The forming of laws is as much the responsibility of the ordinary citizen as it is for elected Members of Parliament. By our interest, or lack of interest, we shape the kind of society we live in.

The Congenital Disabilities (Civil Liability) Act 1976

A child who suffers damage or injury as a result of negligence in the duty of care of his mother, may be able to claim damages. This could be up to the age of 19 and in some instances to 21 years. The claim would be made against those who have a duty of care.

(Clarke, 1982)

The Mental Health Acts and Amendments

The acts of relevance are: The Mental Health Act 1983; The Mental Health (Scotland) Act 1960; and The Mental Health (Scotland) Act 1984.

Although the content of these Acts is similar, the differences in the Scottish legal system have occasioned the need for separate legislation. One of the main aims of the Mental Health Acts is to provide safeguards for mentally disordered people who could be deprived of their liberty. Another is to enable these mentally disordered people to have access to the same facilities for treatment and care as people suffering from purely physical problems.

The 1959 Act for England has recently been amended and the 1983 Act is a consolidating Act incorporating the 1959 Act with its amendments. The 1960 Act for Scotland and the 1983 amendments are consolidated, in the Mental Health (Scotland) Act 1984.

Definition of mental disorder as used in the new consolidated Acts

In England the new legal term is mental impairment whereas in Scotland it is mental handicap (HMSO, 1983). Where a mentally disordered person in Scotland is required to be compulsorily detained the legal term used will be mental impairment. This corresponds with equivalent terms in England.

In England, The Mental Health Review Tribunal is responsible for review of mentally disordered people who are under compulsory detention in hospital. Mental Health Commissioners will monitor the care of mentally disordered people. In Scotland, the body of people who provide independent protection for the rights of mentally handicapped people is the Mental Welfare Commission. Under the new consolidated Act this body is given wider powers than previously. Previously local authorities in Scotland had the power to appoint mental health officers, but under the new Act they have the power to approve these people with reference to 'qualifications, experience and competence in dealing with persons who are suffereing from mental disorder' (HMSO, 1983).

Acts within the Social Services

These are Acts which provide services where the responsibility for implementation lies either directly with central government or indirectly with local government.

Some Acts give specific guidance as to what must be done; others leave room for adaptation to local needs. Central government however has ultimate control since it allocates the money to local government. Ultimately the service provided depends on the level of contribution from society generally. Mentally handicapped people may function at a level which handicaps them in normal society. Their mental disability, however, need not handicap them if the correct types of aids and resources are provided for care. The Acts relating to the Social Services can help to ensure such resources are made available. Increasingly mentally handicapped people have access to resources which enable them to live within the community. These resources include special education, further education, cash benefits, occupation, housing, voting rights, as well as the ordinary citizens' rights of consumer protection and rights under civil and criminal law.

Special education

The report of Committee of Enquiry into the Education of Handicapped Children and Young People (The Warnock Report 1978) led to changes in the expectations some care staff had of their children suffering from mental handicap. Instead of merely ensuring that children were kept occupied, teaching staff went into hospital wards to carry out assessments and create teaching programmes developed specifically for them. The Education Act 1981 made changes along the lines of the Warnock Report proposals by placing the onus on local authorities to ensure assessment is carried out for people in need of special education whatever their disability. Local authorities should also advise as to placement and should ensure the wishes of parents are observed.

Further education

At local levels, further education colleges in some areas may provide facilities for special classes for mentally handicapped people who are over school age. This is encouraging since many mentally handicapped people only begin to grasp certain concepts when they are due to finish full-time education. Responsibility for further education rests with the local education authorities.

Colleges of further education may also assist in providing adult tutors who work within a hospital, teaching mentally handicapped adults. This type of provision has given a new direction to care and in the author's view considerably enhances the quality of care.

Cash benefits

The Department of Health and Social Security is responsible for benefits and allowances. Some benefits can be claimed through local social security offices, but others require a claim to be made to a central department.

Some benefits are dependent on contributions being made over a minimum period of time, but others are non-contributary allowances. For details of the range of benefits, see Chapter 5, pages 95–98.

Occupation

With reference to mental handicap occupation need not mean actual employment. Attendance at an adult training centre or further education college can be termed occupation. Employment itself is facilitated by the services of a Disablement Resettlement Officer, through the specialist help section of the Employment Services Division of the Manpower Services Commission.

Housing

The Housing (Homeless Persons) Act 1977 requires local housing authorities to give help to people who are, or might become, homeless. This Act may have some relevance for mentally handicapped people who are in hospital only because they have no home in the community.

Voting Rights

Representation of the People Act 1983 — Section 12 — is of relevance to the voting rights of people with mental handicap.

People with mental handicap who are in voluntary institutions can be enrolled on the Electoral Register, provided they complete the required form which is provided by the institution, and provided that this form is authorised by a responsible member of staff. This form (Form Z) may be obtained from the Regional Health Boards.

People with mental handicap living in the community may vote provided they are on the Electoral Register.

In the final analysis, voting is at the discretion of the Presiding Officer, who decides whether or not someone is competent at that point in time to register a vote.

Summary

Laws can only give guidance for certain areas of care. They can state what must be done and provide the resources to enable the laws to be carried out. Laws however do not change people's attitudes overnight and it is in this area that moral and ethical issues are allied to legal factors in care.

REFERENCES

Beardshaw V 1981 Conscientious objectors at work. Social Audit, London, Appendix E, p 99, ch 7, p 80
Clarke D 1982 Mentally handicapped people living and learning. Bailliere Tindall, London, ch 3, p 45
Dunkerley D 1975 Occupations and society. Students Library of Sociology, ch 5, p 55–56
Family Welfare Association 1983 Guide to the social services. The Family Welfare Association, London
Fletcher J 1972 Medicine and the nature of man. In: Veatch I, Robert M et al (eds) The teaching of medical ethics. Proceedings of a conference sponsored by The Institute of Society, Ethics and the Life Sciences and Columbia University College of Physicians and Surgeons, New York, June 1–3, 1972, p 52–57
Fowler H W, Fowler F G 1951 The Concise Oxford Dictionary, 4th edn (revised by F. McIntosh). Clarendon Press, Oxford
Fromer M J 1981 Ethical issues in health care. Mosby, St Louis
Griffiths N 1983 Mentally handicapped children and adults. Welfare Rights Guide; Area 5 Action Group, Edinburgh, p 2–9
Henderson V Royal College of Nursing Publication — The Nature of Nursing.
HMSO 1972 Report of the Committee of Inquiry Into Whittingham Hospital. Cmnd 4861. HMSO, London, Appendix II, p 52
HMSO 1974 Health and Safety at Work Act. DHSS Cmnd. HMSO, London, Part 1, Section 7
HMSO 1967 Children and their primary schools. A Report of the Central Advisory Council for Education, vol 1. HMSO, ch 2, p 25
HMSO 1983 Department of Health and Social Security Mental Health (Amendment) Scotland Act 1983 HMSO, London
Phoon Wai On 1971 Occasional Papers Commonwealth Foundation: The role of the professions in a changing world.
UKCC 1983 Code of Professional Conduct for Nurses, Midwives and Health Visitors (based on ethical concepts). UKCC, London
UNO The Rights of the Handicapped. United Nations Organisation to the General Assembly
Wright D 1971 The psychology of moral behaviour. Penguin, Harmondsworth.
Wright A, Taylor D S et al Introductory psychology — An experimental approach. Penguin Education, Harmondsworth, ch 22, p 588
Wright E 1977 What right have you got — Your rights and responsibilities as a citizen. BBC, London, ch 5, p 132

FURTHER READING

Marshall E 1975 General principles of Scots Law, 2nd edn. W. Green & Sons, Edinburgh
Young A P 1981 Legal problems in nursing practice. Lippincott Nursing Series, Philadelphia

Index

Care (cont'd)
  facilities and provision, 77–104
  group allocation, 164–5
  individual, 290–1
  management, 291–304
  multidisciplinary approach, 290, 298
  NHS hospital provision, 79–87
  philosophies, 322
  purpose, 290
  short-term, 272, 280
  'task allocation', 164
  UK historical aspects, 77–8
  see also Community care;
    Institutional care
Care records
  information and assessment data, 293–5
  problem-oriented system (Weed), 292
  problem/progress oriented, 292–301
  problems definition, 294–5, 296, 299
  progress reports, 297–8, 301–2
  treatment programmes, 297, 300
Care staff, 98–104
  behaviour changes, 153
  burn-out, 12–13, 306
  conscience development, 320–1
  emotional involvement, 314–15
  family help, 275–81
  financial aspects, 99–100
  human weaknesses, 319–20
  morale, 162–3, 304
  numbers, 99
  organisation, 99
  personal values, 320–1
  physiotherapist cooperation, 180–1
  structure, 102–4
    local authorities, 103
    NHS, 102–3
  training, 99
Caregivers
  interactional synchrony, 215–16
  movement adaptation, 218
  see also Care staff; Family;
    Parents
Carrow auditory comprehension test, 246
Case conferences, shortcomings, 291
Cataract, congenital, 59
Cattell Infant Scale, 151
CCETSW, 99, 100
Central Council for the Disabled, 96
Central Council for Education and
    Training in Social Work, 99, 100
Central deafness, 60
Centration, development, 118
Cerebellar stimulation, epilepsy, 54
Cerebral palsy, 40, 55–8, 165–8
  care, 57–9

causation, 55, 165–6
classification, 56, 166
dental problems, 167
feeding, 57–8
hip dislocation incidence, 58
inheritance, 55, 165
maternal virus infections, 55
music and rhythm, 57
physical deformities, 167–8, 186, 189
physiotherapy, 57–8
speech problems, 166
spinal deformities, 168, 186, 189
surgery and drugs, 58
Cerebromacular degeneration, 29, 31, 34–5
Charity Organisation Society, 78
Chest infections, profound multiple handicap, 169–70
Chewing difficulties, 175
Chief Area Nursing Officer (CANO), 102
Child-parent interaction, social class, 19
Children, stranger anxiety, 114
Children's homes, 89–90
Chiropody, 87
Chlorhexidine
  mouthwashes, 195
  tooth gel, 195
Choking and gagging, feeding, 174–5
Chromatin positive males, 28
Chromosomes, 24–9
  abnormalities, 24–92
  autosomal, abnormalities, 24–8
  deletion, 25
  glossary, 43
  mosaicism, 25
  sex, abnormalities, 25, 28–9
  translocation, 24–5
Clothes, selection, 191
Cocktail party syndrome, 235
Cognitive changes, adolescence, 122
Cognitive development, 116–21, 226
  stages, 117–20
Communication 196–7
  abilities' assessment, 227–302
    results, 230
  cerebral palsy, 57
  expression interrelationship, 212–13
  inter-staff, 305
  movement interaction, 210–12, 216–21
  skills teaching, 108
Communication, non-verbal, 196–7, 239–41
  adverse messages, 209–10
  channels and codes, 205–6
  components, 206–10
    regulatory functions, 210
  decoding, 213

infant, 213–14
interactants' orientation, 207
leakage, 209–10
limited channels, 205–6
physical contact, 208
role, 204–10
written systems, 241–4
Communication, pre-verbal, 214
Communication, verbal, 224–39
  see also Language; Speech
Community care, 88–9
  institutional care and, 264–6
Community mental handicap
    nurses, 100–2
  consultant liaison, 101–2
  tasks and services, 100–2
Complaints, moral and
    ethical problems, 309–13
Comprehension and expression
    problems, 234–6
Conduct disorders, 73–4
Conduction deafness, 60
Congenital Disabilities (Civil
    Liability) Act (1976), 325
Conscience, development, care
    staff, 320–1
Constipation, 179–80, 181
Continuous quantity conservation
    tasks, 119
Contractures, cerebral palsy, 167, 186, 189
Conversational interaction, gaze-
    direction, 210
Cooperative and competitive play, 252
Coping, parental, 267–9
Cornelia de Lange syndrome, 36
Cottage and Rural Enterprises
    (CARE), 95
Counselling, 277–81
  see also Emotional counselling;
    Genetic counselling
County Asylums Act (1808), 78
Creek autistic behaviour scale, 64
Cretinism, 31, 37
Cri-du-chat, 25, 28
Cuddling, multiply handicapped
    child, 260
'Cultural deprivation', 17–18

Dancing eyes syndrome, 47
Deafness, 59–61
  types, 60
Decentration, 120
Decubitus ulcers, 193–4
Dehydration, 176
  brain haemorrhage, 41
Delirium, 70, 71
Dementia, 70, 71–3
  aetiology, 71
  care and management, 72–3
  childhood, associated disorders, 71
  clinical features, 71–2